Dave
Merry Christmas)!
Creel
2015

Vietnam
to
Western Airlines

11-11-13

[signature]

A VAL-4 Black Pony, U.S. Navy OV-10, firing a Zuni rocket somewhere in the Delta, 1970–1971.

Vietnam to Western Airlines

An Oral History Of The Air War

Edited *by*
Bruce Cowee

Alive Book Publishing

Additional copies may be ordered at: VietnamToWesternAirlines.com
Books are available in quantity for educational, business, promotional
or premium use. For information, contact ALIVE Book Publishing at:
alivebookpublishing.com, or call (925) 837-7303.

Book Design by Elham Sedaghatinia

ISBN 978-0-9857367-4-3 Hardcover
ISBN 978-0-9857367-5-0 E-Book
ISBN 978-0-9857367-8-1 Full Color Collector's Edition

Library of Congress Control Number: 2013942447

Library of Congress Cataloging-in-Publication Data

LC Control no.: 2013942447
LCCN permalink: http://lccn.loc.gov/2013942447
Vietnam to Western Airlines : an oral history of the air war
/ Bruce T. Cowee; [edited by] Bruce T. Cowee.
Edition: 1st edition.
Published/Produced: Alamo, CA : Advanced Pub. LLC, 2013.
Description: pages cm

ISBN: 9780985736743 (pbk. : alk. paper)
        9780985736750 (ebk. : alk. paper)

Published in the United States of America by ALIVE Book Publishing
and ALIVE Publishing Group, imprints of Advanced Publishing LLC
3200 A Danville Blvd., Suite 204, Alamo, California 94507
alivebookpublishing.com

Printed in the United States of America

10   9   8   7   6   5   4   3   2   1

DEDICATION

There are many monuments around the country dedicated to those who were lost in Southeast Asia. One of the most moving is the Missing Man Monument at Randolph Air Force Base in San Antonio, Texas. The inscription at the base of the monument reads as follows:

WE WHO CAME HOME

MUST NEVER FORGET THOSE WHO COULD NOT

One of many who could not come home was an Air Force ROTC cadet and friend of Jim Erdos at the University of Notre Dame:

1st Lieutenant Joseph Stanley Smith, USAF

Date of birth: 07 May 1945

Date of loss: 04 April 1971

Country of loss: Cambodia, Kratie Province

Presumptive status: killed in action/body not recovered

Aircraft: F-100D, #563120, call sign Blade 05

CONTENTS

PREFACE

The purpose of a preface is to acknowledge those who helped in the production of a book, and that is an easy task for me. To those fellow pilots, all but one of whom were hired by Western Airlines after returning from Vietnam, and one Marine infantry lieutenant, who so generously shared their Vietnam experiences and their photos, I offer my profound thanks. I have put the stories together in somewhat chronological order from 1964 to 1973. Most of the stories stand alone, but there is one group of stories by three pilots involving the same incident, and there are two stories that relate separate impressions of the horrific B-52 mid-air collision on July 7, 1967: one by a pilot who was involved in the accident, and another by a pilot who witnessed it. There are coincidences throughout the book, proving that the world of military aviation is a small one indeed. I have taken the liberty of writing a short introduction to each of the stories, and my remarks are easy to separate from the main story as they are italicized. I have tried to explain military jargon and aviation terminology as things go along, mostly in parentheses, but in some stories, asterisks and endnotes are used.

My respect and admiration for these men is pretty obvious throughout the book. I always found it fascinating that no matter how harrowing or dangerous I thought a particular airplane's mission was, the pilots who flew those airplanes always thought it was someone else who had a more dangerous job. As F-105 pilot Bob Spielman said, the F-105 Wild Weasels were "the guys with the big gonads!" Bill Wilson's comment, when asked about one of his more harrowing missions in the A-4, was, "We figured we were going to get killed anyway, so the fallback position was always the Marine Corps motto, 'Better dead than look bad.' We just did it."

There was a definite pecking order for those flying combat, and those of us who were there will never forget the signs in the Officers' Clubs and flight line snack bars throughout Southeast Asia that said, "Combat Crews to the Head of the Line."

No matter what the mission, SAR (Search and Rescue) was the key that made it all work. The Air Force pilots and crew members who flew the HH-3 and HH-53 Jolly Green Giant rescue helicopters could never buy a drink anywhere in Southeast Asia. They flew their rescue helicopters wherever a downed pilot might be, on some occasions in sight of Hanoi, and would tell you they were just doing their job and wished they could have rescued more than they did. The Crown SAR C-130s were always on station and ready to coordinate a rescue attempt when a mayday call came through, even when it took their unarmed four-engine cargo aircraft into northern Laos or sometimes into North Vietnam.

I can best sum it up by saying that it was a bunch of guys in their 20s who were thrust into situations of incredible excitement and danger, were given incredible responsibility, and responded with amazing, heroic performances. It's an honor for me to have been able to collect these stories and publish this book.

I wondered for a while, as I was typing and proofreading the final copies of these stories, why so many of the pilots used military and aviation jargon that was going to be difficult for the uninitiated to understand. Then it dawned on me, and a big light came on. These men don't talk about their Vietnam experiences except to guys who have been there and understand—explaining things isn't part of the process. It was another humbling experience for me as I worked my way through and put this book together. Every pilot had a unique mission, whether he was a fighter or attack pilot, a "trash hauler" (I'm a proud member of that group), a gunship or rescue pilot, a forward air controller, or a helicopter pilot, and the fraternities within the big fraternity never cease to amaze me. As Mike Doyle so elegantly put it, "We all had the same zip code while we served, and recognition for that service is long overdue."

Above it all, the Marines are just…well, the Marines. I knew as I neared the end of this project that I had a shortage of Marine stories for the book. I finally got together with Bill Wilson after years of trying, and Bill's involvement opened the door to three stories about the Marine A-4 operation in the early days at Chu Lai. Giving new meaning to "the few, the proud," Bill was my escort, guide, and technical adviser for all things about the A-4 Skyhawk and the way it was operated by the Marine Corps. His personal introductions made everything work, and through him I was fortunate to meet two of his MAG-12 (Marine Air Group-12) mates, who talk about Vietnam mostly with their fellow Marines. Starting at the beginning, in 1965, these three stories have rarely been told outside that inner circle and have never been in print. That statement applies to most of the stories in the book, and they are accompanied by photos that have never been seen outside of personal photo albums. I have received more than one message that said, "Thanks for letting us tell our stories." *Honored* and *humbled* are the two words that come to mind.

In the course of this project I had impressed on me a few things it seemed I already knew innately: You call the F-105 "the Thud" only if you flew it, "the bush" will always remain pretty much a mystery unless you have been in it (flying over it doesn't count), Marines (especially those who served on the ground) usually tell their stories only to other Marines who were there and understand, and most important, you don't say "Semper Fi" unless you are a Marine, and if a Marine says "Semper Fi" to a non-Marine it is beyond the ultimate compliment. If you want to hear a combat veteran's story, you shouldn't throw around phrases like *trap, bolter, take the wire, cat launch, MIG CAP, road recce, burner, JATO, close air support, pipper, coming down the chute, drogue, basket, CAS CAP, hit the tanker,* and so on. Try asking a question and then (using a little aviation terminology) putting your system on "receive" rather than "transmit."

There is a poignant country song titled, "These Are My People," sung by Rodney Atkins. How could someone like me have had the good fortune to share my Vietnam adventure with men like these and then come home and go to work for Western Airlines and work with them for more than 30 years? I still find myself at a loss for words trying to answer that question.

The dust jacket has two photos. On the back is a Western Boeing 737-200 climbing out to the south after a winter takeoff from Butte, Montana, sometime around 1980. It was Western's "junior" piece of equipment and the airplane most of us flew at one time or another in our careers. For the front I chose a photo that Jim Fogg sent me because it represents everything good and decent about the American fighting man. It is the official Air Force photo taken of Jim's Crown SAR C-130 making the first combat refueling of an HH-3 Jolly Green Giant rescue helicopter on the way to a crash site and a downed pilot in northern Laos in 1967. Once the range of the Jollys was increased by refueling, the rescue forces flew into the "danger zone" of northern Laos and parts of North Vietnam on a regular basis. "Guys with the big gonads" indeed!

Search and Rescue was a huge factor in the creation of the high morale of the aircrews, and it amazes me to this day when I read about the incredible rescue attempts that were undertaken. Every pilot knew about the professionalism and dedication of the SAR crews, and the thought that they would come for you if you needed help was an incredible comfort. The themes of survival and rescue run through these stories, and to this day, I doubt any pilot who flew in Vietnam could hear the sound of a mayday call or an ELT (emergency locator transmitter) without feeling a chill run down his spine. That was the source of the common bond we all had, and I have always felt truly blessed to have worked in such company.

ACKNOWLEDGMENTS

The original purpose of this book was to honor Vietnam veterans, and in particular, the Vietnam service of a group of men I had the honor to know and work with as a pilot for Western Airlines. But, it has become much more. I have learned that additionally, it provided a vehicle for several authors to tell their stories for the first time, some having never even told their families over the years. In telling their stories, it is my hope that the negative stereotypes of Vietnam veterans, as portrayed in books and by Hollywood, will change. I acknowledge and honor their service.

One of my most important tasks was to get the technical data for the airplanes right. Special thanks go to Dennis Dolan and Bill Wilson, two Marines who helped with Marine Corps terminology and with the F-4 and A-4. Because of them, I will always remember the difference between a section and a division! Jerry Stamps gave me similar assistance with the F-105 and, after a search, came up with 50 year old slides that have become a part of the treasure trove of photos that grace this book.

I am truly grateful for the good fortune that brought me to Alive Media, where meeting Eric Johnson and his able graphic designer Eli Sedaghatinia, has made this book a reality.

Those who helped with their encouragement and support are too numerous to mention, but you know who you are. Special praise goes to my late wife Angie, who was my typist, proofreader, and the biggest fan of this project in its early stages. It has grown beyond anything either of us could have imagined ten years ago, both in its scope and its historical importance.

INTRODUCTION

On May 12, 1969, I received the following special order:

"EACH INDIVIDUAL LISTED BELOW WILL REPORT TO AIR PASSENGER TERMINAL CAM RANH BAY AB RVN NLT 2100, 16 MAY 69 FOR DEPARTURE ON FLT Q2C4 FOR CONUS DESTINATION. YOU WILL REPORT TO IN/OUT PROCESSING SECTION ON 15 MAY 1969. THIS ENDORSES YOUR SPECIAL ORDERS."

Below this heading was a list of 11 names, including mine:

1LT FR3178210 COWEE BRUCE T 458TACALFTSQ.

Let me translate: I was going home, back to the world, back to the big BX (BX refers to *Base Exchange—the 'Big BX' essentially meaning, "Home to America"*). My freedom flight was scheduled! I was to report to the passenger terminal at Cam Ranh Bay Air Base, Republic of Vietnam, for departure on MAC (Military Airlift Command) charter flight Q2C4 for a Continental United States destination. My rank, first lieutenant, service number, name, and unit, 458th Tactical Airlift Squadron, followed. If that piece of paper seems like a bit of an anticlimax after 12 months of flying in Vietnam, it surely was! So, let me back up a bit.

I flew my last mission in Vietnam on May 10, 1969. It was a regularly scheduled daily mission, call sign Law 470, a C-7A Caribou from the 458th TAS based at Cam Ranh Bay AB. Early in the morning we flew to Nha Trang, headquarters of the Army 5th Special Forces, and then shuttled to Bien Hoa, with later stops at Quan Loi, Song Be, Blackhorse, and Vung Tau. Since the Caribou was originally an Army airplane, its mission in Vietnam was almost 100 percent in support of the Army, specifically 5th Special Forces. My last mission finished with a low-level flight, feet wet (over the water) up the coast from Vung Tau to Cam Ranh Bay. I logged 7 hours and 10 minutes of flying time for the day.

It was always important when flying feet wet to be low enough so that no one could get below you, as the F-100s from Phan Rang, Phu Cat, and Tuy Hoa and the F-4s from Cam Ranh and Da Nang loved to come up from behind and fly under us, pulling up in front in afterburner and generally scaring the bejesus out of us. At least I didn't break off or crack the bottom rotating beacon on the water. That had happened once or twice, and it was always hard to explain a cracked red plastic cover over the rotating beacon with the cover full of salt water. But that's another story. As we used to say, "What are they going to do? Send us to Vietnam?" They could always have sent us to the LBJ (the Army's Long Binh Jail near Saigon), affectionately named after Lyndon Baines Johnson, but then that might have been a bit extreme.

Returning to my hooch after landing and debriefing, I got the traditional soaking with buckets of ice water from my waiting squadron mates and spent the next few days unwinding, turning in my gear, out-processing from the squadron, and packing. Then I started the wait for my freedom flight.

Less than a week after that low-level flight up the coast of South Vietnam, I was sitting in the family car, with my mom and dad driving me home to Berkeley, California, from San Francisco International Airport. A long MAC charter flight had brought me from Cam Ranh Bay AB to Yokota AB in Japan and on to McCord AFB, Washington, where we cleared customs and were released to find our way home. I caught a United Airlines flight from Seattle to San Francisco, and next thing I knew, I was in the car with my parents. I was quite disoriented from being unable to sleep for the previous 36 hours; still, I listened as my dad described the situation in Berkeley.

I had left home about two and a half years earlier, commissioned a second lieutenant in the USAF in December 1966 through the Air Force ROTC program at the University of California. We had dealt with anti-draft, anti-ROTC, and anti-war protests on a regular basis when I was an ROTC cadet, to the point that our weekly drill periods were planned in secret to try to avoid confrontations. All the ROTC detachments—Army, Navy, and Air Force—had traditionally drilled on the center grass of Edwards Field, the track-and-field stadium, but that was definitely out, so we got pretty creative in selecting spots where we would drill. Since wearing our uniforms on campus was usually more trouble than it was worth, I carried mine in a suit bag and changed before and after drill. My grandmother lived in an apartment at the Carlton Hotel on Telegraph Avenue, so I would go to see her, change clothes, then take her to Kips for lunch after drill. The final drill period before graduation was one of the most memorable, as it was on the lower basement level of one of the parking lots on Bancroft Avenue.

I knew from letters and various news sources, among them *The Stars and Stripes* (the military newspaper published daily in Japan and flown to all the major bases in South Vietnam and Thailand every morning), that the protests and demonstrations had continued and intensified since I left Berkeley in early 1967, but I wasn't prepared for my welcome home. The governor of California, Ronald Reagan, had declared a state of emergency in Berkeley at the request of Sheriff Frank Madigan of Alameda County. There were more than 3,000 police officers from various jurisdictions and several hundred California National Guardsmen patrolling the streets of Berkeley, and the city was sealed off from entry except by residents. As my dad took the University Avenue exit from Interstate 80 we were immediately stopped at a roadblock. There was a large group of very nervous-looking California National Guardsmen, probably wishing they were in Vietnam instead of Berkeley, carrying fixed bayonets on their M1 Garand rifles and wearing flak jackets. In charge at the roadblock were several CHP (California Highway Patrol) officers in full riot gear. A CHP sergeant approached the car. First he checked my dad's ID to make sure we lived in Berkeley, and then he looked at me in my Air Force tan 1505 uniform. I was still carrying some Cam Ranh Bay sand that I had put in my pocket before I left, seemingly a lifetime

CHP roadblock on College Avenue at Parker Street, a few blocks from the Berkeley campus, May 1969.

California National Guard in Berkeley, May 1969. Note bayonets and flak jackets.

earlier. As he waved us through the roadblock he said, "It would not be a good idea to wear that uniform in town."

The seed for this project was planted then, more than 40 years ago, and although I didn't know exactly what form it would take until a few years ago, it has never been far from my mind. This book is a tribute to all who served in Southeast Asia and especially to those who could not return. The fact that these stories were all written by men who came home and ended up working as pilots for Western Airlines makes it especially meaningful for me, and I am truly humbled and honored to call each of these men a friend. They represent the cream of the crop of the generation that came of age in the 1960s. They are my heroes, and their stories speak for themselves as a testimony to their courage and flying skill.

As these chapters unfold, they not only give a fascinating historical perspective on the air war in Vietnam but also tell a wonderful story about a truly special group of men. I am extremely honored and proud to say that each story is written by a man whom I know personally. I have worked professionally with most of them as a pilot for Western Airlines and, after April 1987, as a pilot for Delta Air Lines. These individual Vietnam flying stories cover the entire spectrum of the air war in Vietnam. The stories start near the beginning, in 1964, with the Gulf of Tonkin incident; move on to Operation Rolling Thunder; continue through the next eight years to the bombing of Hanoi and Operation Linebacker II in December 1972, which brought about the signing of the Paris Peace Accords and the release of the POWs (prisoners of war); and end with the winding down of our air operations in Thailand in 1973. You will read about everything from heart-pounding, edge-of-the-seat combat to the human interest and even comic events that always happen in war. Through it all, there is an underlying theme that I touched on in the preface: a group of young men in their 20s, thrust into situations of incredible excitement and danger, given an awesome amount of responsibility, responding with performances that defy any measure you could come up with to evaluate them, then having to return to an unappreciative and often hostile home front. It all

makes an annual flight simulator evaluation or an FAA check ride
seem pretty ho-hum.

Since this book both honors Vietnam veterans and features pilots
who went to work for Western Airlines after the war, it is only fitting
to tell a short story about airline hiring and what it was like for me, trying to get my foot in the door with Western Airlines in the early 1970s.

When I separated from active duty on July 1, 1972, I was flying
the C-141 at Travis AFB. As a current and qualified aircraft commander (this meant that I had the required number of takeoffs and
landings in the prior 90-day period and that I had completed my
annual training and check rides, in both the flight simulator and aircraft), I walked across the street and signed up to fly with the Air
Force Reserve in the 349th MAW (Military Airlift Wing). The reserve
unit was a hub of airline hiring activity and I quickly learned who
was hiring, where I could get an application, what the interviews
were like, what kind of tests they gave, what they expected if they
put you in the flight simulator, and my personal favorite, "Which
chair do you take in the shrink's office at the Delta interview, the
straight chair or the rocker?" (Dr. Janus was the infamous shrink
who did a part of the Delta interview; everyone knew his name and
the two chairs he offered when he asked you to sit down.) It was too
much, very funny in hindsight but deadly serious business at the
time. The reserve unit at Travis was full of furloughed Pan Am,
TWA, and Northwest pilots who were mostly older than the age
limit for hiring at the time, so for them, switching airlines wasn't an
option. The majority of these men were Vietnam veterans who,
through no fault of their own, were a constant reminder to all of us
that the airline industry was a minefield. Who knew in 1972? What
would it be, a Braniff or Eastern and bankruptcy, or a Western,
United, Delta, or American and a 30-year career?

As I began to fly with the reserves I soon developed a friendship
with John Theorell. He was a great guy, one of the few pilots I knew
who had flown the Convair 990 (for an outfit called Modern Air,
based in Miami and Berlin), and he was the go-to guy in the Travis
reserve unit for information on pilot hiring at Western Airlines. Back

in the early 1970s there were no computers, e-mail, or cell phones, no courses on how to interview or how to produce a resume, and everything to do with airline pilot hiring was passed around by word of mouth. John was a bit older than the unspoken but well-known maximum age the airlines were looking for, which was 27 or 28, so he had been particularly aggressive and had camped out in the Western employment office in Los Angeles when word got out that Western was about to resume pilot hiring in early 1972. John befriended the secretaries (flowers and candy seemed to do the trick) but made a general nuisance of himself. He observed over time that the Western executives would come through the employment office on the way to their inner sanctum and would go through a door with a coded lock. When John had an opportunity, he went through the door just like he belonged there and was able to corner Captain Bob Johnson, vice president of operations, in the men's room. Rather than being summarily ejected from the building, John was able to drop off his employment application with Captain Johnson, and in a short period of time he and Bob Johnson became friends. That unlikely friendship paved the way for John to be hired at age 30 in April 1972, in one of the first new-hire classes after those furloughed in 1969 had been recalled, and by the time I joined the reserves in July, John was in full swing as the hiring agent for Western Airlines at the Travis reserves. My application made its way via John to the inner sanctum, and I was called for an interview and offered a job in December 1972.

After he was hired in April, John did the ultimate and became the envy of all the aspiring airline pilots in the reserves. He married a beautiful Western stewardess (there still were stewardesses in 1972) and bought a new house with a swimming pool in Vacaville. John was living large! But I remember sitting in his den listening to tape recordings he had made of missions he flew in Vietnam and how they gave me goose bumps.

John had been involved in the flight testing of the first AC-47 gunships that were flown in Vietnam, earning the nickname Johnny Throttles. The AC-47 was affectionately known as Puff the Magic

Dragon, call sign Spooky, and was a modified C-47 (civilian DC-3) fitted with three 7.62mm General Electric Gatling mini-guns pointing out the windows on the left side of the aircraft. The guns were fired by the pilot using a switch on the pilot's yoke (control column); the gunners in the rear of the aircraft were there to keep the ammunition flowing and to help if the guns jammed. The testing was done at Eglin AFB, Florida. John told of banking his aircraft to the left in a 30-degree turn and described how, with the help of a grease pencil line drawn on his cockpit side window, he could aim the guns with pretty good accuracy. Later the AC-47 was fitted with a gun sight in the pilot's cockpit side window. (Compare that with today's AC-130 Spectre gunships, whose guns are integrated with the flight director and autopilot and are totally computerized in their aiming and firing, putting out many times the firepower.) The tape recordings that John played were some of the most chilling I have ever heard. Troops on the ground were begging for help, telling him they were being overrun and to fire right in front of or even on top of their positions. Unfortunately for the reader, John is a very private man and declined to write a story for this book. I wish I could relate some of the tales he told me over the years, but I can only say that for every story I have for this book there are many others that will never be told and will disappear, much as so many from World War II and the Korean War have disappeared. The 2012 movie *Memorial Day* ends with a quote: "The stories will last forever, but only if they are told." If this book helps to preserve a few Vietnam flying stories, my objective will have been achieved.

When I came to work for Western Airlines in December 1972 my new-hire class of 30 pilots was made up of 28 military pilots and two with civilian backgrounds. Almost all of the military pilots were Vietnam veterans, and my recollection is that nobody really talked much about it. The Vietnam War was still going on, and I was flying the C-141 in the reserve unit at Travis AFB, making flights back to Southeast Asia on a regular basis during my time off from Western. To say that was a bit bizarre might be a fair assessment in hindsight, but at the time, a good percentage of the military pilots were in reserve units, flying everything from fighters to helicopters to transports, and every service was represented, from the Army and Navy to the Marines and the Air Force. I flew my last reserve trip into Saigon in early 1975, after the NVA (North Vietnamese Army), in violation of the Paris Peace Accords, invaded South Vietnam and was moving down the coast toward Da Nang and through the Central Highlands near Ban Me Thuot. The South Vietnamese forces were in retreat, and we were evacuating civilian employees of the embassy and other agencies from Saigon. By early April 1975 Operation Babylift was instituted on C-5 aircraft. The pictures of Vietnamese families handing their babies over the wall at the U.S. Embassy in Saigon are heart wrenching. The day Saigon fell, April 30, 1975, I was on a Western trip, on layover in Idaho Falls. I remember sitting by the Snake River on a beautiful spring afternoon after hearing the news, trying to make sense of it all. I had just turned 30 and had spent nearly nine years in the Air Force, both active and reserve, and other than my initial training in 1967-1968, I had either been based in Vietnam or flying the C-141 back and forth on resupply and medevac missions for close to seven years. *Surreal* is the only word that comes to mind.

The group of 30 in my new-hire class at Western had been split in half, and I was in the half of the class that was assigned to train as flight engineers on the Boeing 707/720B. In that position we flew with the most senior captains, the tail end of the World War II pilots who were retiring at a rapid rate in the early 1970s. I had the honor of flying with several of them, and even though listening to their stories required sitting in a hotel room on layover or in the cockpit with clouds of cigarette and cigar smoke billowing about, it was a high point in my career.

At one time, the majority of airline captains in this country were pilots who had flown in Vietnam. But by the time I started this book project, nearly 15 years ago, the Vietnam veterans were rapidly retiring, and these stories, mainly shared over the years in the cockpit and on layovers, could have been lost forever. I doubt there are many Vietnam veterans still flying for the major airlines.

I learned very quickly that it is one thing to hear a story at work, where a considerable amount of trust and a common bond have been established, and quite another to ask someone to write a story of such a private, personal nature to be read by complete strangers. Thus I approached this project with more than a little trepidation.

In March 1997, I flew the whole month with Gary Gottschalk and got the most incredible encouragement from him to pursue these stories. Gary, as you will read, was a Navy pilot and flew the A-1 Spad from the aircraft carrier USS *Oriskany* in 1965-1966. Never having worked together, Gary and I started the month as complete strangers. I was a senior first officer (copilot) on the Boeing 757/767 and Gary was a captain, both of us based in Los Angeles. We began the month comparing flying backgrounds and swapping stories, moved on to bringing pictures and other neat stuff to show each other on the next trip, and ended the month with Gary promising to write a story and also giving me the names of several Los Angeles–based pilots I should contact.

In the midst of our month together an incident occurred that really gave incentive to this project. As we were sitting in the cockpit, ready to push back from the gate in Fort Myers, Florida, with our checklists completed and with the Delta gate agents frantically making a seat count for another oversold flight, a flight attendant came to the cockpit and overheard Gary and me talking about Vietnam. She asked in a very surprised tone, "You guys were in Vietnam? Are you OK?" This book does a lot to answer that question and will introduce the reader to a group of the most "OK" guys anyone could have the honor to know. I have that honor and the incredible privilege of knowing and working with them as a pilot for Western and then Delta Air Lines.

To those few I contacted who preferred to leave their Vietnam experiences in the past, to those who told their stories, and to those who told me they didn't do anything special and didn't have a story to tell, you all have my deepest respect and thanks. I was encouraged in this project by everyone I spoke with, and I'm proud to know all of you.

I have taken the opportunity (I think it is called literary license) to add two additional Vietnam stories at the end of the book that were written by good friends of mine who were not Western pilots, Bob Moore and Peter Foor.

I met Bob Moore in the mid-1970s when he was on furlough as a pilot for Eastern Airlines. He had transferred from the Air Force Reserve at McGuire AFB, New Jersey, to the C-141 reserve unit at Travis AFB, and we became good friends. When Western started to hire pilots again in 1976 after a three-year pause, Bob was able to get an interview, but due to the vagaries of the airline hiring process, he wasn't offered a job and returned to Eastern in 1978. Eastern declared bankruptcy and ceased operations in 1991, ending Bob's airline career, but he went to work for the FAA and became an air carrier inspector based in Atlanta, working exclusively with Delta Air Lines. He eventually became the FAA's POI (Principal Operating Inspector) for Delta, working closely with the Delta flight operations department, helping to develop and approve the training syllabus for the airline as well as supervising all of the FAA air carrier inspectors who flew with and checked the Delta pilots. Bob flew from Atlanta to LaGuardia on Memorial Day weekend 2004 to meet me and fly in the cockpit on my retirement flight. He made it a memorable event.

I met Peter Foor in the fourth grade at Hillside School in Berkeley, and we were good friends and classmates all the way through Berkeley High School. We went our separate ways after graduation in 1962, but he signed up for Marine OCS (Officer Candidate School) while he was a senior at Whittier College in Whittier, California. He had taken the pilot aptitude test and flight physical for both the Air Force and the Navy but had failed both on the depth perception portion of the eye test. Ever persistent, he took the test for the Marine Corps and was told he passed, so he signed up for OCS. You can guess the rest of the story. Just before completing the three-month course at Quantico, he was told he needed to retake the eye test. He failed, but no problem, the Marine Corps needed infantry officers, so off he went to Basic School and Vietnam. Interestingly, our tours of duty in Vietnam overlapped almost exactly: May 1968–May 1969 for me, and June 1968–July 1969 for Peter (the lucky Marines had a 13-month tour). I never knew he was there and our paths never crossed in that year, when the total number of Americans in Vietnam hit its peak at more than 500,000. I only learned that he had been in Vietnam when we met at the 45th reunion of our class from Berkeley High School in 2007. Peter came home from Vietnam to use the GI Bill to go to law school and is currently a superior court judge in Solano County, California. His story has a Berkeley angle to it, and I thought it was appropriate and fitting to hear what it was like in ground combat as a Marine lieutenant. There is a short addendum to Peter's story written by Nick Kosturos, who served with him in Kilo Company, 3/26 Marines. I don't think many of us could come close to understanding what the war was like for the Marines on the ground, and it was only through Nick that I learned the extent of the casualties suffered by the Marines. Peter was among the few lieutenants who were not wounded or killed, and because of that he was constantly rotated among the units that had lost their officers. I asked Peter if he wanted to dedicate his story to a friend who was lost, and he only said that there were too many. He didn't want to single out anyone in particular because it was for all of them.

I honestly believe that those of us who flew in Vietnam and came home to complete our commitments from pilot training (the Air Force and Navy/USMC required a four-year commitment after getting our wings) or those whose commitments were complete and separated from the service, going right to work for an airline, had a relatively easy transition to civilian life. Both in the reserves and at Western Airlines, I was always surrounded by men who had similar backgrounds and experiences. Even though it wasn't talked about much, it was a common bond that was right below the surface. I could not have invented a better workplace and workforce for me to join after Vietnam and the Air Force.

Jim Fogg says it all in two quotes from his story, first as he describes maneuvering his C-130 into position to refuel a Jolly Green Giant rescue helicopter that was on its way to a crash site and a downed airman in northern Laos. "After locating and passing beneath him, I would chop the throttles to idle, yank back on the yoke as I pulled up and reversed course, then slide ever so nicely past him as I declared, 'I have lead.' It was like poetry in motion. Who the heck would ever, in their right mind, trade this for some mundane job like being a lawyer or a CPA?" The second quote speaks to a feeling I always had, knowing that at age 23, while flying in Vietnam, I had more fun, challenge, and responsibility than I would ever have again in my flying career. "It was an emotional high, a rush that aviation in the years since has never approached." I wouldn't have traded the experience for anything!

As a final comment, I can only say how honored I am to have been entrusted with these stories. I will close with a quote from the book *The Vietnam War: Opposing Viewpoints*, by David L Bender. The quote appears under the heading "Transforming Experience."

No greater moral crime has been committed by the critics of the Vietnam War than to depersonalize and discredit the profound personal, transforming experience of the combat veteran....Whether the American wars of this century were a waste because politicians made them so is really irrelevant. Their meaning and significance for the surviving veteran is that when faced with the most personal, intense experience of his entire life he met the test and became part of the Brotherhood of the Brave.

1

THE BEGINNING

Jerry Stamps, USAF, F-105D, 1964 – 1966
{ Date of hire by Western Airlines: 2/26/1968 }

Jerry Stamps, 3rd from left, in front of F-105D #62-4366, ready to depart Takhli RTAB for a"Rolling Thunder" mission over North Vietnam, 1965.

Chronologically, Jerry's story starts with the very beginning of the U.S. buildup in Thailand. It became a huge operation, utilizing six major bases and providing most of the Air Force fighters that bombed North Vietnam over the next nine years. Fighters from Udorn, Ubon, Takhli, Korat, and Nakhon Phanom, and B-52s and KC-135 tankers from Utapao were in the air over Thailand, on the way to their refueling rendezvous and their targets, around the clock. Along with those fighters were the SAR (Search and Rescue) aircraft; C-130s, Jolly Green Giant rescue helicopters, and A-1 Sandys, as well as gunships, reconnaissance, transport, and support air-

craft. A large number of secret missions were flown over Laos and Cambodia by various units, mostly based at Udorn and Nakhon Phanom. Air Force fighters based in South Vietnam flew missions over the whole area, from close air support of ground forces in the south, to strikes over Laos and the north, while the Navy flew missions from aircraft carriers cruising in the South China Sea, launching their strikes from Dixie and Yankee Stations. The USMC flew both land-based and carrier-based missions, also flying close air support for ground operations over the south and hitting targets in Laos and the north.

I never had the privilege of flying with Jerry, but he has been extremely helpful by providing information and some incredible photos for this book. His color photos came from slides that were nearly 50 years old, and although the color is a bit faded, the history of the first days at Korat is there for all to see.

Jerry's story is preceded by a letter he wrote to me. I wanted to add a few words before I start with his letter, as it accompanied his story and is a part of it. My goal in this project was to tell whatever story each individual wanted to tell. If it was about a particular mission, about a humorous event that happened during his Vietnam experience, the story of how he ended up in Southeast Asia, his opinion about the whole situation, or all of the above, it would be fine. It was his story. Jerry, as you will see as you read on in the book, has a very interesting approach, and the fact that he flew multiple missions over Laos and North Vietnam in the F-105 is hardly mentioned.

In the dark days of the Cold War, Jerry's squadron of F-105s went in a matter of days from sitting on nuclear alert in South Korea to flying conventional bombing missions over Laos. He was there from day one in the bombing of the Ho Chi Minh Trail in Laos and then flew the first missions over North Vietnam less than a year later in Operation Rolling Thunder. This is an incredible story, parts of which will make you angry and sad at the same time, but it is one that needs to be told. Jerry mentions the way the flying time was logged when they first flew over Laos in 1964, requiring the pilots to log training time instead of combat time. It was part of the attempt to keep our involvement in Thailand and the bombing in Laos a secret back in those early days of the air war.

Here is Jerry's letter and his story.

....

Dear Bruce,

This may not be anything you would want for your book. In fact, it was not what I had intended to write, but out it came. If you can use it, fine. If not, let me know and I'll do a more politically correct version/revision. Feel free to edit it as you desire.

Regards, Jerry

As I was separating from the U.S. Air Force in 1966, a friend of mine asked me to speak to his Rotary Club to give them my view of the conflict in SEA (Southeast Asia). Being a team player, I explained to them that the U.S. military forces in SEA were doing all that was being asked of them by their leaders to stop the spread of Communism and aggression. As I reflected back on that evening long ago, I felt that there was another story that should have been told, indeed the bad-news part of the good news/bad news story. Those of you who participated in the SEA War Games no doubt have similar tales that cast doubt on the decisions and actions of our political leaders of that era.

My route to SEA started in 1960 with my assignments to Spence AFB (Air Force Base), Georgia, and Reese AFB, Texas, in Pilot Training Class 61-G-1, with subsequent training in the F-100 and assignment to Homestead AFB, Florida, with the 31st Tactical Fighter Wing. When slots began coming down for the F-105 "Thud," I immediately put in for one, and as a newly arrived first lieutenant I was soon off to Nellis AFB, Nevada, for more training, then to Itazuke AB (Air Base), Japan, with the 36th TFS (Tactical Fighter Squadron)/8th TFW (Tactical Fighter Wing). After a too-short assignment there, the 35th, 36th, and 80th Tactical Fighter Squadrons moved to Yokota AB, Japan.

It was early August 1964, and the 6441st Tactical Fighter Wing's three F-105 squadrons had just been notified of an ORI (operational readiness inspection) and were on the flight line at Yokota AB awaiting instructions. The ORI was some three to four hours along when we received orders to stand down and report to our respective squadron operations buildings. No one seemed to know what was going on (as per usual), and when we assembled at operations it was a while before wing personnel arrived to brief us. We were told that North Vietnamese ships had fired on a U.S. Navy ship in the Gulf of Tonkin (wherever that was) and that my squadron, the 36th TFS, had been tasked with deploying to SEA in support of developing operations. We were to take 18 F-105s and 25 pilots, leaving the next morning at "zero dark thirty." I was one of the seven pilots who would not be flying down, but would ride in a C-124 transport, nick-named Old Shaky, to wherever it was we were going. Our opera-tions officer was also going on the C-124 in order to establish an operations area at what turned out to be our destination, Korat RTAB (Royal Thai Air Base), Thailand.

As it turned out, those of us in the C-124 beat the F-105s by sev-eral days in arriving at Korat. The Thuds were delayed at Clark AB, Philippines, by a typhoon, and that really worked in our favor oper-ationally. Those of you who visited Korat later in the war probably were not aware of the stark conditions we found there in 1964, as the U.S. saw fit to invest heavily in the construction of a super-facility at Korat shortly thereafter. The seven of us arrived at Korat to find three open-air wood buildings that represented the sum and sub-stance of the flight line facilities, plus a control tower. Sleeping quar-ters for the pilots would be three open-bay, open-air hooches adja-cent to the flight line. We seven advance squadron members tried to anticipate the needs of an operational squadron and got busy build-ing and setting up shop. Our security for classified messages amounted to cardboard boxes guarded by armed lieutenants; one box for Top Secret and many more for those messages classified Secret. The Top Secret messages were logged in, the Secret were maybe logged in, and Confidential messages were stuffed in boxes out of sight!

The Thuds arrived several days later and were made ready for whatever awaited us. At this point I should mention that our mis-sion at Yokota involved sitting on nuclear alert, and since nuclear weapons were banned in Japan, we sat alert at Osan AB in South Korea. While at Yokota we strictly flew training missions, mostly gunnery and instrument training. You will notice in the photos that some of the pilots were wearing orange flight suits. These flight suits were worn on the flight down from Yokota to Korat because they made for easier sighting in the event of an overwater ejection. Once at Korat we wore the standard green flight suits. Also, our aircraft were silver, as the photo of the Korat flight line shows. Our planes began the camouflage paint program in late 1964, and the painting was done, as I recall, at a USAF facility in Tainan, Taiwan. Even a year later, in the fall of 1965, there was still a mix of silver and camouflage aircraft on the flight line. The weapons configuration on our planes for our nuclear alert duty could be readily changed so the aircraft were ready to fly missions as soon as they arrived at Korat, carrying conventional bombs or rockets externally on hard points under the wings and a 390-gallon/2,500-pound fuel tank in the internal bomb bay.

The initial missions were two-ship flights escorting RF-101 (reconnaissance aircraft) on what were called Yankee Team missions in the Plain de Jars in Laos. We were logging T-1 (training) missions since it was not publicized that military operations involving the U.S. Air Force were being conducted over Laos. However, when we started picking up battle damage we were able to log O-1 (combat) missions. The Yankee Team missions were usually uneventful until the enemy AAA (anti-aircraft artillery) gunners became more proficient. Our squadron's first battle damage occurred when a lucky 85mm hit knocked one side of the stabilator off, but the plane was able to return to base.

Air-to-ground missions soon followed. Initially the strike force provided its own flak suppression in the form of firing the Thud's 20mm Gatling gun while diving in on a target for a 750 pound bomb or a rocket run. Later in the war, as the ground defenses became more concentrated, advance planes were assigned the task of flak suppression for the strike force. Before the SAM (surface-to-air missile) appeared in SEA, it was not uncommon to initiate bomb runs above 20,000 feet, passing through the 85mm and 100mm flak bursts on the way down. The appearance of the SAMs dictated a change in tactics in the target area, where the F-105 strike force would fly into the target at 500–550 knots IAS (indicated air speed) below 1,000 feet above ground level, fly over an IP (initial point), pop up to 8,000 feet to acquire the target, then dive to expend their ordnance and exit the target area low and fast.

In the period 1964–1965, the targets assigned were supply bridges and truck parks and similar low-priority targets along the Ho Chi Minh Trail in Laos. Too often the flights would find that the assigned bridges had been bombed out many times previously so they turned to secondary targets, often road reconnaissance missions along bombed-out hulks of trucks and trailers. We wondered who would send so many valuable strike fighters and their pilots on missions that involved such non-targets. We later learned that it was the number of sorties that mattered, not the damage done to the enemy forces.

The 36th TFS returned to Yokota AB in late 1964, to return to Thailand again in 1965 and 1966 at Takhli RTAB, again in a TDY (temporary duty) status. The spring of 1965 brought a whole new air war to SEA. The USAF took the fight to North Vietnam in the operation known as Rolling Thunder, the first sustained bombing of the north. Targets assigned had real meaning, and the air defenses had a level of sophistication not seen before. Targeting was coming from the JCS (Joint Chiefs of Staff) level and was very specific, with strict limits on what could and could not be hit. Losses were heavy, but rescues were made possible by the courageous actions of the SAR (search and rescue) teams, consisting of a C-130 Crown, several A-1 Sandys and the HH-3 Jolly Green Giant rescue helicopters. F-105 losses were particularly heavy. An in-house "joke" defined an optimist as an F-105 pilot in SEA who gave up smoking for fear of dying of lung cancer!

This is where my bad-news part of the story begins. I was duty officer one night when a Frag Order (an abbreviated version of an operational order, a schedule for the next day's flying) came in calling for two flights of four Thuds to be loaded with six 750 pound iron bombs each for a strike in North Vietnam the next morning. The problem was that there were only seven bombs on the base. Because the number of combat sorties logged was the name of the game, seven Thuds were loaded with one bomb each and the eighth plane was launched with only a load of 20mm ammunition to accomplish the destruction of a very active AAA site. Needless to say, the report to the JCS would show that eight sorties were flown on a bombing mission against North Vietnam.

Shortly thereafter we received a shipment of Snake Eye 500 pound, folding-fin retarded bombs until the 750 pound iron bombs could be delivered. Since the tactic of delivering a retarded bomb was not applicable to our operation, the decision was made to bind the fins with wire and drop the 500 pounders as slick bombs. Needless to say we did not have the ballistic tables for such a configuration, and the estimated bomb-sight settings caused the destruction of many trees and fields not associated with our assigned targets!

It seems that the Navy was able to provide color movies of its BDA (bomb damage assessment) for the JCS's viewing pleasure, while the Air Force was operating under the false impression that we went to North Vietnam, risking our lives, to destroy targets. We found out that the movies were now a required part of our mission, so for a period of time in 1966, every fourth F-105 was equipped with a wing-mounted color movie pod. Unfortunately, the pod was not compatible with most of our bomb loads, so good old number four was going up north naked, just so we could match the Navy's attempt for an Academy Award!

One final story and I'll get on to other areas of interest. It seems the Air Force was not getting its share of MiG kills (shoot-downs), so a plan was devised to remedy this situation. Sixteen F-105s were to fly a route into Route Pac 6* that passed just north of Kep Airfield, en route to a POL (petroleum, oil, and lubricants) storage facility northwest of Haiphong. Flights of F-4s were flying cover for the strike force with the intent to destroy any MiGs that would launch against the F-105s. The operation produced several MiG kills, so it was decided to repeat the mission for another six days in a row, using the same route, at the same time, and at the same altitude every day. After the second day, the North Vietnamese caught on to the plan and didn't rise to the bait. The Thuds, however, continued to be subjected to the ongoing AAA fire along the route.

A final note about an aspect of the F-105 operation in SEA that is little known was a brief attempt to use the Thud in a ground support role, working with airborne FACs (forward air controllers) flying the O-1 Birddog. In early 1965 I was with a flight of four F-105s sent from Takhli to Da Nang AB in South Vietnam to see if such ground support operations were possible. Because of its size and speed, the Thud had a large turning radius, and we were there a week before it became obvious to all that this usage of the F-105 was not practical.

If any of you reading this had some involvement in the air war over Vietnam, you know only too well the dedication and professional commitment of the airmen conducting that war. Those of us who returned must never forget those who did not. I will forever keep and hold dear the memory of those brave comrades who gave their lives so that we who returned could have the choice of the lives that we have lived since our return. Thank you, "John B.," who was hit in the cockpit on his first mission; "Rocky," whose bomb load did not release and who was not able to jettison them before hitting the earth; "Nasty Ned," who was blown up by his own bombs as he backed away from a KC-135 tanker after refueling; "Shu," who was lost while res-capping a downed squadron mate (flying cover for a rescue attempt); "Pogie," who was lost over China, unable to get his damaged Thud going in the right direction. Thank you, guys!

After a short stint at Hughes Aircraft Co., I joined Western Airlines in February 1968.

*North Vietnam was divided into six Route Packages for defining bombing missions in the north. Route Pac 1 was farthest south, adjacent to the DMZ (demilitarized zone dividing North and South Vietnam) and Route Pac 6 was farthest north, divided into Pac 6A and 6B. Route Pac 6 included Hanoi and Haiphong, the two most heavily defended target areas.

....

The following quote is from the Forward to the book Roll Call Thud, *written by Colonel Jack Broughton, author of* Thud Ridge *and an outspoken critic of the ROE (rules of engagement) that put many targets off limits:*

"How does a nuke fighter enter a conventional war? Rather awkwardly at first, but with experienced and dedicated people and a solid Republic airframe, we got the job done rather quickly. The bomb bay became a fuel tank, the cannon in the nose became important again, and the care, handling, and loading of iron bombs all over the underside of the aircraft was of prime concern....The amazing thing is that the Thud did such a great job fighting a war it was not designed for. It hauled huge loads through shocking weather, put the bombs right in the pickle barrel, out-dueled the MiGs, whipped the SAMS, survived some incredible battle damage, and got a lot of us back home. It is no wonder that those of us who had the opportunity to fly and fight up north thought of the Thud with affection."

Silver F-105s on the ramp at Korat RTAB, August 1964. From the group of the first 18 F-105s to be sent to Thailand.

F-105D #62-4358 making what was called a cartridge engine start (where an explosive cartridge was used to spin up the engine) at Korat, 1964. The blue decal on the tail section is the PACAF logo (Pacific Air Forces) from their unit at Yokota. As an indication of the losses suffered by the F-105s, this aircraft was shot down by AAA on June 21, 1966 with the pilot, Lt. J. B. Sullivan, listed as MIA (Missing in Action, not recovered).

Jerry Stamps in Thailand, wearing orange flight suit, 1964.

Flight-line ramp at Takhli, 1965. Fewer than 1/3 of the F-105s sport their new camouflage paint jobs. Note construction and expansion of the ramp.

2

A LONG DAY'S JOURNEY
TO THE FAR EAST

Tom Blair, USAF, KC-135, 1964
{ Date of hire by Western Airlines: 2/26/1968 }

Tom Blair, Western Airlines Logbook, 1986.

I met Tom Blair while doing work with the Air Line Pilots Association, the union that represented the Western pilots. Tom was an elected representative from the Los Angeles base and I was a rep from San Francisco, and we worked together in the early 1980s on all the issues leading up to the merger with Delta. After the merger I flew with Tom on several occasions, after our San Francisco base had been closed and I was flying as a copilot on the Boeing 757/767 out of Los Angeles. I knew he had flown KC-135s in the Air Force, but he never talked much about it when we worked together. Tom invited me to his retirement party in May 1998, and it was at the party that I caught him in a weak moment and asked him if he would write something for this book. Tom had never related this story to me, but after I asked him it showed up in the mail several weeks later. I had no idea what to expect

*when it arrived, and although it is a unique and funny story, it has great
historical significance.*

*Before the big Air Force buildup in Thailand and the beginning of the
sustained bombing of North Vietnam, the planning for what was to be
called Operation Rolling Thunder was well under way. Establishing a massive program of aerial refueling was as important as getting the bombers to
Thailand and building up the bases to accommodate them. This required
SAC (the Strategic Air Command) to make its tankers available and to
modify some of its B-52 nuclear bombers to carry conventional bombs. It
was a huge change in the middle of the Cold War, when SAC was responsible for 24/7 nuclear alert with the B-52 and KC-135 fleets. There was also
a concern about the proximity of China and how the Chinese might react
when this huge operation got under way so close to their border.*

*Along comes Lieutenant Tom Blair, a KC-135 pilot based at Altus AFB,
Oklahoma, in the early 1960s. I will lead in to his story by saying that Tom
is a real character. This is one of the funniest Vietnam tales I have heard—
and I have heard a lot of them!*

*The KC-135 was the aerial tanker that sat on alert with the B-52 fleet
and was set to launch simultaneously with the nuclear bombers to refuel
them and get them to their targets and back home in the event of war with
the Soviet Union. This is the story of the very beginning of Operation
Rolling Thunder, the first serious, continuous bombing of North Vietnam.*

*Rolling Thunder began on March 2, 1965. Tom was a KC-135 pilot who
was taken away from his job at Altus AFB, Oklahoma, in the early-morn-
ing hours and sent on a secret mission that was so classified he was concerned about disclosing dates and unit designations nearly 50 years later.
The briefings he was given and the security documents he was required to
sign obviously got his attention! I can only estimate that this took place in
late 1964. Tom's very funny account of the 24 hours following his 3 a.m.
phone call follows.*

....

Altus Air Force Base, Oklahoma. The sixties. I got the phone on
the third ring. It was 3:03 a.m. You look at the clock automatically
when the phone rings at that time of the night. "Good morning,
Lieutenant Blair. This is Major Jackson in the Control Room."

"Yes sir."

"Tom, we have a message for you from SAC." This meant SAC Headquarters and certainly got my attention. "You are supposed to report to Base Operations ASAP. We will have a plane standing by for you. And, by the way, you better bring your deployment kit."

"What is going on? Where am I going?"

"Can't tell you; just get down there as soon as you can."

"What about orders?"

"Your orders will catch up with you—better get going."

I was at Base Operations 20 minutes later. Their orders were to get me to a SAC base in the northeastern part of Arkansas as soon as possible. That's all they were told.

My idea of a base operations aircraft for this kind of trip was a T-38 or at the very least a Saberliner, the North American jet with the F-86 wing. It was widely used for transporting the brass and for recurrent training of pilots assigned to non-flying positions. There was usually one sitting around the Base Operations area at the larger Air Force bases or at least one on call. The FAA used this aircraft for many years to flight-check navigation facilities around the world. I thought I might even get a little "stick time" during the flight. Not this time. The only aircraft available was a C-47 (a World War II–vintage aircraft that was the military version of the DC-3). A C-47!

We lifted off at exactly 3:40 a.m., just 37 minutes after my notification. That was the last time I remember checking the time that day. It was going to be a very, very long day.

FLYING LOW

I was awakened by the loadmaster tapping me on the shoulder. "Sir, we need you to put this on." He was holding a parachute. A parachute? I noticed he already had his on. "What the f*** is going on?"

"Well, sir, we lost an engine, and the only place this plane is going is down. They are going to try to make it to Fort Smith Muni." He mumbled something about the other engine and started back toward the cockpit. "By the way, sir, they'll have transportation for you in Fort Smith."

"Jesus f***ing Christ."

FLYING HIGH: FROM FORT SMITH MUNI

I was strapped in the back seat of an Arkansas Air Guard RF-84. Man-oh-man, this thing looked old—just like the C-47. I was thinking, I sure hope it runs better! The F-84 briefing: "Bail out! Bail out! Bail out!" The pilot made it very clear that if I was not out of the bird by the third "bail out," I would be flying solo. The ejection briefing was short and to the point. "Lower your visor, head back, arms and legs in, raise and squeeze the handles, any questions?" I was supposed to eject first since I would be in the backseat. If I didn't go first, in all likelihood I would not make it. The pilot mumbled something about the canopy and the blast from the front seat. He discussed, very briefly, the intercom and the use of the oxygen system. "That's all you need to know," he said. I knew by now that stick time was really out of the question and that this guy was not happy that his Sunday brunch was going downhill on a lead sled. I thought the National Guard always flew on the weekends. Evidently, he didn't.

The pilot, a major, was by now becoming quite a bit friendlier. I suppose he realized that this was going to be an easy trip and a good way to earn his flight pay for the month. My goodies, my deployment kit and flight kit, were in the nose compartment in the space where the cameras were normally located. We were on our way. The leg was uneventful, and I liked that!

ACROSS THE POND

The KC-135 was sitting on the taxiway at the end of the runway at the SAC base in Northeastern Arkansas. We rolled directly up to it in the RF-84. I noticed it had two engines already running. It took about five minutes for my goodies and me to be transferred to the KC. What, no breakfast?

I interrupted the boom operator about two sentences into his passenger briefing. After all, I was qualified on the aircraft as an EWO (electronic warfare officer) and a Stan Board (standards board) puke (check pilot). I didn't need to hear his spiel. I was sleepy, hungry, thirsty, and just a little bit perplexed. What was the urgency of this trip? Where was I going?

"Sir, we don't know. The plane is going to Guam. We're getting off in Hickeyloo. You're staying with the plane. That's all we were told." Hickeyloo meant Honolulu. Great!

The flight from Arkansas to Hawaii was routine. I got some sleep and had a couple of excellent meals. The flight kitchen that catered this flight loaded it with great food, SAC's best, including steaks and ice cream with all the fixings for sundaes. I thought only the bomber crews ate like this. The BO (boom operator) was a great cook.

I was looking forward to the layover in Honolulu. The great weather, the warm water, the girls and the cheap drinks at the military club located on the beach in the heart of Waikiki. Wow!

"What, no layover? There must be some mistake. Isn't there something wrong with the airplane? Can't we break something? Can't someone get sick? I guess not." Two hours later and with a new flight crew—aircraft commander, copilot, navigator, and boom operator—I was on my way to Guam.

About two hours out of Guam, the BO informed me that they had received a message addressed to me. It was coded! Must be pretty important. The navigator and I spent the next several minutes deciphering the message. It turned out to be pretty simple. There was a plane waiting for me at Guam. A plane waiting for me! This was getting ridiculous, laughable. I had been up for what seemed like days. My clothes looked about as bad as I did, and my last shower had worn off hours earlier. A shave and pupu juice just wasn't cutting it anymore. To top it off, my inquiries to SAC requesting clarification of my mission were only acknowledged as being received. No information, no orders.

TWO A-TURNING, TWO A-BURNING

The airman was out of his car and shouting at the aircraft commander through the open cockpit window. "Do you have Lieutenant Blair aboard?"

"He's here."

"Good, send him down."

I couldn't help but notice the smile, really a smirk, on his face as he said, "Sir, we have transport waiting for you. I'll run you over to it."

I had never seen a KC-97. It looked like a surviving memorial of something gone by. I think there was a trace of the World War II–era B-50 in its past. It looked old, worn.

I had heard stories about the 97: two engines running, two engines shut down. Two a-turning, two a-burning. I had heard pilots say, "We never made a takeoff without losing an engine, but it flew great on three engines." Someone said he never landed with all of his engines producing power. I was going to be in the back of one of these for several hours, "a long one, and over the water," according to the boom operator who gave me a short airplane and over-water briefing.

The cockpit was huge. I think there were two extra seats, jump seats as they are now called. I couldn't have cared less about riding in the cockpit. I just wanted to get off the thing.

I excused myself and proceeded out of the cockpit to the rear of the plane. I could at least stretch out on one of the bunks. There were no bunks! There weren't even any seats! No seats! No bunks! There wasn't even running water in the john. You had to pump each squirt of water with a little plunger. I was beginning to hope that this piece of junk would go down just to get rid of the thing. There would be water and it would be warm!

WELCOME TO THE FAR EAST

The airman no-class (very low-ranking airman) rushed around the car to open the door for me, and inside sat a captain. "I'm Captain James from Colonel Harris's office. The colonel wants to see you immediately."

It was a three-minute ride to the colonel's office.

I looked like crap. I smelled worse than a horse and I was on my way to a colonel's office.

"Lieutenant Blair, this is Colonel Harris." Colonel Harris was a large man, a bird colonel, a no-nonsense type. He was standing as we entered his office. I snapped to attention and gave him a sharp salute, but I was not a pretty picture. What an impression! Couldn't this have waited until tomorrow?

"At ease! Welcome to the Far East, son. How was your trip?"

Before I could answer, he continued: "Your mission is Top Secret. You are not to discuss where you are, where you came from, or what you are doing here. You are restricted to the base. Is this clear? Report to work tomorrow at oh six hundred." The captain and I jumped to attention. "Dismissed!"

Outside, the captain addressed me. "Tom, Hayes (the airman who had picked me up at the aircraft) will help you get checked into the TOQ."I learned later that TOQ meant Transient Officers Quarters. "Why don't you meet me at the club in a couple of hours and I'll fill you in. Give transportation a call when you are ready to come over. Hayes will pick you up. See you in a while." This Captain James seemed like a nice guy, and it turned out that Colonel Harris was a good guy too.

Fill me in at the club? I thought this was Top Secret. You don't discuss things like this at the Officers' Club! What was going on here? Was I being tested? We spent the next few hours eating and drinking and drinking and eating and watching the sharks circle the Pan Am stewardesses. No secrets were passed.

I was at the office early the next morning, well before the 0600 report time. I was rested and ready to go to work.

I spent the next several weeks flying every third day and working in the office, "12 on and 12 off," the rest of the time. There were no days off. My immediate group consisted of three crews from my home squadron, a couple of enlisted types doing paperwork, Captain James, and Colonel Harris. We crew pukes were not permitted to wander the rest of the building (on the unspecified base, presumably in Thailand). Security! I suppose it was to prevent the exchange of information, the old "need to know" concept.

It turned out that we were planning and testing the tanker support to what was to become known as Rolling Thunder. We also flew missions with tracks heading directly toward Mainland China. We gave them a little tickle here, a little tickle there. We got them to activate their radar and even launch their MiGs occasionally. Would they give more than just moral support to the North? But we had the bomb!

Those were exciting times. We worked long hours, and most of us loved every minute of it. The missions, I suppose, excited Washington, the Mainland, and the North. They also produced a lot of great war stories for us about this little secret war in the Far East that would soon be secret no more.

I was never able to determine why the big hurry to get me to that assignment. I was simply replacing a pilot who had become sick, and not very sick at that. Nevertheless, he was sent home and I was sent over there to be a party in our government's role in the affairs of the Far East. I suppose the urgency to get me there at any cost was more than a little prophetic of the significance of what was to come.

I do not know how long secrets must be kept secret. Therefore, specific dates, bases, units, and names must remain unspecified. I never did receive official orders for this deployment. I guess the Air Force "knew" about me, for I received several forms of official recognition.

3

FLAMING HOOKER

Vern Sluyter, USN, RA-5C, 1965
{ Date of hire by Western Airlines: 10/28/1968 }

Vern Sluyter, Western Airlines Logbook, 1986.

Vern Sluyter was one of the first copilots I flew with at Western Airlines when I was assigned as a second officer on the Boeing 737 at the San Francisco pilot base in early 1974. My initial assignment as a new hire had me flying as a second officer on the Boeing 707/720B out of Los Angeles, but war in the Middle East in 1973 changed everything. The spike in fuel prices caused Western Airlines to realign its flying and reschedule many domestic flights on its smaller, more fuel-efficient aircraft. They ended up parking most of the 707/720B fleet. This bumped me off the airplane, so I went back to school to train for the Boeing 737 and, after completing my training in Los Angeles, I arrived at the San Francisco base in February 1974. The copilot (first officer) group consisted of pilots hired from 1967 through 1969, and almost all were ex-military and Vietnam veterans. There were Marines like Bill McGaw, Charlie Coxe, Hank Lecy, and Bill Wilson, Navy pilots like Vern Sluyter, Tom Rodger, Tom Goldt, Bob Zimmerman, and Greg Bambo, and Air Force pilots Roy Sordi, Don Avary, John Erickson, Pete Kammermeyer, Larry Reisinger, and of course, Bill Horky, a fellow C-7A Caribou pilot and a San Francisco base legend. It was a gold mine of Vietnam flying stories, and I had a wonderful time. What I would have given for a tape recorder!

Vern Sluyter was like a recruiting poster for a fighter pilot from a different era, born a generation or so too late. He fit right into the mold of the World War II pilots I had come to know when I was based in Los Angeles on the 707/720B. Vern was a bit over six feet tall, trim with gray wavy hair, and he always had a toothpick in his mouth. Quiet, competent, and very much a loner, Vern would talk only in generalities about his Vietnam flying, only if asked, and he would change the subject as soon as he could. I probably would have been a good interrogator, as I always tried to learn the correct formula for getting men like Vern to talk about Vietnam—and here emerged a universal truth: The men with the best stories never volunteered them and tended to talk the least about their experiences.

Vern told me he flew the A-5 Vigilante (the Vigy) in a Navy photo reconnaissance squadron. These were the pilots who flew to the target area after a bombing strike to photograph the results for the famous BDA (bomb damage assessment). The Air Force did it with the RF-4 and RF-101 from bases in Thailand, while the Navy did it from aircraft carriers with the RA-5C and RF-8G and the USMC used the RF-4B.

Imagine this if you can: A large strike (called an Alpha Strike) was launched from one or more of the aircraft carriers on Yankee Station. (Yankee Station was a point in the Gulf of Tonkin from which aircraft carriers of Task Force 77 launched strikes into North Vietnam. There were normally three carriers "on the line" at Yankee Station.) A strike could include 40 or more aircraft, including support aircraft (aerial tankers and rescue helicopters), Iron Hand jamming aircraft for SAM (surface-to-air missile) and AAA (anti-aircraft artillery) suppression, fighter bombers, and fighters to fly overhead MIG CAP (to guard the rest of the strike aircraft from attack by North Vietnamese MiG fighters). After the strike the BDA had to be made by one or more reconnaissance aircraft, and of course the North Vietnamese knew the routine and were ready and waiting for the unarmed recon birds. Reason enough to write about Vern Sluyter comes in the words of his friend Mike Doyle, who looked at me very seriously and said, "You know, they didn't let just anybody fly the Vigy."

Now, after that little bit of introduction, we'll go back in time and find Vern and me on a layover in Idaho Falls, Idaho, sometime in the mid to late 1970s.

....

At the Stardust Lounge at the Stardust Motor Lodge in Idaho Falls, Idaho, Vern showed me the Flaming Hooker. We were on a layover, and I soon learned that this was the formula to start Vern talking. The Flaming Hooker was a shot glass of Drambuie, set on fire, then tossed from several inches into one's mouth in a stream of flame. I offered to buy the Drambuie, and if Vern was feeling generous he would not swallow it but return the Drambuie to the shot glass and repeat the procedure. This, of course, made for quite a show in a dark corner of the Stardust Lounge, and we always ended up with a large audience, sometimes including passengers who were flying out with us the next day! There was quite a lot of technique to keep from singeing mustaches or other facial hair, but the main idea was not to drink too many, reuse the Drambuie, and try to keep the aim accurate!

One night at the Stardust, during and after a Flaming Hooker show, Vern began to talk a bit about the Vigilante, and I have since done a bit of research about it. The RA-5C was originally designed as a carrier-based nuclear strike bomber but ended up in the reconnaissance role due to its supersonic speed, its impressive agility, and its capacity to hold sophisticated electronic equipment and cameras. According to my research, there were 98 RA-5C aircraft originally produced. Eighteen were lost in combat and nine were lost in operational accidents, prompting the Navy to order 36 additional RA-5Cs as replacements. So Vern flew an aircraft that sustained close to a 28 percent loss rate. He told me one of the most nerve-racking procedures was lining up for the catapult launch from the carrier, especially at night. The Vigilante was a very large airplane, and the nose gear sat far aft of the cockpit. Turning the aircraft around to line up for launch put the ground crew of 18- and 19-year-olds in complete control as the cockpit swung out over the edge of the boat and over the water on its way to lining up for takeoff. Vern remarked that he was strapped into his seat with the canopy closed, and if the ground crew miscalculated the position of the nose gear, they would dump him and his Vigilante over the side and he would go right to the bottom of the Gulf of Tonkin!

The best I could get from him was that their mission was pretty simple. They flew low and very fast over the target area of the bombing strike, took photos for the BDA, turned around and returned to the boat. What could go wrong in that scenario? Of the 18 Vigilantes lost in combat, 14 were lost to ground fire, 3 were lost to surface-to-air missiles, and 1 was shot down by a MiG-21. Of those lost in operational accidents, Vern speculated that the pilots may have pulled up too sharply when encountering ground fire, putting too much G-force on the airframe. At the high rate of speed they always flew, this may have caused catastrophic structural failure, such as the wings separating from the airplane.

The San Francisco pilot base was closed by Delta after the merger with Western; Vern transferred to the Salt Lake City base and I went to Los Angeles, so we never flew together again. Still, from the early 1980s to the mid-1990s I would see Vern around at one airport or another. My recollection of Vern was as a loner and a bit of a rebel, seldom wearing his hat and with his ever-present toothpick, strolling through the airport as if he were on the way to a night catapult launch. In the 1990s when I would see him, I would pester him about writing a story for my book project, but he would always tell me he needed to look through his logbook and would get back to me. Vern retired in December 1996, and for all intents and purposes it was the end of any chance to get a story from him.

Then, right out of the blue, nearly a year and a half after he retired, I received a letter from him dated April 5, 1998. On first reading, it seemed he was telling me he couldn't come up with anything, but after I thought about it, I decided to use his letter as the basis for a story that would pay tribute to what he did and tell about a vital aspect of the air war that is seldom mentioned. His letter began with thoughts about retirement and what he had been doing in the last year or so. He had moved to a 10-acre place northeast of Portland, Oregon, and had been traveling to Alaska, Montana, and points in between on hunting and fishing trips and to Northern California to go abalone diving. I will begin the letter from this point:

The area [where] I live is in the foothills with minimum development and numerous species of game. I suppose that most folks would classify me as a sort of recluse—whatever, it is a complex world and life seems more complex the longer I hang around.

Primary subject—your book. I hope that your writing is progressing well. Authoring a book has got to be one major assignment and I do wish you success. Contribution from me is just not materializing—unfortunately. After reviewing my logbooks I just cannot come up with anything justifying publishing. I was with an RA-5C recon squadron onboard the USS Independence from September through November 1965 off the Vietnam coast. During that time I managed to fly only 25 combat flights. This low number was due to the low flight availability of the Vigilante (RA-5C). The machine had the latest high-tech recon gear available and was so maintenance demanding that a combat-ready machine was not the norm, as generally the equipment involved for a mission was not operational. What flights I did manage to get were uneventful and went off without harm. I departed and returned to the boat without any hair-raising tales. The most threatening flight that I had while flying the Vigy occurred while Trans Pac-ing (flying across the Pacific) a Vigy from Sanford, Florida, across the U.S., the Pacific, and finally to the USS Ranger off the Vietnam coast in February 1966. That is another tale, however, and is not combat-related.

So, my friend, I do appreciate your invite for your book material but I am unable to offer anything of importance. Sorry. I admire your drive tackling such a demanding project and hopefully will be able to read your accomplishment soon.

Good luck with your Delta career as well as all your other adventures.

Sincerely,

An old Western buddy,

Vern Sluyter

There is an RA-5C Vigilante on display at the Pima Air & Space Museum in Tucson, Arizona. Years after those early days in Idaho Falls, I was on a Tucson layover and made a pilgrimage out to see it and pay my respects to Vern. It is an awesome aircraft, big and threatening as it sits in the museum. If given the opportunity, I might even have tried a Flaming Hooker with a toast to Vern Sluyter.

RA-5C Vigilante off the coast of North
Vietnam, 1967. According to Navy records,
the RA-5C had the highest loss rate of any
Navy aircraft during the Vietnam War.
My hat's off to Vern Sluyter, who said in
all honesty and humility, "I am unable
to offer anything of importance. Sorry."

4

NINE LIVES
"COME WHEN CALLED"

Dick Hathcock, US Army, UH-1B, OH-13, 1965 – 1966
{ Date of hire by Western Airlines: 8/21/1967 }

*Dick Hathcock standing beside UH-1B Huey after an awards ceremony,
1965. Distinguished Flying Cross and Bronze Star have just been awarded.*

*I knew Dick Hathcock's name from Cal football's glory days, when I was in
high school and used to sneak into Memorial Stadium at halftime and
watch the games from the end zone. I first met him when we were both
doing work with the Air Line Pilots Association at Western Airlines just
prior to the Delta merger. Dick was an elected representative from the Los
Angeles base and I was a rep from the San Francisco base. We were
involved in a lot of weighty issues, as Western was in serious financial*

trouble and we were literally fighting for our lives in the very cutthroat airline environment of the early 1980s. When Dick found out I had gone to Cal and was a big football fan, we hit it off, especially when I told him that I used to sit on "Tightwad Hill" to watch the games when I was a teenager and had probably seen him play.

Dick is a big, tough guy, reminding me of the great Marine slogan, "No better friend; no worse enemy," and I'm happy to be on the front half of that slogan! When you read Dick's story you will see what I mean. My favorite Dick Hathcock story from the airline involved his coming back from the cockpit to talk to a belligerent passenger who had been very abusive to the flight attendants. The passenger made a near-fatal mistake by shoving the flight attendant and taking a swing at Dick. Dick hit him so hard he knocked him through the bulkhead wall and into the first row of seats in the center of the L-1011 first-class cabin. Of course a lawsuit was filed, requiring Dick to appear in court in Honolulu, but he prevailed. He said later he had wanted to do that for a long time, and now his airline career was complete!

Dick's story requires a little explanation, but rather than writing it here I will do it at the end so as not to get ahead of things for the reader. Now let me introduce you to Dick Hathcock, football player and Army ROTC at the University of California, Berkeley; Officer Basic Infantry Course, Airborne Training, and Ranger Training at Fort Benning, Georgia; Basic Rotary Wing Training at Fort Rucker, Alabama, solo 10 January 1962; Advanced Rotary Wing Training, then to the 11th Armored Cavalry in Straubing, Germany. Dick returned from Germany to the United States in 1964 and received orders for Vietnam in 1965.

....

Captain Richard B. Hathcock, 05704853, assigned to Company A, 82nd Aviation Battalion, 173rd Airborne Brigade in September 1965, arrived in Saigon, Republic of Vietnam, on September 7, 1965. He had departed the United States from Travis AFB in Fairfield, California, on a Continental Airlines charter flight via Honolulu. He arrived in Vietnam, able to smell the city of Saigon, aptly named the Tainted Pearl of the Orient, from 20,000 feet. After the normal in-country processing in the ever-present heat and humidity, he was released to barracks to wait for transportation to Bien Hoa.

The following afternoon a 173rd UH-1B helicopter arrived to pick him up for the ride, and his first contact with the 173rd Airborne Brigade was Captain Bob Watson. Watson informed Captain Hathcock that the brigade was on a search-and-destroy mission in the infamous Iron Triangle area of War Zone D. Hathcock was told that they would proceed to Bien Hoa AB that afternoon, and then at first light he would be taken to the operation and begin his in-country orientation on how to operate and survive in Vietnam.

Upon arrival at Bien Hoa, he was greeted by other members of the 173rd who had been in-country since July and, according to them, were already seasoned veterans. They could hardly wait to relate their war stories of the past month and a half, especially when they noticed the Ranger tab and jump wings on Captain Hathcock's uniform. All soldiers must take the measure of the FNG (F—ing New Guy) to see if he is going to be able to hack the program!

Captain Hathcock was issued field equipment, armored vest, and M-16 rifle; he already had his own .45-caliber revolver and toad sticker (knife). After a meal of C rations and a group BS session, they all went to bed. Hathcock was given the warning to keep his mosquito net in place because the rats sometimes would try to get in your bunk. The other part of the briefing was what to do in case the compound was mortared. Everyone was to proceed to the nearest bunker, and one guy was designated to enter the bunker first, helmet in hand, in order to chase out the giant rats.

The following morning at 0400, Captain Hathcock was awakened and told to be ready for a 0500 departure for the brigade's area of operations in the Iron Triangle. This was the third day in Vietnam for Hathcock and he was apprehensive as to what lay ahead. The flight was a short one, over intense green jungle, and as the UH-1B approached the infamous Iron Triangle, the jungle canopy seemed to rise and become very thick and heavy. The LZ (landing zone) was in a relatively large opening in the jungle, and the headquarters of the 173rd Airborne Brigade was located next to a paved macadam road.

The pilot shut the Huey down and led Captain Hathcock to the TOC (tactical operations center). As they arrived, two artillery troops, a captain and a first sergeant, were receiving a briefing from the operations officer, who was a lieutenant colonel. Their briefing was an operation order telling them to find a suitable artillery-fire base position that would allow resupply by helicopter, and then to report their findings by radio. The operations officer said the area was secure for several kilometers on the road and told them to report ASAP so they could begin to bring in the artillery for support. The captain and first sergeant departed in a jeep along with a driver and a radio operator.

As the jeep departed, the aviation platoon commander arrived to greet Captain Hathcock and assigned him to a seasoned first lieutenant pilot who was sitting on call (which was called chopper alert). The lieutenant would be in charge of Hathcock's flight operation orientation and field SOP (standard operating procedures) briefing. The briefing began with a map orientation of the brigade's area of operation and the prominent terrain features of War Zone C.

No more than 15 minutes after the briefing began, a call for help came from the artillery captain and first sergeant who had just left the TOC; they were under heavy fire and had hit a land mine along the road. The call sent the lieutenant and Captain Hathcock running to the waiting alert Huey, where two door gunners were already in place. As the engine started, Hathcock was in the right-hand seat and the lieutenant in the left, and as the lieutenant briefed the gunners over the intercom, he took off. The Huey flew low along the road for approximately five minutes until an opening appeared in the jungle canopy. The radio screamed that the jeep was still under fire and that there were two dead and two wounded. The fire was coming from the right edge of the woods, and the Huey gunners opened fire with their M60 machine guns, spraying the trees. The helicopter flared just prior to touchdown near the overturned jeep, and Hathcock could see that the captain and first sergeant were wounded and that the driver and radio operator were down. Just at touchdown, heavy automatic-weapons fire erupted from a different area and the Huey's windshield shattered. At the same time, one of the door gunners was hit and killed. The Huey hit hard and came to a shuddering rest right side up. The lieutenant and Hathcock exited the Huey in a hail of fire and hit the ground. It seemed like a long time, but it was only seconds before reinforcements arrived in the form of gunships from Company A of the 82nd, the Cowboys. As they opened up with supporting fire, the Vietcong made a hasty retreat while the lieutenant, Captain Hathcock, and the surviving door gunner lay in shock as the firefight ended. Captain Richard B. Hathcock thought that after only three days in-country he might not survive the remaining 11 months and 27 days of his tour in Vietnam.

Fast-forward to December 1965, and Captain Hathcock, now a seasoned veteran, relates the following story:

Early on 17 December 1965, the 173rd Airborne Brigade, commanded by Brigadier General Ellis Williamson, conducted Operation Smash 1. The brigade moved from the Vo Dat area (40 miles northeast of Bien Hoa) to the vicinity of the Courtney Plantation Airstrip in a combined heliborne and ground movement. Intelligence summaries indicated that the Vietcong were going to make an attack during the holiday season in the general area of Xuan Loc and Ham Tan (an area just north of Saigon). The 173rd Airborne Brigade, in conjunction with the 2nd Brigade, 1st Infantry Division, was to conduct a swift spoiling operation in Phuoc Tuy Province.

This was a month of continuous combat operations, and the crews of Company A of the 82nd Airborne Aviation Battalion were flying night and day in support of the 173rd Airborne Brigade. When Operation Smash 1 began, it started off with a heliborne airlift to Courtney Plantation Airstrip, and from there we flew the 2/503rd Infantry Battalion to a spot called LZ Prancer. The 2/503rd moved east from LZ Prancer and ran into heavy action with a battalion-size VC force that was employing heavy machine guns and anti-tank weapons. Company B of the 503rd moved through the jungle and smashed a VC ambush that was set up on the trail leading from the LZ to the area of contact by the 2/503rd. Heavy pressure was brought to bear on the VC position, but the VC chose to stay and fight throughout the afternoon, taking heavy losses from the firepower of the 2nd Battalion and the supporting air and artillery. At 1700 hours the two engaged companies made a strong assault on the enemy positions, which convinced the VC that they had remained too long. During the hours of darkness the VC forces hastily pulled back and retreated from the area, leaving mortar and small-arms ammunition behind. Sixty-two Vietcong were confirmed killed in the action.

On 19 December the brigade continued to chase the fleeing VC without much success. My unit took Company C into a small village north of the Courtney Plantation in a helicopter assault and sealed off the village. This action resulted in the capture of 54 suspected VC, and we did not take fire in the assault. The unit S3 (in charge of planning and operations) decided we needed to find the main force VC unit and that an LRP (long-range patrol) would be assigned to do the job. My crew and I were given the task of inserting the LRP at a location in the northern portion of the operations area. The LRP was to remain out three days and locate the enemy. My mission was to take off just before dark on 19 December and to make several fake insertions before finally dropping the LRP team into the chosen position. My crew consisted of a copilot, Lieutenant Ivy Phelps, and two door gunners with M60 machine guns. We picked up the LRP team at LZ Prancer and conducted our briefing with the LRP team leader, an Army Ranger lieutenant, and his eight-man unit. The weather was clear and warm and the evening promised to turn into a very dark night, which was good for the LRP team. After the briefing everyone was on edge, anticipating the upcoming mission. The LRP team leader was nervous and stressed; his biggest fear was to be dropped into the middle of the VC and not have a way to get out quickly. I assured him that in the event this occurred, we would be back to pick up his team; all he had to do was call on the tactical frequency that we had prearranged.

We took off 30 minutes before dark and flew to the first fake insertion area. I was flying the mission, and the first and second areas of fake insertion were no problem. As darkness descended on the jungle, we picked out the real insertion point and I made the approach and dropped off the LRP team, then headed away from the spot to orbit in case of problems on the ground. The night was very dark and our adrenaline levels were very high. We had been orbiting for about 10 or 15 minutes when we heard a whisper on our radio over the tactical frequency. The LRP team leader was calling, saying that they were in the middle of a large VC unit and needed an immediate extraction. I told him we were on the way and would be there in five minutes, telling him to hold tight and we would get him out. The only reply was, "HURRY."

The LRP team had moved from the area of drop-off, and the leader would have to guide us to his location by flashing his strobe light. I immediately proceeded to the area and had the entire crew looking for the light. Suddenly the right-side door gunner picked up the strobe and directed me to the team's location. The LRP team leader said the VC guerillas were getting closer and the team would be discovered soon. Once again, it was very dark and very difficult to see obstructions on the ground. As I began an approach we started taking fire, with the VC using tracer rounds that looked as big as footballs. I kept on the approach, telling the door gunners not to fire because we did not know the exact location of the LRP team. This put us in a difficult position because we were being hit by small-arms fire, so once on the ground, I told the door gunners to cover the tree line but not to fire until we located the team. The lieutenant and his team were now taking fire and were having a hard time disengaging from the VC. There were no lights illuminated on the Huey and it was very dark, so I decided to leave the helicopter and find the team so I could lead them back to the Huey. I left Ivy Phelps in charge and told the gunners not to fire until I had located the team, then told the team I was coming after them and not to shoot to their rear. It seemed like a long time before I found the LRP team and started leading them back to the chopper, but I'm sure it was only seconds.

Heavy fire was coming from the wood line and the door gunners were now firing at the VC. When everyone was in the chopper, I took off in the direction opposite the enemy fire. There were some high trees that I had to get over to make it out of the landing area, and somehow we cleared the obstacles in the dark and were on our way out. The VC must have been really pissed because we could still see tracer rounds being fired as we climbed to safety. Once at a safe altitude, I told Ivy to take over the flying and then I started to shake. I guess I realized I had just used another of my nine lives and the number of remaining lives was getting smaller. I didn't like that feeling!

The LRP team was animated and wired, knowing how close they had come to being captured or killed, and they thanked the entire crew over and over. We knew we had made friends for life, even if we didn't know their names. Back on the ground and after all the celebration and thanks, we inspected our helicopter and found that we had been hit eight times. Luckily for us, the bullets had not hit a vital spot on the helicopter and we had lived to fight another day. The mission had been a success as we had located the VC, and death and destruction were put on them by air strikes and artillery with no friendly casualties. Operation Smash 1 ended on 22 December 1965, and we returned to our base camp at Bien Hoa and a safe Christmas.

Captain Richard Hathcock was awarded the DFC (Distinguished Flying Cross) for this mission. He received a second DFC for a mission flown on 16 March 1966, and I will reproduce the citation to describe the action:

GENERAL ORDERS NUMBER 5650 13 September 1966
TC 320. The following award is announced.
HATHCOCK, RICHARD B. 05704853 CAPTAIN INFANTRY
United States Army Co A, 82d AvnBn, 173rdAbnBde (Sep),
APO 96250
Awarded: Distinguished Flying Cross (First Oak Leaf Cluster)
Date action: 16 March 1966
Theater: Republic of Vietnam
Reason: For heroism while participating in aerial flight. Captain Hathcock distinguished himself by exceptionally valorous actions on 16 March 1966 while serving as an aerial artillery forward observer and controller during an attack by a large Viet Cong force on a friendly perimeter in the Republic of Vietnam. Upon entering the operational area, in which a battle was already in progress, Captain Hathcock's OH-13 helicopter received intense hostile fire. Although repeatedly exposed to the Viet Cong fire, Captain Hathcock remained over the area to relay radio messages from the ground commander to the commanding general and higher headquarters on the battle. During the course of the action, it became necessary to re-supply the beleaguered ground force with ammunition by helicopter. At this time, Captain Hathcock remained in constant radio contact with the ground force commander and the supporting artillery to maintain close and continuous fire support until the re-supply aircraft made their passes over the

target area. During periods of artillery cease fire, his professional assistance in directing armed helicopter air strikes and
controlling the actions of mortar aerial delivery bombers
enabled the rifle company commanders to maintain the fire
superiority which was essential in preventing the insurgents
from breaching the perimeter defense. On one occasion,
Captain Hathcock halted a helicopter air strike which was
misdirected on friendly positions, thus preventing numerous
American casualties. During the final phase of the battle,
Captain Hathcock, with complete disregard for his safety,
landed his light observation aircraft amidst intense hostile fire
and secured vital information for the commanding general
from the ground force commander. Through his courageous
actions, Captain Hathcock was most instrumental in the successful operation. His outstanding flying ability and devotion
to duty were in keeping with the highest traditions of the military service and reflect great credit upon himself, his unit,
and the United States Army.
Authority: By direction of the President under the provisions
of the Act of Congress, approved 2 July 1926.

....

*Here is a brief addition to Dick's story by way of explaining the LRP
team insertion. Long-range reconnaissance patrols and reconnaissance
teams (RTs) were inserted by helicopter, often in close proximity to the
enemy and often in cross-border operations (in Laos, Cambodia, or North
Vietnam). The trust that the team leader had in the helicopter crew that
dropped his team off was absolute. He knew they would COME WHEN
CALLED, returning for his team if things got too hot. Coming back for a
team right after an insertion was a hairy scenario under the best of circumstances and bad enough in the daylight. At night it was worse because
operating with no lights and trying to find a safe landing zone in the dark
was about as challenging as it gets. But to land and leave the helicopter to
go looking for the team was about the ultimate in courage and craziness,
giving true meaning to the phrase "above and beyond." I think both these
human qualities were required in large quantity to do what Dick did.*

His DFC citation reads, "Captain Hathcock returned to his helicopter and hovered from position to position in the perilous battle area until the patrol members were safely aboard."

*From my own experience, I have a good idea of the arbitrary nature of awards and decorations and how they were handled by different units. In my mind this action deserves far more than a Distinguished Flying Cross. One unit would say these men were just doing their job, while another would recommend a Silver Star or Distinguished Service Cross for the same action. I am reminded of Lyndon Johnson, who **asked** to be written up for a Silver Star—and received one from General Douglas MacArthur—while touring the South Pacific as a **congressman** during World War II. He wore it proudly in his lapel throughout his presidency. Then who can forget John Kerry, who was written up for and received a Silver Star, a Bronze Star, and three Purple Hearts in a four-month period in Vietnam. Using a little-known regulation to cut short his one-year tour after receiving his third Purple Heart, he joined Vietnam Veterans Against the War on his return Stateside. His anti-war activities with such notables as Jane Fonda were used by the North Vietnamese to great effect in their interrogations of the POWs. Never questioned about these activities in his confirmation hearings, he is now Secretary of State.*

Personally, I would rather have Jim Fogg (who you will read about in an upcoming chapter) run the search-and-rescue and have Dick Hathcock land his Huey and come into the jungle looking for me if I were in trouble!

LRP (Long Rang Patrol) boarding Dick's Huey, 1965.

*Dick Hathcock training an Australian pilot in the OH-13S
(S for supercharged!), 1965.*

Dick Hathcock in 2012. Uniform still fits and is worn proudly at age 75!

5

SPAD, NIGHT RESCUE MISSION

Gary Gottschalk, USN, A-1H, 6 November 1965
{ Date of hire by Western Airlines: 7/15/1968 }

Gary Gottschalk in the cockpit of his A-1H with his VA-152 patch clearly visible, on the deck of the USS Oriskany, 1965.

Gary Gottschalk provided much of the inspiration and encouragement for me to begin this project. It was something that had been percolating in my mind since I returned from Vietnam in May 1969, and as I thought it through, I realized that putting these stories together was the perfect way to accomplish my goal. I wanted to find a way to pay tribute to those who had served in Vietnam, and what would be better than a series of Vietnam flying stories written by men I had worked with over the years? You will remember from the introduction that I was flying with Gary in March 1997 when he gave me the names of several pilots he thought I should contact and also promised to contribute his own story. In one month Gary and I had gone from being complete strangers to being best of friends. We had developed a level of trust that was completely based on the respect derived from our common backgrounds and a common bond. He told me this story on a long leg from Atlanta to Los Angeles, and it just clicked with me that there were hundreds of stories like it, some that I had heard while flying around the country for Western and Delta, but most that I had not. It became my goal to work my way through his list of names, contact those I had flown with over the years, and see if this concept could become a reality. It has, and Gary has been there right from the beginning. If I were to name all those whose encouragement has kept me going, I would have to list everyone who wrote a story and several who chose not to but urged me on nonetheless. To say that this has been a rewarding experience would be an understatement.

Gary was involved at the beginning of Operation Rolling Thunder, the first sustained bombing of North Vietnam by the United States. It began on March 2, 1965. Just like another Navy pilot featured in this book, Bob Wood, Gary has a brother who was also a Navy pilot and flew the F-8 Crusader in Vietnam. There are a lot of coincidences and lots of exclamations of "what a small world" in military aviation, especially when those military pilots go to war and then get dispersed throughout the airline industry when they leave the service.

Gary had suggested I contact Fred Guenzel, who had flown the A-1H with him aboard the USS Oriskany. All Gary would say was, "Contact Fred. He has quite a story, and get him to tell you about the fire on the Oriskany—he was there." (A tragic fire aboard the Oriskany on 26 October 1966 killed 44 people. Many of them were combat pilots who had just returned from a morning strike.) I had flown with Fred when I was based in San Francisco years earlier but never knew anything about his military background. All I knew for sure about Fred was that he lived in Berkeley and made beer in his garage! When I asked, he just told me he didn't do anything special or worth writing about but wished me luck with my project. Although I would have loved to have Fred's story, I knew that the contributors to this book would be only a small sample of the hundreds of Vietnam veterans who were hired by Western Airlines. The vast majority of the U.S. airline pilots from the mid to late 1960s on through the mid 2000s had flown combat in Vietnam, and they came home to live very productive and rewarding lives. As I have said previously, I'm honored to have known and worked with so many of them over the years.

Now here is Garry Gottschalk's story from November 1965.

·······

It was my first shipboard cruise—all of it spent flying combat, with 90 missions to date as a lieutenant junior grade, United States Navy, and an A-1H Skyraider attack pilot. I was aboard the USS *Oriskany* in the squadron ready room of Attack Squadron 152 on the afternoon of 6 November 1965 when a message came to the attention of the executive officer, Commander Gordon H. Smith. An Air Force F-105 Thunderchief pilot had been shot down in the area west of Hanoi, North Vietnam, and Commander Smith was appointed to lead a two-plane flight to search for and locate the downed airman. He was looking for a volunteer to fly wing with him for the search. I volunteered.

The USS *Oriskany*, CVA-34 (Carrier Fixed Wing Attack, Hull Number 34), was a ship of the Essex class of aircraft carriers, a design of the World War II period but launched later and in time to see action in the Korean War. The ship was also designated as a 27-C , the 27 originally meaning that she displaced about 27,000 tons and C designating her modifications. In this case those modifications included changes from a straight to an angled deck for landings, from hydraulic to steam catapults, and from an open bow to the so-called hurricane bow, which could withstand strong winds without damage. The *Oriskany* also displaced much more than the original 27,000 tons with the modifications. Her namesake is Oriskany, New York, the site of one of the fiercest battles of the Revolutionary War—a fitting name, because the USS *Oriskany*, at the end of the Vietnam War, was the most combat-experienced of any aircraft carrier. Captain William H. House, USN, was her skipper during the ship's opening rounds in the Vietnam War on May 8, 1965, and I was on a flight that day that made one of those strikes. Later that year Captain Bartholomew J. Connolly, III, took command. The leadership of both skippers was so outstanding that the morale of the entire ship and air wing was continually high throughout the 1965 deployment while conducting combat operations.

Air Wing 16 aboard the Oriskany was led by Commander James B. Stockdale, USN. As with *Oriskany* Captains House and Connolly, Commander Stockdale was an inspirational leader who contributed immeasurably to the high level of morale both on the *Oriskany* and within Air Wing 16. Commander Stockdale, later an admiral, was shot down on 9 September 1965 and became the senior Navy prisoner of war until he was released in 1973. He received the Medal of Honor for his incredibly courageous and inspirational leadership as a POW.

My squadron, Attack Squadron 152 (VA-152), was led by Commander Albert E. Knutson, USN. Twenty-two officers and approximately 200 petty officers and men were under Commander Knutson's charge, with a compliment of twelve Douglas A-1H Skyraiders. I was assigned as aircraft maintenance officer in addition to my main role as attack pilot. Our Air Wing 16 also included Attack Squadrons 163 and 164 with Douglas A-4E Skyhawks, Fighter Squadron 162 and Marine Fighter Squadron 212 with Chance Vought F-8E Crusaders, a detachment from Photo Squadron 63 with photo F-8 Crusaders, Airborne Early Warning Squadron 11 with Grumman E-1B Tracers, and Heavy Attack Squadron 4 with Douglas A-3 Skywarriors. Most important, aboard with us was Helicopter Combat Support Squadron 1, Detachment Golf, with its beautiful H-3 Sea King helicopters, known affectionately as Angels. They were there to pluck any of us out of the water when it was needed—and it was. Air Wing 16 had 70-plus aircraft aboard the *Oriskany*.

My squadron was originally attached to Air Wing 15, which operated aboard the USS *Coral Sea*, CVA-43, but during the Vietnam War many squadrons were assigned to other air wings. Rear Admiral Ralph W. Cousins, USN, and his staff were also embarked aboard the *Oriskany*. Admiral Cousins was Commander Carrier Division 9 and was directly responsible for the conduct of the aerial strikes by the carriers of Task Force 77 throughout Southeast Asia.

It was about 1600 hours when Commander Smith and I started to brief for the flight, reviewing available information provided to us through Air Intelligence. A rough plot of the downed pilot's location was known, and we had a fair prognosis for the weather that day.

Commander Smith obtained communication frequencies for contacting the rescue ship that was on station to the north-northwest of the *Oriskany's* position, about halfway to the search area for the downed pilot. We manned our Skyraiders and were catapulted off the bow at 1730 hours into a setting sun. Each Skyraider was armed with four 20 millimeter canons. Internal fuel plus two under-wing 300-gallon tanks would give us an expected endurance of seven hours, plus or minus, depending upon the nature of the flight and the use of engine power. The flight to the search area would take close to two hours, so Commander Smith called and said he was reducing his power toward a conservative maximum range setting. I followed suit as we were flying toward the shoreline and would be arriving "feet dry" (over land). The route of flight took us inland near Thanh Hoa and over hostile areas with anti-aircraft artillery (AAA) and missile sites, most of which were plotted on our charts for avoidance. At an altitude of about 10,000 feet we avoided the small-arms fire and AAA, and we flew around the known missile sites at a wide distance.

The Douglas Skyraider, like the *Oriskany*, was conceived in World War II, and the early models became operational with the U.S. Navy in the late 1940s. The last of the type was built in 1956 and served with U.S. Navy units until 1968; then it served in U.S. Air Force and South Vietnamese Air Force units as a land-based aircraft until 1975. Range, endurance, and load-carrying capability were the plane's strengths—speed was not. It looked similar to some earlier types from the 1940s, though it had much improved systems and capabilities. The single piston engine was the well-proven Curtiss-Wright R-3350, which was extremely reliable in the version used on the Skyraider. The basic aircraft design was adapted to a variety of roles, but it was used mostly as an attack and ground-support aircraft, as was the A-1H version with my squadron. It was known until 1962 as the AD-6 (Attack Douglas Model 6), affectionately called Spads during the 1960s, probably in association with the Spad of World War I fame. In the Korean War era of the early 1950s it was known as the AD or Able Dog. During the period of the Cold War it was configured with nuclear carrying capability, but conventional weapons usage during the Vietnam War became paramount. All ordnance was carried externally; there was a saying that the Skyraider could "carry anything, including the kitchen sink." The planes were not configured to fire guided missiles. It was a big aircraft, with a 50-foot wingspan and a gross weight of 25,000 pounds. In 1965 the plane was used about two-thirds for target strikes and one-third for support of rescue operations. Later in the Vietnam War it was used more for rescue operations, especially in North Vietnam, where the defenses became almost overwhelming for the speedier jets. For rescue operations the A-1s were the aircraft of choice with their great firepower, endurance on scene, and ability to absorb damage while remaining operable. Skyraider pilots were unanimous in their praise for this excellent aircraft, given the effectiveness and reliability that the airplane provided in the face of heavy fire from the ground.

After flying some distance inland, on a westerly course to about 50 miles from the search area, I noticed that my ARA-25 automatic direction finder was pointing decidedly in a southerly direction. The instrument homed in on UHF (ultra high frequencys) that were emitted by the handheld survival radios pilots carried with their personal survival gear on their missions. I informed Commander Smith of the indication, and he decided to turn in that direction to investigate. It was known that many of the survival radios had fallen into enemy hands, even at this relatively early stage of the war, and could be used to lure rescue aircraft into a trap. In spite of this knowledge, Commander Smith headed in the direction that the ARA-25 indicated, since there was the possibility of finding another downed pilot. If it was a trap we would know soon enough, and soon enough we found out. The signal became stronger as we approached the transmitter until we were circling an area about 1 mile in diameter in mountainous terrain. Then AAA and small arms opened fire with tracer ammunition being visible and coming from numerous directions. It was a trap, and we turned away quickly. Several automatic-weapons bullets pierced each of our aircraft but inflicted no disabling damage. (The profusion of tracer ammunition whizzing by was similar to scenes in the "Victory at Sea" documentaries of World War II.) We continued on to the designated search area.

It was twilight as our two Skyraiders approached the search area for the downed Thud pilot, 50 miles west of Hanoi. (Thud was a nickname the pilots gave the F-105 Thunderchief.) We began a systematic search of an area of terrain that consisted of precipitous karst ridges and mountains, with dense jungle canopies and lush vegetation in between. As we searched the area, our communication radios were tuned to the frequency of the survival radio that we hoped the pilot on the ground would have. After perhaps 15 minutes of searching, with a three-quarter moon rising, the downed pilot made contact with us via his handheld radio in response to our attempts to contact him. He described being located under a high, dense jungle canopy. That was a big step toward enabling us to locate his exact position. He attempted to describe his location with reference to how close we were flying to him. We were close, but we needed to know the position accurately enough to call in the rescue helicopter. We continued to try to zero in on the location, but without success. By then the moon was far enough above the horizon to illuminate the terrain so we could safely fly a few hundred feet above the jungle canopy.

After about 10 more minutes, with both of us searching at low level among areas of patchy fog, Commander Smith directed me to climb to 2,000 feet above the ground and circle while plotting as accurately as possible the location of the search area. Meanwhile, he remained low and continued the search for the exact location of the pilot. I climbed and started associating the main features of the immediate area with what was on the charts. Fortunately, the moonlight and the favorable weather made an accurate plot possible.

Commander Smith remained in radio contact with the pilot on the ground but was unable to find his exact location. Finally, he had an idea that was to prove successful. He asked the pilot on the radio if he had a flashlight. The reply was no, but he did have a cigarette lighter. The next question was whether the pilot on the ground was able to determine when the airplane was flying close by or overhead. The answer was affirmative. Commander Smith then instructed the pilot to flick his cigarette lighter whenever he heard the airplane approaching his position. He hoped to get a glimpse of that lighter through the dense jungle canopy. Many more low passes were made over perhaps a one-square-mile area until finally Commander Smith did get a lifesaving glimpse of the lighter. He saw the flicker for a short few seconds in the darkness below, and it marked the position exactly. The next instruction he gave was for me, while still circling above, to plot the position when I saw him momentarily flash his navigation lights (we were flying without navigation lights so we wouldn't make ourselves a target for enemy fire). I knew his approximate position and was looking in the general direction of his aircraft when the navigation lights flashed on for a few seconds. It gave me enough time to see his location and the location of the downed pilot clearly, and I was able to plot this position on my chart. That plot would lead to the successful rescue of the pilot the following day, with the actual operation carried out by the highly respected Air Force crews of the huge HH-3 rescue helicopters known as Jolly Green Giants.

A flight of four Air Force F-4C Phantoms arrived to relieve us and to maintain a presence on the scene. By this time Commander Smith and I had been airborne for more than four hours and had nearly a two-hour return flight to the *Oriskany* ahead of us. We took up a course approximately the reverse of our flight inland and were conserving fuel as much as possible. There were no available friendly airfields where we could divert for fuel on the return route to the *Oriskany*. The closest friendly field was Da Nang, which was farther away than the ship, so with about two hours of fuel remaining, fuel conservation was very much a concern.

After flying east for about 10 minutes, I again received a weak indication on the homing needle of my automatic direction finder, which was still set on the survival radio frequency. I told Commander Smith about the indication, and he decided, in spite of our low fuel situation, to head north in the direction of the signal. It was a similar situation to the flak trap we had been lured into earlier in the flight. Perhaps 10 minutes later we saw a brief fire flare up in the direction of the signal, and then both the fire and the signal disappeared. I plotted that location on my chart, and without much more delay in the area, we continued on the route back to the *Oriskany*. Days later we were to learn that another Air Force F-105 Thud pilot was rescued at that location. He had kept the signal and fire brief so as not to divulge his location to the enemy.

Fuel and flying time were now weighing heavily on our minds. As we continued on a southeasterly course, heading out over the Gulf of Tonkin, we passed near Vinh, one of the most heavily defended areas in North Vietnam. As we continued over the dark ocean, Commander Smith conceived an idea that was to prove vital to our eventual safe recovery aboard the *Oriskany*. The rescue ship was stationed in the Gulf of Tonkin, off the coast near the Demilitarized Zone (the DMZ, which divided North and South Vietnam), and it was coming into radio range as we flew in that direction. The communications frequencies that Commander Smith so wisely obtained before the flight were put to use, and after several attempts he was able to establish contact with the rescue ship. He asked the ship, which had powerful radio transmitters, to relay a request to Captain Connolly on the *Oriskany*, informing him of our fuel state and our route of flight. If Captain Connolly could change course and steam the *Oriskany* toward us for the next hour, it would put us 30 miles closer and would be crucial with our dwindling fuel state.

Most fortunately for Commander Smith and me, Captain Connolly was willing and able to comply with the request. The decision for him to change course on our behalf was complex, involving many priorities. The state of air operations then in progress aboard the *Oriskany* would be the main issue, and fortunately there were none. If air operations had been in progress, Captain Connolly would have had to hold his course into the wind. As it was, he took a course in our direction as we continued flying at maximum-range power settings. (Captain Connolly showed the same leadership and courage that he had shown on 14 January 1943 as a 22-year-old ensign, when he was awarded the Navy Cross for an action near Guadalcanal. His motor torpedo boat scored several torpedo hits on much larger Japanese cruisers in a surprise attack.)

Our low fuel state offered us a frustrating set of options. If we flew toward the *Oriskany*, there was a strong possibility of having to ditch short of the ship, with the hope of being located by a search-and-rescue helicopter. A ditching could have been attempted alongside the rescue ship, with a possible rescue, but that also depended on making a successful night ditching. Another option would have been to ditch just offshore and make it to land, hoping for a pickup in the morning before enemy forces could locate us. In any case, ditching or bailing out were the riskiest options, so continuing on to the *Oriskany* in hopes of making it onboard (or ditching close by) was the course of action we took.

As we flew on toward the *Oriskany* with our big piston engines turning slowly for maximum range, it became increasingly apparent that the fuel situation was deteriorating from that of possible to probable fuel starvation. Commander Smith, in another of his typical displays of leadership, magnanimously instructed me to make the first approach for a carrier-arrested landing. I did not take exception. I was the first of our two successful landings aboard that welcome flight deck as an Angel rescue helicopter orbited on the starboard side. My Spad came to an arrested halt after a very careful night visual approach. As the tail wheel of the conventional landing gear settled to the deck, the big engine coughed its last and stopped of fuel starvation, after a flight of six and six-tenths hours. An aircraft tug quickly towed my now silent aircraft off the landing area with the fuel gauges reading zero. Within seconds, Commander Smith touched down, his engine continuing to run as he taxied away from the arresting cable. It was not until years later that I learned from one of the other ship's officers that Captain Connolly had extended the *Oriskany* into dangerously shallow waters for the purpose of holding course into the wind for our arrested landings. That, in my opinion, was above and beyond any call of duty or responsibility.

As I mentioned, Rear Admiral Ralph W. Cousins, Commander Carrier Division 9, was aboard the *Oriskany* that night, and he was waiting for the two of us to brief him about the search. We were escorted into his quarters just after midnight while still in our sweaty flight gear. As a 25-year old Lieutenant JG, I was in awe of this naval officer and pilot, almost the same age as my father, who was born in 1915. It was more than his rank that held me in awe. Admiral Cousins was a veteran of the Battle of the Coral Sea in World War II and had been awarded the Navy Cross. He was attached to the carrier USS *Lexington* when she was lost in that battle on May 7, 1942.

Admiral Cousins quickly set me at ease as Commander Smith and I began to brief him on the evolution of the flight. One of his first questions to us was "Do you have an accurate plot of the downed pilot's position?" It was my distinct pleasure to cite that position confidently from my chart and, in addition, to pass on to him the position of the other possible downed pilot.

The daring and innovative leadership of Commander Smith enabled me to make the accurate position plots that led to additional daring the next morning with the successful rescue of the two downed pilots by helicopter crews. To say that it is highly gratifying to have been involved in the rescue of two of our pilots would be a severe understatement. Words fail. I flew many other combat missions with various objectives, many of them considered to be successful, mission accomplished. None of them approach the sense of accomplishment that I feel about this rescue mission.

....

Gary Gottschalk was awarded the Distinguished Flying Cross for this mission. The citation is below.

CITATION:
The President of the United States of America takes pleasure in presenting the Distinguished Flying Cross to Lieutenant, Junior Grade Gary L Gottschalk, United States Navy, for extraordinary achievement while participating in aerial flight during an air rescue mission deep in North Vietnam on 6 November 1965. In an attempt to rescue several downed U.S. Air Force men, Lieutenant (JG) Gottschalk, while subjected to intense antiaircraft and small-arms fire, flew for an extended period within surface-to-air missile envelopes. Through his alert actions in calling antiaircraft fire, he saved his flight leader from being hit. Despite the hazards of low-level flight at night in rugged, mountainous terrain, he boldly elected to continue the search after darkness. When the precise position of one survivor was established, he made repeated passes at dangerously low altitudes in order to determine the optimum approach for the rescue helicopter. After the location of anoth-

er downed airman had been established, he remained on the scene, despite a dangerously low fuel state, in order to point out the exact location of the survivor to relieving aircraft. Lieutenant (JG) Gottschalk's superb airmanship, unselfish concern for his fellow airmen, and bold actions in this heroic night rescue were in keeping with the highest traditions of the United States Naval Service.

For the President,

Paul H. Nitze

Secretary of the Navy

Principals:

Commander Carrier Division 9:

Rear Admiral Ralph W. Cousins, USN

Commanding Officer, USS *Oriskany*:

Captain Bartholomew J. Connolly, III, USN

Commanding Officer, Carrier Air Wing 16:

Commander James B. Stockdale, USN

Commanding Officer, VA-152:

Commander Albert E. Knutson, USN

Executive Officer, VA-152:

Commander Gordon H. Smith, USN

Logbook Details:

A-1H BuNo. 137520, 6 Nov 65, 6.6 flight hours, night visual conditions with 0.3 hours of actual instruments, 4.4 hours night VFR (launched late afternoon), "Special CAP, Combat Air Patrol, to protect rescue vessel or plane," one catapult and one night actual CCA, Carrier Controlled Approach, to a night arrested landing.

As a final note, I would like to thank my friend Gary again for his encouragement and help in getting me started on this project. The month after we flew together in 1997, he invited me to come to Los Angeles and visit for the day. He took me to the Chino Air Museum, where he proudly showed me the A-1 Spad on display, a tail number he had flown in the Navy.

3 VA-152 A-1Hs in formation, 1965.

A-1H from VA-152 on the deck of the USS Oriskany, 1965.

L) *Gary Gottschalk on the deck of the USS Oriskany, 1965.* *R)* *Gary Gottschalk with A-1H, 1965.*

Gary Gottschalk after Vietnam, flying an A-4E as a test pilot at China Lake Naval Air Weapons Station, California, 1968.

6

HARRY'S HOG HAULERS

James P. Gibbs, USAF, C-123B, C-123K, 1965
{ Date of hire by Western Airlines: 6/5/1967 }

James Gibbs, Western Airlines Logbook, 1986.

Jim Gibbs told me that he hadn't really done anything of note in his Vietnam tour, but he would give it some thought and see what he could come up with, if anything, for a story. He casually mentioned that in late 1965 he had flown some Hollywood celebrities into a Special Forces camp on a USO tour to entertain the troops. He said he could mention that in his story, and as we talked, a few more things popped into his mind, so he said he would get back to me in a couple of weeks.

The enclosed story arrived in the mail and is a great tale of Vietnam in the "early days," before the big buildup that came two or three years later. In 1965 there was much more flexibility in traveling around the country, and it was much safer to go into town to local restaurants and live off-base in apartments in the larger cities. After the Tet Offensive (Tet is the

Vietnamese lunar New Year celebration) in early 1968, things were considerably more dangerous, and venturing around town in various parts of the country became a dicey proposition. When I was at Cam Ranh Bay in 1968–1969, we were pretty much restricted to the base unless we went into town with an organized group. The doctors and medical staff at the base hospital would regularly set up clinics to give immunizations to children or help the women with their pregnancies. There were a lot of women and children in the villages outside the base, but there weren't supposed to be any Vietnamese men of military age. If we saw any men in civilian clothes, from teenagers to those in their 30s, they could be draft dodgers or deserters from the ARVN (Army of the Republic of Vietnam) or VC (Vietcong), and because of that we always had armed guards with us on those trips. We were still able to go off base in Saigon or Nha Trang and eat at a nice restaurant, but it required constant vigilance, especially in Saigon, where there were strictly enforced curfews for GIs at night.

As you will read in my story, we were still delivering livestock to the Special Forces camps nearly four years after Jim's tour of duty. His story is reminiscent of my flying, as both the C-123 and C-7 flew resupply missions into the Special Forces camps, the main difference being the STOL (short-field takeoff and landing) characteristics of the C-7, which allowed us to fly into the camps with the shortest runways.

Jim Gibbs was in the very first group of Vietnam veterans hired by Western Airlines. During the airline pilot hiring cycle that began in the mid-1960s, most of the pilots had come from civilian backgrounds, as military pilots were not available. Those who were flying in Vietnam in the early days of 1964–1965 were just starting to separate from the service and became available for pilot positions with the airlines in late 1966 and 1967.

Here is Jim's story of flying resupply missions in the early days of the war.

....

I was born in San Diego, California, on May 28, 1938. I lived in National City, graduated from Sweetwater High School, and then went to Loyola University (now Loyola-Marymount University) in Los Angeles. While at Loyola I participated in Air Force ROTC, and I took my first solo flight from Santa Monica Airport in 1960. I passed the flight physical for UPT (Undergraduate Pilot Training);

upon graduation from Loyola I was commissioned a second lieutenant and reported to Bartow Air Base, Florida, for pilot training in Class 62-A. I was then sent to Reese AFB in Lubbock, Texas, where my training was in T-34, T-37, and T-33 aircraft. Upon graduation from training at Reese, I was assigned to fly the C-133 with the 84th Air Transport Squadron at Travis AFB, California.

The C-133 was a huge aircraft designed to carry outsized cargo and was the only production turboprop-powered strategic airlifter ever to fly for the Air Force (the C-130 was also turboprop-powered but was considered a tactical airlifter). We flew to bases in the Pacific and also transported ballistic missiles such as the Titan and Minuteman to their bases in the United States. We also carried the Atlas and Saturn rockets to Cape Kennedy for use in the space program.

My next assignment was the 311th ACS (Air Commando Squadron) based at Da Nang Air Base in Vietnam. Prior to my departure for Vietnam, the Air Force had to "prepare" me to "win the war," so in December 1964 I attended jungle survival school in Panama and then counterinsurgency school at Maxwell AFB in Montgomery, Alabama, in March 1965. In April and May of 1965 I was at Hurlburt Field near Eglin AFB, Florida, to check out in the C-123. (Hurlburt Field today is home to the Air Force Special Operations Command.) We trained alongside the pilots who were assigned to the 12th ACS and would be based at Bien Hoa Air Base, flying Operation Ranch Hand. (Ranch Hand was the mission that utilized specially equipped C-123s, designated UC-123B and UC-123K, to spray defoliants and herbicides along roads and in jungle areas to deprive the VC and NVA of food and cover for ambushes.)

In June 1965 I left my wife and three children and boarded a Continental Airlines Boeing 707 at Travis AFB and headed to Saigon. I then found my way to Da Nang. Upon arrival I found that the 311th ACS commander was Colonel Harry Howton and we were "Harry's Hoghaulers" because we flew, among other things, cattle and hogs on our resupply missions to the various Special Forces camps in South Vietnam. The Air Force had been in the process of modifying the C-123B models by adding underwing jet pods and anti-skid brakes to give them better performance while operating on the short, unimproved runways at remote Special Forces camps. The new designation was C-123K. This was done by the Air Force to compete with the Army's CV-2 Caribou, which the Air Force viewed as an encroachment on its domain of tactical airlift. In 1966 an agreement between the Air Force and the Army turned over the operation of the Caribou to the Air Force and gave the Army free rein in its helicopter operations. The Caribou was then designated the C-7A.

Besides hauling cattle, rice, fuel, ammunition, and troops, I flew night flare missions where we dropped parachute flares that illuminated the area for ground troops in contact with the enemy. I also flew some celebrities who came to entertain the troops on USO-sponsored tours. On one trip I flew Edgar Bergen and his wife, Frances, parents of Candice Bergen. Edgar Bergen was a ventriloquist and comedian who brought along his two dummies, Charlie McCarthy and Mortimer Snerd, which traveled in beautiful, custom-made trunks. We flew to Kham Duc Special Forces Camp to entertain the troops at lunch, and they really appreciated the visit and the show. (Kham Duc was about 45 miles southwest of Da Nang, less than 10 miles from the Laotian border. By mid-1968, after the Tet Offensive, the camp was closed because it was too difficult to defend. It was listed in the 1969 Aerodrome Directory as "not secure, abandoned, airfield surrounded by mountains, ground fire probable all quadrants.") It was unusual for the troops in small camps like Kham Duc to receive USO visits because they were isolated and dangerous; most of the USO tours went to the larger bases. I was quite impressed with Edgar Bergen and his wife as they knew the dangers involved and requested a visit to an isolated camp so they could meet the front-line troops. On that day the American contingent of about 12 Green Berets really appreciated our being there. Unknown to them, Candice Bergen was busily active in the anti-war movement at home while her father entertained the troops just a few miles from the Laotian border.

I really enjoyed our trips to Khe Sanh, and we used to plan our day to be there at lunchtime because they had a great little old Chinese lady for a cook at the camp and she put out a great lunch! By the fall of 1968, after the siege and battle for Khe Sanh that lasted nearly six months, the camp and airstrip had been closed and Khe Sanh was listed in the Aerodrome Directory as "not secure, abandoned, probably mined."

For our R&R (rest and relaxation), each crew would fly to Saigon once a month, where our squadron kept an apartment for those who were there for an overnight stay. We would go out on the town, have a good French meal at one of the numerous restaurants there, and head back to Da Nang the next day. On the trip back we'd fly resupply to places like Nha Trang, Cam Ranh Bay, Pleiku, Gia Vuc, and many others. Gia Vuc earned the nickname the LBJ Ranch because we landed on a cow pasture in the grass. (The Aerodrome Directory entry for Gia Vuc lists a 3,200-foot runway with a surface of sod! It also mentions that a "mine field surrounds camp.")

Once or twice during my tour we went to Thailand, where we would overnight in Bangkok and shop the next day, then fly resupply to places like Takhli, Korat, and Nakhon Phanom (which was nicknamed Naked Fanny because it sounded like that in Thai). In 1965–1966 those bases were building up quickly to accommodate all the aircraft that were bombing North Vietnam and Laos. It was nice to fly over Thailand because we could relax and not worry about ground fire. Occasionally we would even see an elephant.

As a final note, I had a secondary duty as the squadron awards and decorations officer. I was on duty in the office at Da Nang the day A Shau Special Forces Camp in the A Shau valley was overrun, March 10, 1966. Major Bernie Fisher received the Medal of Honor for landing his A-1E and picking up a downed wingman who had crash-landed and was hiding along the side of the runway. The C-123s from our squadron were flying in and out of A Shau that day trying to evacuate the Green Berets and their ARVN troops. They brought back many exciting stories, and a few of them were awarded the DFC (Distinguished Flying Cross).

I returned to the States in late 1966 and separated from the Air Force a few months later. I was hired by Western Airlines in June 1967 and retired wearing the Delta uniform in May 1998.

7

CAM RANH BAY

Don Avary, USAF, F-4C, 1965 – 1966
{ Date of hire by Western Airlines: 3/3/1969 }

Don Avary and his F-4C at Cam Ranh Bay AB, 1966.

Don Avary was part of the group of first officers (copilots) with whom I flew when I arrived at the Western Airlines San Francisco pilot base in February 1974 as a second officer on the Boeing 737. The copilot group was almost all ex-military, nearly all Vietnam veterans hired in the 1968–1969 hiring cycle that ended abruptly in a furlough in mid-1969. Don was a fellow graduate of U.C. Berkeley who had missed the excitement I experienced there from 1964 to 1966. His story of the early days at Cam Ranh Bay is especially interesting, as I found a fairly modern facility when I was based there in 1968–1969. In 1968, the aluminum mat runway that the F-4s had used in 1965 was reserved for the two C-7 squadrons that occupied the east side of the airbase. The F-4s occupied the west side of the field and were using a parallel 10,000 foot concrete runway that also handled most of the transient aircraft that visited Cam Ranh. By 1968 Cam Ranh Bay AB was a very busy facility, with takeoffs and landings going around the clock.

Cam Ranh Bay was the staging area for the Japanese attack on the Philippines in World War II. The Japanese also assembled their warships and transports there for the invasion of Malaysia, which led to the fall of Singapore in the early days of the war. As we flew our C-7s over the bay on final approach for landing on runway 02R, a sunken Japanese submarine was visible in the clear, pristine water off to the right on final approach. Cam Ranh Bay was the deepwater port that the Russians wanted, and they took it as their payoff for years of support of the North Vietnamese when the south was conquered in 1975.

Don Avary was a pleasure to fly with at Western, and his story came about in a very interesting way. I had asked him if he would write about his Vietnam experience when I last saw him, close to 15 years ago. Years passed, and then we had a chance meeting at a sad event, the memorial service for one of our San Francisco–based pilots, Al Kneier, in January 2013. Don was there and asked me about my project, and in less than a week he delivered the enclosed story. As much as we had flown together, he had never talked about his flying in Vietnam. I knew only that he had flown F-4s in the Air Force and had been based at Cam Ranh Bay in the early days.

Here is Don Avary's story.

....

When I finished college I didn't have a clear idea of what I wanted to do with my life, so I decided to go into the Air Force and learn to fly. My father had been a pilot, first in the Army Air Corps and then with Pan American Airways.

I applied to and was accepted by the Air Force as a pilot candidate. Having taken only the mandatory two years of ROTC in college, I was sent to Lackland's 90-day-wonder school, Air Force OTS (Officer Training School).

I was at Lackland AFB, received a commission, and went on to Craig AFB in Selma, Alabama, for UPT (Undergraduate Pilot Training). There I flew the T-37 Tweetie Bird and the T-33 T-Bird. On graduation I got my first choice of assignment: the F-4C. All of us who got F-4 assignments at that time started out as GIBs (guys in back, backseaters).

This was in March of 1963, and as yet I had given no thought, nor had anyone else for that matter, to the notion that we would soon be involved in a shooting war in Vietnam. I truly believed that I would have the pleasure of flying a world-class aircraft around friendly skies. I went on to combat crew training at Davis Monthan AFB in Tucson, followed by my first operational assignment with the 43rd TFS (Tactical Fighter Squadron), 12th TFW (Tactical Fighter Wing) at MacDill AFB in Tampa.

In the early part of 1965 we were deployed TDY (temporary duty) to Clark AFB in the Philippines, and events caught up with us. The Gulf of Tonkin incidents had occurred on August 2nd and 4th, 1964, and that had started the expansion of our involvement in Vietnam.

Our sister squadron, the 47th TFS, deployed to Ubon RTAB (Royal Thai Air Base) in Thailand and began flying sorties into North Vietnam. The 43rd became their supply squadron. We would fly in our good aircraft and fly out their aircraft that were in need of maintenance and repair, but that lasted only a few months. The 43rd stayed at Clark, but the original pilots returned to MacDill and became part of the 557th TFS. There we received orders and were sent to Cam Ranh Bay AB, Republic of Vietnam. Along with the rest of the 12th TFW we rejoined the 43rd, which had redeployed from Clark and had become the first F-4 squadron at Cam Ranh Bay.

In the fall of 1965, Cam Ranh was a work in progress, with lots of building going on throughout the time I was there. A permanent concrete runway was being constructed but wasn't completed that year, so we flew off a 12,000 foot long and 100 foot wide aluminum mat runway. It was a perfectly good runway, though very slick in wet weather, especially where the epoxy resin had worn through. Facilities were quite primitive. We lived in Quonset huts that had large fans making heroic attempts to cool things down a bit. The mess hall was nothing but a tarp-covered framework with mosquito mesh on the sides. None of this seemed to matter to us much. We were all young enough, and this seemed like just part of one hell of a great adventure.

We were truly blessed by having as commander of the 12th TFW a gentleman by the name of Colonel Levi Chase (he retired in 1973 as a major general). He had been a WWII fighter ace and had 12 aerial victories to his credit. We learned to respect him immensely. He never asked anyone to do something he wouldn't do himself. He flew in the first flight each day, never as lead, just as a wingman.

Because the flight crews had the most available time off, he assigned them the job of building the clubs on the new base. First we built a club for the enlisted men, then an NCO club (noncommissioned officers' club), and only when those were completed did we build an officers' club. Every man in the wing, from the lowest-ranking airman to the most senior officer, was impressed and moved by that. They would have followed Levi anywhere.

He established an unwritten R&R policy. He had one simple rule for us in order to be released for R&R. All sorties had to be flown, all aircraft had to be maintained, and all assigned work had to be done. It meant that we could be gone as much as a week every month, and how very nice that was. It also meant that we often flew more than one sortie a day when on base.

The operations officer for the 12th TFW was a different kind of leader. I won't mention his name. I remember the time he noticed, while flying a sortie, that several pilots in the formation lit up and were smoking in flight. He prominently posted a bulletin citing the appropriate Air Force regulation that dealt with smoking in fighter aircraft—strictly taboo, of course. The bulletin ended with a comment from him: "I intend to enforce this reg. Don't try me." Shortly thereafter, even the nonsmokers were smoking while flying. I suppose we were all hoping that he would catch us in the act and ground us, or maybe even relieve us of duty and send us home in disgrace.

On one occasion he was supervising the landing of aircraft. The runway had been closed because a couple of aircraft had engaged both runway barriers, and that had to be sorted out. Aircraft were holding all over, waiting for the runway to be cleared. One new pilot advised tower that he was going to divert to Phan Rang AB because he was low on fuel. Our operations officer told him to continue holding as the runway would be opened shortly. He flamed out (ran out of fuel) on a base turn to final and he and the GIB punched out (ejected). The aircraft crashed into the bay and was lost. Our good colonel tried to hang the loss on the pilot, but fortunately Levi Chase came to the pilot's defense and actually booted his own operations officer off the base, to everyone's delight. Now and then this guy would be spotted hanging out at some officers' club. He never returned to Cam Ranh Bay.

We had a great flight surgeon, Bill Simmons, who loved to fly and would volunteer to fly in the backseat whenever possible. He was allowed to do this and ended up with more than 30 combat sorties. On his last one, the F-4 disappeared while returning to base in bad weather. Henceforth the Air Force forbade fight surgeons from flying combat.

After the novelty wore off, we all settled in to our year at Cam Ranh Bay. The base was pleasant enough and there never was any real threat to it, so we all felt perfectly at ease. My squadron was designated to train for and qualify for night dive-bombing, and since that meant we had to sleep during the day in order to fly at night, we got air conditioners. We were the only ones with them.

There is an interesting sideline to the air conditioner story. I was returning from one of my many R&Rs through Tan Son Nhut AB in Saigon and was in need of a ride to Cam Ranh Bay. I was told that there was a C-47 Goony Bird heading up that way but that the pilot was not accepting any passengers. The pilot, Lieutenant Colonel Dwyer, was based at CRB and flew a periodic base-operations flight, carrying passengers and cargo between Cam Ranh and Saigon. Since I knew him, I pleaded for a ride as I had to get back for a flight the next day. He finally said OK. Another half-dozen guys had talked him into a ride as well. There were no seats available; the entire airplane was filled with crates, so we had to sit on the floor. None of us minded. We all boarded, and Dwyer immediately started up and taxied out. Halfway down the runway on takeoff roll, with all of us sitting at the rear in front of the large side-entry door, which was open with just a cargo net covering it, the copilot stuck his head up above the crates and yelled, "EVERYONE MOVE FORWARD!!!!" There wasn't much room between the crates and the sides of the fuselage, but we all obeyed instantly. After endless sickening bounces, Dwyer finally unstuck the Goony Bird from the runway and we were airborne. We actually flew between some palm trees on our departure.

I learned a few things later on. The crates were our air conditioners, and the aircraft exceeded the war-time maximum gross weight for takeoff. Lieutenant Colonel Dwyer was an awfully nice guy, but he should have refused us our ride. He truly did not need the extra weight that day!

The flying was great, actually all that you could ever wish for, and I flew 230-plus sorties during my tour at Cam Ranh Bay. Because of our location halfway up the coast of South Vietnam, our sorties were mainly flown in the south or in Laos on route interdiction strikes along the Ho Chi Minh Trail. The trail ran along the entire western border of South Vietnam through "neutral" Laos and Cambodia. Of the 230 sorties that I flew, only around 40 were into North Vietnam. Those were relatively easy missions as they were in the southern panhandle and not over the much more heavily defended northern area. I heard only a handful of SAM (surface-to-air missile) alerts. The policy in force at that time was that one month would be deducted from your year in-country for every 30 sorties in the north, so my year's tour was shortened by a month.

In the south, ground fire was sporadic at best, and only rarely did we encounter much resistance. Quite often our preplanned targets were "suspected VC (Vietcong) concentrations." We ended up targeting their obvious support areas, which as often as not were the villages that served as a source of food and supplies. While that was true, it didn't make us feel particularly heroic flying our aircraft against unarmed villagers and destroying their homes. I recall a particular strike against a small herd of water buffalo in a stream and one elephant chained to a tree! The elephant and water buffalo were used to carry supplies and belonged to the VC, so the target was "fair game."

We all felt good whenever we were flying air support for ground troops who were engaged in combat. One engagement that I will never forget occurred on 9 June 1966 near Dak To, an Army Special Forces camp close to the Laotian border. Our flight was diverted from a preplanned strike to Laos because friendly troops were heavily engaged and needed immediate support. When we broke out below an overcast sky at around 1,200 feet, the FAC (forward air controller) briefed us. A company of the U.S. Army's 101st Airborne Division was fighting a VC regiment at very close quarters. The FAC marked the location of the VC with a Willy Pete (white phosphorus) smoke rocket. On our initial pass on the target, we dropped short, right into the friendlies. The FAC said, "That wasn't the kind of support they had in mind," told us to stand by, and then talked to the ground commander on his FM radio. When the FAC called us back, he said the ground commander wanted us to drop into that same location, as they were in hand-to-hand combat and would at least take as many as they could with them. We dropped our remaining ordnance there and went home pretty shaken up.

On debriefing back at Cam Ranh, we learned that our strike had actually stemmed the enemy onslaught. This strike is memorable because the ground commander, a West Point graduate and football All American in 1959 by the name of Bill Carpenter, was awarded the Silver Star on the spot and put in for the Medal of Honor. His award was later upgraded from the Silver Star to the Distinguished Service Cross and his company was henceforth known as Carpenter's Crispy Critters for the napalm that was dropped near their position. Carpenter went on to become General William Westmoreland's aide and subsequently became a major general. Here is a quote from the citation for the Distinguished Service Cross for Captain Carpenter:

> Captain Carpenter ordered supporting jet aircraft to drop napalm directly on the company's position. The napalm bombs hit the top of the trees in the center of the company position and detonated 25 feet above the ground. As a result, the fiery napalm carried directly into the charging insurgents and passed over most of the friendly troops. The skillfully directed air strike completely subdued the Viet Cong attempt to overrun the company.

Another particular strike of note was on a target late in the day near the town of Tchepone in eastern Laos. Our assigned FAC reported a truck in the middle of a river ford. He thought the whole thing was pretty fishy and in fact was so worried that he was orbiting well away from the scene. There was a forested area next to the river and in it was an AAA (anti-aircraft artillery) gun. As they opened up on us their guns produced a large cloud of smoke, giving their position away. It was then a veritable shootout, as they were shooting at us and we were launching our rockets at them. There were shells flying past us on all sides, but we weren't even scratched. We did knock them out, though, and that remains, to this day, one of the most memorable sorties of my entire tour. It was me against a real enemy, not some civilians. That was immensely important to me.

I flew about a dozen MIG CAP sorties (missions in which the F-4s protected other aircraft from MiGs, North Vietnamese fighter aircraft), but no engagements resulted. We were assigned to cap two Elint aircraft (electronic intelligence aircraft, which monitored MiG and SAM launches by radar and other electronic means) about 30 miles off the coast of North Vietnam, just east of Haiphong: an EC-121 at around 6,000 feet and a C-130 at 25,000 feet. These were long, tedious missions lasting, on one occasion, 12 hours and requiring numerous in-flight refuelings. Flying "S" turns next to an aircraft going half your speed gets awfully tiring after a while. On a daily basis MiGs would launch at us and our Elints would tell us they were inbound and vector us toward them. At that point the MiGs would abandon their attack and fly back inland. Since our job was to protect the Elints, we didn't pursue them but broke off the engagement and returned to our boring "S" turns. It was actually very unsatisfying, as we would all have loved to get into some actual hassling (an air-to-air engagement).

We had an awards and decorations officer whose job it was to pass out appropriate medals and citations. I did receive the DFC (Distinguished Flying Cross) for valor, for the abovementioned action on 9 June 1966. Air medals were awarded for accumulating combat sorties and I think we got one AM for every 20 sorties. I ended up with a bunch of those.

Throughout the year we waged a sortie war with the Navy, and we won if we flew more strikes than they did in a month.

Sometimes, in order to do that we'd launch with little or no ord-nance on board so we could add up more sorties. I imagine the Navy did that sort of thing as well.

I have other memories of this period in my life, but these are the ones I remember most vividly.

In October 1966 our replacements began to arrive and I returned to the States, flew a couple more years in the Air Force and then went back to civilian life in 1969. I was truly fortunate to be hired by one of the best flying outfits in the world, Western Airlines.

Cam Ranh Bay AB as it was in 1969, looking to the south. The F-4s had the right or west side of the base with the concrete runway. The C-7s had the left or east side with the PSP runway.

8

THE LUCKIEST MAN
YOU EVER MET

Robert Tieken, USMC, A-4C, A-4E, TA-4F, 1965 – 1968
{ Date of hire by Western Airlines: 9/3/1968 }

*Bob Tieken in front of the operations bunker for 2nd Battalion,
7th Marines, during his tour as a ground FAC.*

*I never had the privilege of flying with Bob Tieken. Everyone I spoke with
who knew Bob at Western Airlines said he was a great guy to fly with but
very private, and to a man they doubted that he would ever write about his
Vietnam experience. Bob is a big, strong guy, and at 6 feet 4 inches tall
probably was way too big to fit in the A-4 cockpit. With the seat bottomed
out he said his helmet often hit the canopy, and his movement in the cockpit
was quite restricted. As to what kind of a guy Bob Tieken is (and Bob claims
not to remember this story), Bill Snider, a friend from our San Francisco
base who flew with Bob at Western, told of getting sick on a layover in
Chicago. He made it back to the hotel but nearly collapsed in the elevator.
Bob picked him up and carried him to his room. It turned out Bill had*

appendicitis and had to be rushed to the hospital. Bill relates that as he was moaning in pain in the back seat of the cab, Bob looked at him and said, "Hey pussy, can't you handle a little pain? Candy ass!" He then carried Bill into the emergency room at Northwestern Memorial Hospital.

As I mention in several stories, the Marines are a very tight bunch, and entry into their world is definitely by invitation only. Over the years I flew with several Marines who never talked much about Vietnam (except among themselves), but if I was lucky enough to hear an occasional "Semper Fi" greeting in the hallway and stood to the side and eavesdropped, I never knew what I might hear! Bob Tieken was often the subject of those conversations, and he became more of a legend than most for one main reason. He spent nearly 2½ continuous years in Vietnam, from December 1965 until April 1968, repeatedly extending his tour until the powers that be thought he had become "too salty" and sent him to the infantry as a ground FAC (forward air controller). He spent his final months in Vietnam as a FAC with the 2nd Battalion, 7th Marines. They operated in the bush, but you need to read the book Matterhorn *by Karl Marlantes to get a true flavor of what that was like.* ("Finally the driver could contain himself no longer. 'Where did you get the sword?' he asked. Mellas was amused. 'Out in the bush,' he said....There were some things he couldn't tell the uninitiated. For them, the bush should, and would, remain a mystery.")

You learn quickly that in the presence of Marines you only get to talk about or ask about the bush if you have been there. I flew over the bush, I saw it from the air, but that doesn't remotely qualify.

My good friend Bill Wilson provided an introduction to Bob Tieken and urged him to write a story for this book. I want to thank Bill for his involvement and interest in this project. To be trusted by men like these is the ultimate compliment, and I am honored to have Bob's story for this book.

....

Following two summers as an E-3 in the USMC Platoon Leaders Class, I was commissioned a second lieutenant in the USMC Reserve, and in June 1963 I went directly to Pensacola, Florida, for Navy Flight School. There I flew T-34, T-28, F-9, and F-11 training planes and received my wings in September 1964. I was ordered to

MCAS (Marine Corps Air Station) Cherry Point, North Carolina, where I was checked out in the A-4E and was assigned to VMA-332 (Fixed Wing Marine Attack Squadron 332). There I received training in both conventional and nuclear weapons and was designated a nuclear, biological, and chemical warfare officer, LSO (landing signal officer), received training in the use of the then new AGM-45 Shrike anti-radiation missile, and was trained in SATS (short airfield for tactical support) operations.

I should mention that the A-4 cockpit was a tight fit for me, but I soon learned the tricks of the trade. The A-4 did not have a fore and aft seat adjustment, only up and down. The issue with the seat was that the hard canopy bow might take off your toes during an ejection, so the designers kept the seat well aft. The rudder pedals were adjustable so I flew with them all the way forward for comfort.

In December 1965 I received individual orders to Vietnam and arrived that same month at the expeditionary airfield (an airfield that was planned for temporary use of 30 to 60 days) at Chu Lai, RVN (Republic of Vietnam). I was assigned to MAG-12 (Marine Air Group 12) as a squadron pilot in VMA-223. Living conditions were fairly primitive as we had six-man tents on the sand, with outdoor showers and toilets, but we had good, hot chow and sometimes cold beer! Later, things got modern and we lived in plywood "jungle huts" with metal roofs. The runway was 4,000 feet of aluminum planking laid out over leveled earth/sand, and it was very rough. All takeoffs used JATO (jet-assisted takeoff) bottles, which were solid fuel rocket bottles on either side of the fuselage that were jettisoned over the South China Sea after takeoff. All landings used hydraulic arresting gear. Later there was a land catapult that used a cable-and-dolly system with a J-79 jet engine for power. MAG-12 flew 24 hours a day, every day. At night the runway was illuminated with flare pots with a lighted mirror for glide path guidance, just like on the ship. For navigation there was a TACAN (tactical air navigation) station as well as radar and a GCA (ground control approach) for approaches in bad weather.

There were four squadrons of Douglas A-4 Skyhawks. MAG-12 flew both A-4Cs and A-4Es, with the E model having four underwing ordnance pylons, a more powerful J-52 engine, and an enhanced avionics package. The group schedule rotated every day with one squadron flying early, one flying late, one on hot pad alert, and one on stand down for maintenance. Most of our missions were in direct support of our fellow Marines on the ground in South Vietnam, but we also flew sorties north of the DMZ (Demilitarized Zone, the border between North and South Vietnam) and interdiction missions along the Ho Chi Minh Trail in Laos.

I stayed in VMA-223 until the squadron rotated up to Japan. In order to stay in Vietnam, I volunteered to go to MAG-12 to be the Group S-3, (the operations section of the group) where I became the flight briefing officer and wrote the group flying schedule. I continued to fly while there and eventually joined VMA-121, rejoining VMA-223 when they rotated back in-country. In the fall of 1967, after my second tour extension, I took a 30-day leave and went back to CONUS (continental United States)—a big mistake! While on leave, the group executive officer decided that I had become "too salty" for my own good and sent me to the infantry as a FAC. By April 1968 my orders to CONUS came through, my tour with the 2nd Battalion, 7th Marines was over, and I was out of Vietnam. It was an interesting 2½ years! I joined VMT-103 (Fixed Wing Marine Training Squadron 103) at MCAS Yuma as a gunnery/instrument instructor flying TA-4Fs, and I was released from active duty on 30 August 1968. I went to work for Western Airlines a few days later, training as a second officer on the Boeing 707/720B.

WAR STORIES

Some missions were easy and some were a bit more exciting. In the photograph of me giving the "You're number one" gesture, I am standing in front of an A-4E loaded with a 300-gallon centerline drop (fuel) tank and four Shrike anti-SAM (surface-to-air missile), beam-rider missiles on the wing stations. The concept was to fly up north, loiter in a high-threat area, and try to get the people on the ground to "light you up" with their radar. In the cockpit there were aural and visual warnings to let the pilot know when his aircraft was being tracked and also when the SAM fire control radar locked on. All that was required to fire the Shrike was to arm the missile, turn to center the vector and dive angle needles, and pull the trigger. The Shrike was designed to fly the radar beam back down to the radar van and destroy the SAM site. Sounds simple enough, but in a state of high anxiety, with the offshore ECM (electronic countermeasures) aircraft broadcasting on Guard frequency the day's code word for SAM alert, with all the bells and whistles going off in the cockpit, even simple tasks are challenging. Because I was one of the few pilots to have gone to school on the Shrike, I was fortunate to be able to fly these "dream come true" missions. I can tell you, my instrument scan was never better! The photograph was taken by Jack McLaughlin, one of my VMA-121 squadron mates and a new-hire classmate at Western Airlines.

Another mission that not many people wanted and was easy to get was the "midnight special." This was typically a two-ship mission that briefed late, carried a full load of Mk 82, 500 pound low-drag bombs, and a 300 gallon centerline drop tank, and was assigned interdiction along the Ho Chi Minh Trail in Laos. I should add at this point that my good friend and squadron mate Pete Kruger and I had a contest going to see who could hit the 500 mission mark first, so I volunteered for everything.

Most of the traffic on the trail moved at night, so that is when we would show up. After the intelligence/weather briefing at the Group, the pilots would go to the squadron ready room for the flight briefing. Next we went to the flight line to preflight and man our aircraft, starting engines so as to take off at midnight. Depending on the length of runway available for takeoff at Chu Lai, JATO might be required for launch. (Only on your first night JATO takeoff did you forget to turn your rearview mirrors out, as JATO would totally destroy your night vision!) Next it was out over the ocean to jettison the JATO bottles, join up in two-ship formation and climb on course. Depending on the weather, the join-up could be between layers or on top of the clouds.

En route to the target area, the flight would check in with the TACA (tactical air controller airborne), giving call sign, number of aircraft, time and fuel available, and ordnance load. The controller would assign an altitude to orbit and a location. Typically, parachute flares were visible from quite a distance so the flight would orbit in loose cruise with the wingman stepped up so he could observe the target area and see what was going on. The controller was usually in the aircraft that was dropping flares and marking targets on the ground, so when it was your turn on target the controller would describe the target, give the elevation (it was always in steep mountainous terrain), tell you how many runs to make, give you a run-in and pull-out heading, then clear you in "HOT." At this point you turned lights-out and earned your flight pay.

The pattern was usually 8,500 feet above the target, a 45 degree dive angle at 450 knots, bomb release at 3,500 feet above the target, and a 4-G recovery as you turned downwind for your next run. (If you have never dropped bombs at night under flares, you have no idea what VERTIGO is all about!) Because everyone was lights-out to minimize targeting by AAA (anti-aircraft artillery) sites, there was quite a bit of chatter on the radio trying to keep the pattern safe. After the last run you would call "clear," get the BDA (bomb damage assessment) from the controller, go lights-on, and climb to altitude on your pre-briefed heading back to base. Weather permitting, the flight would join up and we would do a visual check of each other for hung ordnance (bombs that had failed to release) and battle damage. For recovery perhaps the mission ended with an instrument approach and an arrested landing. By the time you finished with the paperwork and debriefed, the club would be closed, but there were always cold beers in the ready-room fridge. I will end this section with a heartfelt sentiment: I continue to be the luckiest man you ever met. I only remember the GOOD TIMES.

A MK-4 GUN POD STORY

Strafing is fun! Everyone likes to strafe. There is something in it for everyone. First of all, you get to do it at high speed and relatively low altitude. Next is the joy you feel when you can hear the guns firing, feel the vibration, and—best of all—see your hits. Strafing is fun!

The A-4 Skyhawk had two internal MK-12 20mm guns, one mounted in each wing root. The two ammo cans were internal, in the front "hell hole" just below the engine, and they carried linked 20mm ammo. If my memory serves me, they held 100 rounds each.

The 20mm cannon is a very effective weapon against soft, non-armored targets such as trucks, boats, and personnel on the ground, and therefore is ideal for CAS (close air support) and RES CAP operations (holding over a downed pilot, trying to keep the enemy away while the search-and-rescue people come in).

At some point in my Vietnam flying career, an ECM package was retrofitted in the A-4. It was called Shoehorn and was designed to protect us from radar-controlled guns (AAA) and missiles. The A-4 was a very small aircraft with no room to spare, so in order to fit the Shoehorn gear into the airframe, the two ammo cans were removed and replaced with serpentine ammo belts wrapped around the engine. It was a good idea but not an effective fix. The installation did not feed well and resulted in jammed guns most of the time. As an aside, we felt "bulletproof" with our new ECM package, but only months later we discovered that the black boxes were not hooked up. No brains, no headache!

Eventually, it was recognized that we needed reliable guns for strafing. Enter the Hughes MK-4 gun pod. It could be mounted on the A-4 centerline or inboard wing stations. The pod itself weighed 1,350 pounds, held 750 rounds of 20mm, and could fire 4,200 rounds per minute. Routinely we would fire 1 to 1.5 second bursts, and it was a joy to shoot! No rata-tat-tat, just a purring noise: "WOOOOH!"

As I mentioned earlier, I was assigned to write the squadron flight schedule. That was a great job because you would schedule the Skipper (squadron commander) for whatever he wanted, give the next good deal to yourself, and then take care of the other schedule writer. Sometimes this approach caused hard feelings among the other squadron pilots, so you would have to schedule yourself on a night radar-controlled mission to even the score. But I digress.

I was drinking beer at the club when the message came from Air Group Operations that our missions for the next day were available. I walked up to the S-3 and picked up the assignment, then went to the squadron to write the schedule. The Skipper got his and I scheduled myself for a CAS hop carrying two MK-4 gun pods, a real plum.

The operations briefing officer gave us the mission information, weather, and intelligence. We were to fly a CAS CAP (close air support / combat air patrol) in support of our fellow Marines operating in an area called "Arizona," south and west of the air base at Chu Lai. The CAS CAP designation meant we were to orbit and wait until we were needed. The ordnance load was two MK-4 gun pods and four 19-shot, 2.75-inch FFAR (folding-fin aircraft rocket) rocket pods for my wingman. The 2.75-inch rockets could be fired singly, ripple, or salvo, but the pods were quite bulky and created a lot of drag, like flying with the speed brakes extended.

We went down to the squadron for the flight briefing and pre-flight. Engine start, radio checks, taxi, ordnance arming, and takeoff were normal. We were operating off the expeditionary runway, 8,000 feet of aluminum planking, while the fighter group next door was operating off a 10,000 foot concrete runway, Chu Lai West.

The flight joined up and we headed south along the South China Sea, checked in with the DASC (direct air support center), and were told to contact an airborne FAC who needed air support for troops in contact. We found the FAC, gave him our ordnance load and time before bingo (fuel level at which we would have to return to base), and began to orbit while he described the situation. He gave us the target elevation, run-in heading, and direction of pull-off, marked the target with a white phosphorus smoke rocket, and then cleared us in "HOT." I rolled in, turned the master arm switch on, and charged the gun pods. After firing a burst, "WOOOOH," I pulled off to turn downwind for another run. Suddenly there was a loud bang followed immediately by a violent rolling yaw. This was followed by another loud bang and rolling yaw in the other direction. My helmet bounced hard on both sides of the canopy, and my first thought was that I had been hit twice by the largest AAA in the NVA (North Vietnamese Army) inventory. I broadcast, "I'm hit! I'm hit! Going feet wet," applied maximum power, and turned toward the ocean. I looked in my mirrors and could see that there were huge, gaping holes in both wings, that the starboard slat was missing, and that fuel was streaming out of the wet wings (internal wing fuel tanks) at an alarming rate. My engine instruments looked good so I continued to climb on the way to the shoreline.

By this time I had switched to Guard channel (243.0 MHz on the UHF radio) and was squawking "Emergency" on IFF (the beacon used to identify the aircraft to ground radar stations). All sorts of interesting people started talking to me wanting to know what my situation was and what my intentions were. My wingman had lost sight of me and was trying to join up, but my airplane did not have four rocket pods and was "cleaner" than his. He finally caught up, came up next to me, and said, "What happened to your gun pods?" I had been so fixated on getting out over the ocean, and on my bent and leaking A-4, that I failed to notice that both gun pods were missing! More encouraging words came from my wingman: "Your wings are bent and pretty ripped up."

As we progressed north toward Chu Lai, using fuel out of the internal fuselage tank (1,200 pounds), my engine instruments and hydraulic system appeared normal, so we decided to try slow flight to determine if the airplane was controllable in the landing configuration. The landing gear came down and the flaps extended. At about 170 knots, right aileron was required to keep the wings level, and at 140 knots, full right aileron and some rudder were required to keep wings level. So far, so good!

When we had launched, the weather at Chu Lai was CAVU (ceiling and visibility unlimited). Now there was a solid layer of clouds below. The tower said the bases of the clouds were at 3,500 feet and requested my intentions. I declared an emergency and stated my intention to shoot a HPA (high precautionary approach). At this time in the evolution of the A-4 series, the aircraft had a "zero-zero" rocket ejection seat with a spreader gun to open the parachute canopy. This meant that a pilot could safely eject with zero airspeed and zero sink rate. The HPA was designed to allow a pilot to retain enough energy and altitude to pull up and eject or shoot a flame-out approach.

As the needle swung on the Chu Lai TACAN (needle swing indicates passing over the navigation aid, which was at the air base), I started the HPA from 9,000 feet. In the clouds, estimating abeam the runway on downwind, the altitude was 4,500 feet. I broke out below the clouds at 3,000 feet, high and fast, passing abeam and close to the end of the runway on downwind. Throttle to idle, I turned base and crossed the runway threshold going about 200 knots and tried to land. The airplane touched down about 1,000 feet down the runway but it wanted to fly again so I told the tower I was shutting the engine down and would roll to the end. God bless those fighter jocks and their 10,000 foot concrete runway! Every crash truck in RVN was there with flashing red lights. Somebody brought a ladder, so I unstrapped, climbed down, and looked at my A-4. The wings and fuselage were bent, there was torn metal on top of both wings, and the starboard wing slat was missing. I hitched a ride back to the squadron, filled out the yellow sheet (maintenance log sheet), debriefed at the Group, and went to the club!

The aircraft was later classified as a "strike" (total loss) by the Douglas representative. Maintenance salvaged everything usable and sent the rest to the graveyard. Post-flight analysis revealed that the ordnance crew had failed to safety-wire the aft adjustment bolt subsequent to bore-sighting the gun pods. Vibration and G forces caused the aft locking mechanism to fail, allowing the gun pod to rotate down, forward, and over the top of the right wing. This created a violent rolling/yaw event, and the gun pod on the left wing separated in a similar fashion.

All I can say is that Douglas built one tough little airplane! Unfortunately I do not have photographs.

DEFEND 14

After 30 days of leave, following my second tour extension in the summer of 1967, the Air Group executive officer sent me to be a forward air controller with the grunts (infantry troops). My good friend Pete Kruger (later a Continental Airlines pilot) and I were having too much fun flying A-4s out of Chu Lai. We had a contest going to see which of us could hit 500 combat missions first. This so disturbed the establishment that they sent him to fly O-1s at Marble Mountain as an airborne FAC, and they sent me to be a ground FAC with the 2nd Battalion, 7th Marines. (As an aside, I ended up with 476 combat missions.)

Each Marine infantry battalion has two aviators attached. The senior one is the ALO (Air Liaison Officer), who typically stays with the battalion command group, advises the CO (Commanding Officer) on aviation matters, and coordinates requests for air assets with his counterpart at the regiment. The junior aviator is the FAC. He is typically with the forward or lead element and coordinates and controls fixed-wing air strikes and helicopter support (resupply and medevac). In reality the jobs are interchangeable, and either person can and will do both. The 2nd Battalion's call sign was "Defend," so the operations officer was Defend 3 and the CO was Defend 6. I was "Defend 14."

The 7th Marines were assigned the job of defending the "rocket belt" around the city of Da Nang, the air base, and the helicopter base at Marble Mountain. The VC (Vietcong) and NVA were in the habit of firing their 122mm rockets at the city and airfields, causing great anxiety among the recipients of those attacks. It was our job to try to interdict the enemy supply routes and prevent the attacks. The area of responsibility extended from Hai Van Pass to the north, Elephant Valley and Charlie Ridge to the west, and Happy Valley to the south. I was a full-time grunt. In the field I carried a Winchester Model 12, a 12-gauge shotgun. The early M-16 rifle was a terrible weapon, prone to jam, and many of our troopers died because of it. In the field we all wore jungle utilities with helmet and flak jacket and carried a backpack containing as much ammunition as possible, personal hygiene items, change of socks, poncho, and C-rations. Everything came and went by helicopter. The "search and destroy" missions were always at least platoon events and sometimes involved as much as a company, which would be three platoons reinforced with guns and mortars from the weapons platoon (a platoon could have 26 to 64 men, while a company from 80 to 225, depending on the mission and strength of the unit).

Most people think of Vietnam as being flat with lots of rice paddies. To be sure, the delta south of Saigon and the coastal regions are relatively flat, but the interior is dominated by steep, rugged mountains with high plateaus and deep, heavily forested valleys. Each valley was a travel corridor for the enemy, with a river or stream accompanied by a network of trails or a road. The dense vegetation (triple-canopy jungle) made movement difficult, severely restricted visibility, and made (pre-GPS) map and compass navigation all but impossible. The terrain and vegetation were ideal for small-unit

ambushes and booby traps. With this in mind, it is easy to understand why the French sought to establish and fight out of forts.

The 2/7 did not move the entire time that I was with them. Most
of our activity involved squad-size patrols and night ambushes to
interdict VC/NVA movement. All patrol activities, including
ambushes, were plotted at the battalion operations bunker in the
event air or artillery assets were needed. Typically a patrol would
involve a reinforced squad, meaning an MA-2 machine gun crew
from the weapons platoon was attached. The FAC/ALO did not
carry the radio but had a radioman from the communications platoon who never left his side while in the field. Because of the
reduced visibility and terrain, any fixed-wing assets
(fighters/bombers) were controlled by an airborne FAC, as his view
and ability to spot a target was vastly superior to anything that I
could do from my position on the ground.

Another consideration was our poor radio equipment. In those
days most fighter/bomber aircraft only had UHF radios. Our only
UHF radio was a 40-pound PRC-41 that used a wet battery, and if
the radioman was on the ground in a prone position (sometimes
useful in combat!), the battery would go dead. Our other radio was
a much lighter, 25-pound AN/PRC-25 that had a dry battery and
used FM bands. With it we could talk to other units, artillery, helicopters, and the airborne FACs.

The patrol would leave base just before dark and return at first
light, checking in by radio once each hour. Ambush sites were selected at known or suspected areas of enemy activity, and all unscheduled nighttime activity was considered hostile. The preferred formation was an L-shaped ambush, allowing concentrated fire without
the danger of engaging friendlies, and flares were available for illumination from artillery support. The FAC and his radio operator
would not go out on a night ambush unless there was a specific reason or requirement for them to be there; however the patrol had a
radio operator who made the hourly check-in with base. The small
operations did not utilize patrol dogs, but I did see them on big
operations.

THE TET OFFENSIVE, 1968

In late January of 1968, while I was the ALO/FAC with the 2/7 Marines, things were pretty quiet in the 2/7 TAOR (tactical area of responsibility), the rocket belt around Da Nang. I asked the CO for permission to go to Da Nang and snivel some flight time to earn my flight pay. By this time the Marines had some TA-4Fs (two-seat A-4s) in-country. They were supposed to be used as fast FACs but in reality were used by staff personnel to fly/earn their flight pay, so I would sit in the backseat and watch some field grade officer (major or above) "yank and bank."

I put some personal items in a light pack, picked up my shotgun, and hitched a ride to the airfield. There I found a place to sleep and went to the Officers' Club for a meal and some drinks. Sometime later, I don't remember exactly when, it became apparent that the airfield was under rocket attack, so I found a nearby bunker and spent the night. The next morning after chow, being an independent thinker, I determined that "things" were happening and set out to return to 2/7. I walked to the front gate, said good morning to the guards, and entered the Twilight Zone.

Outside the front gate, nothing was moving. The normally noisy and busy city streets were deserted. Even the birds were quiet. With no other course of action, I continued to walk through a completely quiet and deserted city, eventually coming to Route 1, where I turned north toward my battalion. Still there was no traffic and things were very quiet. The fields along the highway were deserted.

Eventually there was the noise of a vehicle approaching me from behind, so I turned to see a civilian fuel truck coming from the south. I threw out my thumb and flagged it down. Inside was an oriental gentleman, clad in an old baseball cap, cutoffs, a Hawaiian shirt, and go-aheads ("flip flops"). We exchanged pleasantries and I asked him for a lift. He smiled and motioned me in. We were able to converse in a limited fashion using hand gestures and pidgin English. On the normally busy Route 1 we passed no other vehicles, and eventually he dropped me off near the 2/7 headquarters. As I got down from the truck, I thanked him and asked, "How can you drive when there are no other vehicles moving?" He smiled broadly and replied, "We sell to both sides."

I had been riding in the most secure vehicle on Route 1.

Evidently everyone in Vietnam knew of the 1968 Tet Offensive except the U.S. forces!

My relief arrived in April 1968 along with my rotation date, and I returned to CONUS. My experience with the 2/7 Marines was incredible and one of the most rewarding of my time in Vietnam. The young Marines were amazing, and with the right leadership would do anything for you. To this day I am still in touch with some of my radio operators and I continue to be *the luckiest man you ever met*.

....

Bob's 2½ years in Vietnam ended with his flying 476 combat missions and being awarded four Distinguished Flying Crosses, 27 Air Medals, and a Purple Heart.

After he was released from active duty, he was court-martialed while he was in the Marine Reserve for a "mooning" that took place at the Officers' Club at NAS Los Alamitos. To satisfy the Navy for this "serious breach" of the behavior expected of an officer, Bob received a freeze in rank as a captain for five years. Everyone but the Navy knew this was a good deal for Bob. As a captain he got to fly more and avoid the administrative jobs he would have had as a major—and flying was the only thing he wanted to do. (The Marine Corps has always shown clever ways to protect its own.) When asked about the extensions of his tour in Vietnam, he answered, "It was the only war we had. Why would I want to go home?"

Bob Tieken in front of an A-4E loaded with 4 AGM 45 Shrike missiles, before launching for a "Dream Come True" mission, 1966.

Bob Tieken with his hand on an AGM 45 Shrike missile, delivers the "you're #1 gesture," prior to launching for a mission, 1966.

View from the ground of Marine A-4 close air support.
Note: Shirtless Marine hunkered down on hilltop at left.

Officers' quarters at Chu Lai, late 1965–early 1966. Note walkway
made of wood pallets.

9

ONE HELL OF A RIDE

Mike Doyle, USMC, A-4C, A-4E, TA-4F, 1966 – 1967
{ Date of hire by Western Airlines: 9/3/1968 }

Mike Doyle in A-4 cockpit (self-portrait), 1966.

On April 4, 2000, Mike Doyle had his 60th birthday and retired from Delta Air Lines after nearly 32 years of service with Western and Delta. Also on that day he retired from the Army National Guard after more than 43 years of involvement with the U.S. military. That involvement began at age 16 when he was living in the small town of Collinsville in eastern Oklahoma. He lied about his age to join the Oklahoma Air National Guard and soon thereafter signed up for Air Force ROTC when he was accepted at Northeastern Oklahoma A&M College. He ended up at Oklahoma State University in Stillwater and upon leaving OSU was accepted into the MARCAD (Marine Aviation Cadet) program. He reported to Pensacola for Navy flight training and was commissioned a second lieutenant in the Marine Corps in 1963.

I met Mike in Prescott, Arizona, on March 11, 2013, and learned a lot about him. He is someone about whom you can truly say, "After him, they broke the mold." Mike talks about wanting to have been a cowboy in the old West, or to have ridden with Teddy Roosevelt's Rough Riders. He wishes he could have been a World War II fighter pilot or served with the French Foreign Legion. There were some things that were impossible for him to do, but of the possible he hasn't missed much. The only war he had was Vietnam, and he flew in it to the maximum as a Marine attack pilot. There seems to be one overriding philosophy by which Mike has lived his life. When the Army Reserve personnel center called him as his 60th birthday approached, urging him to retire, he was asked why he had stayed so long. "I only did it because it was fun," was his reply. He retired with 24 years, 3 months, and 22 days of credited service, long past the point at which he could have retired and drawn a full pension. He retired as a Marine Corps captain, but he spent more than half his service time as an Army CWO (chief warrant officer), flying attack helicopters for the Utah Army National Guard.

How do you introduce a man like Mike Doyle? He moved to Prescott around 1970, decided he liked cowboying, went to rodeo school, and then became a pro, riding bulls and saddle broncs in competition until he was 41 years old. He is a man who, after retiring from both Delta and the military, spent a month in Marseilles, France, where he met a group of professional international paratroopers and was invited to join them for a jump. Never having been qualified at a military parachute jump school, he took a "quick-ie" civilian course, got jump-qualified, and then jumped with a group of current and retired paratroopers from all over the world: American, Rhodesian, South African, French, German, Israeli, and Jordanian. They jumped into the Jordanian desert from a Royal Jordanian Air Force C-130.

When his Marine A-4 reserve unit at NAS Alameda became overstaffed and he lost his slot, Mike gave up his Marine rank of captain and joined the Utah Army National Guard and the attack troop of the 167th Armored Cavalry. He became an Army chief warrant officer and got an in-house transition to the UH-1 Huey and then to the AH-1 Cobra attack helicopter. Mike's key role in the development of air-to-air tactics for helicopters, to take on both fixed-wing and rotary-wing opponents, won him the Army Aviator of the Year award in the 1980s. (In Mike's words: "Nineteen-eighty-something-or-other. Got a plaque.") Using his experience in Army helicopter tactics against fixed-wing aircraft, Mike was able to finagle orders to fly the A-4 again. He called this "just one more ride on the merry-go-round." He flew the A-4 one last time with Navy Squadron VF-126, the Navy's adversary squadron that did air-to-air workups (tactics for dog-fighting) at NAS Miramar near San Diego. They were flying the two-seat A-4F (Super Foxtrot), training Navy and Marine fighter pilots in air-to air-tactics.

Mike flew in the following Marine Corps squadrons while on active duty:

1) VMA-332: A-4C, MCAS Cherry Point, North Carolina, 1964
2) VMA(AW)-242: A-6, MCAS Cherry Point, North Carolina, 1965
3) VMA-225: A-4C, MCAS Cherry Point, North Carolina, 1966
4) VMA-311: A-4C, A-4E, Chu Lai Air Base, RVN, 1966
5) VMA 214: A-4C, A-4E, Chu Lai Air Base, RVN, and Trans-Pac Chu Lai to MCAS El Toro, 1967
6) VMT-103: TA-4F, MCAS Yuma, Arizona, 1967–1968

[VMA: fixed-wing Marine attack squadron, VMA(AW): fixed-wing Marine attack squadron, all weather, VMT: fixed-wing Marine training squadron, MCAS: Marine Corps Air Station, NAS: Naval Air Station, RVN:Republic of Vietnam, Trans-Pac: ferry flight across the Pacific.]

Mike is very private about his Marine Corps experience, especially about his time in Vietnam. I was able to meet with him through my friend-ship with Bill Wilson, and as you are about to read, Mike's story is pretty incredible. I am honored that he trusted me to tell it; my invitation into the Marine Corps fraternity continues to be a humbling experience. As you will read, Mike Doyle is really one-of-a-kind.

Now, here is Mike's story about the Marine Corps, the A-4 Skyhawk, and Chu Lai Air Base, Republic of Vietnam.

....

When I joined the Marine Corps I knew I had found a home, and I often thought that I could not have been landed from another planet at any better place than the USMC. My first assignment upon completion of flight training was VMA-332 at MCAS Cherry Point, North Carolina, where I checked out in the A-4C. My love affair with the little single-seat attack bomber began there and was only briefly interrupted when I was selected to transfer to VMA(AW)-242 and be a part of the first Marine A-6 Intruder squadron. At the time it was considered an honor to be selected to a squadron that was getting a new type of aircraft with a new mission. It was exciting at first and I had a lot to learn, especially having a bombardier/navigator (who sat to my right) to work with. I was flying a brand-new aircraft that was a lot more complicated than the A-4C. It had two engines, more power, and flew mostly at night. After a while I settled into the squadron and the night flying, but I really missed the A-4.

My squadron needed a new design for its patch, as the old one did not reflect its new mission of mostly night and all-weather flying. I submitted my idea for a new squadron patch—a bat and a lightning bolt—and my design was accepted. However, this did not lessen my ongoing attempts to get back to an A-4 squadron, and after a year flying the A-6, I talked to everyone I knew and managed to work out a transfer back to A-4Cs and to VMA-225 at Cherry Point. VMA-225 was made up of a bunch of "retreads" like me who needed to requalify on the airplane, so the squadron had us flying round the clock. After two months I had flown about 140 hours in the A-4 and was considered requalified. Several of us then went on individual orders to Southeast Asia. In March 1966 I reported to MAG-12 (Marine Air Group-12) at Chu Lai AB, RVN, and was assigned to do my flying with VMA-311. MAG-12 had four Marine A-4 squadrons, flying both the A-4C and A-4E models. There were so many incredible experiences packed into the next 12 months; I will relate a few of them to give the reader the flavor of my year in combat.

NIGHT OPERATIONS

About half of my missions in Vietnam were flown at night, often in weather, and the concept of formation flying took on a whole new meaning. There was no radar flight following in Vietnam, and as wingman you had to rely on your leader. If you lost him you were in serious trouble. First of all, you probably wouldn't know where you were, and if you were lost in the clouds in hostile territory, you were just an accident waiting to happen. As wingman, you flew formation on lead aircraft by visually sighting his wingtip light against a spot on his fuselage and tried to stick there like glue. The expression coined by Bill Wilson was, "You put a lip lock on that wingtip light, suck it in as close as you can get, and stay there." Your trust in your leader was complete. If he flew into a mountain, you would be right with him.

For target illumination, night bombing was usually done under parachute flares. They were either dropped by aircraft like A-4s or airborne FACs like 0-1 Birddogs, C-130s, or C-47s; or fired by artillery or from mortars by ground troops. When the Marines on the ground called for help, it always came. The flares we carried were contained in flare pods under the wings and were dropped on missions when we needed a target illuminated. The flares fell under a small parachute and created a powerful type of vertigo as they swung back and forth, reflecting off the clouds and the jungle below. At times they could also be a real hazard when they burned out before they hit the ground, often in the path of our high-speed bomb runs. Another intense vertigo-inducing experience came about when flying formation in weather at night and encountering St. Elmo's fire. This is a phenomenon caused by static electricity in the clouds that creates a bright blue or violet glow. You could hold up your hand and your glove would be outlined in blue fire, the gunsight would be outlined in blue fire, and looking at the other airplane, the pilot's head would be outlined in blue fire. It was disorienting, to say the least, and when we encountered it, we often flew back to Chu Lai independently rather than try to fly back in formation.

We had a night operation called the "midnight special," also known as the RLAF 501 mission (Royal Laotian Air Force). The bombing over the Ho Chi Minh Trail in Laos was a nightly event and was done with our aircraft lights turned off to avoid attracting enemy gunfire. During our bomb runs, ingress and egress headings and altitudes were called out by a FAC in an orbiting aircraft. The targets were dark, often in weather under flares, and in rugged mountainous terrain. These missions were dangerous, and the targets often turned out to be of minimal value. The BDA (bomb damage assessment) of the targets we attacked often showed marginal results for our efforts and the risk involved. The RLAF 501 was at the top of the list of missions to avoid.

One mission over Laos comes to mind, and even though it occurred in the daytime, it helps to show the difference between the mission types. It was monsoon season, which seemed to be most of the time, and I was on a two-ship mission over the PDJ (Plain of Jars in northern Laos) operating under a 5,000 foot overcast ceiling. We were bombing track vehicles (bulldozers used by the North Vietnamese to repair bomb damage along the trail). Our ordnance load for each airplane was eighteen MK-81 (250 pound general purpose, low drag) bombs plus our two internal 20mm cannons. On my first bombing pass I heard and felt a thump, and shortly my wingman, Butch Miller, called and asked if I was jettisoning fuel. I said no, and he replied, "Yes you are." I had been hit by small-arms fire and was losing fuel from my wing tank at a very rapid rate. I immediately pulled the emergency jettison handle, dropping everything except my centerline fuel tank. That included the inboard and outboard racks and bombs under both wings; the MERS (multiple ejector rack) and TERS (triple ejector rack) that held the bombs. This was called "chaining off" my load. I started a zoom climb to 25,000 feet to conserve fuel and headed east toward the relative safety of the South China Sea, hoping to make it back to Chu Lai. It soon became apparent that I didn't have enough fuel to make Chu Lai, so I turned toward Da Nang, which was the closest air base. My fuel transfer light had come on shortly after I was hit, indicating that I had about 1,400 pounds of fuel remaining in the main tanks. Da Nang was about 100 miles to the southeast of us, so I set glide power on my engine and headed that way. My wingman called the tower and told them we were inbound for a straight-in approach to the south. The tower advised us that they were landing to the north and to proceed accordingly. In typical Marine fashion, my wingman explained to the tower controller that we were not landing north but were making a straight-in approach to the south, as we had battle damage and were in an emergency low-fuel state. We were cleared to proceed and landed to the south with my fuel gauge reading empty. I taxied to the nearest Marine parking area, which happened to be my old A-6 squadron, VMA(AW)-242. As soon as I pulled into a revetment the maintenance men checked the damage, and by use of a dipstick told me I had just 10 gallons (64 pounds) of fuel remaining on the aircraft! Butch and I caught a helicopter ride back to Chu Lai while the Marines at Da Nang were busy repairing my aircraft.

After it had been repaired, I returned to Da Nang in a few days to pick it up, and when I saw it I couldn't believe my eyes: It was totally covered with stickers, graffiti, and squadron logos for VMA(AW)-242. It appeared that nearly every member of my old squadron had signed or otherwise defaced my A-4. I learned a lesson the hard way: You never leave your aircraft overnight and unguarded with another Marine squadron!

A CAS (close air support) mission at night was always challenging. When we were supporting our fellow Marines on the ground, these missions were often under the most difficult circumstances. I flew them to the maximum of my ability and tried to give the ground troops all the help they so desperately needed.

A second mission I recall was a night-alert launch for a Marine unit in contact and in serious trouble. They were in an area south of Chu Lai where there was a solid low overcast with the ceiling at about 1,500 feet AGL (above ground level). There were two conical peaks about 2,000 feet high with the tops sticking out above the clouds, and the Marines were between the two peaks. The FAC knew me and my wingman and knew our capabilities, so he directed a heading for our dive through the clouds, telling us we would break out in the clear at 1,500 feet. He explained that we would have about two seconds to line up on the target, release our ordnance, and then climb back up into the clouds with an immediate hard right turn to miss the northernmost peak. Breaking out below the clouds, we were in a confined space, backlit by mortar-fired parachute flares that were swinging and causing a most disorienting sensation between the clouds and the treetops. We lined up on the target, dropped our ordnance, and then pulled up through the clouds in a 4-G right turn. After several runs we received a thank-you from the troops on the ground, relayed from the FAC, and headed to Chu Lai. It was a rewarding mission and one repeated many times as our Marines were constantly in contact. The FACs learned quickly what we could handle and worked us right to the limit.

CHU LAI MORTAR ATTACK

Chu Lai was built as an expeditionary airfield for the Marine Corps, which meant it was originally planned for just 30 to 60 days of operation, but the base lasted for the duration of the war. In 1966 the base perimeter security consisted of three layers of concertina razor wire, sandbagged bunkers and trenches for the Marine security force, and tin cans in the wire to alert them to any attempted breach of the perimeter. There were also several Marine tanks at Chu Lai, and we would hear them rumbling and clanking around the base while we were trying to sleep. It was pretty primitive for a front-line Marine Corps fighter base. The tanks would fire their guns for H & I (harassment and interdiction) when they had a target spotted outside the wire, but that required coordination to be sure they were not firing on friendly patrols.

The VC (Vietcong) and NVA (North Vietnamese Army) would fire an occasional mortar round or a 122mm rocket at the base, but it was usually more of a nuisance than anything else. There was one major rocket and mortar attack that occurred on a night when I happened to be working at group (MAG-12). In addition to writing the "frag order" that night (the schedule for the next day's flying), one of my responsibilities was to sound the air raid type siren in the event of an attack, so everyone could get in their foxhole-type bunkers. I remember crouching under my desk with my hand reaching up to the table and my finger on the button setting off the siren. At the same time the VC/NVA mortars were "walking" across the ramp and flight line, heading for the operations office. The enemy got pretty good at "walking" or "free tubing" their mortars, moving the tube slightly with each firing rather than using a spotter to adjust their targeting. The end result of this attack was the destruction of several airplanes and several buildings, including the officers' shitter (latrine), and damage to the fueling area and bomb dump. I was glad the VC blew up our new latrine, as I had recently stolen the door to make myself a new bed. No one knew who had taken it, and its disappearance had become a mystery and a source of rumors.

The enemy was trying to terrorize us, but it didn't work with Bob Tieken, who was lifting weights in his hut and refused to leave. A mortar hit a tree just outside his hut and he was slightly wounded. The Marine tanks rumbled into position and had zeroed in on the mortars with their guns, but due to the ROE (rules of engagement), they were still awaiting permission to fire when the attack was long over. I will never forget the sounds: a soft "thwunk" as a mortar was dropped in the tube, a scream of "F***ing incoming!" followed by a loud "ker-blam" seconds later (they were that close to the wire), and the clanking of tank tracks as they maneuvered through the sand and mud.

CLOSE CALL

There was a lieutenant colonel attached to MAG-12 who was notorious for his weak piloting skills and bad vision. He wore Coke-bottle-lens glasses and was allowed to fly only when he was least likely to get himself or anyone else in trouble. On this particular day he was returning from a harmless trip to the Philippines, where we sent our airplanes for occasional modifications. I was sitting in the cockpit of my aircraft in the arming area, which sat adjacent to the parking revetments at the end of a 4,000-foot-long, 35-foot-wide taxiway made of aluminum matting. I was being fueled and loaded with ordnance, with my engine shut down, my canopy open, and my hands up and visible to the armorers who were swarming under my aircraft, arming my bombs and charging a round into each of the 20mm cannons. I happened to look to my right and saw an A-4 that was preparing to land, except he was lined up on the taxiway for landing! As he got closer and closer, I thought surely he would realize his mistake and move over to land on the parallel 8,000-foot aluminum runway. On he came, touching down on the taxiway heading directly for me, and there was nowhere for me to go. All of a sudden a huge cloud of smoke and sparks billowed out from beneath his aircraft as he hit the brakes. He flattened and shredded his tires and ground off the bottoms of his wheels on his way down the aluminum taxiway. He came to a stop barely 20 feet from my aircraft in a cloud of smoke and flaming sparks. The vision that will always stay with me is of his aircraft bobbing up and down on the nose gear oleo strut just feet from my cockpit. He had managed to "arc weld" the main gear wheels to the aluminum matting, and the maintenance crew had to use blowtorches to free them and remove his aircraft from the taxiway.

HUGHES 20MM CANNON

At some point in the fall of 1966, it was decided that a 20mm Hughes cannon gun pod would be mounted externally on the A-4, so several civilian Hughes tech reps came to Chu Lai to teach us how to use it. The cannon had two barrels with a rotating cylinder, held about 1,600 rounds of 20mm ammunition, and put out a tremendous rate of fire. It was in a pod that in size and shape looked similar to our fuel drop tanks. At first we mounted two cannons, one under each wing on hard points. However, if one cannon didn't fire and the other one did, it would cause the aircraft to yaw violently (as much as 45 degrees), so we decided to mount just a single gun pod on the centerline station. (It was Bob Tieken's experience in the previous story that contributed to bringing about this change.) The centerline mounting worked much better, and the tech reps warned us to limit firing to 2 to 3 second bursts or else we would overheat and burn up the barrels and the motor. It was so much fun to fire and did such a great job on ground targets that it was hard to limit the bursts to 2 or 3 seconds. After a few guns were burned up, the Hughes tech reps went home and the Marine Corps gave up on the idea of the Hughes cannon. It was expensive and turned out to be too maintenance-intensive. I can guarantee you that anyone lucky enough to get a mission with the Hughes cannon gun pod came back without any ammo or with a burned-out pod.

On one memorable sortie I was returning from a bombing mission north of the DMZ (Demilitarized Zone, at the border between North and South Vietnam), looking for a suitable target of opportunity for the cannon. There was an old French fort near the DMZ that would occasionally be rude enough to fly an NVA flag from a flagpole on the roof. The flag was up and so was I. I made my run on the fort, laying on the trigger and continuing to push the nose over in a dive. I kept the cannon rounds on the target and watched the concrete building explode as it was reduced to a pile of rubble. The flag disappeared!

When you flew on the wing of an A-4 firing the Hughes cannon, it was incredible to experience the sound of the gun and watch the flame and smoke spewing from the barrels. Firing it was more fun than any young Marine attack pilot could hope to have!

HOT REFUELING

There were several occasions when all the safety rules and procedures were waived for a tactical emergency, usually involving Marines in heavy contact with the VC/NVA. One situation lasted nearly three days, with the ground action taking place less than 10 miles southwest of Chu Lai. A Marine reconnaissance patrol of about 20 men had been surrounded by a much larger enemy force and were literally fighting for their lives. The enemy force was large enough to prevent Marine reinforcements from being landed by helicopter, so we flew round the clock, night and day, dropping bombs and napalm, firing rockets and flares at night, and strafing with our 20mm internal cannons. We would fly mission after mission, not leaving the cockpit but just taxiing to the flight line, leaving the engine running, and parking while the fueling crew pushed up a roll-away stand and brought the fuel hose up to the aircraft. They refueled us through the inflight refueling probe by putting an attachment on the fuel hose that allowed them to clamp it on the probe, fueling the aircraft with the engine running. At the same time, the armorers were under the aircraft loading and arming "napes and snakes" (napalm and snake-eye retarded fin bombs, which we were dropping from such a low altitude that we needed the fin to slow their trajectory so we could fly away before they exploded), and reloading the ammunition for the 20mm cannons. There was only one ground casualty, when an A-4 caught fire during refueling and the pilot was killed. All of this was being done in front of the "No Smoking" signs on the ramp!

At night we dropped flares and had the beleaguered Marines flash strobes and flashlights and flick their Zippos to mark their positions for our bombing and strafing runs. The battle went on, 24 hours a day for nearly three days, and we felt helpless hearing the Marines on the ground begging us to drop our ordnance closer and closer and finally on top of their positions as they were being overrun by the enemy. On the last day, we asked them to pop a smoke canister to mark their position, and the last voice we heard told us to drop right on the smoke as they were fighting the enemy hand-to-hand. Then the voice said, "We're finished." My recollection is that of the 20 recon Marines, some of the toughest of the tough and the bravest of the brave, very few survived. It was a very sad day for all of us.

VMA-214 TRANS-PAC FERRY FLIGHT

At some point in late 1966, the Marine Corps decided to have VMA-214 ferry the A-4C models from Chu Lai to MCAS El Toro in Southern California. The plan was to replace the C models at Chu Lai with E models because they could carry more ordnance, had a more powerful engine, and had a more advanced avionics package. It was an historic first for the USMC to return an entire squadron from a combat zone to the States while a war was still ongoing, and it was an incredible experience for me to be involved in the operation. MAG-12 transferred several pilots to VMA-214 in advance of the move, as their tours were coming to an end and it was a good way to get them home. I was one of the lucky ones, so in November 1966 I was transferred from MAG-12 to VMA-214 in preparation for the Trans-Pac and continued to fly combat missions with VMA-214 until March 1967.

On March 29, 1967, about 14 A-4Cs left Chu Lai on that historic trip flying to Guam, Wake Island, Midway Island, Honolulu, and on to El Toro. There were multiple in-flight refuelings, well coordinated with Marine C-130s, and the only glitch came when one aircraft developed engine trouble and was forced to return to Midway after we had departed. The plane required an engine change. It was Bill Wilson's section leader, so Bill landed with him while the rest of the squadron continued on to Hawaii, where the highlight of my flying career occurred.

VMA-214 was the famous Black Sheep squadron of World War II and Pappy Boyington fame, and our airplanes had the black sheep painted on them along with our squadron logo. The J-65 engine on the A-4C had a "total-loss" oil system that was designed to burn and vent oil, so the airplanes had a coating of oil that picked up all the sand and red dirt that surrounded our base at Chu Lai. They had been in constant combat since the base was opened in 1965 and had never been washed, so the airplanes were a proud but very dirty sight. When we landed at MCAS Kaneohe Bay in Hawaii we were given a reception that I will never forget, and I still get choked up talking about it. I think the following expression might not adequately explain my feelings: "If I live a thousand years, nothing could ever top this."

We had pre-briefed our arrival at Kaneohe on the way from Midway, and the plan was to arrive in flights of four aircraft, pitch out and land, and when everyone was on the ground we would taxi in a line to the ramp, where dignitaries were waiting to greet us. Kaneohe Bay was the first American soil for VMA-214 to touch and represented the historic first for the Marine Corps.

In addition to the dignitaries on the ramp, the highlight of the arrival was the brigade band playing "China Night," a song of great significance to the Marine Corps. From an article in the November 1979 *Leatherneck* magazine is the following quote: "'China Night' is the unofficial regimental song of the Fourth and Ninth Marines who have both seen service at one time or another in China and are considered to be the Corps' old Asian hands." To say I was overwhelmed and bursting with pride is an understatement.

The next day we left for the final leg of our journey to El Toro. Upon arrival we were greeted by a small contingent of El Toro Marines, their families, and wives of some of the pilots and crews. There was a TV camera crew that shot some film, but the event was broadcast only locally. We were released to go on leave, with some of us headed to our next duty assignment and some returning to Chu Lai after a two-week break. The A-4 had an armament bay called the "hell hole" where the ammo cans were located for the internally mounted 20mm cannons, and it was used to carry our baggage on trips like this. We all scattered, changed into our uniforms, and went in a group of taxicabs to LAX (Los Angeles International Airport) for flights to different parts of the country, to go home and start our leave. It all happened so fast, with little time to say good-bye to my fellow Marines, with whom I had just been flying combat a few days earlier. We had trusted each other with our lives many times over. As we poured out of the cabs at LAX, proudly wearing our Marine "khaki summer service Charlie" uniforms, we had to step around and through a group of orange-robed Hare Krishnas beating drums, chanting, and blocking the entrance to the terminal. Shouts of "baby killers" and "murderers" greeted us as we worked our way through the crowds to the ticket counter and to the gates. My emotions went from the very high at Kaneohe to the extreme low at LAX in 24 hours.

VMT-103 TRANS-PAC FERRY FLIGHT

My next duty assignment was VMT-103 at MCAS Yuma where we trained new A-4 pilots and tried to teach them everything they would need to know to survive in combat. I arrived there in April 1967, and it was my final assignment before I separated from active duty.

In January 1968 I was "volunteered" to join a group of four instructors from VMT-103 to fly four TA4-Fs to Da Nang. The two-seat models we used for training were in demand as FAC aircraft in Vietnam, and they were going to be used for everything from spotting targets for other aircraft to calling in coordinates for naval gunfire. On January 17, 1968, we left MCAS Yuma for MCAS El Toro in a flight led by my good friend and VMA-214 squadron mate, Bill Wilson. He was the flight division leader, and I was the section leader of two of the four aircraft. Bill had been tasked with the overall planning of the mission, and not one of us was really excited about going. The night before we were scheduled to depart from El Toro, we were all at the Officers' Club still hoping that it would somehow be called off at the last minute. Flying over the Pacific for hours on end in a single-engine A-4 left a lot to be desired.

Other than a couple of scares (such as trying to find our C-130 tankers so we could get fuel and not have to ditch in the middle of the Pacific), the flight was uneventful until we arrived at NAS Agana on Guam. The Marine A-4 maintenance crew was riding in one of the C-130 tankers, and in the process of servicing the airplanes found that mine was totally out of oil. I received a phone call in the Officers' Club informing me that they had to add 23 quarts of oil to my engine. I asked, "How many quarts does it hold?" and the reply was, "Twenty-three." They determined that my engine had a cracked oil seal and I would need an engine change, so the other three airplanes had to leave me behind while I waited for the work to be done. They found a spare engine in the Philippines and flew it to Guam. Two days later, with me helping the maintenance crew, they got the engine changed and I went to the transient quarters at about 2 a.m. to try to get a little sleep. Early that same morning I got a call informing me that the C-130 had to leave and that I needed to get out to the flight line and go with him in my repaired A-4. The destination was NAS Cubi Point in the Philippines. Although the C-130 provided long-range navigation and was a refueling tanker, it cruised at 20,000 feet and 210 knots so it was going to be a long flight. The weather was forecast to have us flying in and out of clouds or between layers most of the way.

About 400 miles from the Philippines, en route to Cubi Point, I noticed my oil pressure gauge begin to quiver and then drop to zero. According to the A-4 Emergency Handbook—and everything I knew about the A-4—if the engine lost oil pressure, you were to set the power at 87 percent RPM to put the least load on the engine, and this would enable it to run the longest before it seized up and quit. You were to lock the throttle at 87 percent and not touch it! Some engineer, somewhere, had tested this and determined that the J-52 engine would run at 87 percent with no oil pressure for an undetermined length of time: not 86 percent or 88 percent, but 87 percent. Of course, the next step in the emergency procedure was to land immediately. The definition of "undetermined length of time" took on a whole new meaning! This would be the ultimate test of that procedure, as I was more than 400 miles from land, over the water, and all alone except for my tanker. (Even my backseater was gone;

he had left in one of the C-130 tankers that accompanied the other three aircraft.) I didn't have much interest in ejecting and then floating around in my orange raft hoping that someone would find me, so I set the power and evaluated my situation.

With the throttle locked at 87 percent, I could operate only in a very narrow speed range. In order to maintain airspeed and stay with the tanker, I elected to reduce my weight by dumping some of my fuel. I calculated the maximum weight of the aircraft that would allow me to maintain airspeed and stay with my tanker, and then I began to dump fuel to get down to that weight. Since I would be carrying a lower fuel load, I would be required to refuel about every 30 minutes.

With the power set at a constant 87 percent level and unable to move the throttle to make adjustments, the only control I had of my airspeed was my speed brakes. For each refueling, I had to maneuver over to the drogue (the refueling hose that extended from the C-130) and then run the speed brakes in and out to adjust my speed as I tried to plug my refueling probe into the basket, push the probe far enough into the basket to begin fuel transfer, and then stay plugged in during the refueling. It was speed brakes in, speed brakes out, back and forth, until refueling was complete. Then I had to do it again in about 30 minutes. It was challenging, stressful, tiring, and generally a pain in the ass, but I was able to do it.

As we approached the Philippines, Naval Air Station Sangley Point was the closest airfield, so I headed there and received emergency clearance for approach and landing. Without the use of engine power to control my descent, I used the same procedure of airspeed control with my speed brakes and planned for a "dead stick" (power out) landing. The procedure for a dead stick landing involved using the gunsight with a setting of 110 mils, putting the gunsight pipper on the end of the runway, and that was the point you would hit. If I was high and fast on the descent and approach I could make some adjustment with the speed brakes, but if I got too low and slow I was screwed.

I got set up for an approach that I knew was a one-shot deal, with no option to go around for a second attempt. It worked just like the book said it would, and I got the airplane on the ground in one piece.

And bless the engineer who came up with that 87 percent power set-ting. The engine had run for close to three hours with no oil pressure. When I was safely on the runway, I pulled the throttle back to shut it down. The engine seized and the aircraft shook violently.

After another two-day delay and a second engine change (what a coincidence that I had another cracked oil seal!), I left Sangley Point on the morning of January 29, 1968, and headed to Cubi Point and then to Da Nang, where I delivered the airplane. The Marine side of Da Nang AB was pretty primitive compared with the Air Force side, so I headed to the other side of the field and arranged my transportation back to the States. I left Da Nang late in the evening of January 29 as a passenger on an Air Force C-124 heading for Kadena AB on Okinawa. I arrived at Kadena and checked into the transient officers' quarters at about 2 a.m. Unknown to me until then, that C-124 was one of the last flights out of Da Nang as the Tet Offensive began just after midnight on the morning of January 30. Da Nang city was attacked as well as the air base, and I would have been stuck in Vietnam for an indefinite period.

I returned to MCAS Yuma and VMT-103, where I worked as a combat flight instructor until late 1968, when I separated from active duty. I went to work for Western Airlines on September 3, 1968. I had two Chu Lai squadron mates in my class at Western, Bob Tieken and Jack McLaughlin, while my good friend and squadron mate Bill Wilson followed us in a class in February 1969.

FLOWER POWER

When I went to work for Western Airlines in September 1968, my class was split in half, with one group training to be flight engineers on the Boeing 707/720 and another to be flight engineers on the Lockheed Electra. I was assigned to the Electra group and ended up being based in Seattle. The only Marine Corps Reserve unit in the Seattle area was a squadron flying the C-119 at Seattle Naval Air Station, so I signed up and flew with them for a short period until I was able to arrange a transfer to VMA-133 at Alameda Naval Air Station, flying the A-4C.

Marine reserve units in the early 1970s were an interesting mix of officers, most of whom were Vietnam veterans; senior enlisted men, a good percentage of whom were also Vietnam veterans; and very junior enlisted men who had joined the reserves, for the most part, to avoid the draft. Ninety percent of the unit was made up of "squared away" Marines, but the other 10 percent caused us a lot of problems that we never experienced in the active-duty Marine Corps. Long hair that had to be tucked under their hats and a bad attitude toward the war and the military in general were at the top of the list of disciplinary problems.

One time in the summer, around 1970, we were on two weeks of active duty at NAS Fallon in eastern Nevada. We were using the gunnery and bombing range, practicing for the next war. Most of our "plane captains" were young enlisted men, many of them a part of that 10 percent who were against the Vietnam War. I was just getting strapped into my aircraft when I noticed an "unauthorized attachment" to my gunsight. The gunsight was located right in the center of the windshield, directly in front of the pilot, and one of the ground crew had attached a peace symbol to it. The peace symbol was a pretty thing, a small bunch of flowers. I knew that the perpetrator was one of the "plane captains" and that the entire group on the ground was watching to see my reaction. I ignored the flowers and went through the procedures for starting my engine. I gave the signal to the ground crew that I was ready to taxi. Then I picked the flowers off the gunsight, admired them, and proceeded to eat them. I made sure my eating the flowers was visible to those on the ground. Bill Wilson was in the aircraft next to me, watching the whole thing and laughing his head off. After that we went out to the desert and blew stuff up. It was a great day on the gunnery range!

RANDOM THOUGHTS

We had a large jar behind the bar at the Chu Lai Officers' Club that was full of money. It was a fund to which each pilot would contribute in order to say, "Have a drink on me," in the event he went missing. One of our squadron pilots was Pete Kruger (later a Continental

Airlines pilot), whom we called Custer because of the famous quote, "Ride to the sound of the guns," because Pete always did. On an evening mission he got into a one-on-one duel with a 57mm anti-aircraft artillery site south of the DMZ and lost the battle. He was able to make it back "feet wet" (over the water) before he had to eject. A report came in that he had been shot down, and it was determined that he had gone missing. It didn't take long for everyone to show up at the bar, ready to break into the missing-pilot kitty. However, the first round of drinks had just been served when Pete walked into the bar in his barely damp flight suit! He was immediately booed by everyone for spoiling the party. As he related the story, his boots had barely touched the water when he was picked up by a Navy PT boat (also called a Swift boat) and delivered right back to Chu Lai.

When I first arrived at Chu Lai, we were experiencing all the luxuries of an expeditionary airfield. The runway lights were powered by a generator that was somewhat similar to a Briggs and Stratton lawnmower engine. The generator was very unreliable, and since we were operating 24 hours a day, the runway was alternately lighted by flare pots. Quite an operation for the frontline Marine airbase in South Vietnam!

It may seem a strange thing to remember, but the colors of the threats we faced in a hostile sky are indelibly etched in my mind. Green was the color of the AAA tracer rounds, white puffs for 23mm air bursts, gray puffs for 37mm air bursts, and black puffs for 57mm air bursts.

"Red Crown" was the call sign of the Navy destroyer off the coast that maintained a 24-hour radar watch on North Vietnam. There was a code for different threats, and they broadcast those threats over guard frequency (243.0 MHz UHF) whenever they saw a MiG airborne or when a SAM (surface-to-air missile) radar site became active. An example of a call would be: "This is Red Crown on guard. Cowboy at YD5." *Cowboy* would be the day's code word for a MiG airborne, and YD5 would reference a grid square on the map we carried on our knee board. We would check the grid square and be extra alert if we were close to its location.

There was a lot of black humor as we went about our daily missions, and one of my favorite lines came from my friend Bob Tieken.

I had been on a waiting list at the exchange (base store) for a Sanyo fan for my hooch. It finally came in about a week before I ended up being scheduled for the "midnight special." I was walking toward operations and ran into Bob, who asked, "Hey Mike, don't you have the midnight mission to Laos?" I answered, "Yeah." So he asked, "Can I have your fan?"

In my year at Chu Lai, we lost at least 12 A-4 pilots from the group, most hit by ground fire or SAMs, a few accidents, and one who was burned and killed in his aircraft during one of our "hot refuelings." (A steady stream of replacement aircraft came down from Iwakuni AB in Japan, with replacement pilots coming in on individual orders.) I have the names of those pilots in my head, but over all the years I flew for Western and Delta and had layovers in Washington D.C., I never went to the Wall (the Vietnam Veterans Memorial). I have been active over the past year in the Arizona Veterans Center, and I was honored to be selected as part of a group of 44 to go to Washington and represent the state of Arizona on Veterans Day 2012. We visited the Wall and saw the wreath-laying ceremony at the Iwo Jima Memorial, performed by the most squared-away Marines I have ever seen. At the Wall I was finally able to pay my respects to my friends who were lost.

My story would not be complete without a mention of the French Foreign Legion. When I retired from Delta in early April 2000, I still had one major item on my "to do" list, and that was to attend the Cameron Day celebration with the FFL. It is an annual event on April 30 held at the FFL headquarters in Aubagne, near Marseilles, France. It commemorates the Battle of Cameron in Mexico, where 62 Legionnaires battled to the death with more than 3,000 Mexican Lancers on April 30, 1863. I had heard and read about the celebration for years, and it had been described as the annual Marine Corps birthday party on steroids. Using every contact I had made in my 43-year adventure with the U.S. military, I got in touch with a retired Marine Corps chaplain whose nephew had served in the Legion, and through him was sent a personal invitation to the celebration on April 30, 2000. It lived up to everything, and then some! I spent close to 30 days visiting with the FFL. Of all things, I met a group of American Green Berets who invited me to join them on an upcoming parachute jump with a group they belonged to, the International Association of Airborne Veterans. The jump would take place in Jordan in honor of King Hussein, who had passed away early in 1999.

Never having attended Military Jump School in my years in the service, they told me where to take a civilian course that would involve making five static line jumps and being signed off by a jump master. I came home, found the school just south of Phoenix in Eloy, Arizona, and completed the course. Next thing I knew, I was at JFK International Airport meeting the group at the boarding gate for Royal Jordanian Airlines and a flight to Amman, Jordan. A few days later I jumped from a Royal Jordanian Air Force C-130 into the Jordanian desert with the most incredible group of warriors imaginable. The group included American paratroopers, both retired and currently serving (the oldest was an 80-year-old Marine sniper who was a veteran of Bougainville); British SAS (Special Air Service); Australian SAS; and paratroopers from Rhodesia, South Africa, the French Foreign Legion, Germany, Israel, and the host country, Jordan. The most incredible part of the story was the dinner at the Royal Palace the evening following the jump. King Abdullah's younger brother, Ali Bin Al-Hussein, pinned a set of wings on each of us to commemorate the jump. He was a trained free-fall parachutist and had jumped with us.

I would like to end with a brief statement about the rules I have tried to live my life by, and I think I have succeeded to a great extent. They are not totally original to me, but I'd like to think I have stuck by them pretty well.

1) Don't sweat the small stuff.
2) It's all small stuff.
3) Get dressed up and go on all the rides.

I have a saying that I have used since high school. "I want to squeeze every bit of fun out of the fun plant." I have done that in every area of my life, with my year in Vietnam at the top of the list. I wouldn't trade my experience there for anything, and although I am partial to single-seat attack bombers and have a single-seat mentality

(I'm told that a shrink would call this a case of terminal immaturity, for which there is no cure—but I always felt that two crew members in the A-6 was one too many!), I have a tremendous amount of respect for all who served in Vietnam. We all had the same zip code while serving, and recognition for that service is long overdue. I can honestly say that I have had "ONE HELL OF A RIDE!"

....

My visit with Mike Doyle came about only because of Bill Wilson. As I mentioned in the Preface, Bill has been my escort, guide, liaison, technical adviser, and translator for all things related to the Marine Corps.

Knowing that Mike doesn't talk much about Vietnam, my interview involved listening to Mike and Bill talk, taking notes, and trying to keep up, as once Mike got started it came out in a flood. There were lots of laughs and a lot of "inside baseball" Marine Corps code that Bill graciously translated. When I asked Mike about his flight of more than three hours with no oil pressure and no airspeed control during refueling except for his speed brakes, he told me he didn't have a lot of time to think about it as his options were rather limited.

There were only two times that Mike stopped talking and became emotional. The first was during his description of the taxi in to the ramp at Kaneohe Bay with his entire squadron (VMA-214), canopies up and listening to the brigade band playing "China Night." The second was when he told of walking into the LAX terminal less than 24 hours later with several of his squadron mates, just a few days after having flown his last combat mission, and being called names. This was not the kind of reception they expected or deserved, and was certainly not the reception received by Pappy Boyington and his VMA-214 Black Sheep squadron mates in 1945. In the words of Jim Webb, it represents "a conscious, continuing travesty."

Mike Doyle at Chu Lai, 1966.

Marine Corps tank in the mud at Chu Lai, 1966.

Bunker along the Chu Lai flight line. Bunkers were placed along the flight line for protection against mortar and rocket attacks. In Mike's words, "The Gomers liked to walk mortars down the flight line and the hooch area near the beach. They were damn good at it." Photo from early 1967.

Mike Doyle, "living large" at Chu Lai, 1966.

VMA-214 A-4Cs after arrival at MCAS Kaneohe Bay, Hawaii, on the Trans-Pac to MCAS El Toro in early April 1967.

L) *Mike Doyle inspecting the graffiti stenciled on his airplane after it stayed at Da Nang with his old A-6 squadron, VMA(AW)-242.* **R)** *View of the comments on Mike's airplane, "A6A Dropout" in the center.*

Mike Doyle's A-4, trailing fuel, on his way to an emergency landing at Da Nang. Hit over Laos by a 14.5mm heavy machine gun, he had a hole in his right wing. Photo taken by his wingman, Butch Miller.

A-4Cs and A-4Es on the Chu Lai flight line, 1966.

Mike Doyle at the squadron S-3 Office at Chu Lai, 1966.

Mike Doyle having "ONE HELL OF A RIDE," on a bull the size of a Volkswagen, at a rodeo in Hemet, California, August, 1972.

Army CWO Mike Doyle and AH-1 Cobra attack helicopter with the Utah Army National Guard, known affectionately as the Mounted Mormon Militia, Cobraville, Utah, 1970.

Mike Doyle (left) and Bill Wilson in Prescott, Arizona, March 2013.

10

DARTS WITH THE AUSSIES

Bill Wilson, USMC, A4-C, A4-E, TA4-F, 1966 – 1967
{ Date of hire by Western Airlines: 2/24/1969 }

Bill Wilson with his assigned VMA-214 A-4C at Chu Lai. Note: Black sheep on the fuselage, sheep horns on Bill's helmet, 20mm cannon powder stains around the wing root, 1966.

The last time I flew with Bill Wilson, we had a layover in Washington, D.C., and were looking forward to visiting the Smithsonian Air and Space Museum. The merger of Delta and Western had taken place in April 1987, and we were looking at the closure of our San Francisco pilot base in the not too distant future, so it was a nostalgic but exciting time for all of us. Bill told me he wanted to see the Navy carrier display at the museum. As we walked into the room, we were staring at an A-4 Skyhawk with Navy markings. Bill said, "I flew that airplane." To which I answered, "I know, you flew A-4s in the Marine Corps." Bill replied, "No, I mean I flew that particular airplane. The tail number is in my logbook. It is an A4-B model, and I flew it in Marine markings back in 1962, when it was brand new." That was the beginning of my education about the A-4, MAG-12 (Marine Air Group-12) in Vietnam, and about Bill Wilson.

I spent a weekend with Bill during which we searched through his photos and studied his flight logbooks to put together a story about a man who is somewhat of a Marine Corps legend. I had flown with Bill quite a bit over the years at Western when there was no pilot hiring, so the seniority list stagnated and the only upward movement was due to deaths or retirements. Both of those were infrequent in the mid-1970s to early 1980s, and San Francisco was a small pilot base, so we were all stuck in place for several years and tended to fly with the same people on a regular basis.

Bill is the most unpretentious, self-deprecating man I can remember flying with in an aviation world that is full of big egos and big BSers. There were several stories from Vietnam that he would tell, and all of them involved him either screwing up or doing something that could have gotten him court-martialed and thrown out of the service. They were funny stories, perfect for a layover or in the cockpit. Bill has an infectious laugh, and when I saw him again after more than 10 years, I could have recognized him by that laugh alone.

I always knew there was much more to Bill Wilson than a couple of funny Marine Corps stories, and after bugging him over the years after his retirement, I finally got together with him to work on his story. Little did I know that I wasn't just dealing with a run-of-the-mill Marine Corps pilot who happened to fly the Douglas A-4 Skyhawk. At the time Bill retired from the Marine Corps Reserve at Alameda Naval Air Station in 1978, he was a high-time Marine Corps A-4 pilot who had flown the aircraft for 16 years and probably at one time had more flying time in it than anyone else in the Corps. He knew the aircraft systems backwards and forwards. After several "I didn't do anything special" responses and "I was just having a good time and I loved flying combat," we agreed that it would be left to the reader to decide the definition of "anything special" and I would take on the responsibility for telling his story. The title, "Darts With the Aussies," refers to what is perhaps my favorite cockpit story of all time, but there is a lot more to Bill Wilson, and I learned a great deal of it while sitting at his coffee table, looking at his photos and reading through his Marine Corps flight logbooks.

Bill will never tell this, so it is up to me to introduce you to the man with a little background and a history of Bill and the Douglas A-4 Skyhawk. Douglas produced nearly 3,000 A-4s from 1954 to 1979, and Bill flew every model produced (except the A-4M) over a 16-year period from 1962 to 1978. In the A-4 alone, he accumulated close to 2,900 hours of flight time. Deployed to Guantanamo Bay Naval Base during the Cuban Missile Crisis as a newly minted second lieutenant, he was involved in a flight that nearly triggered an international incident and caused the "red phone" to ring in the White House: a local patrol flight that inadvertently penetrated Cuban airspace. He and his flight leader were unofficially reprimanded upon landing.

He flew the A-4 in the following squadrons:

1) VMA-533 at MCAS (Marine Corps Air Station), Cherry Point, North Carolina: 1962–1964
2) VMA-214 at Chu Lai Air Base, Republic of Vietnam: 1966–1967
3) VMA-121 at Chu Lai AB, Vietnam: 1967
4) VMT-103 at MCAS, Yuma, Arizona: 1967–1969
5) VMA-131 and VMA-133 in the Marine Corps Reserve at Alameda Naval Air Station, California: 1969–1978

[For future reference, VMA stands for Fixed Wing, Marine, Attack Squadron, and VMT is Fixed Wing, Marine, Training Squadron. In VMT-103 Bill was a combat pilot flight instructor who trained and helped prepare replacement pilots for the A-4 and for combat in Vietnam.]

He made three over-water ferry flights. His first was a trans-Atlantic flight with VMA-533. It was the first attempt by A-4s at long range in-flight refueling and involved taking the squadron from the East Coast to Spain to support the Spanish Marines in NATO war games. He made two trans-Pacific ferry flights as well. The first one involved the whole squadron when VMA-214 ferried A-4C models back from Chu Lai to MCAS El Toro near San Diego in March 1967. The second took place when he was "volunteered" to lead a ferry flight of four TA4-Fs from MCAS

Yuma to Chu Lai in January 1968. The ferry flights and the reasons for them are mentioned in Bill's story.

The Marines did several things in combat that were unique to them, and the FAC (Forward Air Controller) program was one of them. The Marine Corps assigned a FAC or ALO (Air Liaison Officer) to operate on the ground with their infantry units. The FAC/ALO was a pilot who was there to coordinate close air support from Marine attack bombers and helicopters when the ground troops were in contact and needed air support or resupply. The FAC traveled right beside the unit radioman, whose backpack radio made him the first target of a sniper or in an ambush (the Marine infantry lieutenant was a close second in targeting), and even though the FAC was assigned a rifleman to guard him, it was often of small comfort. The Marine FAC/ALO program is a little-known part of the war outside the Marine Corps community, and Bill told me quite a bit about how the program worked in combat. It is explained fully in this book as part of a story by Bob Tieken.

A large group of Marine A-4 pilots was hired by Western Airlines and flew out of both the San Francisco and the Los Angeles pilot bases. They were still flying the A-4 in the reserves at Alameda Naval Air Station and NAS Los Alamitos in the mid-1970s. It was a very loose operation relative to today, and Bill was able to take an A-4 to Mather AFB in Sacramento and leave it parked there during the week. It was close to his home and available for him to fly back down to Alameda for his reserve drills. The Marines were always a tight group, and as Bill said, "Nobody gets to drink wine out of one of my Marine wine glasses unless I like them." I played it safe and had a beer!

We discovered a treasure trove of photos that Bill had not looked at for more than 40 years, and a lot of them are shown here due to their unique nature and their applicability to the story.

As a final note, there were two A-4 pilots who were in VMT-103 at Yuma with Bill and also ended up at Western Airlines, Mike Doyle and Bob Tieken. In a funny turn of events (only funny now!), they beat Bill to the airline and were hired several months before him. They ended up more than 100 numbers ahead of him on the Western seniority list, and that translated into more than 700 numbers on the combined list after the Delta merger. Those 100 numbers at Western meant a three-year furlough for Bill and no furlough for them when Western cut back and furloughed pilots in mid-1969.

My goal here was a proper introduction to Bill as I know it will make his story more compelling and enjoyable for the reader. Now in his own words: my friend Bill Wilson. I plan to have a glass of wine in one of those Marine Corps glasses next time I visit!

....

I joined the Marine Corps Aviation Cadet program in 1961. I was sent to Pensacola Naval Air Station in Florida for flight training and took my final carrier qualification at Kingsville, Texas, on the carrier USS *Lexington*. I received my wings, was designated a naval aviator, and was commissioned a Marine second lieutenant in 1962. My first assignment was to MCAS Cherry Point, North Carolina, where I was attached to VMA-533 and qualified on the A-4B Skyhawk. They were brand-new aircraft being delivered from the factory by Douglas Aircraft Company pilots, who then gave us our check-out and flew with us on our first flights. The check-out was a lot of fun as we flew the aircraft "clean," without any external racks or tanks.

The A-4B had such a small cockpit that the sitting height of the pilots had to be measured before they could be allowed to check out in the aircraft. The cockpit was such that even with the seat bottomed out, your helmet would hit the canopy when it was closed if you were above a certain sitting height. The cockpit was so tight that most things had to be done by feel (such as changing radio frequencies) because there was so little maneuvering room. Even reaching both arms up and back to get to the ejection handles was a chore. This changed in the A-4C and later models, but it was still a tight fit. My friend and later fellow Western pilot Bob Tieken, who is 6 feet 4 inches tall, often banged his head on the canopy in the C and E models, even with his seat bottomed out.

My first adventure while in VMA-533 at Cherry Point was the squadron move to Roosevelt Roads Naval Station in Puerto Rico during the Cuban Missile Crisis in 1962 and into 1963. We sent four A-4Bs and crews to Guantanamo Bay, Cuba, with two aircraft to sit alert and two to fly regular missions, taking off from Guantanamo and then flying around the island, staying just outside Cuban airspace. On one mission, as a new second lieutenant, I was flying on the wing of a more seasoned squadron mate and he got lost looking for the Isle of Pines off Cuba, the island that holds their penal colony. I was flying on his right when I looked out to the right side of my aircraft and saw an airbase in the distance with MiGs on the runway taking off. I alerted my leader, and we made a quick turn and flew as fast as possible back to Guantanamo, but not in time to avert a charge by the Cubans of a violation of their airspace that went all the way to the White House. Our two airplanes were met by a Navy captain who read us the riot act while we were still in our cockpits, then ordered us to report to his office, where we had to explain ourselves and do a "rug dance" (explaining your actions while standing on the rug in front of the Skipper's desk). Our CO (Commanding Officer), who was still at NAS Roosevelt Roads, was not amused. It was fortunate that we were able to beat the MiGs back to Guantanamo, as they were armed and mad, and we were unarmed and totally defenseless on that flight.

During my tour with 533, flying our new A-4Bs, we set several records: longest distance flown with refueling and the first trans-Atlantic flights to Europe from the U.S. We called ourselves the Heavy Demonstration and Light Bombardment Squadron.

In 1964 I was sent to be a flight instructor with the U.S. Navy Training Squadron, VT-9, at Naval Air Training Command, Meridian, Mississippi. The war in Vietnam was heating up and we were training pilots and flying seven days a week. I really enjoyed instructing and was building a lot of flight time, and while I was there I was instrumental in writing the NATOPS manual (Naval Air Training and Operating Procedures Standardization) for both the T-2A and T-2B aircraft.

The tour of duty for a flight instructor was three years, and in 1966, with a full year to go before I could expect my next assignment, I was beginning to think the war would be over before I could take part in it. By pleading with my "career planner" at headquarters, I was able to cut my instructor tour short, and in September 1966 I received individual orders to Southeast Asia. I didn't know it at the time, but there was a real need for FACs (Forward Air

Controllers) in Vietnam, and I was at the head of the line for a FAC assignment. It was a job that none of the pilots wanted, as we were not trained for it and the casualties were very high. However, I was sure that with my background and experience in the A-4, I would be assigned to fly once I arrived, even though I was not current in the aircraft, having not flown it for nearly two years.

I flew to McCord AFB in Tacoma, Washington, where I caught a Continental Airlines charter flight, a Boeing 707, to Yokota AB, Japan. From Yokota I flew on a Marine C-130 to Da Nang AB, RVN, where I reported to a grunt (non-pilot) captain in the personnel section. The first words out of his mouth were "FAC" and where I was to be assigned. I managed to bluff my way through with a certificate for an A-4 maintenance refresher course that I had recently taken. I told him there must be some mistake as I was qualified on the aircraft and needed to be assigned to an A-4 squadron. He looked at the certificate and said, "OK. In that case, you are going to Chu Lai to be assigned to VMA-214."(VMA-214 was the famous Black Sheep squadron of World War II and Pappy Boyington fame.)

CHU LAI

MAG-12 at Chu Lai consisted of four A-4 squadrons, flying both A-4C and A-4E models. I reported to VMA-214 and immediately explained that I was not current in the A-4 and had never flown the A-4C model. The operations officer looked at my logbooks, said not to worry, and assigned a pilot to check me out in the new A-4C procedures. I was given a couple of local familiarization hops and was ready to fly combat missions.

Chu Lai was considered a USMC expeditionary airfield, meaning that it was built for operations of only 30 to 60 days. It had outdoor toilets and showers, no hot water, and although some electricity was available, it was very unreliable. However, the base ended up lasting the whole war, operating under very primitive conditions. It was built in a great location, right on the beach along the South China Sea, where there was always a breeze. That made living in plywood huts pretty nice, with sides that could be lowered when the monsoons came. The monsoons brought horizontal rain that could come in one side of your hut and go out the other. Swimming in the South China Sea was not recommended due to strong riptides and numerous sea snakes, but we all swam anyway.

New guys like me, upon checking in, were issued a cot, a blanket, and a space in a hut. All the old-timers in the hut had scrounged up crude furniture made of plywood ammunition crates where they stored their gear. I just had my footlocker, but it didn't take me long to find out where they got their extra stuff. As soon as the word came out that someone was confirmed killed, everyone would rush over to his hut and take what they wanted, always leaving his personal effects alone. It didn't take long for me to have all I needed.

We had an outdoor movie theater and an Officers' Club that had very limited hours, but they were often ignored. There was a large glass jar kept behind the bar, and the pilots would put money into it so they could be remembered in case they went missing. When that happened, drinks were paid for out of the jar until the money was gone or it was confirmed that the missing pilot had been rescued or was reported to be KIA (killed in action). It helped in dealing with the loss of good friends.

The O Club at Chu Lai was famous for a sport called "three man lift," which was the best-kept secret in all of Vietnam. As a new guy, I was treated to it by Bob Tieken and another Marine on my first visit to the club. I will never forget it, nor will anyone who has participated. Once you were in one, you were not allowed to tell how it was played as it was too much fun to watch the new guys receive their initiation. We never tired of it, and there seemed to be an endless supply of new players.

COMBAT—THEY'RE SHOOTING AT US

My third flight in Vietnam was with a major who, I found out later, only flew the easy missions. The mission was a recon just south of the DMZ (Demilitarized Zone, which marked the border between North and South Vietnam), working with an Air Force FAC. We were each loaded with six Mk-82 500 pound bombs, set up for low drag (free fall). When we arrived in the area and checked in with the FAC, he told us to hold as he was working with two Air

Force B-57 Canberras, bombing an NVA 37mm AAA (anti-aircraft artillery) gun position. Green AAA tracers and white smoke puffs were erupting all around us, and I was so scared I could hardly breathe, but I was the one who had wanted combat, and now I had found it! As we were circling, waiting for our turn, one of the B-57s took a direct hit during his bomb run; we watched as the airplane burst into flames and saw the crew eject. The FAC told us we were "cleared in hot" and to bomb the smoke from the B-57 hits. The FAC said to "take them out."

My leader started turning toward the smoke and began his bomb run. I was off to his side, trying to line up on the target, when he exclaimed, "Getting out of here," and dropped all six Mk-82 bombs. He was not even close to being on target, but I continued on my bomb run and dropped two Mk-82s as we had previously briefed. We had briefed for 45-degree dive-bombing runs and I felt good about my drop, but I didn't hang around to see my hits. The Air Force FAC was busy looking for the crew of the Canberra, and with all the chatter on the radio someone reported seeing their parachutes, so I climbed back up and started looking for my leader. I was heavy and climbing slowly so I considered dropping my load, but I didn't dare. My leader was headed for Chu Lai and I finally caught up with him over Da Nang. I still had four Mk-82s on my wing stations and he ordered me to drop them (unarmed) in the water. We were not allowed to bring back any bombs unless there was a malfunction and they wouldn't release.

At the debriefing by my flight leader, he said that he had never seen flak before and had never been shot at, to which I replied, "That's funny, I thought the enemy was supposed to shoot at us." The part about him dropping his load and turning tail was never mentioned in the operations report given to the MAG-12 debriefer.

OPERATIONS AT CHU LAI

Chu Lai airfield was built on soft sand with a runway of interlocking aluminum planks. When you landed, it wasn't hard to stop as the planks tended to roll up in front of you! However, if it was raining, you could hardly walk on the planking without slipping, so we always made an arrested landing (using the tail hook and arresting gear). Most of the time, when you called the tower to tell them you were inbound, they would say something like, "3000 scattered, 6000 broken." You were not sure if they were talking about the weather or the runway condition!

The types of missions were coded with letter designators and I entered them in my logbook along with the aircraft number and flying time. We flew LZP, landing zone preparation for troop insertion; DAS, direct air support (higher-level bombing of fixed targets); HE, helicopter escort; CAS, close air support for troops in contact with the enemy (which would involve lower-level bombing and the use of rockets, napalm, and strafing); and TPQ, radar-guided bombing missions. We flew a lot of these where a mobile ground radar unit would guide us or send a pencil beam signal to the aircraft and take control of the autopilot for a bomb run.

Each of MAG-12's four squadrons was scheduled to fly at a different time and was required to provide crews for alert. We were on a three-day rotation, with alert duty for 24 hours and launches at different times of the day. The alert crews sat in the squadron operations building, where there was a phone connected directly to group operations for MAG-12, called "the barrel." There were six to eight airplanes (sometimes more) fully fueled and loaded with different combinations of ordnance, so we could launch and be airborne within five minutes with whatever load was required for the mission. There were airplanes with bombs only, bombs and Zuni rockets, and bombs and napalm, fueled and ready to go. This brings me to a tale that involved being alerted for a launch in a blinding rainstorm.

In 1966 there was a period of 97 days when it rained continuously and set a record for rainfall in Southeast Asia. On this particular day it was raining so hard that it was difficult to see the flight line from the squadron operations building. Suddenly we heard the phone ring with an alert from "the barrel." The SDO (squadron duty officer) answered the phone and after a few seconds replied, "You've got to be shitting me." A few seconds later he said, "F*** you!" and hung up. We alert pilots went back to playing our backgammon dice game, acey-deucey, and in about five minutes the phone rang again.

The SDO answered but this time promptly said, "Yes, general, yes sir, we'll launch immediately." The request was for a critical launch of two aircraft loaded with Mk-82s for a tactical emergency with troops in contact and in serious trouble. It was requested that the aircraft for this mission have working autopilots, because the critical nature of the situation on the ground required a TPQ bombing run in close proximity to our troops.

The procedure was for the alert pilot to run past the SDO, who handed him a slip of paper with the mission, an aircraft tail number, a set of coordinates, and who to contact written on it. The coordinates identified the point where he would rendezvous with the FAC or controller and be directed to the target. By the time I got to my aircraft I was soaked, the cockpit was soaked, and it was raining so hard that after engine start I had to be towed to the departure end of the runway, as I couldn't see to taxi. I made an instrument takeoff (a takeoff with minimum visual reference) and was told by tower that the weather was below minimums for landing so I would have to go somewhere else after the mission was completed. The message from "the barrel" said to land wherever I could, even to go to Thailand if necessary as the mission was critical. The alert was for two aircraft, but we ended up taking off about 15 to 20 minutes apart and arriving at the target one at a time.

I climbed, coming out on top of the weather and the clouds at about 15,000 feet, and flew to the prescribed coordinates, where I contacted the ground radar unit for a TPQ run. The TPQ ground radar unit sent out a pencil beam radar signal that took control of the autopilot and flew the bomb run remotely, even sending a signal for the time to drop the bombs. I dropped them from 15,000 feet and then checked and confirmed that all the bases in South Vietnam were below weather minimums for landing, so I headed for the closest base in Thailand, which happened to be Ubon RTAB (Royal Thai Air Base). The weather was good throughout central Thailand, so that was not going to be a problem. I had heard about an Australian Air Force unit at Ubon that I wanted to check out, so I was looking forward to my overnight stay.

A few minutes after turning west toward Ubon, there was a huge bang in the cockpit followed by a rapid depressurization, and fog and vapor filled my cockpit. I was momentarily stunned and thought I had been hit by ground fire or by a SAM (surface-to-air missile). When the fog cleared, I checked my instruments and warning lights to evaluate the situation. I saw that the canopy on the left side of the cockpit was open about an inch, and I could see that the canopy locking latch on that side had broken. There is a canopy locking handle on the left side near the throttle, and I pushed it to reclose the canopy. It worked, and the aircraft pressurization returned to normal, but I still had one big problem. I now had to hold the handle to keep the canopy closed. I flew to Ubon with one hand and was getting the hang of this one-handed flying when I got my next surprise upon arrival in the Ubon traffic pattern. When I lowered the landing gear, the standard procedure was to check the brake pressure by pushing on the brake pedals (the top of each rudder pedal controls the brakes upon landing and when taxiing). The brake pedals went right to the floor: There was no hydraulic brake pressure, and I would not have brakes for landing.

I called Ubon tower and asked if they had arresting gear available, as I could use my tail hook to engage the arresting gear and bring the aircraft to a stop. (Much like a carrier landing where the tail hook engages an arresting gear called the wire, Air Force bases had a wire that could be stretched across the runway. It was attached to big, heavy chain links that were stored in an underground container on each side of the runway. When the wire was engaged by the tailhook, it pulled the chain out, stopping the aircraft.) I flew around the traffic pattern while the arresting gear was set up. Then I landed, caught the arresting gear with my tail hook, and came to a stop. A blue Air Force pickup truck came roaring up behind me and a captain jumped out, climbed up on my wing, and handed me a cold beer, saying, "Welcome to Ubon, Marine." I jumped into the pickup truck with the Air Force captain and started one of my more memorable overnights in Thailand. My aircraft was eventually towed off the runway and repaired. The brakes had air in the lines, and the Air Force mechanics fixed the broken canopy latch by fabricating a new part that was better than the original.

There was a little-known RAAF (Royal Australian Air Force) unit called 79 Squadron, which had flown F-86 Sabre Jets from Ubon since 1962 in support of allied war efforts and to help defend Thailand under SEATO (Southeast Asia Treaty Organization) agreements. I was determined to find out if they were there and to check out their club and see if they really drank as much beer as had been reported. As it turned out, I found them—or, better said, they found me—as I located and entered their club at a remote end of the base. Every Australian pilot showed up in the bar and the party began— and boy, could those guys put away the beer! I left a message with base operations for my wingman, and he soon showed up at the club. In the course of the evening I was talked into playing darts with an Aussie pilot who admired my Marine Nomex fireproof flight suit. We ended up betting flight suits over a game, which of course I lost, so I ended up wearing a cotton Aussie flight suit and drinking way too much beer.

At some point in the festivities they told me there would be an awards ceremony on their flight line at 10 o'clock in the morning and asked us to be there. I explained that it would not be possible, but we could make a low pass over their formation and the assembled troops. It was immediately announced to all in the club, "We have a boast. Sergeant major, bring out the Boast Book." Not being one to pass on a challenge and remembering the Marine motto, "Better dead than look bad," I readily agreed to make the low pass in the morning. This was duly noted in the 79 Squadron Boast Book, and my wingman and I each were required to put $100 in a kitty, which would be returned to us if we fulfilled the boast. If we didn't complete our boast, all the money in the boast kitty would be used to help a young Australian girl who needed a cornea transplant.

The next morning my wingman and I discussed whether we should proceed with our boast to the Aussies. We decided that we were probably going to get killed anyway and did not want to look bad. The only smart thing I did that morning was to file our flight plan using Navy call signs and file for a destination called Yankee Station in the South China Sea, where several Navy aircraft carriers were located. The weather at Chu Lai had lifted above landing minimums by morning so that was where we were really headed. We took off about 15 minutes before the awards ceremony was to begin and made a turn to the east, climbing out to 10,000 feet. When out of the Ubon traffic area we both turned off our IFF (identification friend or foe) transponders so we couldn't be tracked on radar, and turned back toward the base. I was flying lead, and the wingman's position is usually back and a bit below lead, but we were planning to be low enough that he had to fly a bit above me to keep from hitting the ground. The plan was for a 500-knot pass at 50 feet, but I'm sure we were lower than that. As we shot over the awards ceremony, everyone on the ground scattered and hit the deck, while the tower began frantically calling us on guard frequency demanding to know who we were and what the hell we thought we were doing. As we blasted across the Australian Air Force flight line, close to the taxiway, I looked to my right and was eyeball to eyeball with an Air Force F-4 pilot who was just rotating on takeoff on a crossing runway. He had a full bomb load, and his wingman was just starting his takeoff roll. I am sure he is still talking about it to this day!

We stayed low and fast and turned east to work our way out of the area, then climbed up to 25,000 feet, and when we got close to Vietnam we began using our MAG-12 call signs (call sign Oxwood). We headed toward Chu Lai, just knowing that our careers were over and that we were headed to arrest and a court-martial at the very least. We landed at Chu Lai and swore each other to secrecy, and amazingly, even with a massive search of the whole area, we were never discovered and no one in MAG-12 or VMA-214 was any the wiser. How that happened was never really clear to me, but not wanting to jinx my good luck, I never told this story for more than 20 years. Barring a statute of limitations problem, I should be safe. Someday I would like to track down RAAF 79 Squadron and the Boast Book. I would like to ask about my $100 and find out if the young girl got her transplant.

When we were not flying or standing alert, we had collateral duties ranging from assistant operations officer to maintenance and flight line duties. What little time off we did have was spent running, swimming, sunbathing, reading, or playing poker. Along with the regular mail, the Red Cross sent packages that contained candy, food, magazines, and paperback books. One day I was rummaging through the books and found one on how to play poker by someone named Bart Maverick! I always thought he was just a TV character, but I guess he also knew a lot about poker. Everyone knew I was a poor poker player, so I thought I should learn how to play, and after reading the book several times and putting what I had learned into the game, I became quite good. Too good, in fact, as soon I was not invited to play, so I had to start losing more often than I wanted just to be allowed to play with my friends.

Late one afternoon I was playing poker in a hut about four rows away from mine, when we all heard sounds we were not familiar with and all at once realized we were being attacked by the VC (Vietcong). The sounds were mortars being dropped into mortar tubes and being shot into the air, followed by the explosion on impact. They were getting louder with each mortar launch.

Every hut had a foxhole that was dug by the occupants, who were also responsible for maintaining it. The foxhole for my hut was the closest to the sea and was the biggest, with the added safety of a cover made of aluminum runway planking and two layers of sand-bags. The cover was supported on all four corners by sandbags so we could see out. I started running for my foxhole, and by the time I arrived I found it was completely full! It seemed that everyone wanted protection from the mortars coming down on us, so I dove in on top of all my fellow Marines and tried to work myself as low as I could.

The Vietcong were "raking" or "walking" the mortars across our flight line and operations. They hit several airplanes and buildings, and the last few mortars rained down on top of us. One was a direct hit on our new latrine, which effectively ended the investigation into the missing front door, which had been stolen. The next mortar hit a tree just outside Bob Tieken's hut, where he was still in his rack lifting weights. (Bob, a big man whom we called Lurch, refused to run like the rest of us.) The next-to-last mortar hit just a few yards from our foxhole, and the shrapnel hit all around us, but luckily not one of us had a scratch. The explosion was so loud that I could not hear for a while and my ears rang for days. The whole attack was seen by one of our tanks. I later met the second lieutenant tank commander who told me he could not get permission in time to fire on the VC as they were inside our perimeter and there was a concern about hitting our own troops.

JATO

During the long period of heavy rain, Chu Lai was seldom below minimums for flight operations, but the weather and winds were such that we often had to take off on the short, 4,000-foot crosswind runway. It was oriented toward the southwest, with the aircraft taking off over the beach and heading over the ocean. The short runway and the heavy bomb loads required the use of JATO (jet-assisted takeoff) bottles, which were solid-fuel rockets strapped to the rear on each side of the aircraft. The empty bottles had to be jettisoned over the water after takeoff as they were high drag and also would restrict the movement of the speed brakes if they stayed on the aircraft. It was a spectacular show to watch, so on days when the short crosswind runway was in use, we would drag folding chairs and a portable radio out to the beach at the end of the runway and watch the show. We would listen to the tower and the pilots talking as we drank our beer, making bets to see if the JATO bottles would fail or the pilot would screw up the takeoff and the aircraft would end up in the ocean. Taking off on the short runway was not on our list of things we liked best. There was always a chance that your JATO bottles would fail to fire and you might have to eject at the end of the runway. Once again we were dealing with a "Better dead than look bad" philosophy, so our gallows humor was on full display.

There were two types of JATO assist takeoffs that we watched for, and we named each of them. One was the "heavy breather" and the other was the "roger boom." In the cockpit of the A-4 there were two buttons beside each other, one on the throttle to talk on the radio, and another on a fold-down catapult handle to fire the JATO bottles. The "heavy breather" went like this. In a high-stress situation like a JATO assist takeoff, in rain and wind on the short runway, it was easy to push the wrong button at the very moment needed to fire the JATOs. If this happened, you would hear the pilot transmitting his stressed-out heavy breathing over the radio. When the pilot realized his mistake, that he had pushed the radio button instead of the JATO button, he would then fire the JATOs. At this point during takeoff, firing the JATO would over-rotate the aircraft and cause it to go almost straight up and nearly into a stall.

The "roger boom" was the worst situation, and it went like this. The pilot would be in position on the runway, and when cleared for takeoff he would hold the brakes while running up the power toward maximum to check his engine. He would then start sliding on the wet metal runway surface. If he pressed the JATO button instead of the radio button to acknowledge his takeoff clearance, it would fire the JATO bottles while he was still holding the brakes. The result, instead of a radio call to the tower, would be a loud boom and the firing of the JATO bottles. The aircraft would career down the runway with tires skidding as the brakes were still on. In both the "heavy breather" and the "roger boom" situations, the aircraft taking off would barely be airborne or would be going almost straight up by the end of the short runway. I can't remember watching an A-4 go into the water after takeoff, but there were some close calls, and some had to jettison their external loads (bombs, rockets, and fuel tanks) to stay airborne!

BEER RUN

Chu Lai Air Base was built from scratch on the coast of South Vietnam on the South China Sea, and the only way to resupply the base was by air or sea. When the monsoons came, the Navy had a tough time getting their LSDs (landing ship dock) ashore for resupply. Therefore we were always running low on critical supplies during bad weather. It was one thing to run out of powdered eggs and milk, but we also ran out of beer. You cannot fight a war if you do not have beer! The air group (MAG-12) knew that the Air Force had plenty of beer at its bases in Thailand, so it was decided that anyone who wanted to go would be randomly placed on a list to fly to Korat RTAB and get beer. Everyone looked forward to making a beer run and kept track of his place on the list.

On March 7, 1967, it was my turn to make the beer run to Thailand "for the troops." I flew an A4-C to Korat RTAB and loaded up with 80 to 100 cases of beer to take back to Chu Lai. I don't recall the brand, but it was either Singha Thai beer or San Miguel Philippine beer. It was in steel cans, and most of them were rusty! But beggars can't be choosers. I flew aircraft #148545, and in the photo you can see my aircraft with a large #7 on the fuselage forward of the cockpit, safely parked in a revetment surrounded by Air Force F-105s.

We all had tremendous respect for the F-105 pilots and their mission. The F-105s were being loaded with bombs and Shrike missiles, soon to head out for North Vietnam, while I was awaiting my beer shipment to take back to Chu Lai. My A-4C was outfitted with two modified 300-gallon underwing fuel tanks that had a door cut into them for use in carrying luggage or any kind of small cargo. We called these modified fuel tanks blivets, and there was a 250-knot critical air speed restriction when carrying them. It was my job to get the beer back to Chu Lai without dumping it all over the jungle or, worse yet, losing one of the blivets en route. I made it safely back to base, to the applause of the troops and my squadron mates. The best part was that after an hour at 25,000 feet, the beer was cold and ready to drink.

VMA-214 TRANS-PAC

After flying combat for about six months, and with the Ubon fly-by in the rearview mirror, the next bit of excitement was a trans-Pacific ferry flight of the whole squadron from Chu Lai to MCAS El Toro near San Diego. The Marine Corps had decided to bring the entire VMA-214 squadron back to the States. It was determined that the A-4C models would be replaced by A-4Es because the E model had a more powerful engine, updated avionics, and two additional hard points under the aircraft so it could carry 1,000 pounds more ordnance. VMA-214 loaded up and on March 29, 1967, about 14 A-4Cs took off for an adventure, flying from Chu Lai to Guam, Wake Island, Midway Island, Honolulu, and on to El Toro. It required multiple in-flight refuelings from Marine Corps C-130s along the way, and it went off without a glitch until arrival at Midway, when one of the aircraft developed engine problems and required an engine change. I stayed behind with him, and after the maintenance was performed we flew as a two-ship to Honolulu and on to El Toro. To my regret, I missed the arrival ceremony at MCAS Kaneohe Bay in Hawaii, which is related in Mike Doyle's story in this book.

BACK TO CHU LAI

Once we arrived at El Toro, they gave us two weeks of R&R and then put us on a Marine C-130 back to Chu Lai. It was a long flight and very cold in the rear of the C-130, so we were happy to get back to the heat and the A-4E models that awaited us. Upon arrival I was attached to VMA-121 and was briefly sent to Iwakuni, Japan, where we were training new pilots to rotate back to Chu Lai. The squadron moved its colors to Chu Lai shortly thereafter, and I flew combat missions with VMA-121 until November 1967. During those months we flew continually in combat and appreciated the additional ordnance we could carry on the E model. We flew a lot of close air support for Marines in contact with the enemy, and we hit targets of opportunity or as directed by the FACs. There was no real flight following from the ground and no radar to keep track of our position, so at times we had free rein to go where needed and a lot of leeway in our targeting. Being right next to the DMZ, there was a lot of enemy activity, and we tried not to come back to Chu Lai with unexpended ordnance. Occasionally our mission would be canceled while we were en route to the target so we would just circle and wait for a call or a target of opportunity. On one occasion we had been circling over a solid overcast just south of the DMZ when the clouds broke below and we got a call from an Air Force FAC. He could see a long line of NVA trucks, tanks, and other military vehicles coming down Route 1, just north of the DMZ. The column of vehicles was halted at a bridge that was out, and they must have felt safe after days of bad weather and solid overcast. We had caught them in the open! I was the wingman, and my section leader was a major from the group. We decided to make three passes over the long convoy, dropping 250 pound bombs and firing Zuni rockets. We had always been warned to make only one pass and get out of the area ("one pass and haul ass"), but the target was too tempting for us to leave. I made a final pass to strafe with my 20mm cannon (the A4-E had two of them, internally mounted) and saw ahead and to my right a gunner sitting behind a truck-mounted machine gun, firing at me from what seemed like a few feet away. I was flying at 450 knots but he wasn't leading me properly; I could see the tracer rounds coming at me and curving behind my aircraft as I flew past him. It persuaded me to call it a day. Both of us did slow rolls as we left the target and the burning vehicles. The FAC had watched the whole show from his position way above us, and as we were hightailing it out of there, he gave us a running commentary on the secondary explosions that were taking place. This was one of my best missions, and I felt that we really took it to the enemy that day.

SAMS

Soon after this mission I reported late for my briefing on a routine night TPQ bombing mission. A friend of mine, Bob Snyder, was already there and told me that he had taken my briefing slot and mission number and I should take his, as he wanted to get back early. We changed mission numbers and he took off 15 minutes ahead of me. Later that night I was awakened by a corporal who told me to get dressed and report to group operations. They wanted to know how it happened that we'd changed mission numbers and if I had heard anything that might explain why Bob did not return. I told them that the last I heard was Bob checking in with the controller for his TPQ bomb run. It turned out that the NVA had installed a surface-to-air missile site near the DMZ and had fired two SAMs. I later learned from a close friend of mine, who was a FAC on the ground near the DMZ, that the Marines in his unit had witnessed the SAM launches and later found the wreckage and Bob's body.

To counter this new threat, all our aircraft were sent to the Philippines to have the ALQ-51 anti-missile warning system installed. This system would help us visually acquire the SAMs after launch so we could turn into them (which was our avoidance procedure: Turn into them and then pull away in a high-G maneuver that the SAM couldn't follow). SAM launches were usually easy to detect visually as large dust and smoke clouds were created, and the boosters tended to have large and bright exhaust plumes. Similarly, most AAMs (air-to-air missiles) would generate visible plumes while accelerating.

This brought about the missions in which an aircraft would be loaded with four Shrike missiles (anti-radiation missiles that locked onto a radar signal coming from the SAM radar van and were fired to ride that signal back to the van and destroy the SAM site). These missions required the pilot to circle around over the DMZ basically as bait, waiting for the SAM radar to lock onto his aircraft, giving him the opportunity to fire the Shrike back at the SAM site. It became one of our most dangerous missions.

In November 1967 my tour ended, and I flew back to the West Coast on a MAC (Military Airlift Command) charter flight from Da Nang to Travis AFB, California. After a short leave at home I reported to MCAS Yuma as a combat pilot flight instructor in VMT-103. The Marine Corps now had the two-seat TA4-F model for training, and my new job was to utilize my combat experience and train new pilots who would be going to Vietnam as replacements for those who had been lost and those whose tours had ended. It was a big job, a huge responsibility, and we tried to pass along everything we had learned in combat to a group of pilots who were just out of flight training and learning to fly the A-4.

ONE MORE TRANS-PAC

One day in early January 1968 I was called in to see the VMT-103 "Skipper," and he had a message for me. "Wilson," he said, "You're the one pilot in the squadron who has the most experience in trans-Pac flights, so you are going to volunteer to lead a flight of four TA4-Fs from here to Chu Lai, RVN. Select three other pilots that you want to go with you, and we'll put four more in the backseats. You're leaving January 17." Now, apparently a decision had been made at a much higher level that the two-seat version of the A-4 would be perfect in the role of a "fast FAC," and they wanted the airplanes flown to Chu Lai, ASAP. The Air Force had a two-seat version of the F-100 flying as a "fast FAC" out of Phu Cat AB, RVN, an F-100F model with the call sign Misty. Apparently it was decided that the Marine Corps was missing out on that part of the FAC action, so off we went, leaving Yuma on January 17.

As part of our pre-departure briefing we were told that if we were unlucky enough to have a problem and have to ditch or eject over water, the Navy probably wouldn't come and look for us. They told us the Navy had such a low success rate in finding pilots in the middle of the ocean that they probably wouldn't bother, so we shouldn't plan on being found. At this point we were pushing the limits of the motto, "Better dead than look bad." It was rapidly losing its luster, but what could I say? After all, I had "volunteered."

When VMA-214 left Chu Lai as an entire squadron, it was a totally coordinated Marine Corps operation, with Marine C-130s positioned along the way to refuel us and to aid us in our navigation on the long overwater legs. When our group of four TA4-Fs left Yuma, I was given frequencies to contact two C-130 tankers that were out of MCAS El Toro, but it wasn't nearly as well coordinated. The funniest radio call I made was when we crossed the California coastline and I asked Los Angeles Center for a radar vector to Honolulu. They asked me to repeat the call, then came back with: "Heading 246 degrees, 2541 miles"! We had no long-range navigation equipment onboard, so we took up the heading and flew it with whatever correction we could make for known winds along the route and hoped for the best.

The long leg to Honolulu required two in-flight refuelings, and the first one came off as planned. We got a course correction from our C-130 tankers and continued on toward Honolulu. The second refueling was a bit of a problem, as the two C-130s out of MCAS Kaneohe Bay, Hawaii, were not where we expected them to be, and when we finally contacted them on the radio we were dangerously low on fuel. The pilots of the C-130s got a UHF (ultra high frequency) ADF (automatic direction finder) fix from our radio transmissions, and they flew toward us at top speed. I instructed them to have their drogues deployed when they saw us, as some of us were approaching 500 pounds of fuel (500 pounds is the margin of error for the fuel gauge, so we were in a critical fuel state with less than 10 minutes of flying time remaining). The drogues were the refueling hoses that extended from each side of the C-130, with a basket on the end that we plugged into with our refueling probe. We made a successful refueling and went on to Honolulu without further incident. The rest of the way to Chu Lai was somewhat uneventful (as uneventful as a ferry flight in a single-engine jet with no long-range navigation equipment can be). Mike Doyle, who was the section leader of the other two aircraft in our formation, ran out of engine oil over Guam and was left behind to fend for himself! We arrived in Vietnam on January 25, eight days after leaving Yuma. The Marine Corps wasted little time in getting me back to MCAS Yuma, and I finished my active duty time as a combat flight instructor in VMT-103.

I separated from active duty in early February 1969 and was hired by Western Airlines to begin training on February 24. I had sent an application to Western and should have been interviewed a few months earlier, as they had called the VMT-103 Squadron Ready Room looking for me. Mike Doyle and Bob Tieken took the call and immediately took off in a TA-4F for NAS Los Alamitos and a Western interview in Los Angeles. They started training in September 1968, and missing that class cost me more than 100 numbers in seniority!

I was based in San Francisco with Western and immediately began flying with the Marine Corps Reserve at Alameda Naval Air Station, flying older A-4Bs. We initially had to share our aircraft with the two Navy squadrons that were also based there. There were two Marine squadrons, and it was akin to a very loosely run flying club. You could check out an aircraft and no one would ask you where you were going or when you might be back! That ended real soon, and we actually became a highly skilled combat-ready outfit. Eventually the Navy changed aircraft and we were given newer models of the A-4, right up to the latest model, the A-4F.

There was a group of Western pilots at Alameda, and we had a great time until the unit was eventually deactivated. I flew my last flight in May 1978 and managed to make a low pass over my house that the neighbors still talk about today! I retired as a lieutenant colonel in the USMC with 26 years of active and reserve service, and I retired from Delta Air Lines as a captain on the Boeing 737 based in Salt Lake City on August 27, 1997.

I would like to pay tribute and dedicate my story to a dear friend, a fellow Marine A-4 pilot and fellow Western Airlines pilot, Henry (Hank) Lecy. Hank was killed in a tragic boating accident in 1992 at age 54. He was a highly decorated combat veteran who had attended a funeral at Arlington National Cemetery for a good friend barely three months before his untimely death. At that funeral he expressed his desire to be buried at Arlington to his wife, and three months later she was there for his funeral. I was able to help design the gravestone for Hank and was there for his service, watching the Marine escort and the caisson carrying his remains wind its way through the most hallowed ground of Arlington in a light rain.

The article about Hank that appeared in the *Sonoma Index-Tribune* from his home town of Sonoma, California, said the following:

For his actions on June 3, 1967, Captain Henry Lecy was awarded the Distinguished Flying Cross for heroism and extraordinary achievement. As leader of an aerial mission in support of Marine ground troops about to be overrun by a numerically superior force of Viet Cong, he encountered intense enemy ground fire.

Upon arriving over the battle zone, he realized extreme accuracy would be required due to the close proximity of enemy and friendly positions.

His precise low-altitude passes, often within 100 meters of friendly lines, forced the enemy to discontinue attacking the besieged Marines. Lecy later received a Gold Star in lieu of a second award of the DFC, and 13 Air Medals.

*Bill Wilson with his assigned VMA-533 A-4B at MCAS Cherry Point,
1962-1963.*

*Bill Wilson headed out for a DAS mission on October 12, 1966.
His VMA-214 A-4C is loaded with 12 Mk 81 250 pound bombs with
instantaneous fuses, 6 on each wing. Photo taken by his wingman.*

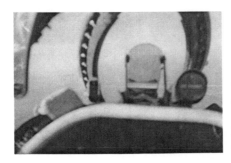

*In Bill's words, "The gun sight in the
A-4C was a WW II era non-computing
'iron gun sight.' To be effective and hit
your target, you needed to get as close
as possible."*

Bill Wilson with his VMA-214 A-4C.

A division of 4 VMA-214 A-4Cs, over the Pacific, enroute to MCAS El Toro on the Trans-Pac ferry flight, March 1967.

VMA-214 pilots before Trans-Pac departure from Chu Lai, March 29, 1967. Bill Wilson is 6th from the left, Mike Doyle is 7th from the left.

Bill Wilson on collateral duty, checking flight line security. The sand bagged emplacements were fortified fox holes for the Marine Secuity Force. Every Marine had his own "fighting hole," dug, built, and maintained by him and his squad. In case of attack, every Marine grabbed his weapon and headed for his hole. The fighting holes were handed down to each Marine's replacement when he left.

Bill's corner space in the hut. Note: Case of Bud on the floor, necklace chain of beer pull tabs hanging on the back of the desk. Back scratcher and folding chair came from a roommate who failed to return from a mission.

Bill's A-4C in the revetment with the ground crew cleaning up what appears to be a fuel spill, 1966.

Bill's A-4C with the #7 clearly visible on the fuselage, parked on the ramp at Korat on the "Beer Run," March 7, 1967. Bill's airplane is surrounded by Air Force F-105s.

JATO bottle clearly visible during JATO takeoff.

11

Condition One

Tom Rodger, USN, F-4B, 1966 – 1967
{ Date of hire by Western Airlines: 1/27/1969 }

Tom Rodger beside his F-4B on the flight deck of the USS Ranger, 1966.

I flew with Tom Rodger only a couple of times when I was based in San Francisco, but when he learned I had gone to Cal we became fast friends. After that, all his letters to me ended with "Go Bears," and he was an enthusiastic supporter of this project. He wasn't as big a guy as his friend Dick Hathcock, but he had lettered at Cal in both rugby and football and was tough as nails. I remember a flight on which the captain questioned whether Tom had really played college football. "You're not big enough" was the line I recall. Tom looked over and gave a classic response: "It's not how big you are; it's how hard you hit!"

In all the years after those flights we had together in the mid-1970s, I never knew much about Tom's military background until his name came up on the list given to me by Gary Gottschalk in 1997. Gary told me that Tom was very quiet about his Vietnam days but was quite a Navy legend, that he was fearless and flew the F-4 the same way he played rugby (better known as "football without pads"). Gary wondered if Tom would write a story, although he said he'd never heard Tom talk about Vietnam. But for whatever reason, maybe the Cal connection, Tom said he would give it some thought and get back to me. He had retired in November 1996 and I was lucky to reach him, but fortunately I did, and the enclosed came in the mail a few weeks later.

That is my friend Tom Rodger, and here is his story.

....

Your request triggered many long dormant memories. Of all the exciting missions in which I participated, I have decided on two that might add some spice to this project, but first I'll start with some personal history.

I was born in Fullerton, California, on November 9, 1936. I attended Fullerton public schools, and in November 1954 I began my military career when I joined the Naval Reserve Surface Unit in Santa Ana, California. After graduating from the University of California at Berkeley, where I lettered in football and rugby, I activated my reserve program and was later commissioned an ensign upon completing Officer Candidate School at Newport, Rhode Island, in October 1960. As a matter of coincidence and interest, when I was in high school I had worked at Knott's Berry Farm, where I became good friends with Dick Hathcock, a fellow Western pilot. Both of us played football at Fullerton Junior College and then at the University of California at Berkeley.

In December 1960 I entered the Navy flight training program at Pensacola, Florida, and during the basic phase of training I played football for the Pensacola Goshawks. After completing the jet fighter course at Beeville, Texas in June 1962, I was designated a naval aviator, and my first duty assignment was Utility Squadron 3 at NAS (Naval Air Station) North Island, California, where I flew the F-6A Skyray. In September 1964 I transitioned to the F-4B Phantom and was subsequently assigned to Fighter Squadron 143, the Pukin' Dogs. I participated in combat operations in Southeast Asia aboard the USS *Ranger* in 1966 and aboard the USS *Constellation* in 1967, and I flew 249 combat missions over North Vietnam. I remained in the Navy Reserve, flying both the F-8 Crusader and the F-4B Phantom. My last military assignment in the reserves was as commanding officer of Fighter Squadron 301 at NAS Miramar, California. I will now transition to my story.

My first cruise on the USS *Ranger* consisted of an introductory or buildup phase, when we worked the Mu Gia Pass along the border with North Vietnam and Laos and then flew missions over South Vietnam for about two weeks. After that orientation we flew the rest of our tour over North Vietnam while operating from Yankee and Dixie Stations in the Gulf of Tonkin. During the cruise we didn't have any DECM (defensive electronic countermeasures) equipment on any of our aircraft, and because of this we were vulnerable to SAM (surface-to-air missiles). Our entry altitudes were restricted as we came across the coast of North Vietnam. A typical mission was an Alpha Strike of more than 30 aircraft rendezvousing over the carrier at 500 feet. We would then head out on course toward the target and refuel en route, crossing the coast of North Vietnam as a group below 100 feet in altitude. We had a predetermined pop-up point where we would hit the target and then leave the area at a very low altitude, trying to stay below the SAM Fan Song radar acquisition height.

On every cruise each fighter squadron was required to have one fully functional aircraft on the flight deck, ready to defend the carrier at all times. This aircraft was known as the Condition One plane, and it was always manned and armed, 24 hours a day. During my tour of duty with VF-143 I was launched on the Condition One aircraft five times. Twice I intercepted Russian aircraft, a TU-95 Bear bomber and an M-4 Bison bomber (also used as an aerial refueling tanker); once it was a live missile exercise; and twice I was launched to protect ships in the Tonkin Gulf. My memory of one such occasion is as follows:

The USS *Ranger* was the day carrier during the month of June 1966. At 10 p.m. on June 13, it had completed its daily operations. Earlier that day I had been a member of an Alpha Strike into North Vietnam. That evening I was on the schedule for a two-hour assignment in the Condition One aircraft, from midnight until 2 am. Since the ship was standing down, with no aircraft activity, the Condition One aircraft was spotted (positioned) on the waist catapult with a starting unit attached and ready to go. I noted during the preflight that the aircraft had two Sparrow (radar-controlled) and four Sidewinder (heat-seeking) missiles and four 37-shot 2.75 rocket packs. I manned the aircraft at midnight along with my designated RIO (radar intercept officer), Ensign Dave Vermilyea. It was a very dark night, overcast with no moon whatever, but quite pleasant with a cool breeze blowing across the deck. At this point I fastened myself into the ejection seat and promptly went to sleep.

At 0038 I woke to the voice of the Air Boss announcing, "Launch the Condition One" over the PA system. The flight deck became a hub of activity, and by 0040 I was off the end of the ship and told to switch to the carrier strike control radio frequency. My call sign was Taproom 305. I was told that friendly naval forces were under attack by enemy aircraft approximately 300 miles to the north. Since this would be an air-to-air engagement, I elected to jettison my rocket packs with the plan of getting to the combat area as quickly as possible. I remember that while making this decision, I never got higher than 1,000 feet, and after releasing the rocket packs I initially dropped down to 500 feet. I increased my speed to 600 knots, and as soon as I was comfortable flying my instruments I dropped down to 300 feet. Just over 100 miles from the combat zone, I could see flares reflecting in the distance below a cloud cover. At this point we were switched over to the USS *Coontz* (DLG-9) for radar control as we dropped down to 100 feet above the ocean.

The number-two Condition One aircraft from our sister squadron, being flown by Lieutenant Commander John Tibbs and his RIO, Lieutenant Fred Trupp, was a little more than 20 miles behind my aircraft and at an altitude of 10,000 feet. At this point, the enemy aircraft broke off their attack and descended to a lower altitude. The enemy aircraft were getting GCI (ground-controlled intercept) information from a ground station in North Vietnam as they had their IFF (identification friend or foe) transponders activated, but I don't think my aircraft was visible on their radar as I was engaging from such a low altitude. I'm sure they did see the trail aircraft at 10,000 feet. The ensuing engagement was conducted completely on instruments as a full all-weather night operation.

The USS *Coontz* gave us an initial vector turn toward the enemy aircraft and said they were at a low altitude, approximately 500 feet. When I was about 20 miles from the targets, the number-two F-4, which was Dakota 201, said he had a contact at 20 miles. Thinking he could possibly be locked on me, I said I would do a 360 degree turn to the right. Because of poor resolution in the pulse mode of the F-4 radar, when looking down he probably did not have an actual target at that time. Upon completing my 360 degree turn I reacquired two aircraft 15 miles on the nose of my aircraft. I was cleared to fire by the *Coontz* but worried about Dakota 201's position as he was now out in front of my aircraft. As a result, I told Dakota to turn to a heading of 090 degrees. I was locked onto one of the bogies, but the speed gate (speed differential) went from about 250 knots down toward zero as I was approaching minimum range for the Sparrow missile. I decided to try to identify the target, making sure that I wasn't locked in on a friendly aircraft. Keeping the target on my nose and alternately flying my instruments and glancing ahead, I passed within approximately 20 feet of two aircraft which I recognized by their interior red lights glowing on their canopies. These bogies were in a hard left turn toward me at 700 feet. The cockpits were large and rectangular, and I judged them to be propeller aircraft because of their shape and speed. At this point I executed a 360 degree turn and dropped to 300 feet. I regained radar contact at 12 miles from the bogy and got a lock on the target. At 0116 hours I fired a Sparrow missile at a range of four miles. I did not see the initial ignition of the missile, so I fired a second Sparrow at 3½ miles. Approximately two to four seconds later I saw a double flash as the warhead expanded and then hit the target. Both the controlling ship (*Coontz*) and Dakota 201 observed the explosion, and one target subsequently left the ship's radar screen. After firing, I exited to the east and then south. Dakota 201 chased the remaining enemy aircraft as it went feet dry (crossed the coastline) but had to turn back as he encountered heavy enemy fire as he crossed the coastline.

As a result of this engagement, it was estimated that one North Vietnamese Colt aircraft had been downed. The initial battle action had involved the two Colts dropping flares while MiG fighters were strafing United States Navy PT boats, which were operating just south of Haiphong Harbor. This engagement took place in the early morning hours of 14 June 1966 and terminated with a safe arrival aboard the USS *Ranger* at 0200 hours. This was the first night engagement of the Vietnam War, and both my RIO and I were awarded the DFC (Distinguished Flying Cross) for the action.

The second story took place during my cruise on the USS *Constellation* in 1967. This cruise was very different from my USS *Ranger* cruise in that we now had DECM equipment throughout the air wing. The two F-4 squadrons had the new ARC 25/27 radar that painted the ground radar vans and gave indication of missile flight. This allowed the air wing to operate at higher altitudes and away from small arms fire. Thus, this cruise became one of missile dodging. If you could see the missile you could make it miss, but if you didn't see it you were going to get bagged if you weren't jinking your aircraft (making erratic maneuvers).

On 21 August 1967, I was part of a coordinated strike against the heavily defended Doc Noi Railroad Yard, five miles north of downtown Hanoi. There were eight of us, four F-4 Phantoms and four A-6 Intruders. We were to serve as a diversion for a large attack group from our carrier that was going to come in from the south at a low level, with the Hanoi Thermal Power Plant at the south end of town the target. The idea was for us to be a definite threat to the capital and to strike the railroad yard exactly two minutes prior to the power plant strike. Our group of eight crossed over land just north of Haiphong and headed straight for Hanoi at around 20,000 feet. This triggered an immediate response from the North Vietnamese Air Defense System as more than 100 SAM missiles and continuous AAA (anti-aircraft artillery) were directed at our group.

Prior to 30 miles from the target, the number-two A-6 was hit by AAA but elected to continue to the target (each A-6 had a load of eighteen 500 pound bombs). The eight of us were jinking and evading missiles while maintaining tactical integrity (staying in formation). As we neared the target, the four F-4s raced ahead and went after SAM sites that were guarding the railroad yard. After releasing our weapons, four 1,000 pound bombs per aircraft, we reversed course and departed at a low altitude. Immediately behind us the lead A-6 aircraft, flown by the squadron's commanding officer, was hit by a SAM at the top of his dive. As the missile hit the plane, both he and his bombardier/navigator were ejected into the air and the other three A-6s narrowly missed them as they dove for the target.

Upon pulling off the target the number-two A-6 (which had been previously hit by AAA) made a wide turn to the north to go around a storm cloud. The number-three A-6 tried to talk to him but discovered that number-two had lost his radio. This was bad news because two was flying the wrong direction. With three and four in pursuit, number two flew up Kep Valley and all three aircraft were lit up by AAA fire. Number three was just edging up on two as he was headed across the border into China. At that point the pilot of the number-four aircraft, who was lagging because he knew the location of the border with China, called, "MiGs, MiGs at nine high." Numerous Chinese MiGs attacked the two A-6s and shot them down. The fourth A-6 made an immediate turn to the southeast and headed into a large storm cloud. He made it safely to the ship as the sole survivor of a flight of four A-6s.

There were numerous friendly fighters along the egress path for our eight attacking aircraft, but the two A-6s had passed west and then north of the line of protection and were not accounted for. As I was heading south over the Gulf of Tonkin I heard the MiGs call being transmitted and figured I'd missed the excitement. After landing on the *Constellation* my RIO and I went straight to the squadron ready room and were told to relieve the crew in the Condition One aircraft immediately. We ran to the flight deck and had no sooner strapped in when the Air Boss announced, "Launch the Condition Ones" (one F-4 from each squadron). We thought the Condition One planes were being launched due to the MiG activity, and as we headed north we began piecing together the puzzle of what had happened. Our sister squadron launched an aircraft with us, and we were told we would be searching for two downed aircraft. We proceeded in a spotter/shooter formation (one F-4 looking for the A-6s and one guarding against a MiG attack) and were vectored beyond the Chinese border. As we entered the area we had Chinese bandits (MiGs) on our radar but they flew away from us. We proceeded to search for approximately 30 minutes. Each time we turned and headed south, the bandits would turn and follow us. When we turned north they would retreat. We eventually left the area, never having sighted the downed planes.

Each A-6 had two crewmembers, and of the four crewmembers only one survived. Two were shot while descending in their parachutes and one died during the shoot-down. We learned this from the lone survivor, who was released by the Chinese years later when President Nixon went to China on a goodwill tour. The fate of the crew of the number-one A-6 was never known to us. We hoped they were captured and realesed with the POWs in 1973.

During those two cruises I flew 249 combat missions and was awarded the DFC, 21 Air Medals, 3 Navy Commendation Medals, 2 Navy Achievement Medals, and 2 Navy Unit Commendations. In January 1968 I reported to Fighter Squadron 121 to become an instructor pilot in F-4 aircraft. I left active duty in January 1969 and was hired by Western Airlines on January 27, retiring in November 1996 as a Boeing 737 captain for Delta.

12

MR. TOAD

Dennis Wills, USAF, F-105D, 1966 – 1967
{ Date of hire by Western Airlines: 4/22/1968 }

Dennis Wills with "Mr. Toad," F-105D tail number 59-1749, at Korat RTAB, 1966.

In 1997 Gary Gottschalk gave me Dennis Wills's name and urged me to contact him about writing a story for this book. Little did I know at the time that Dennis would introduce me to Jerry Stamps and that between them I would have two great stories about the F-105. Dennis was also kind enough to share his photos with me, especially one that shows him with Mr. Toad, the F-105D that carried him through his missions "up north" and enabled him to return safely from Thailand. I never had the pleasure of flying with either Dennis or Jerry, mainly because they were longtime Los Angeles-based pilots and I spent most of my Western years flying out of San Francisco and Salt Lake City, not going to Los Angeles until after the Delta merger. However, I knew them both in passing and feel honored to be able to preserve a little bit of their personal history in this book.

Thrust into a combat situation in a closed group of men who were facing the same dangers every day, it was easy to think it wasn't such a big deal; everyone else was doing the same thing, and you were just doing your job. This often gave way to the gallows humor that Jerry Stamps mentions when defining an "optimist" in his F-105 squadron. When one steps back and takes a more detached look, it is amazing that these men went out to fly day after day, constantly aware of the rules of engagement that came from Washington that put many targets off-limits, losing friends and in some cases being shot down, sometimes being rescued and returning to the flight schedule in a few days. It certainly wasn't for the pay: In 1968 a first lieutenant received about $500 per month with base pay, flight pay, and combat pay. The government generously gave a $500 per month exemption from federal income taxes, so it was a tax-free deal. There was a running joke that if the government had to contract out the flying, it couldn't have afforded the war!

Now buckle-up and let Dennis Wills take you on a mission over North Vietnam in the F-105...

....

I grew up in California's San Joaquin Valley, where there was plenty of World War II military activity to captivate any young boy's imagination. There were Army convoys passing through town, glider training at Chandler Field for the D-Day Normandy invasion, and across town was Hammer Field with its P-61 Black Widows lined up along the fence. An Army Air Corps lieutenant moved in behind our house, and as luck would have it, he was a P-61 pilot. That young airman was the most influential figure in my life at the time, and unbeknownst to either of us, that random crossing of paths would lead to my long love affair with aviation.

I had discovered that by joining the Air Force ROTC program after entering college at Fresno State, there was a chance I might learn to fly while still in school. That possibility became reality, and after flying a Piper Super Cub in the Air Force FIP (Flight Indoctrination Program), I had a private pilot's license. In June 1961 I graduated with a degree in biology and was also commissioned a second lieutenant in the U.S. Air Force. My flight school assignment was Big Spring, Texas, where the T-37, T-33, and the brand-new T-38 were the training aircraft. After my arrival there in October 1961, it was announced that my group, Class 63D, would be the second class to enter basic flight training in the supersonic T-38. Even though our class graduation was delayed two months, to February 1963, due to operational and maintenance problems with the new aircraft, the machine was superb in every way and a delight to fly.

After earning my wings, my aircraft of choice was the F-100, and the transition to this airplane was at Luke Air Force Base, Arizona. Before this training took place, we all had to attend survival training in the Sierra Nevada range at Stead AFB outside Reno, Nevada. After completing my F-100 training at Luke, I received an assignment to Bitburg, Germany, where I was to get a theater checkout in the F-105. I was assigned to the 22nd TFS (Tactical Fighter Squadron), 36th TFW (Tactical Fighter Wing). Shortly after my arrival in Germany in December 1963, I went to Wheelus AFB, Libya, with a squadron mate who checked me out in the aircraft. This was before the two-seat F-105F models were built, so it was a particularly memorable event for me. There is nothing quite as exciting as climbing into a machine when your first flight is a solo!

I spent nearly three years sitting nuclear alert in Germany during the Cold War with the Soviet Union. At one time during that period we escorted airliners through the Berlin corridor after Soviet MiGs had made threateningly close passes at them. It was a tense period in our Soviet relations, but living in Europe during those days was an enviable assignment.

The war in Southeast Asia began to occupy more of our news, and there was talk of our airplanes being transferred to that theater and replaced in Europe by the new F-4C Phantom. Our rotating pilots began getting assignments to Thailand, where two F-105 bases were being developed. Soon we began ferrying our aircraft across the Atlantic, delivering them to bases in the U.S. from which they would then be flown to Thailand. In August of 1966, after almost three years in Germany, I was ordered to Korat RTAB (Royal Thai Air Base), Thailand. Most of the heavy bombing of North Vietnam was being staged from Korat and Takhli, and already many of my squadron mates from Germany had been shot down and taken prisoner or listed as missing in action. It was a difficult time for our families, knowing we would all soon be in the fray.

After finding a house for my wife and two infant children near our parents in Fresno, I departed from Travis AFB on 15 October 1966. My first stop was Clark AFB in the Philippines for jungle survival training prior to being assigned to the 469th Tactical Fighter Squadron, 388th Fighter Wing at Korat. After arriving at Korat and greeting many old friends, I was given a quick theater orientation and scheduled on a few combat missions into the lower-threat areas just to get my feet wet. Completing that, the pace quickened abruptly, with predawn takeoffs into the more heavily defended areas closer to Hanoi. Now flight integrity became more vital with the MiG threat as well as the SAM (surface-to-air missile) threats. It was of extreme importance for each pilot to be in the proper formation position and to be looking at his assigned 90 degree portion of the horizon for possible MiGs, AAA (anti-aircraft artillery), and SAM launches.

Nearly all flights were of such duration that refueling was required going into the target as well as going back to Korat. I recall the first time I switched onto combat frequency as we crossed into North Vietnam and was stunned to hear the stress in voices I recognized. I remember the chaos coming off some of the heavily defended targets as airplanes became separated from their flights and radio frequencies became so jammed with transmissions that they were unintelligible. Add to that a shoot-down or a bird that had taken some hits and was in trouble, and you had a real three-ring circus.

A mission that will always stand out in my mind started out well. We were four flights of four ships, 16 F-105s, targeted for the petroleum tanks at the end of Phuc Yen Airfield, a MiG base across the Red River from Hanoi. The date was 2 December 1966, with a 4 a.m. wakeup so we could launch just before dawn and be over the target early. Learning the previous evening what our target assignment would be, we had already prepared our route maps. The only item left to cover in the morning was the actual briefing by the mission commander, who was the flight leader of Panda flight. Panda would be carrying deadly CBU bombs (cluster bomb units). These weapons contained hundreds of steel spheres the size of tennis balls that would shower out of their bomb casing when it opened in midflight. These balls would detonate when they struck the ground, sending hot shrapnel in all directions. It was Panda's job to release these on the gun sites defending the target. The weather en route and over the target was briefed by the meteorologist and was forecast to be clear. The intelligence officer then called our attention to the expected defenses and most recent locations of SAM sites as well as the relatively safe areas to use if one had to eject. After this group briefing, each flight adjourned to a separate briefing room to talk about the finer details such as time to start engines, taxi, takeoff, rendezvous points for meeting the tankers, refueling, and emergency procedures on takeoff as well as over the target.

As Anzac 03, it was understood that I would lead my flight if the lead ship had to abort the mission for any reason. Each flight always had a fifth plane and pilot who was the spare and would fill any missing position, with the exception of lead. This spare had to attend the briefings as though he would fly the mission and actually would taxi to the end of the runway with his flight in case he was needed.

We had already examined target photos and decided where each pilot would drop his bombs. During this period of the conflict, in the finest tradition of the political leaders who were running the war from Washington, we were warned repeatedly not to fire on any MiGs unless they were aggressive toward us. We all found this a distasteful order from Washington. We knew that on this mission, after bombing the petroleum tanks some distance off the airfield, it would be easy to then strafe all the MiG-17 and MiG-21 aircraft and related support equipment on the field as we pulled off the target. Unfortunately, we had been warned that if any gun camera film showed that we had done so, we would be subject to a summary court-martial. The flight leader reminded us of this.

Our takeoffs were single-ship because each airplane was so heavily laden. There was a 10-second brake release spacing between aircraft, and water injection was added once the afterburner had lit in order to add the necessary thrust for a safe takeoff.

After all the wingmen had joined their airborne leader, we headed for our in-flight refueling tankers that were circling in a designated track over Laos. Each flight member in the entire strike force hooked up to an assigned tanker, one at a time in proper order, to top off his tanks before departing for the target. Flying northward through Laos and approaching the North Vietnam border, we all test-fired our 6,000-round-per-minute 20mm GE Gatling guns, checked our headsets for a tone indicating that our heat-seeking missiles were ready to be fired if we should encounter MiGs, and turned on our wind-generated ECM (electronic countermeasures) pods to ascertain that they were functioning properly. As we approached the target flying southeast on the north side of Thud Ridge, aptly named after all the F-105 Thuds forever scattered in the mud there, the target was clear of weather and we experienced only sporadic SAM signals on our onboard QRC-160 radar scopes.

We were preceded into the target area by Buick Flight, a specialized SAM-hunter flight (code-named Wild Weasel and/or Iron Hand) that used anti-radiation Shrike missiles to destroy the SAM launching sites. These specially equipped two-seat models of the Thud carried an electronic weapons officer in the rear seat to operate the equipment. Also, about 10,000 feet above us and following us in to the target, were multiple F-4 MIG CAP (combat air patrol) aircraft from Ubon AB, Thailand. The strike force was composed of Panda, Anzac, Vampire, and Satan flights, each ship (with the exception of Panda flight) carrying six 750 pound iron case bombs of World War II vintage. As Panda lead began his roll-in over the target, ground fire began erupting from everywhere. His flight was well into its 45 degree dive angle as my flight, Anzac, rolled inverted to begin the plunge from 18,000 feet. I rolled out, keeping the bombsight on a large, backfilled steel fuel tank on the ground, and watched the airspeed build toward 450 knots as I looked for the release altitude of 5,000 feet above ground level. The gunfire from the ground was intense and included small arms, 37mm, 57mm, 85mm, and 100mm anti-aircraft guns. I remember the impossible hail of tracers that seemed to lace all the space that we were diving through. In an instant I was there and hit the bomb-release button. *Not one* of the six 750 pound bombs released! I continued tracking and quickly switched from ripple to salvo position (in ripple position all bombs drop at once, while in salvo they drop in a single bomb sequence) and tried again. Still nothing. Closing with the ground at a rapid rate, I jabbed the emergency jettison button and everything came off the plane at once. The bombs were on the external centerline rack and came off still attached to the rack and not armed. Both 450 gallon fuel drop tanks departed as well, with their pylons. It was now obvious that the pullout was going to be from a very low altitude and in the firing range of small arms, one of the things we all tried to avoid. As I pulled out I could see what appeared to be masses of twinkling lights on the ground, with each twinkle the muzzle flash of a barrel pointed directly at me!

I pulled as hard as I could and kept the jet right on the high-speed stall shudder (the aircraft was shuddering and experiencing heavy vibration because it was on the verge of an aerodynamic stall), which gave me the smallest turn radius at that speed. I rolled toward the northwest and the relative safety of Thud Ridge. My flight members had pulled out well above me and were climbing up the north side of the Red River. Seeing the white golf balls (anti-aircraft fire) now whizzing past me from every quadrant, I maneuvered the airplane erratically, something known as jinking, to complicate the tracking solution of the gunners who were intent on hitting me. I kept the afterburner engaged since the high-G pullout had bled off a great deal of airspeed. As the speed began building and I was into a hard rolling jink to the left, I looked directly to what had been my 6:30 position. There, a couple thousand yards away, I was startled to see a MiG-21, and between us an Atoll heat-seeking missile was coming my way. The MiG was pulling lead on me in a left turn, so my reflexive reaction was to roll right and pull for all I was worth. I saw the missile pass off my left wing, unable to negotiate the turn with its high overtake speed.

My pleas for help after pulling off the target got quick results. My wingman, Jack Spillers, who was Anzac 04, noticed my predicament and was making a large barrel-roll descent to the right in order to close on me for support. Apparently the MiG pilot was aware of this repositioning of my wingman, which would have sandwiched him ahead of Jack and behind me. He must have broken off his attack, descending to the left toward Hanoi, for Jack didn't see him and reported my tail clear. We both began scissoring northward along the ridge in order to clear each other's tails. Once out of the threat area, we continued climbing and scissoring our way southward toward Laos and our tanker orbit.

While I was in a left turn, with Jack behind me and crossing my flight path to his right, he yelled, "Break right!" Not sure what was coming toward me, I made another high-G rolling pull to the right. Looking to my right, I saw my wingman was inside and slightly ahead of my turn, and beyond him was a MiG-21 pointed at us and firing his cannon. Our pull into him was now causing him to overshoot, and he pulled up and over us, rolled inverted, and headed for the cloud deck below. We both turned after him in full afterburner and watched as he disappeared into the clouds. We disengaged and headed for the tanker orbit, both relieved that we had finished the hardest part of our day.

It was very common during this period of the war for MiG pilots to make hit-and-run attacks, perhaps due to their lack of training, but that was to change in the following years when they became very aggressive and used teamwork in their engagements against our fighters. The perverse satisfaction I had was knowing that while we were at the Officers' Club that evening and having what I think was a good time after this tense three-and-a-half-hour mission, several poor devils were probably down in a hole trying to disarm what they thought was a new delivery system. Watching those two 450-gallon tanks falling had to have made some of those gunners duck for cover for a few moments, so I suppose it wasn't a total loss on my part.

My aircraft, Mr. Toad, tail number 749, was named after my son Toby, whom I called Toad when he was small. It also carried the inference of Mr. Toad's wild ride from the book *The Wind in the Willows*. There are photos of the airplane in several books written about the F-105. Mr. Toad was destroyed in 1971 after taking an 85mm round in the right wing root. Unable to lower the landing gear, the pilot ejected safely in a friendly area and was rescued.

I left the Air Force in July 1967 and began working for Martin Marietta in Denver as a human factors engineer on the Apollo Applications space program. I had talked to Pan Am and was told I would be contacted for the next pilot class date. But when I felt out some people I knew who were already employed in the airline industry, more than one individual suggested I try getting hired by Western Airlines, which appeared to be a small, up-and-coming airline. Fortunately I was accepted by Western and hired in April 1968, and I have been domiciled in Los Angeles continuously since then. I retired in October 1996 as a Boeing 727 captain wearing the Delta uniform.

....

In a letter Dennis sent to me in October 1999, he related a visit he had with John McCain at a book-signing event for Faith of My Fathers. *In the book Senator McCain relates how the lessons he learned from his father and grandfather enabled him to survive his years as a POW at the Hanoi Hilton with his honor intact. Dennis briefly related their conversation. "He knew some of my friends from "the Hilton" and said he enjoyed our low supersonic flights over Hanoi. He said our sonic booms reminded him that he hadn't been forgotten. For us it was simply the best egress out of the nearby targets. My memory was of the hundreds of people on rooftops pointing their rifles at me, unaware that the aim point should be way out in front of the machine at that speed!"*

As Dennis mentioned, Mr. Toad, F-105D tail number 59-1749, was shot down in 1971, but fortunately the pilot, Major D. S. Aunapu, ejected and was rescued in Laos. The aircraft Jerry Stamps is pictured with, F-105D tail number 62-4366, was hit by AAA near Hanoi and crashed in Laos in November 1966. The pilot, Captain Dean Elmer, ejected and was rescued.

Dennis Wills and "Mr. Toad" on the Korat flight line prior to a mission up north, 1966.

13

STRAYGOOSE

Richard H. Sell, USAF, MC-130E, 1967
{ Date of hire by Western Airlines: 4/22/1968 }

Richard Sell with his MC-130E, somewhere in South Vietnam, 1966.

Richard Sell's story is a fascinating piece about the "black" or secret war that was carried out in Laos and North Vietnam, right alongside the war we all read about in the news. That secret war was waged in part by the CIA using civilian contractors such as Air America and Continental Air Services, and by clandestine groups like the Ravens, USAF pilots who disappeared into the mysterious Steve Canyon Program and reappeared flying as FACs (forward air controllers) in Laos, wearing civilian clothes. Within the special-operations community in the active duty military, an organization called MACVSOG (Military Assistance Command Vietnam — Studies and Operations Group) was formed to utilize active-duty military units on

*special-operations missions. Mostly Army, with men coming from units
such as 5th Special Forces (Green Berets), the Rangers, and other elite
units, SOG also drew from the other services to complete its missions.
Richard Sell, as an experienced combat crew member flying the C-130, was
assigned to a new group, the Straygoose detachment, in early 1966. They
would be flying a specially equipped MC-130E for missions into Laos and
North Vietnam.*

*I never had the pleasure of flying with Richard over the years at
Western, but it was a small airline, and with only about 1,200 pilots at its
peak, we all knew or at least had heard of most of the guys on the seniority
list. We had a lot of pilots who commuted, and when the flights were full
and a pilot was going to work or on the way home, he would ride in the
cockpit on a jump seat. I met Richard when he was traveling home from
work and was riding in our cockpit. He was wearing a very distinctive
MACVSOG lapel pin on his uniform necktie and was surprised that I recognized it and knew what it represented. As we talked, I related that I was
a collector of Vietnam military memorabilia, which includes unit patches
and other items related to the Vietnam War, and that I had an extensive col-
lection of SOG-related items. That started a conversation that ended up
with Richard's writing the story that follows.*

*Some will ask how a piece of the war could be kept secret with so many
American troops in Vietnam, more than 500,000 at the peak in 1968–1969.
I can only speak from my experience as a pilot flying the C-7 on resupply
missions to the 5th Special Forces camps along the Laotian and Cambodian
borders with South Vietnam. I really gave little thought to the idea that
Americans were going on cross-border missions with their Montagnard
troops (the Montagnards were from mountain tribes in Vietnam and were
utilized as mercenary soldiers). We were told that the camps were strategically placed to guard against incursions from Laos and Cambodia where the
Ho Chi Minh Trail ran along the other side of the border. As far as our
flight operations went, we were warned about crossing the border and spent
a lot of time learning the landmarks that marked the border areas. The western border of South Vietnam, running alongside Laos and Cambodia, was
marked on our topographical maps with hash marks and a warning,
Military Operational Boundary. As far as secrecy goes, it worked pretty
well. I had some suspicions but didn't think too much about it, and I don't
remember that it was talked about very much. It has been only in the past*

few years that the special-operations side of the war has been written about and those secret tales have been told.

My squadron's C-7 aircraft flew to Nha Trang every day as it was the headquarters for Army 5th Special Forces. We would pick up loads to deliver and a rough itinerary for the day's flying. I always marveled at the mysterious aircraft at various spots on the Nha Trang ramp, parked in revetments to protect them from rocket and mortar attack. Richard's MC-130Es, totally unmarked and painted green and black with scissor-like blades on the front for the Fulton Recovery System, always fascinated me.

This story shows the great lengths to which the U.S. military would go in its attempts to rescue downed pilots. The Fulton Recovery System was tried but without much success in combat. Less than a year later, when in-flight refueling was perfected for the HH-3 Jolly Green Giant rescue helicopters, the problem was solved. The in-flight refueling gave the rescue choppers the range to fly far into northern Laos or North Vietnam and return safely to their bases in Thailand. This did not make the rescue of a downed airman a sure thing, but it surely boosted morale to know the Jollys would be on the way when a pilot went down.

In this book you will read of several historic firsts among the Western pilot group, especially with regard to the C-130. Richard Sell flew the first C-130 with the Fulton Recovery System in combat and flew the first successful resupply mission over North Vietnam. Jim Fogg flew the C-130 that made the first in-flight refueling of a Jolly on a combat mission.

Here is Richard Sell's story.

....

I was a pre-World War II baby, born on May 29, 1940, in Lafayette, Indiana. It's likely I was conceived at around the time France and Great Britain declared war on Germany in September 1939 but before America entered the fray on December 7, 1941.

One of my earliest memories is seeing, at age four, long, olive-drab troop trains rolling through the Indiana farmland, packed with soldiers heading for the West Coast to fight in the Pacific War.

In 1946, at age six and after the war, I built my first play version of an airplane. When I was ten, the Korean War was in full action and I saw the neighbors' young sons go away again to fight in the Pacific.

In the 1950s, the Cold War experience was brought home to me personally. My older brother, after earning an aeronautical degree and officer's commission at Purdue University, became an Air Force pilot and was flying the Convair B-36 Peacemaker on interminably long missions, again in the Pacific.

On October 4, 1957, the Soviet Union launched the first artificial earth-orbiting satellite, *Sputnik*. A junior in high school, I had already made up my mind to join the military. I was studying the Russian language and had a heavy load of science and mathematics courses, so I applied to my congressman, Representative Charles Halleck, for an appointment to the recently opened United States Air Force Academy in Colorado. After a battery of mental and physical tests, I was admitted to the fourth class at the academy.

Of some 6,000 applicants, 454 entered my class in May 1958, and 298 graduated on June 6, 1962. Vice President Lyndon Johnson presented our diplomas, and the legendary, cigar-chomping General Curtis LeMay awarded our second lieutenant commissions.

I was privileged to be able to choose one of the two pilot training bases that had the new, supersonic Northrop T-38 Talon for advanced training. After a year (August 1962–August 1963) in the cotton, cattle, and oil country of West Texas at Webb Air Force Base, our class was offered a mixed bag of pilot assignments: F-100 Super Sabres, KC-135 tankers, B-52 Stratofortresses, helicopters, and the C-130 Hercules. Though I once aspired to be a fighter pilot, I'd just had a good friend die in an F-100 accident (known famously as the F-100 Sabre Dance), so I opted for the more staid C-130.

My first assignment was to Pope AFB, in Fayetteville, North Carolina. The 464th Troop Carrier Wing was transitioning from Fairchild C-123 Provider transports to the Lockheed C-130 Hercules, and I was to be in the first combat-ready squadron, the 776th Troop Carrier Squadron. First, I had to go through C-130 transition training at Sewart AFB, Tennessee. My partner in training was a crusty major who was a Korean War vintage KB-50 tanker pilot. I learned several things from him: how the real Air Force operated, how to play golf, and how to roll dice. Nobody ever said it had to be all work and no play!

Pope AFB was adjacent to the Army's Fort Bragg, home of the 82nd Airborne Division and the U.S. Army's Special Forces, the Green Berets. Our primary mission was to support these airborne troops in any deployment, anywhere in the world, and we were also assigned to airlift humanitarian aid.

We were soon put to the test. The shattering 8.3 magnitude earthquake on March 27, 1964, in Anchorage, Alaska, killed 131 and had every one of our crews deployed to Alaska carrying medical units, food, supplies, and rebuilding equipment.

Regional brushfire wars soon occupied most of our flying. I had two deployments, in August 1964 and March 1965, to the Republic of the Congo, the former Belgian colony, to assist the friendly army fighting the Communist-backed rebels. It was there that I first got the notation in my records that I had experience in COIN (counterinsurgency) fighting. In another deployment, in April 1965, we airlifted supplies to forces fighting in the Dominican Republic.

We also had an ongoing commitment to provide airlift in the European and Middle East theaters. On a 90 day rotation in the fall of 1965 to Evreux AB, France, I was happily flying to Finland, Cyprus, England, Germany and the Berlin Corridor (I saw Berlin before and after the Wall was built), Turkey, Iran, Greece, Libya, Tunisia, and Spain.

On March 8, 1965, President Johnson started the massive U.S. military buildup in South Vietnam by ordering the U.S. Marines to land near Da Nang. Every available airlift resource was needed in the next several years, and our C-130 squadrons deployed on a two-month rotational basis to airfields at Kadena, Okinawa, and Mactan Island, the Philippines. Nearly all missions were to, from, or inside South Vietnam, and we sometimes spent two weeks in-country. These many combat support flights resulted in numerous Air Medals and further notations in my records of counterinsurgency experience.

In the spring of 1966, while back at Pope AFB for a breather from jungle flying, a group of us experienced combat crew members, and others who had transferred in from other Air Force units, were given orders to join a new unit at Pope, the Straygoose detachment. "What in the world is that?" we all asked. It seems we all had similar backgrounds and notations about COIN experience in our records.

We soon found we would be flying specially equipped MC-130E Skyhook aircraft outfitted with the Fulton Recovery System, known as Skyhook. The Skyhook system was designed to drop a bundle to a downed pilot who needed rescue. Within the bundle was a jumpsuit and harness attached to a 500-foot braided nylon line, and at the other end of the line was a large balloon to be filled by the pilot with helium from a compact bottle. After dropping the bundle, the aircraft would return in about 20-30 minutes and snatch the line with the scissor-like attachment on the front of the airplane. This would pull the pilot out of the jungle or out of his raft if at sea, and then we would reel him in to the back of the airplane. The system had been tested on a de Havilland DCH-5 Buffalo and on a Boeing B-17 Flying Fortress, but this was going to be the first combat deployment for it in the long-range, modern Lockheed C-130 Hercules.

Rescuing downed pilots deep behind enemy lines was ostensibly our primary mission, in support of the JPRC (Joint Personnel Recovery Center) in Southeast Asia. Rescue helicopters at that time did not have the range to go deep into Laos or North Vietnam, so we trained at Pope and became proficient in pickups (and not just in the local saloons!). We studied low-level flying tactics, anti-aircraft avoidance, and means of escape and evasion.

Deemed combat ready, our six crews and four Skyhook aircraft and support personnel went to the Pacific. We arrived at Ching Chuan Kang Air Base at Taichung, Taiwan, in September 1966. CCK for short, it was the home of the 314th Troop Carrier Wing and was to be our maintenance base and home away from home. We barely had time to enjoy the noodles and rice (and ice cream—an extreme rarity in the Vietnam War) before we deployed to our permanent base at Nha Trang, South Vietnam.

Nha Trang had once been a delightful French seaside resort town with white-sand beaches and inexpensive restaurants serving *langouste* (lobster) and excellent imported French wines. Now the French were gone, the beaches had barbed wire containments, and the city was occupied by a conglomeration of allied military forces.

Nha Trang was home to the U.S. Army's 5th Special Forces Group (Airborne). They conducted a commando training center there, providing forces for raids and covert operations into North Vietnam, Laos, and Cambodia. These raiders were members of MACVSOG. We learned at this time that we would be augmenting and eventually replacing a clandestine C-123 unit called First Flight, which had been supporting SOG. In addition to our Skyhook rescue mission, we would be carrying men and supplies into forward airstrips, dropping propaganda leaflets, resupplying, inserting and extracting SOG personnel behind enemy lines.

Early in January 1967, SOG headquarters in Saigon requested a Combat Spear (one name given to cross-border re-supply operations), Straygoose mission to re-supply an Ops Plan 34A road watch team that had been inserted into North Vietnam some four months earlier. (According to Lieutenant Colonel Ian Sutherland in his book *Special Forces of the United States Army*, "Op-34A used all indigenous teams [all Vietnamese with no Americans], designated by the cryptonym Earth Angel, in Cambodia, Laos and, early in the war, in North Vietnam. North Vietnam was a very difficult area to operate in because of their tight security organization.") The task of this team was to provide surveillance of the North Vietnamese men and materiel moving down the Ho Chi Minh Trail to South Vietnam and radio this data to SOG. Numerous teams had been inserted, and this one reported it was out of food and supplies.

Since our Straygoose crew, SG-5, was next up for a combat mission, on January 16, 1967, we started the briefing process with a detailed analysis of the drop zone location. It was in the middle of the jungle behind a low ridge of mountains, 90 miles southwest of Hanoi. We would have a TOT (time over target) of 0100 with a 30-second leeway on either side. Our signal to identify the drop zone would be a cross of five flare pots to be lit 30 seconds before and extinguished 30 seconds after TOT. We would drop five pallets of supplies within one minute from an altitude of 1,200 feet.

We next sat down at a huge planning table and prepared our track of ingress and egress. Since the route would be flown at night, at low level (500 feet above the terrain), and would have to avoid early-warning radar and known anti-aircraft batteries and SAM (surface-to-air missile) sites, we plotted it with a very, very fine pencil and a magnifying glass. Our aircraft was equipped with terrain-following and terrain-avoidance radar. However, the software to run it was from an F-4 fighter, so we did not have the performance capability to match its climb or turn commands. In other words, while flying at 500 feet at night, it might command a sharp climb or turn to avoid a mountain, a simple operation for an F-4 with afterburner and nearly instant climb capability, but for us it would be just a heads-up that we were about to hit the mountain. Our navigation equipment was also minimal. We had Doppler radar to give us course and speed information, and we had Loran-C navigation. Unfortunately, there was only one Loran-C station in Southeast Asia at the time, so we could not get an accurate fix. We only knew we were somewhere on one line on the chart, so we went back to basics.

Our primary navigation mode became map reading! Thankfully, the Lockheed C-130 was designed with a large cockpit and lower side windows for ease of vision in getting in and out of small, unimproved airfields. We used this to our advantage because we had three pilots, two navigators, an electronic warfare navigator, two flight engineers, two loadmasters, and a radio-man—lots of eyeballs!

After planning our route around the known enemy defenses and plotting the easily visible landmarks such as isolated mountains, river junctions, and small towns, we next had to consider the weather. One of our requirements was that the moon had to be more than half-full and we had to have about 10 to 15 miles flight visibility. The forecast for this night was marginal, but due to the urgency we opted to go.

Continuing the briefing, we covered communications. We would not have fighter escort and we would maintain radio silence other than several quick code busts to headquarters of success or failure of the mission. Our own GCI (ground-controlled intercept) radar sites would be told only that a friendly would pop up at 0100 at a certain location about 90 miles southwest of Hanoi. We reviewed our escape and evasion procedures, knowing it was one long walk out (would we trust that one of our own would come in and pick us up? That would be much better than a bamboo cage!) All insignia and identifying personal articles were collected in bags and held for us. We

checked our green mesh survival vests for the emergency radio, the
E & E (escape and evasion) survival kits, and the Smith & Wesson
Combat Masterpiece .38 caliber revolver (the enlisted men also had
M-16 rifles, which was the total of the armament on our aircraft).

Normally for our cross-border missions we would fly to Nakhon
Phanom Air Base (NKP) in Thailand on the border of the panhandle
of Laos. It was a forward field nearly on the same latitude as the
DMZ (demilitarized zone) between North and South Vietnam. It
was heavily used by allied commando aircraft to interdict the flow
of munitions and troops along the Ho Chi Minh Trail. The A-1
Skyraiders (call sign Sandy) were also there providing air cover for
rescue operations. We often used this base to rest before the night
missions as it was many miles closer to our targets than Nha Trang.

However, due to the secrecy of this mission and its deep penetra-
tion into northern Laos and North Vietnam, we would start and end
the flight at our home base of Nha Trang. We would depart Nha
Trang and fly up the coast to Da Nang, then over Laos to Udorn
RTAB, Thailand. Instead of landing, we would make a low pass over
the field as if we were landing, then continue on a low-level route to
the north. On return we would again make a low pass over Udorn
before proceeding to our home base. Hopefully this would confuse
any spies, but it made for a long, seven-hour mission.

The night of January 16 we launched for our mission and for once
the weatherman got his forecast right; visibility was marginal at
best. This was the dry season in interior Vietnam and Laos, and the
farmers were burning off their rice fields. We had flown nearly half
of our route to the target when our Doppler radar failed. This, and
the poor visibility, was cause for an automatic abort of the mission,
so we returned to Nha Trang.

Our crews used a first-in, first-out rotation for our missions but
since we had already briefed and planned this mission, we were told
we had to do it again until we got it right! So we crawled into our
air-conditioned barracks (a real rarity in Vietnam; even the base
commander did not have AC) and slept the day through. That night
the weatherman came into the briefing room smiling like the
Cheshire cat, with a forecast of 15 miles visibility and a bright moon.
The mission was on.

We launched about 2200. Everything on the airplane was working perfectly and the crew was full of adrenaline, feeling the fear and excitement of being in enemy territory in a large, unarmed transport airplane. After crossing over Udorn Air Base, Thailand, we raced along at 500 feet above the ground, observing orange flashing anti-aircraft fire tracking us from the Ho Chi Minh Trail in the mountains below us on the right as we proceeded north up the 250 mile track in Laos to our target in North Vietnam. The gunners did not seem to have a clue to our altitude as the shells exploded well above us. Our navigator, Captain Les Smith, commented, "Wow! That sure looks close." Major Howard Reeve, the aircraft commander, responded, "No, it's way off. They're just firing for effect." Captain Smith came back with, "Well, it's effective as hell as far as I'm concerned!"

At our speed of 250 knots, it would take us about one hour to get over the target once we crossed into northern Laos. We were easily able to pick out the lights of towns (Vientiane and Luang Prabang come to mind on the way in, and Dien Bien Phu on the egress), and silvery river junctions and dark mountains stood out plainly in the moonlight. Two minutes before drop time, we lowered our wing flaps and slowed the airplane to 115 knots, opened the back cargo door, lowered the ramp, and prepared to drop the five heavy pallets. One minute out and we popped up to 1,200 feet. We could plainly see the lights of Hanoi some 90 miles away, but we did not think we had been detected by enemy radar.

Thirty seconds to go, and suddenly we saw the lighted flare pots in the form of a long cross. We were only a few hundred yards out of alignment so we kicked the rudder and made a shallow turn to line up.

"Green light!" Just 15 seconds off our planned TOT. Verbal, mechanical, and electrical signals immediately dumped the load out the aft door in a matter of seconds, dragged by heavy cargo parachutes. (This procedure was called low-level extraction. The floor of the C-130 cargo compartment had tracks with small wheels so the pallets could be loaded with a forklift, then rolled into position and secured by hand. A cargo parachute was attached to the end of each pallet, and when coming up on the drop zone the cargo door was opened and the pallets were released from their tie-downs. The aircraft was flown with the wing flaps extended, in a nose-up attitude and at a low speed. The pallets then rolled back to the end of the ramp, where each parachute would deploy in the slipstream and pull its pallet out. The pallets then would basically free fall from 1,200 feet.)

"Red light!" The navigator signaled the end of the drop, and the loadmaster declared, "Load away." Buttoning up the cargo door and raising the wing flaps, we turned left off the target and accelerated to 250 knots as we started our descent to 500 feet for radar avoidance on the egress south back toward Laos, then to Thailand and on to South Vietnam. Suddenly the sky lit up with tracers and flashes as anti-aircraft shells exploded around us. We ducked and dodged left and right for what seemed like minutes but was really just a few seconds, then soon found ourselves back in the serenity of a quiet, moonlit sky, coasting along the ridge tops and karst peaks and down into the valleys. A damage report on interphone said, "No hits, no damage. Let's go home." The radio operator sent his specially coded "Mission successful" message out on his secret HF radio frequency (which went to an operator named Bugs in the Philippines), and we all took a deep breath and wiped our sweaty hands.

Three and a half hours later, we made our recovery back at our home base, Nha Trang. During the debriefing, the intelligence officer was surprised (really!) by the report of anti-aircraft fire at that position. We told him he should have been there. Our compassionate flight surgeon had provided the debriefing team with some Bushmill's medicinal whiskey, so we all congratulated one another on this, the first successful C-130 resupply mission over North Vietnam.

Our crew soon received a personal message from General William Westmoreland, Commander of U.S. Forces in Vietnam, commending us for flying a critical combat mission in support of unconventional warfare operations in a hostile environment (unclassified version). For this mission, the entire crew of SG-5, six officers and five enlisted men, received the Distinguished Flying Cross. We also heard, in a report from the team on the ground, that four of the five pallets had hit directly on the drop zone and the fifth was 100 meters to the left (we needed more wind correction).

I had six more missions over Laos, North Vietnam, and the Gulf of Tonkin, dropping leaflets and supplies. There were many in-country flights (in South Vietnam), resupplying the Special Forces SOG teams at forward airstrips. I was also the unit intelligence officer and helped plan several Skyhook rescue attempts of downed pilots in North Vietnam using the Fulton Recovery System in the spring of 1967. Regrettably, one pilot was captured before we could get there, and another lost radio contact and was presumed killed.

I recall one humorous event of interest: Our mascot was a white duck named Maynard, even though he should have been a "stray goose." We brought him all the way from Pope Air Force Base, and he was familiar with every Officers' Club and bar we frequented. His favorite drink, I believe, was a martini, very dry (shaken, not stirred). In any event, he died of cirrhosis of the liver, and his owner, who was on another SG crew, buried him at sea from 20,000 feet while on a psychological warfare (leaflet) drop over North Vietnamese waters.

As our time in Vietnam wound down and we got close to rotation stateside, we began receiving replacement crews from the U.S. We briefed and trained them on what we had learned, but the war was getting hotter. We later learned that one of these 11-man crews, S-01, was lost on a mission over North Vietnam on December 28, 1967. The crash site was finally found in November 1992. One of my gnawing thoughts is this: Did we miss something in our training and briefing of these replacement crews? There is now a memorial at the headquarters of the Air Force Special Operations Command at Hurlburt Field, Florida, to this crew, the only MC-130E lost in combat in Vietnam.

I had five years of active duty and was told I would be stuck in transports for the duration of the war. I didn't want that. Therefore, I resigned my commission and separated from the Air Force in August 1967, not looking back. I enrolled in Purdue's graduate business school, but after one semester of boring economics and statistics classes, I decided to try the airlines. An application to Western Airlines in early 1968 netted me an interview, and in April 1968 I was hired and trained to be a flight engineer on the Boeing 720B. I completed 32 years of service with Western and Delta, flying international flights, again to the Pacific! I retired in June 2000 as an MD-11 captain at the Portland, Oregon, base. Now it's fly-fishing, study, writing, and travel—my suitcase is always packed (I guess I had too many years commuting)—and I wish the best to those who follow.

In researching my logbook and memory bank for this story, I wrote to Leslie Smith, now a retired federal judge, who was the navigator on this mission. I will quote a bit from his letter to me as it adds some interesting points.

On January 17, 1967, we flew up the coast to Da Nang, then direct to Udorn where we made a fake landing/low approach (tower even directed us to a parking spot after we were "on the ground"). We then resumed low-level flying north/northwest to the bend of the river where most of our missions started, and then on north into Laos. In fact, when we crossed the river we could see the lights of Vientiane in the distance. At the northwest corner of the route we could see Luang Prabang, Laos, in the distance. I had asked whether we could use it as an emergency landing base if we were shot up, since Air America was flying in and out of there. We were advised that we could. We also had the use of two secret TACAN (tactical air navigation) stations in Laos, but they weren't much good at our low altitude. I've since talked with an Army friend who resupplied those TACAN sites by helicopter, and he said both TACAN sites were overrun a number of times. We flew out along a slightly different route and diverted a number of miles from it when, on the way out, we flew through some AAA. We made a turn and flew down a different valley and then intercepted our planned route. Then back to Udorn for a fake takeoff and on to Nha Trang. Mission length was a little over seven hours total. —Leslie Smith

....

As an interesting footnote, Richard said the last two MC-130E aircraft he flew in Vietnam, tail numbers 64-561 and 64-562, were just retired by the Air Force in October 2012. They were flown from Florida to Davis Monthan AFB in Tucson, Arizona, and now reside in the Air Force "boneyard."

Richard Sell's totally unmarked MC-130E, with the scissor-like yoke attachment on the nose for the Fulton Recovery System.

Scissor-like attachment for the Fulton Recovery System.

14

SEARCH AND RESCUE

Jim Fogg, USAF, C-130P, 1967 – 1968
{ Date of hire by Western Airlines: 5/26/1969 }

Jim Fogg at Tuy Hoa, 1968.

Before Jim's story begins, I want to make a short introduction to one of the most interesting men I have ever had the good fortune to know. In his story Jim uses the term "100 percent warrior" in describing one of the Sandy pilots he worked with in search and rescue. Now anyone who knows Jim knows that he is pretty much the definition of 100 percent warrior, yet his tour in Vietnam consisted of saving, not taking, lives. The courage and flying skill displayed in this story truly speak volumes about Jim Fogg.

When Jim was furloughed from Western Airlines shortly after he was hired in May 1969, he flew the C-141 in the Air Force Reserve at Norton AFB and went to work for the Orange County Sheriff's Department in Southern California. As a deputy sheriff he spent most of the next two years and five months doing extraditions and other dangerous things. He is a tough guy, yet his story is one of survival and rescue. It is a tribute to a good friend who has been supportive of this project from the very beginning.

Jim Fogg was involved in the rescue of Jim Pollak, another contributor to this book, and you will read both men's accounts of the episode later in this book, along with that of a third participant, Kirk Clark. It is an incredible coincidence that these three pilots, thrust together in a harrowing incident on January 4, 1968, all ended up flying for Western Airlines after their service in Vietnam.

Now, here is Jim's story.

....

The following history is an account of my Southeast Asia tour, which was from March 14, 1967, until March 14, 1968. During that stretch the infamous Tet Offensive, which greatly intensified the war, was launched by the enemy. In this narrative, I shall attempt to give a general overview of my mission in Vietnam, then relate a couple of the dozens of war efforts in which I was involved, and finally I'll give my perceptions of the conflict, both during and since those tumultuous years. Please note that I chose the word *perceptions* because Vietnam, like thousands of controversial issues that we all face during our lifetime, was and is to each of us as we perceive it. I can see the world only through my own eyes.

My sole purpose in Southeast Asia was to save lives, flying the C-130P, a rescue aircraft. On each and every mission I prayed that no American pilot would be shot down, but if it happened, my crew, along with all the other rescue forces, was prepared to rescue and recover the downed airman as expeditiously as possible. We hoped this could be accomplished without further loss of aircraft or crew, but unfortunately that was not always the case.

In the middle of March 1967, I picked up a brand new C-130P at the Lockheed factory and, with my good friend Captain Bill Delony, flew it from Georgia to Udorn RTAB (Royal Thai Air Base) in Thailand. During that one-year tour of duty we would be stationed for three months at Udorn AB and nine months at Tuy Hoa AB in Vietnam—and wow, what an experience! Both bases were seriously dedicated to the war effort, but each seemed unique and very different to me. Udorn was huge, with what seemed like about every plane in the Air Force inventory (with the exception of F-100s and F-105s) stationed there. There were F-4 Phantoms, F-101 Voodoos for reconnaissance purposes, F-102 interceptors, F-104s, and some cargo aircraft painted jet-black that I was told were not actually there (and therefore I could not actually be seeing them, if you catch my drift). And to think, this was years before stealth aircraft were included in the Air Force inventory! (These black aircraft, with no markings, were flown by various civilians and contract organizations working for the CIA and for other clandestine organizations.)

All three of the aircraft types used for search and rescue were stationed at Udorn. Those were the C-130, the A-1 Skyraider, and the HH-3 (later the HH-53) Jolly Green Giant rescue helicopter. Combat flying out of Udorn was almost always exciting, often dangerous, and sometimes resulted in the loss of aircraft and crew members. This fast-paced lifestyle, with possible disaster always lurking, made for great celebration after mission accomplishment. Without exception, night life at the Officers' Club was a riot of fun, particularly when a downed pilot was safely rescued and returned, or when a fighter pilot successfully cheated death and accomplished his 100 missions. Whenever pilots hang it all out on the edge, they are surely ready to celebrate after returning from such close calls. The more harrowing the experiences of the day, the more intense the revelry of the night!

No Officers' Club before or since, in my experience, has ever surpassed Udorn during a wild night. I can still visualize the numerous holes in the ceiling from the butt imprints of fighter pilots being shoved into it upside down after completing 100 missions. Their name and the date of the last mission would be written on the ceiling beside their tail print. That also signified that they would be returning safely to their families at home. The club was also lined with knife pockets that had been ripped from pilots' flight suits. Woe unto the poor neophyte pilot, new to the war zone, who had the audacity to enter the Udorn O Club still sporting a survival knife pocket with all these hardened and seasoned veterans stalking about. That pocket would soon become another club adornment and its pilot an object of amusement. You see, longevity in the war zone was reason enough for a smug pecking order.

When we were nearing the end of our combat tour, the term "getting short" was used, and we would pity the poor, unfortunate newcomer with one whole year or 100 missions to go. I actually heard over the radio, during a relaxed lull in action, the phrase "Speak quickly, man, I'm getting short and don't have time for a long conversation."

Now, Tuy Hoa AB Vietnam was a contrast in style to Udorn. Even though the flight crews encountered the same dangers, it was low-key, and everyone seemed more subdued. Tuy Hoa was a newly opened base right on the coast, much smaller than Udorn, with only two primary aircraft types assigned, three F-100 squadrons and one squadron of C-130 rescue aircraft. This C-130 squadron was mine— the 39th ARRS (air rescue and recovery squadron), and my crew was one of the first two crews sent from Udorn to prepare for the eventual full squadron transfer. We immediately began flying our standard rescue missions from there to assist the Udorn operation.

Tuy Hoa, being new, had none of the standard conveniences when we first arrived. The runways and taxiways, instead of concrete, were PSP (pierced-steel planking), which was a challenging change from the norm. There were no permanent quarters for us, officers or enlisted. Our temporary lodging consisted of large tents holding roughly 30 men, each with his bed, a small metal closet to hang up clothes, and a footlocker at the foot of his bed. Do not picture these tents as resting on plush grass. They were right out on the sandy beach with tents, beds, etc. plopped down on the loose sand. This arrangement proved quite an inconvenience when, during one very long night in the summer, a monsoon storm with incredible winds blew down all our tents and closets. We were forced to hold tightly to our belongings to prevent their loss into the South China Sea. There was no sleeping that night—we could only try to shield our face and eyes from the sand blizzard. Though exhausted from the ordeal, it was a pleasure to fly a mission the next morning and get away from the mess. I only hope God will forgive me for my many unkind utterances that evening! Our showers and bathroom facilities were a large communal affair situated about half a block away. Fortunately for us, permanent air-conditioned quarters were built in about two months and base living greatly improved. The base remained, however, more primitive and less celebratory in mood than Udorn.

The fact that enemy forces frequently threatened our base may have been a contributing factor. The 95th North Vietnamese Regiment was a particular nuisance for a long time. I thought it incredibly ironic that during their siege of our base, our wing launched a squadron area beautification project. My squadron, being highly competitive and ingenious, had imported palm trees and sod grass from the Philippines. My squadron commander, whom I greatly respected and admired, stated at commander's call that he would personally participate in the planting along with all officers and enlisted men. I agreed and gladly chipped in. At the same time that we were diligently digging huge holes, planting palm trees, and laying sod, F-100s from our own base were screaming overhead in a dive, dropping bombs to drive back and prevent the NVA from overrunning the base, and B-52 bombers were constantly laying a bomb barrage on the base perimeter from a high altitude.

One day in the midst of this melee, a strange, perverse thought crossed my mind. I turned to the man beside me, also sweating profusely in the hot sun, and said, "Please tell me that I'm crazy and the rest of the world is sane. Please tell me there is nothing weird about planting grass and palm trees as fast as we can while just across the field they are busy blowing grass and palm trees to smithereens just as fast as they can." Thank heavens we did succeed, with tremendous help from the South Korean (ROK) forces stationed nearby, in driving those pesky intruders away.

When the threat was most severe for a couple of weeks, the flight crews frequently stated our desire to have possession of our individual rifles, which were kept in the armory. This situation brought back memories of Joseph Heller's famous book *Catch-22*. Every man on base was assigned a rifle (an M16), but we could never check it out of the base armory and take it back to our BOQ (base officers' quarters) for protection. All those rifles were locked in one location, and if the enemy had overrun our base, it's easy to guess where they would have gone to obtain more firepower. The response to our plea was always the same: "You flyboys would probably blow your foot off if we gave them to you." We each had a .38 Smith & Wesson revolver that was part of our flight gear, but we had to check it out at the start of each combat mission and turn it back in at mission completion. This procedure did afford us, though, the opportunity to peer into the next room and view our trusty rifles.

The following is a description of the search and rescue forces as they were utilized in Southeast Asia. A standard recovery team would consist of one C-130, a flight of four A-1s whose call sign was always Sandy, and at least two, preferably four, HH-3 Jolly Green Giant helicopters with the call sign Jolly. Our operation in a rescue effort was a total, choreographed, team effort. It was truly poetry in motion. Midway through my tour, there were two improvements to the SAR mission that I felt greatly improved our overall effectiveness. First, during the summer of 1967, we began air refueling the Jollys. This became a new task for my C-130, hooking up and delivering fuel to the giant helicopters whenever they were running low. This added immeasurably to their range and made them available for the duration of the rescue, and I had the good fortune of being selected by my squadron commander to fly the first air refueling mission in combat. Until then it had been tested in training in the States but had not been used during an actual combat mission. However, it soon became common practice and greatly improved the Jollys' range and usefulness. (*A photo taken of that mission is on the dust jacket of this book.*)

Primarily, these three aircraft types were assigned to the task, though rescue efforts could sometimes involve more than 100 planes in a single SAR. This would occur when rescue forces had to operate in an area, often North Vietnam, where protection from hostile fire from MiGs, SAMs (surface-to-air missiles), or AAA (anti-aircraft artillery, also called triple A) was necessary. Small arms fire was always possible, but our own A-1 Skyraiders were assigned the task of eradicating those threats. For protection from MiGs, SAMs, and triple A, we would proceed into the more dangerous areas with fighter aircraft orbiting high overhead. We called all overhead fighters MIG CAP no matter what type they were. It was important to know whether our MIG CAP planes were F-4s, F-105s, or F-100s and, if they were Navy fighters, what weapons they carried. For example, it could be missiles; 1,000, 750, or 500 pound bombs; 20mm (or "20 Mike Mike," as it was affectionately called); or Willie Petes (white phosphorus).

I would meticulously copy plane and weapon types and their intended targets up north during the pre-mission briefing for the strike. This was very useful information during a rescue mission, because certain planes and ammo loads were more beneficial than others, depending upon the threat. I would always take what I could get and be thankful, but my preference was F-4s when MiGs were the greatest danger, while F-105s, with their air-to-ground missiles, were more desirable for SAM suppression. Nevertheless, I always felt much better with any of them up there on the perch. The only problem with the jet fighters was their incredible fuel burn. It often required that they be recycled to an assigned airborne tanker to take on a fresh fuel load.

Each flight generally consisted of four aircraft, and they used the term "bingo fuel" when they had to leave high station to go and hit their tanker for more fuel. "RTB" meant a flight, for whatever reason, was returning to base and had left us for the day. Whenever a flight would RTB or reach bingo fuel, one or more flights would replace them if we could arrange it. Fighters, whether they were Air Force stationed in Thailand or South Vietnam or Navy from the Gulf of Tonkin (off any of several aircraft carriers), were always most cooperative and would stay as long as necessary if they could. They would come up on guard frequency and volunteer their services. They did this, I felt, because they appreciated the extreme measures taken to recover every downed airman, and they always had the thought in their minds, "There but for the grace of God, go I." It was such a reassuring feeling to know that every effort humanly possible would be put forth for the rescue and safe return of each combatant, should misfortune befall him. Such is the value that America has always put on the life of the fighting man, and no other nation, to my knowledge, has ever matched this compassion for the individual in combat. This exemplifies why our nation is so unique and so special.

The moment a "mayday" distress signal was transmitted, all attention swiftly turned to the pilot's recovery, and the war effort seemed to be momentarily put on hold. As you might imagine, pilots were almost always shot down in the jungle or in a small clearing where only a helicopter could make an actual pickup. I was involved in the safe return of 38 pilots, and only once did I actually land and retrieve a downed airman. Sadly, though, we lost more than we saved because the enemy would capture them before we could arrive. Sometimes a plane was reported down with no observed chute, and no radio contact could be established.

The air refueling procedure for the Jolly differed substantially from the air-to-air refueling of fighters from their tankers. Fighter aircraft had to locate their tankers, which were orbiting in a pre-planned area, and then join up for a drink. Airspeed was not a problem for them as the fighter and tanker were mostly compatible in speed. In our case, the fuel-receiving aircraft, the Jolly, would continue on its steady course toward the downed pilot, or homeward bound if returning from a rescue operation. The Jolly would be dependent on my C-130 aircraft to locate and intercept him to transfer fuel. They were not easy to see from any angle, as they, like our C-130, were painted a jungle camouflage that blended closely with the surroundings. The trick was to fly 500 feet lower than the chopper's reported altitude to make him easier to see and to prevent a midair collision. After receiving a call for fuel, I would usually come toward the Jolly from the front at high speed: balls to the wall. After locating and passing beneath him, I would chop the throttles to idle, yank back on the yoke as I pulled up and reversed course, then slide ever so nicely past him as I declared, "I have lead." It was like poetry in motion. Who the heck would ever, in their right mind, trade this for some mundane job like being a lawyer or a CPA? Anyway, just as I declared "lead," I would extend both refueling hoses (each extended 82 feet) to prepare for fuel transfer. The Jolly would always declare, "I'm in," as he hooked his refueling probe into the basket, but it was really unnecessary as I could feel his presence. By the time he was in position to receive fuel, his rotor blades would be close enough to my empennage (tail) that I could feel a constant vibration in my flight controls and throughout the entire aircraft. Our left hose was considered the primary one, but both hoses could be used simultaneously to refuel two Jollys if time was of the essence.

There was one minor flaw to this operation, however, and that was the chopper's slower speed. In order to match speeds, his maximum had to be equal to my minimum. I would extend my wing flaps and slow to 110 knots, which was near my stall speed, especially at the heavy gross weights we maintained during the early part of a mission. As the Jolly took on more and more fuel and became heavier, it became increasingly difficult for it to keep up, and soon we would get a standard request. "Crown, give me five" (my call sign was always Crown in the early days—later it was changed to King). This meant for me to slow five more knots to 105 knots, which was now *very* close to my stall speed. I would always oblige, of course. Occasionally I would have a Jolly driver, as he neared his top-off, state, "Crown, give me another five." This would instantly tip me off that I had one of those poor neophytes on my hose (the veterans knew better than to ask), and I would have to give him a short lesson on fixed-wing aerodynamics. In fact, I would tell him, "No can do," but I would give him a gentle 400 fpm (feet per minute) descent. The descent allowed the helicopter to accelerate and he could keep up with the tanker until he reached his full fuel load. In the mountainous areas, that brought us rather close to the terrain, and small arms fire sometimes became a problem.

This speed differential problem was eliminated when the second improvement to the SAR mission occurred in the fall of 1967. At that time, a new rescue helicopter slowly began to replace the trusty HH-3 Jollys. It was the new HH-53, which is still used today in rescue operations. The official call sign was still Jolly, but we informally referred to them as "Super Jolly." They were much more powerful and much faster, and their pilots never had to say, "Crown, give me five!" However, the old Jollys and their pilots will forever have a special place in my heart.

As soon as air refueling was complete, I would reel in my hoses, climb, and dash back to the crash site. Generally the Sandys would still be there keeping up their vigil, ready to strike at the first sign of hostile fire. As courageous as the Jolly pilots were, certainly the Sandy pilots were no less so.

One Sandy pilot I shall never forget was Captain Jack Cockran who flew Sandy out of Udorn in 1967. During one mission, enemy MiGs jumped Jack's two-ship formation just as it was getting dark. With no fighter cover available to assist them, they tried desperately to dodge the MiGs, but Jack's lead was blown from the sky and the airplane went down with no chute. Then the MiGs turned their full attention on Jack, but he eluded them. All alone, Jack flew back from the North Vietnam/Laos border country in the dead of night to his base at Udorn. The lead pilot was one of Jack's good friends, and any normal man could be forgiven for requesting a brief grieving period for a lost comrade-in-arms or asking for a day or two of rest to get his head back on straight— but not Jack! Before the sun rose the next morning after that terrifying night, Jack was back up north at the same location, leading a flight of four Sandys. Jack was 100 percent warrior.

Shortly after this incident, Jack paid me a compliment that I have never forgotten. All SAR crews—Crown, Jollys, and Sandys, were briefed together, and one early morning as we left the pre-mission briefing room, Jack and I walked out into the silent darkness. As we started for our planes, Jack turned to me and said, "It's good to see you, Jim." I replied, "It's good to see you too, Jack." He came back with "It's *really* good to see you, Jim," whereupon I shot him a quizzical glance. I thought for a moment, "Oh no, don't tell me that combat has finally gotten to Jack and he has taken a fancy to me!" He quickly relieved me by stating, "You don't know what I mean, so I'll tell you. We go up north and risk our lives every day. That's all in the cards, but what makes all the difference is the confidence that if we do get shot down, someone will come and rescue us. On each briefing, the first thing I do is look around to see who is manning Crown. If I see you and that crazy Indian sidekick of yours, I am immediately reassured. I know that if things go wrong, you two will come and get me no matter where it is. Some guys will call off the rescue if things get hot."

Jack was very close in his assessment of how I felt about my job. You see, fighter pilots took great pride in hitting the target dead-on. I received my satisfaction from going in and recovering a downed airman from almost certain capture or death and returning him to his base and his buddies. It was an emotional high, a rush that aviation in the years since has never approached. Besides, it got me free drinks for the night at the O Club if we brought him back to our base. And, incidentally, my "crazy Indian sidekick" was not crazy at all, as Jack well knew. This was Captain Tom Baines, a very bright officer from Tahlequah, Oklahoma, who happened to be part Cherokee. He was my dependable, capable copilot for the entire year in Southeast Asia, and we had good chemistry in the cockpit, which was essential in a rescue operation. My primary task during a typical mission consisted of talking to the downed pilot, finding out his physical condition, pinpointing his exact location, reassuring him that plans for his rescue were under way, and calling the Jollys to find their location as they raced in our direction. They would usually navigate to the crash site by keying their mike for five seconds. Upon their request of my location, I would state, "Give me a short count." They would reply, "One, two, three, four, five—five, four, three, two, one, out." By this time an instrument in my cockpit would point to the location of their transmission, and I would then give them the correct heading to fly to come to my position.

Tom generally tracked the MIG CAP flights and their tankers, once bingo fuel was reached. He was especially gifted at this, as some rescue missions would involve 20 or more flights shuttling in and out as they were required to leave, hit their tanker, and return with a full fuel load. Through it all, Tom could keep everything straight, remembering everyone's location, call sign, frequency, flight condition, bingo fuel time, and tanker call sign and location. Tom was very good and I was lucky to have him. His efficiency allowed me the luxury of concentrating almost entirely on the specific rescue operation itself without having to worry about protective cover.

My crew consisted of eight members. In addition to two pilots, we had a navigator, two flight engineers, two loadmasters, and a radio operator who kept Saigon headquarters abreast of ongoing rescue operations. The call sign for headquarters was Blue Chip, and messages between Blue Chip and our C-130, while we were working a rescue, were relayed by my gifted radio operator, Sergeant Sellers. He was from Sacramento, California, and not only was he very good at his job, but he was the comedian of the crew. My chief NCO was Master Sergeant Furr, who was very professional, congenial, and cooperative and was one of my very favorites among my crew. One of my wishes for a nostalgic trip through yesteryear is to reassemble my old crew for a reunion, and I intend to do that.

Blue Chip was, naturally, in overall command of every rescue operation. Those folks were good, but as with any operations headquarters located hundreds of miles away, they were only as good as the information they received from the field. My radio operator's duty was to keep Blue Chip abreast of what we were doing. They generally would agree with our actions but occasionally would call with a change of plans, such as to call off a rescue operation if all efforts seemed futile. The on-scene commander of any SAR operation was the rescue crew commander of the C-130 Crown aircraft, and that was my responsibility for my year in Southeast Asia. The Crown aircraft would be in orbit, and it was the obligation of the rescue crew commander to go into action at the first, often frantic, call of "Mayday, mayday, mayday." Silence would be shattered by a hastily transmitted notification of a downed bird or an impending disaster, and from that first call my copilot and I would jot down every bit of information we received. The caller would barely have finished his distress message before I would be calling him on guard frequency (243.0 MHz on UHF) to get any additional information we needed. My navigator would relay the location of the downed plane to me, whereupon I would turn toward the crash site and fly at our best possible speed unless I considered it a hopeless situation. Such a case would be a fighter downed anywhere near Hanoi, Vinh, Haiphong, or a similar location. Nothing would have pleased the enemy more than to watch us attempt a rescue in one of those heavily fortified areas. If I called off a rescue in one of those hot areas, Blue Chip would always agree, but if I thought we had a reasonable chance of success, all operations would be set on go unless Blue Chip disagreed.

The following story involves a rescue mission that occurred on the afternoon of April 30, 1967. My factual information is exact since I kept notes stating events, call signs, locations, and precise times in detail. I will use abbreviations during the mission description and will give actual times at which events took place. I will be as accurate as I can because someone reading this story may have been involved or had a friend who was lost during this mission. The times will be Zulu time (Greenwich Mean Time) in all cases, just as I'm copying them from my notes, and locations will be identified as channels and numbers, since that is the quick way we referred to them at the time. For example, Ch. 97 (North Station), the northernmost navigational aid we used, was a TACAN station with 97 as its frequency. It was situated in northern Laos, near the North Vietnamese border, and was used by fighters for navigation to and from their targets. It was also used in rescue missions to locate downed aircraft and pilots. If a pilot stated his position to be "090 slash 25 off Ch. 97," it meant he was 090 degrees, or due east, of Ch. 97 for 25 miles. Also, military bases were identified by this system as every large Air Force base had its own TACAN station for navigational purposes. For instance, my base at this time was Udorn Air Base Thailand, and it was referred to as Ch. 86. Ch. 89 was the military base at Nakhon Phanom (NKP). Additionally, we used numbers to denote airports and runways in Laos. We called these Lima sites. For example, Lima Site 108 (L-108) and Lima Site 34 (L-34) were well-known locations to all pilots, especially those of us in rescue. To save time and space, I'll use the letters S and J to indicate the other two aircraft types of my rescue team. S-1 was Sandy 1, the lead ship or commander, usually of a four-ship formation. J 1, 2, 3, and 4 signify a flight of four Jolly rescue helicopters. All F-105s were based at either Korat Air Base or Takhli Air Base in Thailand, and most Air Force F-4s that were assigned targets up north were from Udorn Air Base and Ubon Air Base in Thailand or Da Nang Air Base in South Vietnam. As mentioned earlier, "bingo fuel" meant the time an aircraft had to leave duty station to refuel, and RTB stood for "return to base," usually signifying the end of a flight's services, during the recue attempt. With that as an explanation, we will now get on to April 30, 1967.

From our pre-mission briefing I copied down the following information. Fifty-nine fighter aircraft would be going into North Vietnam on a strike from over Ch. 97. Note, this includes only those planes coming overland from Thailand and South Vietnam, not from the Gulf of Tonkin side, where both Navy and Air Force strikes also originated. These 59 strike aircraft included call signs Zipper 1, 2, and 3 and Fallon 2 and 3—all B-66s. Wedge flight of four F-4s would serve as cap for the B-66s. Two more flights of four F-4s, call signs Thrush and Cactus, would provide MIG CAP for the mission. All remaining planes heading up north would be F-105s. Among them were Carbine and Leopard flights, both Iron Hand missions (using two-seat F-105s), which meant their primary concern was to locate and knock out surface-to-air missile sites. Other F-105s were Tomahawk, Waco, Oakland, Cleveland, and Neptune flights. In addition to my flight, Crown 2 out of Ch. 86 (Udorn), were S-1, 2, 3, and 4 and J-09 and J-53. S-5, 6, 7, 8 and J-36 and J-37 were coming out of Ch. 89 (NKP). J-52 and J-56 were at L-36.

Mid-afternoon local time (0815Z), rescue forces are on station and all fighter aircraft are heading north in a routine fashion. All is well. Suddenly there is a call on guard, "Mayday, mayday, mayday." At 0821Z Waco flight reports that someone has been hit. Then Carbine 1 states that Carbine 3 has gone down at 2118N10500E (longitude and latitude). There is a good chute, and now two ELTs (emergency beepers) are going off in addition to the continuous transmission on guard by the downed aircraft. The three transmitters are quite distracting now, but I copy on guard that the front-seater is OK. He has landed about halfway up the ridge above a narrow valley. I receive no word on the back-seater, but I can surely hear his ELT. Waco, Tomahawk, and Oakland flights are now on high perch for MIG CAP and any other needed assistance, along with Carbine 1, 2, and 4. At 0855, Carbine 1 reports that Carbine 4 has been hit and is going down. I hear, "Smoke, two to three miles east and slightly north."

Confusion reigns; constant chatter on guard with steady transmissions from two downed aircraft and four pilots. Carbine 1 and 2 must leave to hit their tanker for fuel. Cleveland 1 and 2 are coming in to help from their tanker. They are armed with 20mm. Detroit flight now arrives, also with 20mm. Now my C-130, along with S-1, 2, 3, and 4, are in northern Laos near Ch. 97 but south of the crash sites, which are well up in North Vietnam. Meanwhile, I have been vectoring the Jollys in our direction, planning to go in only when all rescue forces are prepared for a recovery. The crash site area is damn hot! Detroit and Cleveland flights are holding high over Ch. 97. There is a report that Carbine 4 is located at 054/86 off Ch. 97. At 0916Z Detroit flight has bingo fuel and leaves for the tanker. Neptune flight was up briefly but RTB at 0922Z. Likewise, Zipper flight is low on fuel, RTB at 0923Z. Thrush and Cactus flights arrive. That's good. Both are F-4s and well suited against MiGs. At 0929Z I hear, "Number 4 has been hit," followed by additional pilot and plane ELTs. That's Tomahawk 1, calling to report that Tomahawk 4 has gone down with a good chute (only one pilot this time, not an Iron Hand). He is located at 040/74 off Ch. 97. S-5, 6, 7, and 8 and J-53 and J-09 are heading north from NKP at 0957Z. J-52, much farther north, has an emergency and is forced to turn back. S-3 and 4 will escort him. Wedge, Cleveland, Waco, Thrush, Detroit, Carbine 1 and 2, and Tomahawk 1, 2, and 3 are periodically reaching bingo fuel, shuttling to their assigned tankers and reporting back on station after refueling. This keeps me and my copilot very busy assigning the tanker and the radio frequency for refueling. (For example, "Waco flight hit Orange Anchor, frequency 225.8.") In addition, we are marshaling all rescue forces farther north, though it is beginning to look bleak as to our chances of mounting a rescue this late in the afternoon. If the most sophisticated fighters of the time, with all their warning signals, are being blown out of the sky, how are we ever going to get in with our ensemble of slow-moving, low-flying aircraft to attempt a helicopter pickup?

Yet steadily northbound we move, hoping our fighters may have the chance to pound our rude and unwelcoming host into submission and give us a chance of a successful pickup. Finally, at 1015Z, Sandy 1 reports that he and his wingman, S-2, are over the crash site of one of the downed Carbine aircraft. He sees both chutes are empty, with no sign of either pilot. We now know that both successfully ejected but were probably captured since we could not get either pilot to respond to repeated radio transmissions. S-1 recommends that we discontinue our SAR and withdraw. I decide to hold off a bit longer, hoping for further contact, either visually or by radio, with one or more of the downed pilots. At 1040Z Waco 1 calls and states he has radio contact with Tomahawk 4. He is in good condition and is on top of a ridge at an elevation of 3,000 feet. His position is 055/77 of Ch. 97. Though this is good news, there appears no hope of getting a Jolly to this location and recovering the pilot before dark.

Remember J-52, who would have been closest, has turned back with an emergency. With a heavy heart and Blue Chip's approval, I call off the SAR at 1055Z. Most fighters begin to hit their tankers one final time and RTB. However, Tomahawk 1, 2, and 3 remain at high station a while longer, hoping to hear more from Tomahawk 4, but to no avail. Rescue forces begin pulling back to the south. S-5 and 6 are to go with S-1 and 2 to L-108 and then RTB Ch. 86. J-52 lands at L-111 and the crew is picked up by their sister ship, J-56. S-3 and 4 are to escort J-56 to Ch. 86.

Our day is not over yet, however, as more bad news awaits us. Tomahawk flight calls and says, "There is a ball of smoke down below." Sandy lead, S-1, announces over the radio, "Sandy 2, jump, jump!" Then he tells me at 1115Z that S-2's chances of survival look pretty grim. He relates that S-2, hit by ground fire and with his aircraft burning, spun down through a low overcast. Without an ejection seat in the Skyraider, it is doubtful he had time to get out. Five minutes later, at 1120Z, I hear on guard, "Crown 2, this is Sandy 2. I regained control just above the treetops and will try to fly it out, but it doesn't look good. I have put the fire out, but this plane is buffeting so badly that the instrument panel is nothing but a blur in front of me." At 1121Z he is 095/38 off Ch. 97, and S-1, 5, and 6 are to escort S-2 to L-108. I call Skyline (call sign for L-108) and tell him to turn on the runway lights at L-108 to assist Sandy flight in the emergency landing. Praise God, S-2 is able to land his crippled bird and is brought back to Udorn that night.

At this time my attention is quickly diverted from S-2 as I learn that S-1 has been struck by gunfire. He was due east of Ch. 97, 20 miles out when hit. S-1 states that his plane is flyable but his wings are shot up and he is losing fuel from the wing tanks so rapidly that his fuel state is fast becoming critical. I immediately begin suggesting every friendly Lima site that I think he can reach, but there are two problems. Only a few of the Lima sites are secure. Choosing any of the others is risky since they change hands so often, and our pre-mission intelligence briefing noted that fact earlier in the day. I certainly do not want to put him into an enemy-held airfield! The other problem is that darkness is fast approaching. S-1 vetoes every suitable friendly field that I suggest because of his low and rapidly decreasing fuel state, while all during this time I am rushing Jolly Greens in his direction as fast as they can fly.

There is one gamble we can take that might pay off for Sandy 1. There is a Lima site in the huge basin known as Plaine des Jarres (Plain of Jars, or PDJ) on the border between Laos and North Vietnam, but it is not often considered friendly. (This was an area where the French had been defeated in one of the big battles of the Indochina War of the 1950s.) Sandy 1 says he doesn't have enough fuel to go farther than this site so I come up with a plan. Since I don't feel it is prudent to call the site on the radio to alert whoever is there of our impending arrival, surprise has to be the order of the day. I tell S-1 that I will lead him down the final approach to the runway, dropping night illumination flares to light his way to touchdown. I promise him that the moment his crippled plane comes to a stop on the runway, a rescue Jolly will sit down beside him. Naturally, he is to jump from his plane to the Jolly in all haste since we don't want to wait for a welcoming committee.

Once we settle on the Plaine Des Jarres plan, I instruct my loadmasters to load the flare tubes as fast as they can. This is time consuming, since each million-candlepower flare is sealed in a metal container. They can load the flares but only I can fire them, since the sequencing switch is to the left of my seat in the cockpit. There are enough tubes to hold 12 flares, but my loadmasters have time to load only six of them. Regardless, I pull in front of S-1 and lead him down the final approach, dropping all six flares in sequence. Just above the runway, I pull up and turn left on a crosswind climb. Then, the next shocker comes: As I am in my turn, S-1 makes a transmission to me that I shall remember until my dying day. His voice seems so calm, cool, and relaxed that you would think he was in a rocking chair on his front porch. He said, "Crown 2, what say we call that a practice approach and try again?" To my dismay, I find that he is not on the runway but is following me on the go-around. The early evening is dark as pitch, and when I ask him the nature of the problem, he states, "Only two of your flares illuminated (the other four were duds) and they were drifting too far to the right to light the runway for landing." I say, "Do you have enough fuel for another approach?" He says, "I don't know. I hope so."

I intend to rectify the situation if Lady Luck will just hold out. I tell my loadmasters to load flares as fast as they have ever done before, because a man's life hangs in the balance. Also, this time I know the wind direction and its approximate speed on final approach. I received it, of course, from S-1 himself, since there was no control tower to call for the wind and altimeter setting! Coming around to final, I tell S-1 I will lead him down, but instead of lining up with the runway, I will fly all the way down about 150 yards left of centerline to allow for the wind drift of my flares. We have five good flares this time, and then my eyes behold a beautiful sight: S-1 touching down safely on the runway as the Jolly swoops in to sit beside him as he comes to a halt. The flares, drifting directly over-head, are turning the darkness into a bright, beautiful day! S-1 (who will tell me later that he ran out of fuel just as he touched down) wastes no time abandoning his wounded, now silent bird and climbs aboard the chopper. Jolly quickly launches and brings S-1's pilot back to join his wingman, S-2, at Udorn, where both of them are stationed.

It is ironic how fate works. As I stated previously, all rescue crews were briefed together prior to a mission. At the briefing that day I knew most of the pilots, especially the Sandy pilots, since we were quartered nearby on the base. I noticed at the briefing that Sandy 1 was Major Russell, a man in his mid-30s, while Sandy 2 was Major Gould, also about 35. I was 28 years old at the time and a captain. Who could have ever guessed, at that midday briefing, the twisting, perilous journey that awaited us that day? Needless to say, there was a party going on that night at the O Club. We laughed a lot on the outside, celebrating the safe return of the two Sandy pilots, but cried on the inside. Deep in our hearts we mourned the loss of five of the most valiant warriors our nation could produce. The loss of three F-105s and five crew members was huge, and over the years I have hoped and prayed that they were among those returned from the Hanoi Hilton at war's end.

I would like to express my thoughts concerning the aftermath of our tours in Vietnam. Most of us long ago recovered from any detrimental effects of the war and went on to successful careers. We have prospered, as has our country, since those difficult times. I know, however, that many veterans fell through the cracks of society, and we were told this was from trauma caused by horrifying experiences in combat. I cannot speak to that because it occurred mostly to those involved in the ground war who faced horrors along the jungle trails. They do have my deepest sympathy and respect for their sacrifices.

It seems that those of us involved in the air war in Vietnam returned home with far fewer emotional scars, almost certainly due to the fact that our experiences were so different from those of the servicemen on the ground. Our fighting was done from a fast-paced, emotionally packed but clean, air-conditioned cockpit, not a sweaty, leech-infested trail. Our world was mostly one of thrilling excitement, with a general feeling of security derived from that beautiful piece of aluminum wrapped around us. We felt, most of the time, snug and secure as we sat high above the fray. An aircrew member's life was filled with all good or all bad; there was not much in between. The threat was always there for a pilot, but we developed a necessary, though sometimes false, sense of security. Those unlucky aircrew men who were hit and went down found their world instantly shattered beyond any previous imagination. For everyone else, it was all in a day's work. It was mostly for these reasons that the morale of those involved in the air war was exceedingly high. We kept our spirits high through esprit de corps built up by daily association with buddies in similar circumstances.

What I've just written about was not a problem. The problem was what we read in the *Stars and Stripes* (the military newspaper published daily in Japan and flown to the war zone) and in other news sources from home. Many Vietnam veterans, including me, have never really gotten over the resentment we felt when we returned from the war to an unappreciative and often hostile American public. True, we had our supporters, but the rabble-rousers received most of the attention on the news and in print. I just hope and pray that we are never involved in a serious war for survival and have to leave it up to each individual to decide for himself if it is a "just" war and if he will serve. We know that during the Vietnam War, some young men conveniently found their way to Canada or England, smoking weed as their way of showing support for the American fighting man.

My reward on returning home was a free round of golf. My brother-in-law and I went to play at the Augusta Country Club in Staunton, Virginia, in 1968, and he told the club pro that I had just returned from Vietnam. The pro informed me, "You may play all you want today but your money is no good here. This is on the house." This was very kind—and the extent of the freebies. No tickertape parade awaited any of us.

To say that I haven't any deep affection for the Jane Fondas of this country is an understatement. Hanoi Jane, as we dubbed her, will forever stick in my craw. It was during my tour of duty that she traveled to the North Vietnamese capital and consorted with the enemy, giving them encouragement to fight on against our forces. The word *treason* comes to mind.

In my own way I have extracted my pint of revenge, although I fully realize that thousands like me can't put a financial dent in that woman. She, being no fool, fully understood when Communism was no longer cool and was happy to step aboard the Ted Turner capitalism train. It was good-bye Tommy and hello Teddy. Just the same, she can count her billions without thanking me for my support. The last movie I saw with her in it was *Cat Ballou*, which my wife and I saw in 1967, just before I left for Vietnam. We saw it mainly because of our fondness for Lee Marvin and Nat King Cole. My son is 43 now and my daughter is 40, and they have never seen a Jane Fonda movie in their life. None of us feel culturally deprived. We feel good!

To sum it all up, I love my country intensely and pray with every fiber of my body that America and the rest of the world will enjoy lasting, tranquil peace. I would love to live in a world where understanding and tolerance overcome bitterness and greed. I'm now growing older and tired of war. "Gonna lay down my burdens, down by the river side. Ain't gonna study war no more."

Long live the U.S.A.

Jim Fogg with his SAR C-130P at Tuy Hoa AB, Republic of Vietnam.
Note: Scissor-like yoke attachment for the Fulton Recovery System on the nose, 1967.

Jim Fogg at squadron headquarters for the 39th ARRS at Tuy Hoa, 1967.
Note: Small palms and sod grass planted during the base beautification project.

Jim Fogg is flying the C-130P in this photo of the first combat refueling of an HH-3 Jolly Green Giant rescue helicopter, 1967. Official Air Force photo.

15

MIDAIR

Wilcox (Will) J. Creeden, USAF, B-52D, July 7, 1967
{ Date of hire by Western Airlines: 2/24/1969 }

Will Creeden sitting in a T-33 trainer in pilot training, 1959.

This story involves a tragic midair collision and is an incredible tale of survival. It really speaks for itself, and I only want to add that it involves one of several coincidences related in this book. The chapter that follows this one is by Dick Dixon, who was not only a pilot training classmate of Will Creeden but also the Aircraft Commander of Red 3, the third B-52 in Creeden's flight of three aircraft. Also coincidentally, both Dick and Will were hired as pilots by Western Airlines, Dick in June 1968 and Will in February 1969. Since I was based in San Francisco and Will in Los Angeles, we never worked together, but I heard his story when he was relating some of the details in the Los Angeles crew lounge. When I contacted him years later and asked if he would write it for this book, he very graciously agreed. It is really an amazing story.

Will Creeden graduated as an Aviation Cadet with class 59-H in June 1959 and was assigned to SAC (Strategic Air Command) as a copilot in the B-47. He was assigned to the B-52 in 1964 as a copilot and served at Castle AFB and March AFB, both in California. Amazingly, after this horrific incident, Will resumed flying exactly one week later and completed his six-month temporary-duty assignment to Anderson AFB, Guam, in September 1967. He then flew the B-52 as an aircraft commander and separated from the Air Force in January 1969. He was hired by Western Airlines a month later and retired from Delta on June 1, 1997, as a Boeing 727 captain.

Now here is Will's story.

....

In 1965 I thought, "This war will be over and I'll never fly combat. I'll miss the opportunity I have trained for throughout my career."

I was a 28-year-old Air Force pilot, flying the B-52, attached to the 486th Bombardment Squadron, 22nd Bombardment Wing of the Strategic Air Command, based at March AFB, California. Our job was nuclear retaliation; we sat on alert ready to respond to a nuclear strike. The B-52 was designed for high-altitude bombing of hard targets with nuclear weapons. At that time, the war in Vietnam was a guerrilla war, with small units and no hard targets held by the enemy, so I didn't see how a nuclear bomber could be used.

Then someone thought of pattern bombing: having a formation of B-52s bomb with conventional bombs, striking and destroying a one to three mile area of South Vietnamese jungle. With good intelligence, we could destroy stored weapons, supplies, and the Vietcong's ability to wage war. The biggest risk was bombing the wrong place and killing the very people we wanted to defend. Therefore, the planes would be vectored in on most targets by ground radar, much like ground-controlled landing approaches. However, on the very first mission two B-52s collided in the air refueling area and were lost, getting the program off to a bad start (this occurred on June 18, 1965).

Our wing was not the first to go to Vietnam, and there was still a chance that I would never serve there, but in March 1967 my turn finally came. On St. Patrick's Day, our squadron landed at Anderson AFB, Guam, to replace the crews that had been there for six months. I was the copilot on the lead ship. Buses drove us through a tropical downpour to the concrete barracks, and on the balconies hundreds of men stood in the rain, cheering their replacements. Maybe the next six months weren't going to be so great.

The first three months went quickly. Weekly, each crew flew two missions, about 15 hours from briefing to landing, and most of the bombing was done at night. We flew the missions in a three-ship formation called a cell, and often there were several cells on a bombing mission. Most of the targets were in the DMZ (the demilitarized zone, between North and South Vietnam) in support of the Marines. Our bombing was an attempt to disrupt the flow of supplies on the Ho Chi Minh Trail, from the Mu Gia Pass in North Vietnam to Khe Sanh in the South. We occasionally bombed a Vietcong base camp in the Mekong Delta south of Saigon.

By July 1967 my crew had flown 40 missions, more than any other crew, and we were to receive an award as the best crew from the 3rd Air Division Commander, Major General William J. Crumm. General Crumm was in charge of all B-52 bombing missions and KC-135 aerial refueling in Southeast Asia. Because we were a select crew, my aircraft commander and radar navigator flew with other crews as instructors, so to keep my hours up, I volunteered to fly extra missions. On the afternoon of July 6, a scheduler assigned me a mission the following morning with a select crew from the 2nd Bomb Squadron, our sister squadron. Major John Suther was the aircraft commander and the mission was unusual: It was to be a daylight raid. Also, General Crumm, who had just been promoted and was soon to return to the States on a new assignment, would be flying with us.

At the 1 a.m. briefing I met an old pilot training classmate, Captain Dick Dixon. I had not seen him since 1963, when we were both flying B-47s at Topeka, Kansas. Newly arrived at Anderson, he was on his first mission, and I was envious because he was an aircraft commander with his own crew. The other wingman was

Captain George Westbrook, with a new crew from Columbus, Mississippi. Our target was a Vietcong base camp in the Mekong Delta. Because it was a daylight strike, we would fly a visual formation and the bomb run would be directed by ground radar.

Six planes lifted off from Anderson AFB at 3 a.m. on July 7; the rain was coming down in sheets. The takeoff was always hazardous because the B-52D model was old and underpowered. Our formation consisted of two cells of three planes each, with my crew in the lead as Red 1. We flew in a trail formation with Red 2 and 3 spaced two miles behind and 2,000 feet higher (Red 2 at two miles and 2,000 feet; Red 3 at four miles and 4,000 feet above lead). The second cell followed 40 miles behind. The six-hour flight to the target was routine, with the only excitement being the air refueling near the Philippines.

For the bomb run we would visually move into a formation with our wingmen flying just 15 feet off each wing. The formation was exacting, physically fatiguing, and seldom used. We were to start forming up about 30 minutes away from the target and be in formation for the last 10 minutes of the bomb run.

We all knew our duties. My aircraft commander, Major John Suther, would fly the airplane while I talked to the ground radar controller on the radio. Major Paul Avolese, our radar navigator, would arm and release the bombs. Captain William Gabel, our navigator, would monitor our position. Captain David Bittenbender, our electronic warfare officer, would monitor the emergency frequencies for last-minute withholds (mission cancellation) or emergencies. Sergeant Lynn Chase, our gunner, would watch the formation from his isolated position in the tail and notify us of trouble. General Crumm would sit behind and between the pilots on the fold-down jump seat and listen to the radios.

As the sun came up behind us, John signaled the wingmen to join in close formation. We were approaching Point X-ray, the beginning point of the bomb run. As I looked toward the target area, I saw a low cloud deck that started at 5,000 feet. Out my right side window I saw Red 2 moving into position. Our navigator reported Point X-ray and asked for a right turn to the northeast. John began the turn and I contacted the ground radar controller. I could see that Captain

Westbrook in Red 2 was having a hard time maintaining position, and I could see his aileron move as he tried to stay in place. He was too close, and I thought his left wing was overlapping our right wing. At this point the ground controller called, "Red 1, your beacon (transponder for radar position) is inoperative. Suggest Red 2 take lead." I replied "Understand you want Red 2 to take lead." As I looked out to the right, Red 2 started to pull off to the right; suddenly his airplane rolled into a hard bank back to the left. Alarmed, I keyed the interphone and told John, "Number two is coming in on us! Roll out!" Our aircraft was still in a right turn at that point.

John smoothly rolled our wings level and I watched Red 2 just miss our right wing and move quickly under us, still in a left bank. As I released the interphone switch, I heard part of a transmission to us from Red 2. Most of the transmission had been blocked during my call to John, and because I had not heard what Red 2 transmitted, I radioed to the entire cell, "Red 1 turning to a heading of 020." My intention was to get Red 2 back on our right-hand side and give him our new heading.

At the same time, John shouted, "Oh my God!"

When I looked over at him, I saw a B-52 filling his side window, coming up from below.

The collision occurred a heartbeat later. The ripping, grinding, tearing lasted an eternity. I tried to grab the controls but it was like trying to grab a speeding freight train. All the forces from the crippled airplane were transmitted back through the cables to the control column. My hand was slammed into the right side panel and the entire airplane flipped and dove to the left. The right wing and tail section rotated over the nose. The cockpit was filled with flying clipboards, pencils, and trash and, as the airplane decompressed, a smoky mist filled the cockpit. I was amazed at how clear my mind was, focused on one goal: survival.

The G-forces from the spinning forced my head down into my lap and all I could see was different shades of gray as the airplane spun around the horizon. I couldn't move when I tried to reach the ejection handle in my armrest. As the airplane rotated, I was immobile for most of the spin but, for a brief second, the G-forces let up and I grabbed the handle on the second spin. I was able to jettison the hatch above me and arm a lever in my armrest, but before I could squeeze the lever that would fire me out, the G-forces pushed me back to the left and I couldn't hold on. On the third rotation I lunged at the handle and squeezed the trigger.

I knew I was in the wrong position to eject; my right arm was going to be outside the ejection envelope and my head would be on my lap. To eject properly I should have been sitting up straight with my arms and legs in position to clear the small hatch. However, because of my small size, I felt my head would clear the hatch, though my right arm would not.

As the shell in my ejection seat fired, my head hit my left knee and the G-forces kept me pinned until I hit the slipstream. The airplane was traveling at about 500 mph just prior to the collision but I have no idea how fast the wreckage was going when I left. The wind threw me back into my seat and ripped off my helmet and oxygen mask.

Through closed eyelids, I saw a giant ball of fire and I was going right up into it. I thought, "I'll hold my breath so I won't breathe in the flames." My left hand reached up and patted out the flames in my hair above my left ear, and then I fell out of the fireball and tumbled through the air. My training reminded me that if I would just spread-eagle, I would stabilize the tumbling. I stretched out and ended up face down, spinning slowly to the right. I still had my right arm and hand, but they were cut and possibly broken.

Since the collision, everything had moved in slow motion, and at this time it became a problem; I had no idea how long I had spent in the airplane. I couldn't calculate my altitude because I was still in a slow spin and couldn't focus on the cloud deck below. If I was still above 14,000 feet, my parachute would deploy automatically at 14,000 feet. If I had fallen below 14,000 feet, my parachute would not open automatically. I could deploy it manually with the risk of hypoxia (loss of consciousness from lack of oxygen) if my altitude was far above the 14,000 foot level. I decided to risk it and open the chute. To do so, I needed to use my damaged right hand, so I reached over and got a grip on the T handle and pulled. My parachute deployed more slowly and with less opening shock than I expected.

For the first time I was able to focus on the world around me. I was higher than I had estimated, probably above 20,000 feet.

Unrecognizable pieces of airplane fell around me; sheets of metal were dropping like gigantic leaves. Below me, other chutes began to open, and I said to myself, "There are other survivors. I don't know who made it." I thought I was the only one from my airplane because it had exploded. I counted six parachutes and one that looked like a drag chute (used to slow the aircraft on landing roll) as I fell for approximately 15 minutes. Then I began to plan my landing. The low clouds would conceal me from anyone on the ground until just before I landed, and I might have a little time to hide or escape. Although we'd been flying over South Vietnam, we were so close to the target that I had to assume anyone I would see was the enemy.

I pulled the handle on my seat pack to deploy my survival gear. The life raft fell out, inflated, and then started to deflate—it must have had a leak. Below me, two of the other survivors were just entering the clouds, and it looked like I would land close to them. As I approached the clouds, I was shocked at how fast I was falling. I passed through the cloud deck very quickly and below was water, brown and muddy. I was drifting beyond the brown water toward the blue ocean so I inflated my Mae West life vest in preparation for a water landing. I reached up for the parachute canopy releases and decided to wait until my raft hit the first wave to open them.

When my raft hit, I opened the releases and pulled the rings to release the parachute canopy. I hit the water, went under, and then popped to the surface. My raft was attached to my leg and I pulled it toward me but it was only half inflated. I swam around it until I could find the oral inflation tube, but there was no valve cover so I blew and inflated the raft, held my thumb over the end, and climbed in. How could I stop the leak? I looked in the storage pocket for the oral tube, found the valve cover, and jammed it on the end of the tube. It held and the leak stopped.

I sat back in my raft. I was alive, and even with the pain and anxiety, I was elated. The waves were at least 10 feet high, occasionally breaking over the raft and filling it with water. Would I capsize? I secured the survival gear to the raft and rechecked that the raft was still attached to me. I washed off my right hand and arm in the water in the raft. I did not want the blood in the ocean because it would attract sharks. My right forearm had deep puncture wounds and my right hand was swollen double and felt broken. Otherwise, I was OK.

I took out the radio from my survival gear but when I turned it on I received only an emergency beacon. I remember thinking, "Someone didn't turn off the emergency beacon activated by his parachute." It never occurred to me that it was my own.

Within minutes, fighter jets flew low over me, and when the two other survivors nearby set off orange smoke flares, the jets dipped their wings in response. Help was on the way. I was within a mile or so of the other survivors, but because of the waves and distance, I could not see them.

The clouds had given way to blue skies when two helicopters appeared. One came very close to me but continued on to the survivors nearby. I watched as they lowered the sling to the first survivor, and after he put it around himself the helicopter started to climb. When he was 100 to 200 feet off the water he fell. Perhaps he was wounded and could not hold on. I thought that the fall had probably killed him and I watched to see if anyone jumped in after him, but no one did.

I watched as they picked up two other survivors and headed for shore. What if they hadn't seen me? Quickly I set off a smoke flare and they turned toward me. I had decided that when the helicopter came for me I would point to my injured hand and arm and shake my head no. But when the sling was lowered, I was ready. The sling was like a rigid horse collar and it was too big for me. If I put my hands together, it hung down behind my back. If I rested my back on the bottom then I couldn't get my hands together at the top.

The helicopter was hovering only about 25 feet above me and I felt I could hold on with my left hand long enough to be lifted. So I closed my eyes (I'm afraid of heights), grabbed hold, and held on. As my raft cleared the water, I realized it was a mistake to have left my raft attached to my leg. The raft caught the downwash of the rotor blades and pulled down like a reverse parachute. My hands slipped; I opened my eyes so I could see if I fell....

Now I was about 200 to 300 feet above the water and no longer below the helicopter. I was being trolled behind like a piece of bait and I had to hang on because the fall would probably kill me. I was slowly being cranked up to the open hatchway. The crew chief reached out and grabbed me, but the weight of the raft pulled me out again. He grabbed me a second time, cut the lanyard to the raft, and as the raft fell away he pulled me into the cabin.

As I looked around I saw three crew members, two from Red 2 and my pilot, John Suther. I said, "John, how did you get out? I thought I was the only one to survive from our airplane." John answered, "As I ejected, the plane blew up and I thought *I* was the only survivor."

The flight to Saigon was a blur. We landed at a small Army base in the Delta to get Captain Thompson, the copilot of Red 2, immediate medical help. There we learned that our gunner, Sergeant Lynn Chase, had been rescued, alive but badly burned. Also rescued was the aircraft commander of Red 2, Captain Westbrook, who was also badly injured.

As John and I talked about the accident, I found out for the first time that only our two airplanes were involved. Luckily, my friend Dick Dixon in Red 3 had somehow avoided this whole mess.

At the hospital in Saigon I received a tetanus shot, x-rays, and stitches in my arm. I felt as if I had been beaten with a hammer; every part of my body hurt. In the next bed was Captain Endo, the ECM officer from Red 2. When I told him about seeing someone drop from the helicopter sling he exclaimed, "Tell me about it. That was me." I asked him if it hurt. He said, "You got that right. But the good thing was I had my life raft attached. I went under only 25 feet when it jerked me back to the surface."

After a few hours in the hospital, we were offered a flight back to Guam. When I boarded the transport, I saw Captain Gabel, our navigator. Both John and I could hardly believe it—four survivors from our airplane—unbelievable!

The investigation took a week. As best as I can recall, this is what happened. As Red 2 joined up, Captain Westbrook had a problem holding formation. The airplane wanted to turn right and the pilot was using a lot of control force to keep the left wing down. He trimmed left wing down and even asked his copilot to check the fuel balance. The fuel tanks were in the wings, and if they were not properly balanced that could have been the cause of the problem. The tendency for the airplane to turn to the right also could have been caused if he had actually overlapped his left wing over our right wing.

When the ground radar asked for Red 2 to take the lead, Captain Westbrook started to move his airplane slowly out to the right. He knew that we would have only a short time to change lead if we were going to be in a position to make the bomb run. From my position I could not tell if his wing overlapped ours; with a wingspan of more than 150 feet, it was hard to see. As his wing cleared the top of ours, all that force and trim he had been holding took effect and rolled him sharply into us. When we rolled out of our turn into him, his plane slid down and under us. At this time I believe he was trying to recover his airplane from an unusual position and probably never saw our plane again. It didn't matter, because once he was under us there was no way a collision could have been avoided. The air pressures between the airplanes would suck them into each other regardless of control forces.

Investigation revealed that the Boeing Company had warned the Air Force not to fly these airplanes in a wing formation closer than 150 feet wingtip separation. About a month before our accident they'd had a training accident in the States, when the #2 ship in a visual formation rolled hard to the left, going beneath and a little behind the lead ship. When they were sucked up they collided, although only minor damage resulted to the wingtip of the lead and some part of the #2 ship.

John Suther said that when we hit, our left wing folded and broke at the wing root. While we were tumbling after the collision, he was able to brace himself in his seat and move his hands down to the ejection levers. As he ejected he saw the airplane explode.

Captain Gabel, our navigator, attempted to eject right after the collision. His seat was a downward ejection model with a handle between his knees. It required him to pull the handle twice, once to blow a hatch beneath him out and another to eject himself. He pulled once and the hatch fired. When he pulled a second time, nothing happened, and shortly after that, because he did not have his oxygen mask on, he lost consciousness. When he regained consciousness, he saw blue water through the open hatch beneath him, so he unfastened his lap belt and jumped through the hole. He immediately deployed his parachute and hit the water within seconds. Investigators later speculated that he had fallen almost three minutes in that piece of the airplane. His last sight of Major Avolese was of him sitting in his seat without his oxygen mask on and his head rolling on his shoulders as if his neck was broken.

Our gunner, Sergeant Lynn Chase, said he had gotten out right away. The gunner's compartment was back in the tail of the plane and didn't have an ejection seat. Lynn had to pull a handle and the whole back end fell away. Next he unfastened his seat belt and jumped out. Because the plane was still moving forward, all the flames and heat from the explosion went aft, and Lynn was badly burned. (Sergeant Chase wrote an account of his ejection that is included at the end of this story.)

I can only speculate about the other two crew members. General Crumm was sitting between and in back of John and me, on a fold-down instructor's seat that had no ejection capability. When I last saw him, he had his parachute and oxygen mask on, and his only possible escape would have been through either of the holes that John and I left after we ejected. Captain Bittenbender sat about 25 feet aft of the pilots in an upward ejection seat. No debris was ever found to give us a clue as to what happened to him.

My life raft was found to have a type of glue on the oral inflation tube that degraded in the tropical climate. When I inflated it at such a high altitude, it popped the valve right out.

On Red 2, which had a six-man crew, Captain George Westbrook and his copilot, Captain Harold Thompson, survived, along with the ECM officer, Captain Toki Endo. The navigation team of Captain Charles Blankenship and First Lieutenant George Jones were not found. The gunner, Master Sergeant Olen McLaughlin, positioned about where the impact occurred, was also missing.

I am still amazed that seven men survived. Although I didn't see a final copy of the report, I felt confident that most of the blame would go to the people who thought up that close formation. We should never have flown those B-52s so close together. We never did again.

General Crumm was the highest-ranking officer to be killed in the Vietnam War. He had entered the Army Air Corps in 1943 and had been a B-17 pilot in the European theater in World War II.

As a prologue, in 1995 a newspaper reported that a Vietnamese fisherman had recovered some B-52 parts from a wreck in the South China Sea near the mouth of the Mekong River. I knew it must have been from our planes, and I wrote to the newspaper to see if I could be of any help or get any more information. I received no reply.

Then, just weeks after I started writing this account, in July 1997, I received a call from someone who said his name was Eric Bittenbender. I said, "I know who you are! Your dad was with me in a crash in Vietnam in July 1967." He said that was right. He had been meeting with survivors and would like to meet with me. Luckily for both of us, he also lived in Seattle, so we were able to get together easily. He had been collecting reports about the accident and much of the information Eric had was new to me. I found it fascinating. The Vietnamese fisherman not only had parts of the airplane but also dived on the wreck and found some human remains, identified as Captain Blankenship and Lieutenant Jones, navigators of Red 2. The fisherman also reported seeing more wreckage and more remains.

The U.S. Navy also dived at the site but found only wreckage and no human remains. The divers quit because weather conditions became hazardous. I hope to encourage more investigation of this site with the hope of bringing home Eric's dad and the others who were left behind.

....

Incredibly, after this horrific collision, Will returned to Guam and began flying again, finishing his copilot tour and then returning to March AFB, California. At March he was upgraded to aircraft commander, was given his own crew, and was selected to go back to Guam on a short, three-month tour, during which he flew 21 bombing missions. He put in his paperwork to separate from the Air Force and was immediately sent back for a six-month tour, this time flying out of Utapao RTAB (Royal Thai Air Base) in Thailand, where he flew an additional 55 missions. On the three-month tour to Guam, Will had another harrowing experience that was written up for a

DFC (Distinguished Flying Cross), but sadly it was not awarded due to a paperwork mix-up. On that particular mission he was departing from Kadena AFB on Okinawa, a far more populated island than Guam.

I will reproduce that letter of recommendation here, and add it to my earlier comments on the totally arbitrary nature of the awards and decorations that were processed by different units and the different services during the war.

Recommend the DFC for the following crew members:
Crew E-74
Captain Wilcox J. Creeden, Aircraft Commander
1/Lt. Donald A. Becker, Pilot
Captain Larry E. Peterson, Radar Navigator
Captain James C. Akers, Navigator
Captain Darryl W. Smith, ECM (electronic countermeasures officer)
Tech/Sergeant Paul L. Clark, Gunner

May 1, 1968, while on takeoff for an Arc Light Mission (the B-52 bombing missions were code named Arc Light) this B-52 crew found itself in extreme danger. Just after liftoff, engines #5 and #6 blew up. T/Sgt. Clark reported flames all the way past the tail of the aircraft. While Capt. Creeden fought for control, Lt. Becker began emergency procedures to fight the fire. With full rudder and all other engines at maximum power and a 10 degree left bank, Capt. Creeden was able to level off at 800 feet. Because of a full bomb load and full fuel tanks (52,500 lb. bomb load and 240,000 lb. fuel load), the airplane would not climb. At this low altitude, ejection was not an option. They were over a populated area so jettison of the bombs would have resulted in certain casualties. The fire in the #3 pod (there were eight engines on the B-52 in four pods of two engines each) was located only 15 feet from an external bomb rack and 10 feet below the #3 main fuel tank. Lt. Becker was able to reroute fuel from the fire area and it slowly started to burn itself out. T/Sgt. Clark advised Capt. Creeden of how the fire looked from his tail compartment. Capt. Smith maintained contact with the Command Post and kept them informed of the situation. Capt. Peterson and Capt. Ackers tracked their position over the island and gave directions to the nearest unpopulated area to dump the bombs. The command, "prepare for bailout," was given. With the fire almost out and approaching a safe area to jettison the bombs, Capt. Creeden had the crew check their emergency equipment and stay in their seats. Still below the minimum safe altitude for ejection, the plan was to be ready to eject in case of loss of another engine or any other degradation of the situation. An attempt would be made to roll the airplane just prior to ejection to aid the downward ejection seats. After arriving over the ocean on the other side of the island, the procedures were started to safely jettison the bombs. Capt. Peterson noted that there were numerous vessels in the area, so the decision was made to delay until the aircraft arrived at a safe area. While proceeding to the safe area, Capt. Creeden was able to climb slowly above the minimum safe bailout altitude. After consulting the Command Post, a decision to maintain configuration was made. Capt. Creeden, feeling that the main wing spar might have been damaged, decided that any sudden weight change, like the salvo of the bombs, might cause a greater problem. The decision was made to maintain an altitude above minimum bailout altitude over the safe area until the fuel weight would allow a landing. A successful landing was made about five hours after takeoff.

Capt. Creeden was told that the wing spar had been damaged and that the airplane would only be used for spare parts, never to fly again. Will Creeden was told by the commander of the 4233rd Bomb Wing that he and his crew would receive the DFC. These awards were never received.

I will end with the following comments made by Sergeant Lynn Chase, the gunner on Red 1, in a short story he wrote titled "Vietnam Veteran's Stories."

On a warm rainy night on the island of Guam, six aircraft awaited the order to launch. Aircraft Commander Major John A. Suther of the 22nd Bomb Wing, flying in cell position Red One, was in charge of the mission. Having flown 34 previous combat missions, he was designated a well-qualified aircraft commander. Other members of Major Suther's crew (Crew E-06) were: copilot, Captain Wilcox J. Creeden; radar-navigator, Major Paul A. Avolese; navigator, Lt. William R. Gable; electronic warfare officer, Captain David F. Bittenbender; and tail gunner Sgt. Lynn O. Chase. Also flying as an observer for this mission was Major General William J. Crumm, Commander 3rd Air Division. With the execution order to launch, all six aircraft were soon airborne and en route to their target. It was 0303 hours, July 7, 1967.

Jumping ahead:

As the two aircraft came out of the turn they were both trying to occupy the same airspace. Red Two's fuselage contacted Red One's left wing between the external wing tank and the number one engine pod. The outboard wing section of Red One broke off as it made contact, severing the tail of Red Two. Explosion and fire ensued, most probably initiated by the rupture of the wing fuel tanks on Red One. Red One was immediately engulfed in flames and went into a left spiral dive while Red Two pitched into an immediate severe dive.

At the moment of contact it was immediately apparent what had happened. My pilot, Major Suther, told me later that he had given the order to bailout but I never heard this order nor did I need to. The tremendous explosion and heat were all that one needed to experience to know that it was time to leave. It was 0737 hours, July 7, 1967. I had been flying for about two years at the time of this accident and had become quite comfortable back in my gunner's compartment, away from the rest of my crew. Anyone who has been a tail gunner on a B-52 knows this feeling of being king of all he surveys. Usually I flew in a very relaxed mode, unstrapped from my parachute and not having my oxygen mask attached. This day was different. The erratic flying of Red Two had been a concern to me and I was strapped in and cinched up as tight as I had been since gunnery school. When we hit, my first reaction was to reach out with my right hand and grab hold of a strap to pull myself forward. When I did this the heat was so intense that the skin on my right arm peeled off. Then I reached for the lever with my left hand that would eject the turret so that I could jump out. This resulted in the skin from my left arm peeling off. I had always flown with my sleeves rolled up—I have often thought of myself as sitting inside a tin can in a bonfire.

The turret section ejected just the way it was supposed to and away I went into the open sky.

Jumping ahead again, after the rescue:

After spending two days at Vung Tau I was transferred to the naval hospital on the island of Guam. I spent 30 days in isolation in the naval hospital and then was flown home to March AFB in Riverside, California. Two months later my unit rotated back home and I was assigned to another crew and began flying again.

Twenty-four years after the collision I met Eric Bittenbender, who was five months old when his father died. Through Eric, my wife Clara and I have established relationships with Marilyn Avolese and Eric's mother Kathleen.

Will Creeden

16

MIDAIR (PART II)

Dick Dixon, USAF, B-52D, July 7, 1967
{ Date of hire by Western Airlines: 6/3/1968 }

Dick Dixon, Western Airlines Logbook, 1986.

This is a continuation of Will Creeden's story about one of the most shocking aircraft accidents of the Vietnam War, not only because of the loss of two aircraft and five crew members, but also for the loss of General William J. Crumm, the highest-ranking officer to be killed in the war. As I stated in the previous chapter, amazingly, there was an eyewitness to this midair collision, and it was Dick Dixon, aircraft commander of Red 3, which was the surviving B-52 in the three-ship formation. The fact that Will and Dick not only knew each other from pilot training but both ended up as pilots for Western Airlines, is one of the most incredible coincidences that I discovered in my research for this book.

I had flown with Dick when I was based in Los Angeles in the early 1990s as a first officer on the Boeing 727 when he was a captain. He was very quiet and very serious. He was what Western and Delta called a line-check airman, a check pilot who gave annual check rides, instruction, and checks to pilots moving into a new position, either as first officer or captain. Dick was not one to socialize on layovers, and as I reflect on the times I flew with him, I never really engaged him in personal conversation and never knew of his involvement in this incident. As a matter of fact, I didn't even know that he had been a military pilot, as he never talked about his flying background.

When Will sent me the first draft of his story for this book, he asked if I had spoken to Dick Dixon. He told me the connection between the two of them, and I was floored. I contacted Dick right away, but he put me off. He told me it was such a horrible accident, with loss of life and a subsequent investigation by the Air Force, that he didn't want to put anything in writing that might cast aspersions on the crew members involved or say anything that could possibly reflect poorly on the deceased. Then Dick retired in January 1996 and I lost track of him. Will retired in May 1997 and we stayed in touch periodically as he asked about my progress with the book. I got a letter from Will in December 1998 with a general greeting and then the following: "I promise to call Dick Dixon and get him to contact you. I think he is instructing in the Delta 737 flight simulator in Salt Lake City." Soon thereafter, in January 1999, I received a two-page letter from Dick that was his story. It came without a cover letter and I have not heard from him since, making it obvious that he wrote to me only because Will prevailed on him to do so.

It is obvious that Dick remembered everything, and he added a lot of detail that made the accident sound all the more dreadful. The three B-52s had just refueled near the Philippines before turning toward Vietnam for their bomb run, and each airplane had close to 240,000 pounds of fuel onboard. Each was loaded with 52,500 pounds of bombs: 105 500 pound bombs carried both internally in the bomb bay and externally on pylons under the wings. There are a couple of minor differences in Will's and Dick's recollections, but the main story seems indelibly etched in both their minds. Here is Dick Dixon's letter.

....

On July 7, 1967, I was on a bomb run over Vietnam when there was a midair collision involving three B-52s. We had taken off from Anderson AFB, Guam, and had flown six hours to the target. We had air refueled in the vicinity of the Philippines and took on 90,000 pounds to bring us up to the 240,000 pounds of fuel we'd had at takeoff.

This was my second combat mission and my first mission in command, after being signed off by a check pilot to fly combat. I had been an aircraft commander in the B-47 for five years before switching to the B-52. After qualifying as a B-52 aircraft commander, I had been placed on a crew that had recently returned from combat. We had been assigned to a six-month tour at Anderson and my crew was not too happy about returning to combat so soon. But the crew was professional and competent and morale was good.

Because the plan was to fly close formation in a cell of three airplanes, we had been given one training flight in close-formation flying. The separation was nose to tail, and laterally, wingtip to wingtip. The wingspan of the B-52 was 185 feet while the fuselage was 165 feet long. We could not see the wingtips from the cockpit windows.

My position was number three in the first cell. There were 21 aircraft in cells of three, the cells separated by 40-mile intervals. Each cell flew in trail (following each other in a line) until near the target and then formed into the V formation. I was call sign Red 3, on the left side. We were to perform a ground-radar-directed bomb run. Number one, Red 1, was to be identified by ground radar controllers with a transponder, but it was inoperative, and Red 2, who was on the right side, was told to move forward to assume the lead.

As Red 2 moved forward, I moved aft and to the left to give them extra maneuvering room. At this point I saw the collision and my mind would not accept what I saw. I reported that Red 2 moved forward and contacted Red 1, but later I found out what actually had happened. Red 2 had been tucked in so close to Red 1 that the wings had overlapped, and the pilot of Red 2 had trimmed out the wing wash pressure with aileron trim. When the plane moved out and forward, his left wing dipped and he went under and to the left of

Red 1. Red 1 dipped his wing to the left and chopped off the tail of Red 2.

This took place above 30,000 feet. My first thought was to perform a barrel roll to the left to escape but I was very heavy. I had 105 bombs on board, each weighing 500 pounds, and our fuel tanks were full. In that moment of time I knew I could not survive such a maneuver so I flew through the fireball and wreckage at a 45 degree bank angle.

My radar navigator made a position report. The ground controller asked if we heard any ELTs (emergency locator transmitters, set off by the opening of parachutes). I reported that I heard six or seven. Sure enough, the helicopters picked up seven survivors in the water 25 miles offshore from Saigon.

My radar navigator directed us to an alternate target since we were off course for the primary target. The six-hour flight back to Guam seemed very long. Every unusual sound and movement filled us with concern because of the heavy concussion we had experienced.

My friend Will Creeden, who was my classmate in pilot training many years prior, was in Red 1. A general was also in Red 1, and it was to have been his last mission. Sadly enough, it was.

Image on the cover of "Combat Crew" magazine, Nov. 1967, showing the view Dick Dixon would have had from aircraft #3 in the cell of three B-52 aircraft.

17

IRON HAND

Bob Wood, USN, A-4E, A-4F, 2 cruises: 1966 – 1969
{ Date of hire by Western Airlines: 5/9/1969 }

Bob Wood on the flight deck of the USS Ticonderoga with a fully loaded A-4E, 1967.

During the period from November 1966 to January 1969, Bob Wood was deployed on two cruises to Vietnam on the aircraft carrier USS Ticonderoga. The Ticonderoga was a World War II–vintage, Essex Class carrier, complete with a wooden flight deck. Bob was a pilot attached to VA-192, the Golden Dragons, flying the A-4E. As a matter of interest, his brother Don was also an A-4 pilot in the Navy and went on two cruises whose time frames were the mirror-opposite of Bob's, so their parents had at least one of them in harm's way for three years. (Don returned safely and flew for American Airlines for nearly 30 years, retiring as a Boeing 767 Captain.)

Bob's first cruise began in November 1966 and took place during the heavy bombing of North Vietnam known as Rolling Thunder. This was a time of intense daily combat missions, with periodic bombing halts declared from Washington. The bombing halts were aimed at getting the North Vietnamese to the bargaining table but only served as a reprieve that allowed them to improve and refine their already formidable air defenses.

VA-192 deployed with 11 airplanes and went through more than 20 on Bob's first cruise. Combat losses and accidents required a fairly steady stream of replacement aircraft. The odds of being rescued in the event of a bailout were very good, though, and morale was high. From all the aircraft losses suffered by VA-192, only one pilot was killed—Lieutenant Commander Michael J. Estocin, killed in an action over Haiphong, North Vietnam, on April 26, 1967, for which he was awarded a posthumous Medal of Honor. Two other fliers were captured and became prisoners of war.

In flying more than 270 combat missions in the A-4, Bob was involved in everything from Alpha Strikes, road reconnaissance (known as road recce), and air refueling missions where an A-4 flew as a tanker, to Iron Hand missions. Iron Hand was the Navy's version of the Air Force Wild Weasel program, initiated after the Shrike missile was developed as a response to the increasing SAM (surface-to-air missile) threat. The Shrike was designed to intercept and fly back down the radar beam sent out by the SAM radar site when it locked onto a target. Since that target was you, there was a fair amount of stress as the Shrike was fired and the SAM, which often had been launched, was evaded.

Bob was part of the first Iron Hand mission flown by the Navy in August 1967. There were no training missions, and although it was a totally new concept, later improved in combat, the Shrike aircraft were launched that day to lead a large Alpha Strike and, in theory, take out the SAM threat in advance of the Alpha Strike bombers reaching the target area. As Bob relates the story, you will see that in this case, the plan went awry. He also had a very exciting flight when he got involved in a rescue mission for a downed pilot while flying an A-4 that was serving as an air refueling tanker.

Bob has been most supportive throughout this project, and he has my eternal gratitude. I will make a final comment at the end of his account.

....

My tour in the Navy, from February 1964 to January 1969, included two West Pac (Western Pacific) cruises on the USS *Ticonderoga*,

CVA-14. The *Tico* was a World War II carrier that was retrofitted with an angled deck. She still had her wooden deck and carried a brass plaque on the island that told how she had survived several kamikaze hits at the end of World War II. My squadron was VA-192, the world-famous Golden Dragons. We flew the A-4E Skyhawk on my first cruise and then the latest model of the Skyhawk, the A-4F, on my second cruise.

We flew strikes into North Vietnam from Yankee Station, an area off the coast of North Vietnam in the Tonkin Gulf. Our mission was to try to keep the North Vietnamese from moving men and supplies into South Vietnam. The story that I have chosen to tell took place during my first cruise and is a good example of how sometimes the best-laid plans don't always work out.

While we were on Yankee Station a new weapon system was developed for the Navy called the Shrike missile. The Shrike was an anti-SAM weapon designed to track and fly down the same radar signal that the enemy was using to guide the SAM and then blow up the radar van that was emitting the guidance signal. Our squadron was the first to use this missile for the Navy, and we were given the task of developing the tactics used to deploy it. The Shrike would require the pilot firing the missile to spend a lot of time with his head in the cockpit, monitoring his ECM (electronic counter measures) receiver in order to turn toward the radar signal and line up a couple of needles on his instruments. This was necessary to aim the missile correctly before he pulled up the nose of his aircraft to fire it. We knew that the Shrike aircraft would need an escort to help watch for incoming missiles, AAA (anti-aircraft artillery), or enemy aircraft that the pilot would need to evade. Our squadron decided to escort this Shrike aircraft with another A-4.

My story begins on that first mission. I was not even on the schedule to fly on this particular afternoon. The *Tico* was a very hot ship since only a few areas were air-conditioned and it was summer in Southeast Asia. My stateroom was two decks below the hangar deck and therefore *extremely* hot. I had decided to go up to the squadron ready room and read a book as it was one of those few air-conditioned spaces on the ship. I was there reading when the pilots who were flying this mission got back from their A/I (air intelligence) briefing. This was an Alpha Strike, which is a large strike force of about 40 aircraft including fighters, bombers, and support airplanes, and all the pilots going on the mission had been together for the A/I briefing. This briefing consisted of what your target was, what to expect in the area as to enemy defenses, where the SAM sites were expected to be, how the strike force would fly into the target area and how it would fly out, what to do if your aircraft should take a hit, and all those really nice things to know when you are on one of these big strikes. Then the individual squadrons went back to their ready rooms to continue briefing on how they would conduct their own smaller parts of the strike. This brief included things like who would be the section leaders and who would be the wingmen, who would hit what part of the target the squadron had been assigned, and in this case, how the Shrike planes and their escorts were to conduct their part of the mission.

Since this was the first Iron Hand mission (the name given to the Shrike mission by the Navy), I was curious about how they were going to fly the hop, and I was eavesdropping on their briefing. They talked about how the Shrike aircraft would be leading the entire strike force into the target area and how they would be trying to suppress the SAMs as they came up at the strike group. They also talked about how the escorts would fly cover around the Shrike planes while the pilots were performing this task.

Each Shrike aircraft was loaded with four Shrike missiles and one centerline fuel tank. This was a very aerodynamically clean load. The escort aircraft was loaded with one centerline tank, two Zuni rocket pods (containing four five-inch Zuni rockets in each pod), and two 2.75-inch rocket pods (containing 19 2.75-inch rockets in each pod). None of the rocket pods had nose cones on them to make them a little more aerodynamic, so this was a very aerodynamically dirty load.

After the brief was completed it was time to man up. Everyone got into their flight gear in the rear of the ready room and went up to the flight deck to man their aircraft. Now the ready room was quiet again, with only the duty officer and me remaining there, so I went back to reading my book. After a few minutes the silence in the ready room was broken by the squawk box on the duty officer's desk. They were calling down from the flight deck to say they didn't have a pilot to man the spare Shrike escort aircraft. The duty officer looked straight at me. I immediately began whining about how I didn't go to the A/I briefing and I didn't even know what the target was, much less how they were going to get into and out of the target area. But I knew what he was going to say next. He was going remind me that it was only the spare, and "they never have to launch the spare." I did eventually let him talk me into it so I put my book down, climbed into my flight gear, and went up to the flight deck to man the spare. I did my preflight checks and strapped into my airplane. Then I got settled down to watch the launch. I was always fascinated with the production of a launch from the flight deck of a carrier. It is a masterpiece of coordination, discipline, and timing and goes off just like clockwork.

My plane-captain was standing beside my aircraft and got my attention by spinning his two fingers in the air, which meant he was ready for me to start my engine. I knew this had to be a mistake because I was only the spare, and "they never have to launch the spare." I confidently gave him the hand signal that I was just a spare and shook my head meaning that I wasn't supposed to launch and didn't need to start my engine. This time he nodded his head and again gave me the signal to start my engine. We went back and forth like this a couple more times until I decided I would settle this dispute once and for all. I was going to call the Air Boss on the radio. The Boss runs the launch from his position up in the island of the ship overlooking the flight deck. I called him and explained that my plane-captain wanted me to start up and that I was only the spare. The Boss very quickly informed me that the "go" escort had gone down and I was to launch.

Normally the launch sequence went something like this. The first to be launched were the tanker aircraft, followed by the support aircraft, then the fighters, and finally the bombers. But today, since I was positioned on the deck as a spare, I was actually the first airplane off the deck. This was great! I didn't even know where I was supposed to rendezvous with the rest of the Shrike aircraft. There were four of them, and each had an escort, so I decided to just circle over the ship until I saw one of them launch and then wait to see which Shrike plane didn't have an escort. I would join him and go from there. Actually, this part of the plan did work out OK, and after the entire strike group got together, we headed out for the target with the four Shrike aircraft and their four escorts leading the pack.

As we approached feet dry (nearing land), the strike leader called for everyone to power up to increase our speed so that when we went across the beach we would be up to required speed. It didn't take long to figure out that something wasn't working out as planned. First, all the Shrike aircraft quickly pulled away from their escorts because they were so much more aerodynamically clean than we were with those flat-ended rocket pods. Next came the fighters, and then came the entire strike group. Even the bombers were able to fly faster than we were. We escorts felt like we were going backwards. We had our power tube locked (for maximum power), and everyone was continuing to pull away. I can still see them all, the entire strike group going out of sight ahead of us. I wasn't feeling very good about what was happening because, as you remember, I didn't know how we were going to get in to the target or even what the target was. I decided that the best thing for me to do was just to hang in there with the other escorts.

To reach the target—whatever it was planned to be—we went in quite a bit south of Hanoi and continued west until we were over a mountain ridge. Then we turned north and flew until we were abeam Hanoi, at which time we turned east. I could tell that we were now getting close to the target because a lot of the strike aircraft had already dropped their bombs and were heading back out the same way we were coming in. I noted this in the back of my mind for use later. I could see the bombs hitting a bridge just southeast of Hanoi, and now, for the first time, I knew what the target was. The sky was full of flak, the smoke hanging thickly in the air, and a lot of SAMs were still being fired at the retreating strike group. I looked around to see if I could find any of the Shrike aircraft so I could do the job that I was supposed to be doing. I couldn't find any of them, and just then I spotted a SAM coming toward me that had my name on it for sure. I did the escape maneuver, which was to turn into the missile and start a steep dive to try to get the SAM to follow, and then when the missile got close enough you would pull up and over. The missile couldn't follow this maneuver because it was going so much faster and couldn't make as tight a turn as you could. It would then pass under and blow up harmlessly away from the aircraft. After I evaded that missile I ended up really low and slow. I tried to climb back to a safe altitude, but with all the drag on my aircraft from my weapons load I just wasn't accelerating or climbing very fast. I looked around for another airplane from the strike group but I didn't see anyone. I really felt all alone at this point, which isn't what you should be feeling in any combat situation.

There were still more SAMs being fired and a lot of flak in the sky. I was still down low and slow, and I knew I had to get rid of the drag on my airplane that was keeping me from accelerating and being able to maneuver to protect myself. I quickly decided that my rockets wouldn't do any good against a bridge and I didn't have anything else good to shoot them at, so I reached down and set up my switches for bombs instead of rockets and pickled off (jettisoned) each of my four rocket pods. I felt bad about not firing them, but that didn't last very long because just about then I had to evade another SAM that was coming up at me. Now I was light and clean and had no problem evading this missile. As I climbed back up to a safer altitude and headed out of the target area, I caught up to one of our fighters that had taken a hit and was trailing a lot of smoke. He had one of his squadron mates on his wing helping him back to the ship, so I joined up with the two of them and we flew back out to the ship together.

It was a clear day at the ship so I entered the break (traffic pattern) with the two fighters and came aboard uneventfully. The fighter that was trailing smoke also made it back OK. I didn't find out until the debriefing that the other three Shrike escort aircraft made it back too, except that all three of them had taken some small arms hits on their aircraft while trying to evade the SAMs. I was the only one of the four of us that didn't get hit.

After the debriefing of this mission, and after everything that had unfolded during this strike had been thoroughly discussed and debated, it was decided that the Shrike aircraft would have to be escorted by a clean F-8 fighter, which could keep up and do the job that was required of the escort. This arrangement worked out great, and we stuck with it for the rest of the cruise.

The Shrike missile worked so well that after the North Vietnamese learned what was going on, they would shut down the radar that was guiding the SAM as soon as they saw a Shrike missile being fired back at them, and the SAM would go ballistic and explode far above the strike group.

My second story took place later on that cruise when I was flying an A-4E as an aerial tanker. What began as a routine tanker hop for me wound up as a rescue mission for a downed pilot. Every launch of strike aircraft was accompanied by air refueling tankers that would orbit over the ship until the strike force returned and recovered safely. The tankers were on hand in the event someone returned with battle damage or had trouble getting aboard and needed more fuel. We always launched the A-3 tanker, a twin-engine jet that had been converted from a bomber to a tanker and designated the KA-3B. Since it was the largest aircraft to operate off the carrier, it was called "the whale." We also launched an A-4 buddy tanker outfitted with a refueling store, carried on a centerline rack. It consisted of a 300-gallon fuel tank, a hydraulically operated hose reel, 50 feet of refueling hose, and a drogue. The drogue, or basket, was a funnel-shaped device at the end of the hose. Navy aircraft that were designed for in-flight refueling had a compatible probe that plugged into the basket so refueling could begin.

I would launch with the whale and stay over the ship until recovery, when another A-4 tanker would come up and relieve me. It was usually about an hour and a half until a strike force returned. Often, when planes were returning from a strike and waiting for their recovery time, they would hit the tankers for a little more gas so that they could jump each other in a massive dogfight over the ship.

This particular tanker hop was routine until I got strapped in and was about to launch from the ship. The Air Boss called me on the radio and said there had been a change in plans for me. It seemed that an Air Force aircraft had been shot down and the pilot was evading the enemy while a massive rescue attempt was being mounted. Since rescue operations took top priority, all available assets were made ready to help out. I was given the location of the rescue operation and it turned out to be only 60 miles from the ship, so I was to launch ahead of the strike force and get to the area as soon as I could. Once there I was to contact the on-scene commander (a pilot over the scene who was in charge of the rescue operation) and coordinate with him to refuel support aircraft as needed, then return to the ship and recover with the returning strike force. That sounded pretty straightforward to me.

I launched from the boat and headed for the rescue. It didn't take long to get there, and as I had been given the radio frequency for this operation, I was listening to what was happening as I approached the scene. It was very exciting. The on-scene commander was directing airplanes to strafe, bomb, or fly high-speed low passes to try to keep the enemy away from our downed pilot. Everybody was there to help, including Marine F-4 and A-4 fighters along with Army gunships and rescue helicopters. There was a lot going on and a lot of chatter on the radio. A couple of the aircraft had taken hits from small arms fire, but they continued to stay on the scene and help. As I got closer I could see quite a bit of flak in the air so I just headed for that and checked in with the on-scene commander. I told him I was a tanker and asked him what he wanted me to do. He was very happy to see me because people were getting low on fuel and would have had to leave the area to refuel. He asked me to set up an orbit right around the rescue at 5,000 feet and he would send airplanes to me. I had only 15,000 pounds of fuel to give away, and that doesn't go far in a situation like this, but every little bit would help.

As soon as I set up my orbit and extended the drogue I had three Marine F-4s on my wing and I asked for the lowest on fuel to come in first. While we were refueling I couldn't maneuver very much or the receiving aircraft would fall out of the basket. This got pretty dicey because the enemy on the ground could see what was happening, and we became a great target for them. We could see a lot of tracers coming up at us and some flak over our heads, but everyone hung tight as we transferred fuel. The F-4s were good and it didn't take long for them to hook up, transfer about 5,000 pounds of fuel each, and say good-bye! I called the man in charge, told him I was out of fuel and had to go. He thanked me very much and went back to the business at hand.

As I headed back to the boat I reflected that this had been a first for me; I had never been shot at while refueling! I calculated how much fuel I would need to get back to the boat and make a recovery and, since I had given most of my fuel to the Phantoms (F-4s), I would need priority in the landing sequence as I was pretty low on fuel myself. I made it back on board without any problems and had a little more time to think things over. What made this hop so exciting was the way it came up so unexpectedly and was over so quickly. The whole evolution took only about 30 minutes. The best part was that I had helped in what turned out to be a successful rescue. I checked with air intelligence as soon as I got back onboard ship and was told that the Air Force pilot had been picked up safely. He had been shot down in Route Package I, which was just to the north of the DMZ. This enabled a quick response by the F-4s and A-4s from Da Nang, plus the Marine and Army helicopter gunships from one of the many fire bases just the other side of the DMZ. A quick massive response like that, with a Navy A-4 tanker thrown in for good measure, made for a good day! I mentioned earlier that our morale was high because we knew that no effort would be spared to rescue us if we had to bail out over enemy territory. This experience proved that beyond a doubt, and I was happy to have been involved.

....

I flew with Bob Wood on several occasions while I was a copilot and he was a captain on the Boeing 757/767 in Los Angeles. He told me both these stories while we were flying and was happy to write them for this book. He was also very supportive of the project. It always amazed me to hear his casual description of the SAM avoidance procedure, especially the first time he did it for real on his orientation ride on his first cruise. The Shrike escort story is really funny, especially the way I first heard Bob tell it in an Irish pub on a layover in New York. Probably anything would have been funny that night, but I think you will agree that it is a great story!

Bob claims to have two A-4 tailhooks in his garage at home and has offered me one. I might take him up on it, but then it would probably involve drinking a "flaming hooker" or two.

*Battle damage from a SAM hit under the wing of an
A-4E, after a Shrike mission, 1967.*

Bombs being dropped from a VA-192 A-4E over North Vietnam, 1967.

Bob Wood boarding the USS Ticonderoga for his first cruise, 1967.

L) A-4E at sunset over the South China Sea, 1967. *R)* A-4E returning to the USS Ticonderoga at dusk, 1967.

Bob Wood's photo, kept on file to be used to identify him in the event he was shot down.

18

PAUL DOUMER BRIDGE

Bob Spielman, USAF, F-105D, 1966 – 1967
{ Date of hire by Western Airlines: 4/7/1969 }

Bob Spielman with F-105D at Takhli RTAB in 1967.

Bob Spielman has written the most unique story in this book. In telling about the Doumer Bridge raid on August 11, 1967, he not only relates his story but includes a personal letter from his friend and fellow F-105 pilot Jon Reynolds, a classmate of his from Trinity College. Jon had been shot down and was a prisoner of war at the time of the Doumer Bridge raid. He confirmed Bob's thoughts about the effect on the morale of the POWs as the F-105s flew their egress route at high speed over Hanoi after dropping the bridge.

The first F-105 pilot I ever met was a new T-38 instructor who arrived at Williams AFB in the fall of 1967, when I was about halfway through the T-38 portion of my training. The Air Training Command had strict rules about what patches were to be worn on our flight suits. The "100 Mission" patch wasn't one of them, but he wore his proudly, and the powers that be didn't ever ask him to remove it. My most vivid memory was that he was just a couple of years ahead of us trainees but somehow looked and acted much older. To say we were in awe of him would be an understatement. He chain-smoked and couldn't get through an hour-and-a-half training flight without a cigarette. I remember flying in two-ship formation, with him in the backseat of the other aircraft, his oxygen mask pulled aside, puffing away, using a small, hand-held ashtray that he kept in his flight suit pocket. This was totally against all the rules, but the chance that he could have blown us all up with the flame so close to the 100 percent oxygen supply never occurred to me at the time. I was just trying to hold formation on the other T-38—at times, being blown up would have been a relief!

The students didn't have a lot of social contact with the instructors, but I remember hearing that he had gotten an F-105 as his initial assignment out of pilot training and had gone to Southeast Asia with a group of five pilots. Three were shot down, with one killed in action, one missing in action and assumed to be a POW, and one rescued. It was a ritual for the instructors and students to go to the Stag Bar at the Officers' Club for our Friday evening "debriefings," but being mesmerized by that 100-mission patch, none of us students dared ask him about any of his combat experiences and he never talked about them. (The Stag Bar was for males only and is long gone in today's politically correct world.)

Williams was right next door to Luke AFB, which was a very busy fighter training base. A lot of interesting aircraft would stop at Williams on weekend cross-country trips, and a great weekend activity for those who lived in the Bachelor Officers' Quarters was to head down to the flight line and see what was parked out in front of Base Operations on a Saturday afternoon. It was on the Williams flight line that I saw my first F-105 up close and personal, and I have been in awe of it and the men who flew it in combat ever since.

I consider myself very lucky to have known the three F-105 pilots who wrote stories for this book. In particular I owe a debt of thanks to Bob Spielman, who generously lent me his photos, including the gun camera *filmstrip taken from his aircraft on the Doumer Bridge raid, and his letter from Jon Reynolds. Bob's story, just like Dennis Wills's, seems to say, "That's what we did, and when we did it 100 times, we got to come home." All I can say is a well-deserved "Wow!"*

....

I was commissioned a Second Lieutenant from ROTC at Trinity College in Connecticut and went to UPT (Undergraduate Pilot Training) Class 61B at Spence AB, Georgia, and Laredo AFB, Texas. My initial assignment was the F-100 with training at Luke AFB, Arizona, followed by an assignment to Itazuke AB, Japan. I then transitioned to the F-105 and went on to Yokota AB, Japan.

In the summer of 1967 the air war over North Vietnam was getting hot, and the code name for the operation was Rolling Thunder. The JCS (Joint Chiefs of Staff) began to designate new and more important targets than had previously been hit. The F-105 (the Thud) was carrying the bomb load north while the F-105 Wild Weasels put down the SAMs (surface-to air missiles) and AAA (anti-aircraft artillery) threat and the F-4 Phantom flew top cover (MIG CAP) against an increasing MiG threat.

I was based at Yokota with the 36th TFS (Tactical Fighter Squadron). The fighter wing formed a new squadron, the 34th TFS, and sent it to Korat RTAB, Thailand, to help out with the war effort. When the squadrons in Thailand ran short of airplanes or pilots, short-term replacements would be sent from Kadena AB, Okinawa, or Yokota AB, Japan, until permanent replacements came from the States. I missed being in this new squadron because I had been sent to Nellis AFB, Nevada, to attend Fighter Weapons School, but when I returned I was sent from Yokota to Takhli for a 90-day TDY (temporary duty). Five of us were sent on that TDY, and out of our group three were shot down, two were rescued, and the third pilot, Art Mearns, would die in prison camp in North Vietnam. I was 30 years old when my TDY to Takhli was assigned.

The mission I remember so well was the raid on the Doumer Bridge on August 11, 1967. This bridge spanned the Red River on the edge of Hanoi and had been off-limits to us until this time. It was the main rail link between Communist China and Vietnam and carried most of the major Soviet equipment from China south to Hanoi. This equipment included SAM missiles, aircraft, AAA weapons and ammunition, and general armament.

We were planning our mission the day prior and debating whether to egress across Hanoi after the bomb run or do a 180 degree turn and exit to the north, the way we came in. One of our young pilots, First Lieutenant Dick Guild, convinced us that even though the enemy's defenses were concentrated around Hanoi, we would have the element of surprise in our favor, and exiting across Hanoi would be the fastest way out. That turned out to be a good decision.

Colonel Bob White (of X-15 fame, and *fearless*) was leading our task force. On the day of the mission, we arose at 0230, ate breakfast, and went to the mission briefing. We started engines at 0400 and our 16 Thuds plus 2 spares taxied out for departure. We each carried two 3,000 pound bombs that day, plus a Sidewinder air-to-air missile and an electronic warfare jamming pod. We taxied to the arming area at the end of the runway, and here was the procedure: We stopped the aircraft, set the brakes, and held our hands up in view while the arming crew pulled the pins on the bomb fuses and charged a live round into the 20mm Gatling gun. The arming crew followed the same procedure for all of us and then waved us off, cleared for departure. As we left the arming area, the chaplain was always there off to the side of the taxiway to bless us before we got under way. I don't think that was as reassuring as it was intended!

Our aircraft gross weight was about 52,000 pounds. Our Pratt & Whitney J-75 engine would put out 25,000 pounds of thrust, and we used water injection for an additional 2,000 pounds of thrust on takeoff. It was still pitch-dark when we lined up for takeoff. As each pilot ahead of me lit his afterburner for takeoff it became bright as could be, and until the Thud ahead of me came out of burner it was very difficult to see to join up as we climbed out of the traffic pattern. It took nearly 30 minutes for the 16 Thuds to climb out and rejoin on the way to the rendezvous with our KC-135 tankers over Laos. It was just getting light as we each refueled and then topped off again before we pushed off to North Vietnam. Due to our weight we refueled at a fairly low altitude, perhaps 18,000 feet. We were at such a high gross weight for so long that we were using the J-75 engines at much higher thrust and temperature than was intended, thus reducing their useful life by a huge amount.

We pushed off for the north at 480 knots in four flights of four, spaced so that our jamming pods covered each other. We flew 500 feet out and 500 feet vertically so that #4, the farthest back, was within 1,500 feet vertically of lead, and this effectively overlapped our pod coverage and degraded the North Vietnamese radar ability to develop azimuth and range information. I was #2 in the last flight of four and flying on Mo Baker's wing. (Mo was shot down and captured later in the war but luckily returned home with the POWs.) I do not recall our call signs, but one squadron used cars—Buick, Olds, etc.—and another used fish—Marlin, Shark, and so on.

We could see the four F-105 Wild Weasels—the guys with the big gonads—out ahead of us. There was another flight of 16 Thuds from Korat behind us, another 16 F-4s from Ubon behind them, and we could hear the F-4 top cover escorts on the UHF radio, so we knew they were with us. Over Yen Bai on the Red River, about 100 miles northwest of Hanoi, AAA always shot at us if they had gotten their weekly supply of ammunition. They did this morning, but no sweat; we were at 14,000 feet and it gave us incentive to push up to 600 knots. We headed southeast and crossed Thud Ridge as it pointed our way to Hanoi. The Wild Weasels radioed that the target weather was clear. Two MiG-17s slid in above us, head-on as we were inbound, but by the time they could turn around there was no way they could catch us, and the F-4s would, we hoped, chase them away. I could see a couple of SA-2s (SAMs) explode far off to the right ahead of us.

Lead rolled in over Gia Lam airfield, which was located on the northeast side of the Red River, and aimed for a 45 degree dive angle with an 8,000-foot release altitude. This would enable us to pull out of the dive at least 4,500 feet above the ground and keep us out of range of small arms fire. We went in four at a time, and as our flight of four was coming down the chute, a 100mm AAA round went off between Mo Baker and me, turning our two 50,000-pound Thuds upside down, but luckily no shrapnel hit either of us. We rolled out and continued on our bomb run. I watched Mo and when he released his bombs, so did I. My F-105 had the camera pod and it captured a beautiful photo of bombs from the first flight of four dropping a span of the Doumer Bridge, AAA firing, and for the first time that we know, Thuds going as fast as they could in afterburner across Hanoi. We thought the POWs were in and around Hanoi, and we hoped they could see or hear us because we wanted them to think they were coming home soon. As it was, it only took five more years!

Only one aircraft was hit on this mission. He took a piece of shrapnel in his windscreen but otherwise had no major damage. We all made it home. It was a three-and-a-half-hour mission, and we were wringing wet with sweat but happy as we pitched out over Takhli and landed. The flight behind us called from Korat and congratulated us—the bridge was down before they rolled in for their bomb run. The brave RF-101 Voodoo pilots flew over later and took photos that proved it. We had expected to have to go again the next day unless someone was lucky enough to hit it on the first mission.

In doing research for this story I contacted my friend Mo Baker and asked for his recollection of the mission. He confirmed my memory of that day, including the 100mm AAA round that exploded between us and turned us upside down. Keith Ferris said he could see the shiny round coming up in the photo he used to paint the picture of the Doumer raid. I also contacted Jon Reynolds, a friend from Trinity College who was a POW at the time of this bombing mission. Some of the POWs were moved around Hanoi during these raids and he refers to this in his note. Here is his message to me:

Your story of the raid on the Doumer Bridge was also great—must have been that great English teacher you had at Trinity Freshman year. I was also on the Doumer Bridge raid—in fact I made every one of them until 1972 when they moved us up to the China border. Summer of 1967, however, was the most exciting. They had moved several of us to a power plant not far from the bridge. That was one of Ho Chi Minh's dumber ideas. It seemed like it was early afternoon in late July or early August when the first strike took place. The bombs were close, but the prison walls were thick. The problem was that big hunks of the ceiling were coming down and we had nothing to hide under. One bomb must have hung up, as it hit so close as to crack the wall enough to see light in the cell next door, the sole occupant of which was Bob Peel. That prison was a real pit, known as the Dirty Bird because of all the soot from the power plant. We could sure hear you all flying. Wish I had known you were there. Dick Guild flew with our squadron when he first got to Yokota. There were three new guys right out of Nellis and Guild was one of them. We later heard that it was Guild who dropped the bridge. Was that true? The air strikes during that period really picked up our morale. And it helped the time pass. Another exciting event was the night of the Son Tay raid, when they had just moved us to a new camp and we thought the war was almost over. As Bruce Seeber said one day when the bombing was especially close, "Sometimes I have mixed emotions about these air strikes!" We really did appreciate your efforts on our behalf.

From the book *The Raid*, by Benjamin F. Schemmer:

One dark November morning in 1970, an elite, helicopter-borne force of American raiders landed inside and outside the walls of Son Tay prison, only 23 miles from Hanoi. Its mission was to rescue 61 American prisoners of war who were believed to be held captive under brutal conditions. Minutes later, after a fierce firefight, the Son Tay Raiders were again airborne without suffering a single serious casualty. But they left without a single American POW; the POWs were not there.

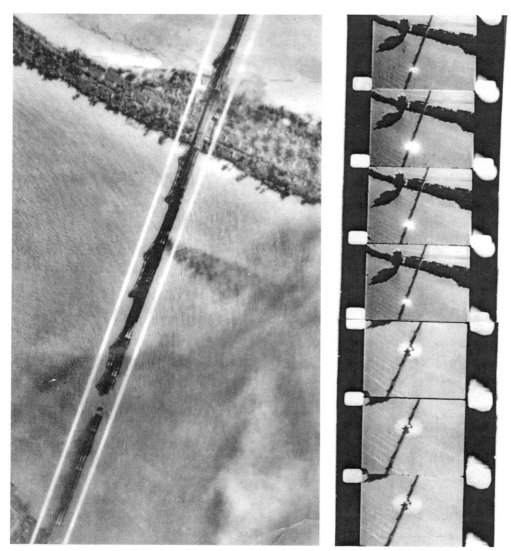

L) Paul Doumer Bridge with span missing after the raid on August 11, 1967.
R) Gun camera film strip from Bob Spielman's F-105, taken during the Doumer Bridge raid on August 11, 1967.

Gun camera photo taken from Bob Spielman's aircraft of another F-105 egressing after the Doumer Bridge raid, August 11, 1967.

Bob Spielman, far left, in a photo of 5 pilots who went into combat together. 3 were shot down, 2 rescued, and Bob's friend Art Mearns, far right, was shot down, captured, and died as a POW in North Vietnam.

19

Khe Sanh

Bill McGaw, USMC, UH-1E, 1967 – 1968
{ Date of hire by Western Airlines: 1/27/1969 }

Bill McGaw in front of the S-3 "office" for VMO-6 at Quang Tri.

When I arrived at Western Airlines' San Francisco pilot base in February 1974, Bill McGaw was the copilot on one of the first trips I flew. What's not to like about an old Marine Mustang (an enlisted man who became an officer) who thought he was pretty tough when he arrived at boot camp at age 18, but got taught what "tough" really was by his drill instructor, a veteran of Saipan who took him behind the barracks for a little talk? Tough, brave, courageous, heroic—words fail when you read Bill's story and realize that he flew in and out of Khe Sanh throughout the 77 days of the siege. The Marine helicopter crew members of VMO-6 (Bill's Squadron) provided the lifeline to the hill outposts around Khe Sanh, supplying ammunition, food and water, and bringing in replacement troops while carrying out the dead and wounded.

There is something about helicopters that has always intrigued me, and I never tired of hearing Bill's stories, although getting him to talk took some doing. The small group of Marines based in San Francisco was pretty tight, and several of them flew A-4s in a reserve unit at Alameda Naval Air Station. Two in particular, Hank Lecy and Charlie Coxe, always told great stories (with the proper encouragement), but sadly, both passed away at a very young age and their stories went with them. Hank was buried at Arlington National Cemetery and his good friend Bill Wilson accompanied his remains and attended the service. I am just sorry I didn't get started on this project sooner so I could have included Hank and Charlie.

As for Bill McGaw, his prior service as an enlisted Marine gave him a pretty good idea of how the system worked, and he had a very colorful time in the USMC. His casual mention of being selected for the initial cadre of the helicopter program for the Marine Corps is really typical of Bill, who was the definition of unassuming and understated. He was involved in a lot of firsts, as were several other pilots included in this book. He told me that he had to write this story in such a way as to minimize all the bad memories that came with it, and that the flying in and out of Khe Sanh was so compressed on a daily basis that the individual missions became little more than a blur. I have been told by more than one pilot that the whole process of remembering and writing these stories was therapeutic, and for the part this book played in that, I am extremely grateful. Several of the chapters in the book, including this one, relate stories that are being told for the first time.

The siege of Khe Sanh is an incredible story. While the actual Battle of Khe Sanh took place from January 21 to July 9, 1968, there was a 77-day period during those months when the combat base was completely sur-rounded and under siege. The North Vietnamese wanted it to be the American Dien Bien Phu, the battle that brought about the departure of the French from Indochina in 1954, but they failed due to the courage and tenacity of the U.S. Marines. I am reminded of a Marine infantry captain I met years ago at a book signing, by the name of Dick Camp. Dick was at Khe Sanh with Lima Company, 3/26 Marines, and wrote a book about his experience in Vietnam called Lima-6. Trying to think of anything he could volunteer for to get away from Khe Sanh, he jumped at the opportunity to *be the aide to Major General Ray Davis, a Medal of Honor recipient in the Korean War. Dick was flown out of Khe Sanh to Phu Bai to meet General Davis and interview for the job. Dick wrote the following after being offered the position:*

> As I walked out of General Davis's office, it occurred to me that I had no idea what the hell an aide did. I didn't even know where I was supposed to work. I didn't know where I was supposed to live. I didn't know where my seabag was. I didn't know what I was supposed to wear. I didn't know what weapons I was supposed to carry. I didn't know a damn thing about my new job, but I knew one thing—I didn't have to go back to Khe Sanh.

Now, here is Bill McGaw and the story of the part he played in the siege of Khe Sanh, where the word terrifying *is not adequate to describe what he experienced. The courage and flying skill displayed in this story are a testimony to Bill and the young Marines he worked with every day.*

. . . .

I enlisted in the Marine Corps in 1954 while still in high school and served as an enlisted man until 1956. I was selected to become a NAVCAD (naval aviation cadet) while I was based in San Diego attending an electronics school as a corporal. After flight school I flew transports until 1962, when I was picked along with 54 other regular officers to transition into helicopters. We became the initial cadre of the future helicopter program for the Marine Corps.

Backtracking a little, I was involved in a shooting war called Lebanon in 1958. That was the first time someone tried to kill me. Later, in 1960–1961, I was involved in a fracas called the Laotian War. By this time I had acquired about nine months of combat, none of which was officially recognized. During 1965 I was assigned to a three-star general's staff in Hawaii, and while on the staff I was sent to Vietnam, where I served from 1965 to 1967. I flew mainly transport helicopters during this time, acquiring another six months of combat. The missions I flew were mostly resupply, with a few medevac and extraction missions (extraction of ground reconnaissance teams). I also flew fixed-wing transport (R5D/C-54) into and out of Pleiku, providing transport to R&R for the Army's 1st Air Cavalry. R&R was usually a break of a week to 10 days for a trip to Bangkok, Hong Kong, or Sydney for the single guys, or to Honolulu for the married men, who could meet their wives there. They would be taken to Cam Ranh Bay or Tan Son Nhut in Saigon to go on their MAC (Military Airlift Command) charter R&R flights.

I was with the 1st Marine Air Wing in 1967, assigned to VMO-6, a Huey (UH-1E) helicopter gunship squadron. I had never flown the Huey, and my first flight, an orientation ride, turned out to be a real "shit sandwich," as we later called such missions. The flight was an eight-hour battle with a company of NVA (North Vietnamese Army), and at the end of the day I was a Huey driver! Our mission in VMO-6 was to provide close air support for the grunts (ground troops) and cover for the medevac helicopters. It also included calling in artillery and controlling fixed-wing aircraft in close support. Though most of the time we provided close support and escort for the medevac helicopters, we often ended up as emergency medevac ourselves, as picking up WIAs (wounded in action) and KIAs (killed in action) was a daily occurrence. That was one part of our mission that I did not like, and the memory of the smell and the screams of the wounded still bother me. Of course there were times that the silence was overwhelming.

VMO-6 was assigned to Phu Bai and later to Quang Tri. We were the first squadron to be permanently assigned to Quang Tri, but until we arrived there I did a lot of work out of Phu Bai with the Army Special Forces, 5th SF Group, which was based at Nha Trang but worked out of several FOBs (forward operating bases). I was involved in several reconnaissance team insertions and emergency extractions, with the team being pursued by Charlie (the Vietcong). I was also involved in several other types of missions with the SF until we were permanently assigned to Quang Tri.

When I was first assigned to Quang Tri, the so-called McNamara Line was being built as an electronic barrier across the DMZ (demilitarized zone, the border between North and South Vietnam). The Marines had three battalions in the DMZ to protect the Seabees

(Navy construction crews) as they bulldozed a strip about 500 meters wide from Gio Linh to Con Tien and sowed it with listening devices and land mines. We were worked to the nub trying to protect the units from the NVA until the Seabees were finally pulled out of the DMZ after two months. During this time we also flew a lot of gunship support for medevac missions, most of them under a ceiling of 1,000 feet or less, putting us well within small arms and AK-47 range. The period following was primarily one of extensive reconnaissance team insertion and extraction, with most extractions occurring with the team in contact with the NVA.

I was involved with the siege at Khe Sanh from beginning to end. In January and part of February 1968 we stood alert at Khe Sanh for 24-hour periods so we could be instantly available for close air support and medevac. We lost too many Hueys in those two months, so we had to move the close air support mission to Quang Tri, still refueling and rearming at Khe Sanh. Charlie had their mortars zeroed in on every refueling and rearming spot, and we became very adept at refueling and rearming with 25 seconds of ground time. The 82mm mortar took about 35 seconds from dropping in the tube to impact, so while the crew chief pumped the gas, the gunner threw the ammo on board. After getting airborne, the crew chief and gunner would stand on the skids and reload the rocket tubes. As I remember, we had to refuel after about 40 to 50 minutes of flight time, so each mission was fuel-critical. Often we would just make a rearming stop, as some of the sorties around the hill positions were only 10 to 15 minutes long, and due to the elevation and temperature we were limited to less than 400 pounds of fuel, which enabled us to carry more armament.

We carried two seven-shot rocket pods and six fixed forward-firing M-60 machine guns, plus two door-mounted M-60s that were manned by the crew chief and gunner. There were two stations equipped with rocket launchers for 2.75mm folding-fin rockets. We were normally equipped with a seven-shot pod, although there was also a 36-pod launcher. The normal load for the rocket pods was seven rounds of white phosphorus (Willy Pete) for marking targets and seven rounds of high explosives for fire suppression. We never knew in advance which type of mission we would be flying, but it usually involved close air support, medevac escort, artillery targeting, resupply of positions that were under fire, and, to a limited degree, search and rescue. During the two-month period that VMO-6 sent two Hueys to Khe Sanh for a 24-hour alert mission, the crews would remain on station for quick response to whatever mission was required. Whenever one of the hill outposts needed resupply or a medevac, we would do a fly-by reconnaissance and then lay down suppressive fire while the medevac helicopter made its pass to the hill position.

There were six hill outposts, with Hill 950 to the northeast of Khe Sanh and manned by a reinforced platoon. Unlike the other hills, Hill 950 was rarely in need of close support. The other hill positions were Hill 881 North, Hill 881 South, Hill 861 A, Hill 861 B, and Hill 558, with Hill 881 North being lost to Charlie early in the siege. The hill positions ran from north to northwest of Khe Sanh. The toughest position that we resupplied was Hill 881 South, as the battle there raged 24 hours a day.

When the siege began we would park our Huey in a revetment and spend the night in a bunker, but we did not get much sleep as the incoming was continuous, and if there was an emergency medevac or close air support mission, we would launch. VMO-6 lost several Hueys to incoming artillery and mortar fire while they were parked in revetments, so as I mentioned previously, the 24-hour alert mission at Khe Sanh was abandoned and moved to Quang Tri.

Most of the takeoffs from the arming and refueling pits at Khe Sanh were over the maximum gross weight for hover in ground effect (too heavy to fly), so we would just bounce along until we got transitional lift at 14 knots. One of the biggest problems we faced was trying to suppress the mortar and ground fire for the transport helicopters trying to take in or pick up supplies or troops, and also trying to function as medevac at the hill positions. We would lead the H-34 or H-46 helicopters to the hill, putting rockets into areas known to be mortar positions. Then we would swing around to give suppressing fire along the perimeter while the transport bird was on the ground. Timing was everything, and time was always short, so when Charlie got too good, we came up with what we called "the super gaggle." This was a coordinated effort of fixed-wing, artillery, and helicopters to get in and out of the hill positions, and it worked quite well.

The story that follows is not of any one mission but more as I remember what a day was like to fly in support of Khe Sanh.

After the move to Quang Tri, we would plan the next day's missions and assign the crews in the late evening. Everyone took a turn, with the crews being rotated first in, first out in the morning. (I never had to make a night launch from Khe Sanh, but several of our crews did and it was not pleasant.) Knowing you were going to Khe Sanh the next day did not help with sleep, and since Quang Tri was attacked most nights with 122mm rockets, 82mm mortars, or sniper fire, sleep was not that common anyway. Each mission was a section of two Hueys, and it was about 15 minutes of flying time to Khe Sanh, depending on the weather. After a breakfast of B rations at the mess hall, it was on to the flight line for the briefing. If the weather was bad, we would fly out a TACAN (tactical air navigation system) radial to a point and then use a GCA (ground-controlled approach) to the airfield. Once we were VFR (visual flight rules) under the clouds, we would break off the approach and start whatever mission the ALO (air liaison officer) of the 26th Marines at Khe Sanh assigned.

Usually the first mission of the day was to escort a medevac helicopter to one of the hills. If possible we would call in a flight of fixed-wing attack aircraft to soften the position before we started, and we quickly learned just where Charlie would have his mortars and heavy machine guns. We would try to hit those spots while escorting the medevacs and keep it up while the chopper was in the zone. Since Charlie had troops within meters of the wire and would start small arms fire at the helicopter immediately on its arrival, they were limited to roughly 20 seconds on the ground. After the medevacs were completed, the resupply would start. Most of the resupply was done with an external sling load, limiting the supply choppers to a minimum exposure time in the zone, but if there were troops, KIAs, or equipment to be picked up from the hill, the tactics would change. The gunships basically did the same job trying to find and eliminate any known or suspected emplacements prior to the mission, then provide close suppressive fire, usually right outside the wire, while the supply helicopters were in the zone.

We started our rocket and gun runs from about 1,500 feet above the target, weather permitting. I tried to complete the run at about

500 feet, but if the zone was too hot and we were taking fire from the area I was suppressing, I would continue right down to the deck. The Hueys were a higher-priority target for Charlie than the H-34 or H-46, so on most missions the gunship received several hits. I was lucky that only one Marine was ever wounded in a gunship that I was flying. We were responsible for five hill outposts, both to resupply and to pick up outgoing loads, and emergency medevacs always took priority. By nightfall we had spent most of the day in our seats.

The fuel load was limited to allow us to carry more rockets and ammo, and the refueling pit and ammo dump was located just off the west end of the runway. Here is how a typical refueling and rearming pit stop worked. One Huey at a time would land, and the crew chief would jump out and start refueling while the gunner ran to the ammo dump and grabbed as many rockets and 7.62 ammo cans as he could carry. The pilots would be watching the second hand on the clock, and at 25 seconds in the pit we would pull collective (lift off) and leave the immediate area. It took about 35 seconds for a mortar round to arrive, and if the crew chief and gunner were still on the ground, they would jump into a trench. We would circle and land, then finish refueling and rearming, again watching the second hand of the clock. The crew chief and gunner would then stand on the skids and reload the rocket pods while we were circling at about 1,500 feet. They were attached to the Huey by what we called a monkey harness, and as far as I know no one ever fell off the skids. After the rocket pods were loaded they would load the machine guns and we would be ready for the next mission.

In January and early February when we operated totally from Khe Sanh, here is what the end of a day's flying would be like. We would land directly in the revetment and everyone but the pilot would leave the Huey as soon as it was parked. The pilot would shut it down and then set everything for a quick start, so all we had to do for a start was turn on the battery and pull the starter switch. Charlie would start firing 122mm rockets and 82mm mortars at us as soon as we landed, so the crew would run and jump into a trench or whatever they could find for protection from the incoming. My personal favorite was a culvert with PSP (pierced-steel planking) on top, but I got to use that only three times. The last time I slid into the culvert, a long-delay-fused 122mm rocket impacted at the other end of the culvert and was about 15 feet underground when it exploded. I became a human cannonball and was shot about five feet in the air and out of the culvert! The next hurdle was to get across the runway, as Charlie had 12.5mm heavy machine guns aligned to fire down the runway about five feet above the ground. It was a mad dash across to the bunker.

The following was our procedure when we were operating as a medevac. At Khe Sanh the medical bunker was located next to the ramp area, and the idea was to land as close as possible to the bunker, load the wounded and get out of town within that 25 to 35 second time frame. We could usually carry two wounded, and we would drop them off at the field hospital in Dong Ha (which was called D Medical) and then return to Quang Tri.

The procedure of staying airborne except for refueling and rearming worked well, and we had an alert crew at Quang Tri that could respond and be in Khe Sanh in about 20 minutes. As I remember, in the support of Khe Sanh we lost nine crew members KIA. I don't remember the number of WIA, but we lost 10 to 12 Hueys. During my entire tour with VMO-6 we lost 22 crew members and about 25 to 30 Hueys. The 24-hour alert mission at Khe Sanh was finally canceled after less than two months as we lost too many Hueys to incoming artillery and mortars at night.

When we were not flying support for Khe Sanh, we provided support for most Marine units in Quang Tri Province. And, as before the siege of Khe Sanh, the recon business kept us busy. In my last three months in-country I was with Group Staff, working in S-3 (operations and planning), and my main job was perimeter defense at Quang Tri. While I was in charge of security, the enemy never made it through the wire.

From September 1967 to May 1968 I flew more than 400 Huey gunship missions and was awarded 21 Air Medals and a Navy Commendation with a V device (for valor). I had a total of 19 months in Vietnam.

Marine UH-1E Huey gunship.

Crewchief preparing a UH-1E gunship for flight at Quang Tri during the siege of Khe Sanh, February 1968.

20

SHOOTDOWN OF JIM POLLAK

Jim Pollak, USAF, F-100D, January 4, 1968
{ Date of hire by Western Airlines: 1/27/1969 }

Jim Pollak with his F-100D in a revetment at Tuy Hoa AB, Republic of Vietnam, late 1967.

The next three stories are about an incident that occurred on January 4, 1968, and represent one of the more interesting coincidences of all that seem to occur in these stories. There are pilots who knew each other before they were in the service, like Dick Hathcock and Tom Rodger, who met while in high school working at Knott's Berry Farm in Southern

California. Then they played football together at the University of California at Berkeley and went their separate ways to Vietnam, only to meet again as pilots for Western Airlines. Then there was Will Creeden and Dick Dixon, two B-52 pilots who had been classmates in Air Force pilot training. Will was involved in and Dick was a witness to the horrific midair collision of two B-52s on July 7, 1967. Both ended up as Western pilots, Dick in June 1968 and Will in February 1969.

The three pilots in these upcoming stories had a very different experience, but all ended up at Western Airlines as well. Two F-100 pilots, Jim Pollak and Kirk "KB" Clark, had known each other from a prior assignment in Europe and found themselves in the same squadron flying the F-100 at Tuy Hoa AB in Vietnam. The third pilot, Jim Fogg, had never met either Jim Pollak or KB Clark. He was a C-130P pilot flying SAR (search and rescue) missions for downed airmen and was also based at Tuy Hoa, but he was quartered in a separate area on base. At the end of the third story in this series, the uninitiated will learn the importance of an airline seniority number (based on hire date and then date of birth within a particular class). KB Clark was hired by Western in October 1968, Jim Pollak in January 1969, and Jim Fogg in May 1969. There is only a seven-month period from KB's hire date to Jim Fogg's, but in the airline world seven months can be an eternity, and next to a pilot's health, his seniority number is his most important possession! This incredible tale will start with Jim Pollak's account, move on to KB Clark's, and finish with Jim Fogg's.

I never flew with Jim Pollak but was referred to him by KB Clark, who had told me the story when we flew together in the early 1980s. It all seems to come down to coincidence and timing and I feel very fortunate to be able to preserve this great story for three good friends. Jim has been very helpful and supportive over the years and I can't thank him enough. Now here is his story of January 4, 1968, and of a two-hour period that truly changed his life.

. . . .

The 31st Tactical Fighter Wing at Tuy Hoa Air Base, RVN (Republic of Vietnam), consisted of three F-100 squadrons. Each of these squadrons was responsible for having two planes on alert at all times, and if scrambled, an alert plane had to be off the ground in five minutes. On January 4, 1968, the 308th Tactical Fighter Squadron was assigned to lines 3 and 4 in the alert area, and each aircraft was loaded with four 750 pound bombs. KB Clark and I had the alert duty that day, and our call signs were Litter 03 and Litter 04. KB and I flew together a lot since we were in the same flight, and we always swapped lead duties. Since he had led the last flight, I would lead the next one. The flight lead was responsible for the mission, and this responsibility included handling all radio calls, navigating, choosing tactics to be used when attacking the target, and generally making all decisions. The wingman's job was a lot easier: Just stick with your leader and protect him.

It was a slow, dreary day. The sun would peep out every now and then, but it was mostly cloudy. We had all been on duty since 6 o'clock that morning and none of the alert birds had been scrambled. At about 1:30 that afternoon we got the call to launch. All of our equipment—parachute, helmet, charts, survival gear, etc.—was already in the plane, so all we had to do was jump in and hit the start switch. While the engine spooled up, the crew chief took away the ladder and pulled the wheel chocks. I announced to the tower, "Scramble Litter 03 and Litter 04," and immediately got priority clearance to taxi to the active runway. While we taxied, we strapped ourselves into our parachutes and other gear. It took less than a minute to get to the end of the runway, where the armament people charged the guns, pulled the pins on the bombs, and armed the pylons. While this was going on, I called the command post (call sign Surfside) and got the call sign of the FAC (forward air controller) who would be working with us, a set of map coordinates where we would rendezvous with him, and a tactical radio frequency on which to contact him. A minute later we were off the ground and heading southwest to meet the FAC, call sign Helix 41, about 40 miles east of the city of Ban Me Thuot in the central highlands of South Vietnam. As yet, we didn't know what the target was, and this was usually a tense time in the mission, heading out and not knowing what you'd be going up against.

As we got closer to the rendezvous point, the cloud cover got worse, and by the time we called Helix 41 on the tactical frequency, we were over a solid overcast. While we looked for a break in the cloud cover that would allow us to get below the overcast, the FAC briefed us on the target. He told us that while he was patrolling in an area that was not supposed to be inhabited by either ally or enemy, he was fired on by what sounded to him like a heavy-caliber automatic weapon. Since the FACs flew small, light airplanes, they were able to open a window and virtually hang their head out and listen to ground fire. In the F-100, with its pressurized cockpit and with the pilot wearing a helmet and tight-fitting earphones, all you could hear in the target area was the hum of the engine, radio chatter, and strangely enough, the beating of your own heart. The FAC didn't know exactly where the gun was located, but there were a few obvious places in that area where an automatic weapon might be set up. He wanted us to hit a couple of those spots and, if nothing else, blow away some of the thick jungle foliage so he could get a closer look underneath. Charlie (the Vietcong) didn't usually put heavy weapons in an area unless there was something they wanted to protect. KB and I both groaned since we hated targets like this. Charlie would normally stop firing as soon as fighters arrived on the scene, and then all we would do was blow up a bunch of trees and find nothing. But the FAC was determined. Nobody should have been in that area, let alone somebody who was firing a large gun.

A few miles from the rendezvous point I found a hole in the clouds that I could dive through; it was large enough to see that I wasn't going to fly into a mountainside as soon as I got underneath. KB, like a good wingman, was right with me. As bright and sunny as it was on top, under the overcast it was gloomy. The base of the overcast was about 1,500 to 2,000 feet above the terrain, so we slipped into a spread formation about 1,000 feet above the ground and started to look for the FAC. He told us he was orbiting at 500 feet and roughly 10 miles from the target area. We spotted him first, which was normal, since it's easier to see a white O-1 Birddog (Cessna 305-A, a variant of the civilian Cessna 170) traveling at 70 mph against a green jungle background than it is to see a pair of camouflaged fighters streaking along at 350 mph. After making visual contact, the FAC headed for the target area while we orbited and set up our armament switches for the attack.

While we waited for the FAC to get into position, I scanned the surrounding area for as far as I could see. There was nothing but jungle, which in other circumstances would have been a beautiful sight. The terrain was relatively flat, with a few hills about 500 to 800 feet high scattered randomly about. Those mounds made flying at 1,000 feet a bit challenging, and if you didn't pay attention to your altitude and your location, you could very easily find yourself splattered on the side of one of those hills. I could see that we should have been carrying retarded bombs. With a retarded bomb you could fly right down to the treetops before releasing it and still have enough time to get away from the blast. Unfortunately, we were carrying slicks. Slick bombs are not designed to have their speed retarded when they leave the plane, so when they are released, they travel at the same speed as the plane. If the plane is flying level, the bomb will fall directly beneath it until it hits the ground. If the plane is flying at 1,500 feet or lower, it will probably receive damage from the bomb blast. Normal delivery of slick bombs was from a steep dive: rolling into the dive at about 10,000 feet, releasing the bomb at about 4,000 feet, then pulling out from the dive no lower than 2,500 feet, which is well above the bomb blast. The low cloud cover prevented any kind of dive, so we were forced to level bomb, and this required a long, straight run to the target. It was essential to be perfectly level and at exactly 500 knots (about 575 mph) when the bomb was released. Any deviation from level flight or the desired speed would cause the bomb to miss the target. We avoided bomb blast damage to the aircraft with this type of delivery by making an immediate tight turn after bomb release. (We all *hated* to level bomb!)

I mentioned to the FAC that our accuracy might not be too good because of the conditions, but he told us again that there were no friendly forces in the area. He also said he wanted the bombs spread out a bit so it would be no problem. I then told the FAC that I wanted to make a dry run on the target in order to check out the terrain in the target area and see if I would draw any ground fire. I planned to make this run at 300 knots instead of the normal 500 knots since I wanted a little more time to look around. KB continued to orbit while I made my dry run. The target itself was in a wide, flat valley about three miles across that ran north-south. Along the west edge was a row of hills that rose about 1,000 feet above the floor of the valley, and on the east side was another row of hills. They were much higher and the tops disappeared into the clouds, so it looked like our tactics were going to be dictated by the weather and the terrain.

The valley was much too narrow to maneuver in, so I decided that we would attack from south to north. After releasing our bombs, we would break (turn sharply) left, pass over the hills on the west side of the valley, and then fly south again to set up for another attack. As I flew up the valley the first time, I briefed KB on how I thought we should attack and he agreed. I was watching very closely for any muzzle flashes, tracers, smoke — anything that might give away Charlie's position. In doing this, I broke one of the cardinal rules of flying a single-seat fighter, which is, "Keep looking around!" I had been so intent on scanning the ground that I nearly collided with a helicopter that was flying up the valley in formation with four or five other choppers. I really don't know how I missed him as we passed just a few feet apart. Six months in a combat zone and I almost got killed in a midair collision! I started yelling at the FAC, "Who are those guys and what are they doing in this valley? I thought you said there were no friendlies anywhere near!" The FAC stammered out an apology and assured me that he knew nothing of the choppers, but he would contact them on their tactical frequency and advise them to get out of the area. Trying to get my heart back down to a normal beat, I passed over the target area and started an easy left turn, crossed over the hills to the west of the valley and flew back south to rejoin KB.

A couple of things bothered me about the whole setup. Working under a solid overcast made it very easy for gunners on the ground to judge your altitude, and you could be seen a lot more easily against a cloud cover than a high blue sky. Second, we would have to make all of our passes from the same direction, and after the first few Charlie would figure that out. There was always something about a target that you would like to be different, and this one was no exception.

The FAC came back on frequency and explained that the flight of helicopters was out on a patrol and had wandered into our area. He had advised them to stay out of the valley until after the strike was over. He also had a request. He asked if we could drop our bombs one at a time so they would spread out a little more for better coverage. Now, this was a tricky proposition with the F-100! We carried four bombs, two on each wing with one inboard and one outboard on the wing. Normally, when the bomb button is pushed the first time, the two outboard bombs drop at the same time. If you set the switches to drop them one at a time, you must be very careful. When the first bomb drops off, the plane is immediately out of balance, and if you don't get rudder correction in almost immediately, the plane can flip over and go out of control. But KB and I both had a lot of experience in the plane and had both dropped singly many times before, so we agreed to do it.

We were now ready to strike, and the FAC cleared us in hot. I went through my pre-attack ritual: tighten my seat belt and shoulder straps, tighten my helmet chin strap and oxygen mask, switch to 100 percent oxygen (instead of a mix of pressurized cockpit air and 100 percent oxygen), double-check the settings on the bomb sight, set up the armament switches hot, and finally, say a quick prayer. I was to make the first bomb run so I applied full power. With a full bomb load of 3,000 pounds, which is a tremendous drag on the plane, it takes about 10 miles to accelerate from 300 knots to the drop speed of 500 knots. As was standard procedure, as soon as the first plane started on the attack the FAC would fire a Willy Pete (white phosphorus) rocket to mark the point where he wanted the first bomb dropped. As I accelerated toward the target, I made the mandatory call, "Litter 03 is in hot." The FAC answered, "Cleared in hot; rocket's away," signifying that he had just fired his marking rocket. Now came the tough part: Get that beast up to 500 knots, keep it exactly 1,000 feet above the ground, keep it perfectly level, hit the bomb release button the instant that the bomb sight passes through the smoke of the rocket, and keep an eye out for ground fire. Not to mention that the sweat really started to pour now, coming out of my helmet and into my eyes. My heart rate picked-up and the adrenaline started to flow.

Aircraft #765 was a good bird and accelerated as well as any in the squadron. Flying at 500 knots at 1,000 feet over the jungle is quite a ride as the air is usually turbulent at that altitude and high speed magnifies every bump. The ground goes by in a blur, but amazingly, the adrenaline is flowing so fast and you are so keyed up that at times everything seems to be moving in slow motion. As I got near the target, I started to scan the terrain ahead a little more closely, trying to spot the smoke from the FAC's rocket. Up ahead I picked up the telltale spot of white smoke in the all green jungle and called, "Lead has the mark," making a minute adjustment so that I was heading directly at the target. As the bomb sight passed through the FAC's mark, I mashed the bomb release button with my right thumb. The familiar thump and a slight jolt on the plane told me that a bomb had been released. There was no doubt that the left outboard bomb came off because I immediately had to jam in left rudder to keep the bird flying straight and simultaneously roll into a very tight turn to the left to clear the bomb blast.

That row of hills to the left of the target had seemed harmless the first time I had flown through but was now coming directly at me *very fast!* Things seem to happen about 10 times faster at 500 knots than they do at 300 knots. I eased off the left rudder just a hair and the nose of the bird came up just enough to allow me to rocket over those hills with about 100 feet to spare. That was a little closer than I had wanted, but there wasn't that much clearance between the tops of those hills and the base of the clouds. I eased back on the power and rolled out on a heading of south to go back to the orbit area for another run. About this time KB radioed that he was starting his bomb run. I called and warned, "That damn hill comes at you real fast when you break left after bomb release, and there isn't a lot of room between the hilltops and the clouds." He acknowledged and the FAC cleared him to drop. The FAC also commented in a rather ho-hum fashion, "By the way Litter 03, they were shooting at you on that last pass." I don't care how many missions you have flown, you always get a chill when you learn that somebody is shooting at you.

As I got back to the orbit point and was about to start my second run, KB transmitted, "Litter 04 is off dry." My ears perked right up because pulling off dry (not dropping a bomb) meant that he had a problem. Before I could inquire, KB grumbled, "I couldn't get this dog up to 500 knots." (If you don't have 500 knots on a level bomb run, the fuse will probably not have time to arm and the bomb could be a dud.) He added, "I'll tap the burner next time." (We didn't like to use the afterburner at low altitude because it used fuel at a tremendous rate, and we didn't have that much fuel to begin with.) KB also commented, "The damn hill really does come at you rather quickly."

By now I was on the run-in heading at full power and making small adjustments to my speed, heading, and altitude. The FAC cleared me in hot and instructed, "Drop this bomb about 50 meters short of your last one." Up ahead I could see the smoke from the first bomb that I had dropped and made a mental note that the nose of the bird was going to yaw badly again as the other outboard bomb came off the wing. This time the plane would yaw in the other direction. As I approached the target, I could still hear in the back of my mind the FAC saying, "They were shooting at you."

My altitude was right, my speed was right, and as my sight passed 50 meters short of my last bomb, I pickled off the other outboard bomb. I'd been scanning the area pretty well but still didn't see any sign of ground fire. As the bomb left the wing the nose yawed right, as I had expected, and I corrected immediately as I rolled into my tight left turn. I was even feeling a little smug about how much more smoothly I had corrected the yaw this time as compared with my first run. I was pulling about 5 Gs (five times the force of gravity) in the turn and was watching the hills that had surprised me the last time. They didn't seem to be coming at me nearly as fast this time, but then, the second pass on any mission always seemed slower and more controlled than the first. I guess it had to do with knowing what to expect.

At that instant KB called, "Litter 04 is in hot." I was hoping that he could get his dog up to 500 knots, when suddenly something caught my eye. It was a flash of light that went past the canopy. At 500 knots and a couple hundred feet off the ground, everything is a blur, but this was different. Another flash went by and my heart skipped a beat because this time I knew it was a tracer. Up ahead that row of hills was coming at me rapidly and to my great distress, a string of tracers was coming off the top of those hills and right at me. At the speed I was going there was neither time nor space to maneuver, and I would cross those hills at the exact spot that those tracers were coming from.

I couldn't have been more than 100 feet from the tops of those hills when I crossed them, and that's when it happened. BOOM! The plane was jolted with a deafening bang and I knew instantly that I was in big trouble. Without even thinking, I keyed the mike button and transmitted, "I'm hit!" (KB heard this call but thought it had come over guard channel, which we always monitored. He had no idea that it was me since I didn't use my call sign.) Whatever the reason—whether it was from the impact of getting hit or possibly just from instinct as I tried to get away from the tracers—I found myself in the clouds and completely dependent on my instruments. Smoke was starting to pour into the cockpit, warning lights started to flash, and the engine was beginning to sound like it was having serious problems. I knew I had to get the plane on the ground, and the closest field was at Ban Me Thuot, a civilian strip about 40 miles west of my position. At the speed I was going, I could be there in four minutes, but I had to be VFR (visual below the clouds) because there was no instrument approach at Ban Me Thuot. Besides, with the aircraft severely damaged, I wasn't even sure the instruments were working correctly. All I knew was that the plane would not hold together much longer, and if I wanted to land it, I had to get beneath the clouds again.

I rolled the bird inverted and pulled the nose below the horizon (the fastest way to descend in a high-speed fighter). I was about to roll right side up again when I heard a muffled explosion from somewhere in the engine, and more smoke poured into the cockpit. The annunciator panel, a bank of nine lights that monitors all the aircraft systems, lit up like a Christmas tree. All the systems had failed and the flight controls had frozen. There was no chance of saving the plane now, and I knew I had to get out fast because I was descending in the clouds and didn't know my altitude. For all I knew, I could be rocketing straight down, so I made one last transmission, "I'm getting out!" and ejected. Again I failed to use my call sign.

One of the dangers of low-level attacks is that if something goes wrong, you often don't have time to bail out. To eject from an F-100 you simply raise the armrests and then squeeze the exposed triggers. Everything else is automatic. All of those boring hours sitting in the flight simulator and practicing ejection procedures finally paid off. Once I decided to go, I only vaguely remember doing it: Sit straight, head back, elbows in, feet back. When I raised the armrests, it blew the canopy off. The wind noise was absolutely deafening. I really don't remember squeezing the triggers but I recall the blast of the seat as it ejected, and then I don't remember anything. Although it seemed like an eternity, it was only about five seconds from the time the plane got hit until I ejected.

KB was just approaching the target on his second pass when he heard my transmission and this time recognized my voice. He broke off his attack and started to scan the area for a parachute because he wasn't even sure that I had gotten out of the plane. The FAC never heard my first call but he heard the second. Later he stated that he saw my parachute open and also saw the plane hit the ground a second or two later. Obviously, I didn't get out any too soon.

I have no idea how long I was unconscious, but the first thing that I remember was the silence as I drifted down, suspended from my parachute. It was almost as deafening as the wind blast when the canopy blew off. The first thing I saw was sheets of paper, about 5 to 10 sheets, fluttering in the air around me, probably from the clipboard that had been strapped to my leg. I looked up and saw the most beautiful orange and white, undamaged parachute canopy above my head. I did a quick scan of the area around me and all I could see was jungle. I did not see the plane or any smoke on the ground from a crash site, and that really puzzled me! I did not see the ejection seat that I had ridden out of the stricken bird and then separated from, and I couldn't see my helmet or oxygen mask, which had obviously been torn off by the wind blast. All I could see was endless jungle. And then I got scared. Until that point everything had happened so fast and I had been so busy that I hardly had time to think. I had just made a very high-speed, low-altitude ejection with no severe injuries. The chances of doing that successfully are three to one against you, so somebody was watching over me.

Dangling in that parachute, I guessed that I was 100 to 200 feet in the air, and I finally had the time to realize that I was in real trouble. I kept waiting for the shooting to start but there was nothing but silence. It seemed like I hung in that chute for an hour, but I'm sure it was less than 30 seconds. As I got closer to the ground and began to think that I just might make it down without getting shot, I noticed that I was going to land in a rather large clearing, half of which was covered with water and looked like a swamp. The wind was blowing slightly, and it looked like I would drift over the swamp and land in what appeared to be tall elephant grass on the edge of the water. I tried to remember which risers to pull to control my drift but my mind wouldn't work. In any case, I was more concerned with what was in store for me on the ground.

I was drifting backwards when I landed and the chute just laid me down nice as could be. The tall grass made for a very soft landing, but the real surprise was the water! That entire clearing was a swamp, and the tall elephant grass was really growing in about three feet of water. I came to rest on my back and the thick grass allowed me to sink slowly until only my head and the toes of my boots stuck out of the water. The parachute canopy quickly blew across the open water of the swamp after I released it, and for the first time I heard gunfire. There were two or three bursts from an automatic weapon, but I had no idea which direction it came from or what they were shooting at. I had a very bad feeling that it might have been at the parachute canopy or worse, at me! Fortunately, the three-foot-tall grass virtually covered me, so unless someone knew where I was, they would never find me. Now, for the first time since I had gotten hit, I had a chance to stop, take a deep breath, and take stock of my situation. I didn't like my chances.

The jungle clearing in which I'd landed had looked rather small from the air but was really about a mile wide and a couple of miles long. I was just about in the center of it. Other than my helmet, I had all of my emergency equipment, but of course it was all under water so I wasn't sure how well it would work. I especially didn't want to see the Vietcong coming toward me and have to defend myself with a water-soaked .38 pistol. I had a good bit of blood on my face and my flying suit, but I couldn't tell where it was coming from. My mouth was full of blood because I had bitten my tongue and the insides of my cheeks. This must have happened while I was blacked out because I couldn't remember doing it. I hurt all over, but there didn't seem to be anything broken. I was on the ground and alive and that was reason to be thankful!

About then it dawned on me: my emergency radio!! I dug it out of my G-suit pocket (a G-suit is a flight garment worn by jet pilots that presses on the lower body to maintain the blood supply to the brain during rapid vertical acceleration), shook out the water, turned it on and sure enough, it worked. I could hear the FAC on Emergency Guard channel requesting that a rescue helicopter be scrambled and also fighters to cover the chopper. I heard KB say something and then the FAC again. There was so much chatter on the radio that I couldn't get a word in edgewise. Finally I managed to transmit that I was on the ground and OK. My tongue was so swollen I could hardly talk, but now that I had contact with KB and the FAC again, I was almost frantic to tell them that the gun was on the hill and not in the valley. From where I lay, I could see what looked like "that hill," but I wasn't sure. KB and the FAC were circling overhead, and every time they flew near "that hill," I could hear automatic weapons firing. They were thankful to hear that I was OK and also acknowledged the location of the gun. From then on they stayed well clear of "that hill."

Their major concern was getting me out of there. First the FAC had to find me, so he asked if I could help. All I knew was that I was in the tall grass near a swamp in a clearing. He spotted the water and said that he would zigzag over the area and that I should transmit when he passed overhead. Although I couldn't see him, I could hear the sound of his engine getting louder and louder. Suddenly I could see him directly above me at about 100 feet so I yelled into the radio but he just kept going. I was about to tell him he had missed me when he called to say that he had seen me but would continue to zigzag over the area so as not to give away my exact location to anybody who might have hostile intentions. Smart guy! I may have been lucky enough to live through a high-speed, low-altitude bailout, but if I wasn't careful I could still get myself killed. I was just about to ask if I should move to a different location when the FAC read my mind and said to stay put because I was virtually impossible to see except from directly above. Was I ever glad to hear that! I had no great desire to be sneaking around in Charlie's backyard with only a pistol. Odd as it seems, I had a strange sense of security in that tall grass.

KB was now very anxious to pinpoint my location. Until he knew my exact position he couldn't defend me if Charlie decided to make a move toward me. I listened over the radio while the FAC described to KB my location with respect to some of the nearby landmarks that could be seen from the air. KB thought that he had my position but to be sure, he said that he would make a low pass over the area that I was in and would say "now" as he passed directly over me. That way the FAC could confirm that he had my exact location. Then there was quiet; when there was no chatter on the radio the quiet in the jungle was deafening. When KB said he would make a pass over me he didn't say how low or how fast he would be going, and at 500 knots you don't hear an airplane until it's actually past you. The total silence was suddenly broken by an explosion of noise that was so sudden and so loud that for an instant I thought that it had come from the VC firing mortars at me. He was so low that I swear he would have hit me if I had been standing up. I never did hear KB say "Now," but I did hear the FAC confirm, "Yep, that's him." KB then called me to advise that he still had all of his bombs and ammo so if the bad guys showed up, all I had to do was give him their position and distance from me and he would do the rest. That was a very comforting thought until I remembered that I was lying in water with only my head sticking out, and if he dropped a 750 pound bomb anywhere in that swamp, the concussion would probably kill me. By now my mouth was bleeding quite freely and my tongue had really swollen up, but I frantically mumbled to KB, "Don't drop anywhere within half a mile of me or I'm finished." I also managed to pass along the disturbing news that every time they flew near me, the gun on "that hill" would start firing again.

Suddenly a new voice came up on the radio. The flight of helicopters that I had nearly collided with earlier had been listening in on guard frequency and asked if they could be of assistance. A minute or so later I heard a most beautiful sound, the wop-wop-wop beat of helicopter rotors. The FAC started to brief the choppers as to my location and also to the fact that there was ground fire in the area. He finally told them, "When you get here I'll fire a marker rocket and the downed pilot will be 50 meters north of the mark." As the choppers got closer, I got very nervous again because I couldn't figure out why Charlie hadn't raked the entire swamp with gunfire. They could easily have nailed me. However, I remembered from our intelligence briefings that the VC knew the Americans always sent rescue forces to aid a downed airman and they would just hold their fire until the rescue team arrived. Then they would open up on them and the downed pilot, executing the perfect ambush.

When the lead helicopter radioed, "I've got you in sight, Helix 41," the FAC replied, "Watch for my mark." The FAC's rocket hit about 50 meters from me and sounded like a 20 megaton bomb going off! In less than 30 seconds a helicopter passed directly over-head and the side door gunner waved at me. It was a Huey gunship, and it passed over me at about 50 feet. I then heard the lead chopper call that they had me in sight, and he advised the FAC to stay out of the way. He also asked KB to stand by and be ready in case they needed support, as we all thought the shooting would probably start during the pickup.

With KB on the perch at about 1,500 feet and ready to roll in on any target in the area, the choppers started to fly around me in a cir-cle about 100 yards in diameter and about 100 feet off the ground. About the time that I was wondering what in the world they were doing, one of the choppers transmitted, "I'm in!" and shot into the center of the circle, hovering right on the surface of the water about 10 feet from where I lay. Then all hell broke loose! Every chopper opened fire, shooting away from the circle in every direction to make Charlie keep his head down during the pickup. With all of the noise, I wasn't sure if we were taking any enemy fire or not.

I tried to stand up but only then realized that I was still strapped into my parachute harness, which had my survival kit clipped to it. As I fumbled with the releases to get myself free of the harness, I was surprised to see a Special Forces Green Beret sergeant, standing beside me thigh deep in the water. He was dressed in clean, crisp, starched fatigues and looked like he had just come from a parade ground inspection. He threw me a very snappy salute and said, "Captain, let's get the hell out of here!" He helped me up and we waded over to the hovering helicopter. As water-soaked as I was in all my flying gear, I must have weighed a ton. And I was just about physically drained. So when we got to the chopper, I couldn't even climb the four feet or so to get in. The Green Beret, although smaller than me, literally picked me up and threw me in the chopper door. As he was about to climb aboard, I glanced back to where I had been lying and saw my harness and survival kit. I yelled to the sergeant, "I can't leave that survival kit; it has an emergency radio in it!" When they recovered one, the VC used these radios to send out fake distress signals and try to lure rescue helicopters into traps. Therefore we *never* allowed these radios to fall into the wrong hands. The Green Beret calmly turned around, walked to the harness, threw it over his shoulder, and slowly walked back to the chopper. I think he wanted to show any VC that might have been watching that they couldn't make him run! Of course, every last nerve in my body was screaming, "Let's go, let's go, let's go!" as I just knew the chopper would be riddled with gunfire at any moment. He threw the harness and survival kit in the door and then leaped in himself. Why couldn't I do that? The door gunner gave a "thumbs up" signal to the pilot and we were out of there. The other choppers that had been circling quickly fell into trail formation and we scooted along at about 100 feet above the ground, heading for....I had no idea where.

After a minute or so, when we were clear of the target area and I figured we just might make it out of there alive, I crawled up front to thank the pilot for saving my bacon. He was also the flight leader, and I was surprised to see that these guys were as elated with the successful pickup as I was. It seems that they had flown many types of missions in Vietnam but had never rescued anybody, so this was a first for all of us! The pilot had one request and asked if I would give him an insignia of my rank. My cap was still zipped in my G-suit pocket so I took the silver Captain's bars off, gave them to him, and watched as he proudly stuck them on the overhead panel. I later learned that among chopper crews this was a sign of honor, showing how many men the ship and its crew had saved. At every Air Force fighter base in Southeast Asia there was a custom that at the Officers' Club bar, chopper pilots did not pay for their drinks! The fighter jocks picked up the tab and after this experience, I was all for the custom!

I asked the pilot why we were flying so low, as I didn't want to get gunned down twice in one day, and he told me that since choppers fly so slowly, 50 to 70 mph, the only way to keep from getting shot was to fly very low or very high. Since climbing to 5,000 feet took too long, they preferred to fly very low, so I just held my breath and tried to enjoy the ride. I swear that we were only inches off the ground at times and I'm sure we had to climb over anything that was more than five feet tall. These guys were crazy! But they had saved me, and that made them OK in my book. They informed me that I was going to be dropped off at a Special Forces camp nearby so I could get some medical attention. I really did look a mess, covered with blood and mud and God only knows what else from that swamp. After about a 10 or 15-minute ride, the helicopter landed in a small jungle clearing just long enough for me to hop out. They immediately took off and were gone. I never saw those guys again and never even got their names.

The Special Forces troops showed me to their hospital, which was a one-room underground bunker. The team medic, a kid of about 19, cleaned and sterilized my cuts and abrasions. I was given a clean set of Tiger Stripe Army fatigues and a canteen cup that must have contained at least eight ounces of Scotch. When I started to sip it, the doc told me to drink it right down, saying he thought I needed it. So I drank that entire cup of Scotch in one gulp, and surprisingly it had no effect on me. I think my adrenaline was still pumping so fast that it would have taken a gallon of whiskey to give me a buzz!

The camp commander came by and informed me that Air Force Headquarters in Saigon had been contacted and transportation was being arranged to get me back to Tuy Hoa. The doc made a quick written report for my flight surgeon stating what treatment had been given me, including the Scotch, and I was told to be ready to move out as soon as a C-130 transport landed. My personal equipment—parachute harness, pistol, emergency radio, G-suit, survival vest, etc.—was bundled up for me, and with a couple of heavily armed troops I was taken out to the clearing that these guys called their landing strip. I swear I couldn't believe that a C-130 could land, let alone take off, in that tiny space. It didn't help when my escorts told me that the C-130 would land with its back ramp open, roll to the end of the clearing, turn around and take off immediately in the opposite direction from its landing. We would be at the end of the clearing, and I had to get in the open ramp door as soon as the plane turned around. He wasn't going to wait, as Charlie loved to lob mortar rounds into the clearing when a plane landed in an attempt to disable it. I was beginning to wonder if I was ever going to make it through this day.

I could hear the C-130 long before I could see it. We were sitting at the edge of a clearing that had very tall trees surrounding it, just to make it even more difficult! Suddenly the sky was full of airplane and he just seemed to drop into the clearing. There was a roar of reversing engines and the squeal of brakes, a huge cloud of dust, and there, right in front of me, was the giant transport. My escort screamed, "Go!" and I was up the ramp and into the plane. Immediately the engines roared and we were gone. I couldn't see the takeoff from the belly of that C-130 and it's probably just as well, since I didn't need any more excitement that day! I still don't know how we got over those trees at the end of the clearing.

Again, I went up front to thank a crew for a great job of flying and for sticking out their necks to help me. (Jim Fogg, the pilot of the C-130, and I would meet again years later as pilots for Western Airlines.) In about 30 minutes we landed at Tuy Hoa and I found that KB had landed only about 10 minutes before us. All this time he had been bombing and strafing the hill where the big gun was located. Before that day was over, about a dozen flights of fighters would literally bomb "that hill" into oblivion.

Less than two hours after KB and I had taken off, I was back on the ground at Tuy Hoa. Many things about this mission still remain a mystery. Who were those guys on the hill? A few weeks after this mission the Tet Offensive kicked off, with the VC attacking just about every city and village in South Vietnam during the Lunar New Year Tet holiday, after a truce for the holiday had been declared by both sides. Intelligence guessed that this was an enemy force that was supposed to hide in the jungle until Tet and then attack a nearby town or village, perhaps Ban Me Thuot. But why did they shoot at the FAC, who would never have seen them had they not opened fire on him? And then why didn't they open fire on the helicopters that picked me up? Nobody knew the answers.

Later investigation of my parachute harness turned up something strange and disturbing. The harness still had the D-ring (manual actuator) and the automatic lanyard (barometric actuator) attached to it. Both of these actuators are connected to the ejection seat, and during an ejection they stay with the seat after pilot separation, thus opening the parachute. If both of the actuators were still on the harness, they obviously hadn't gone with the seat, and this brings up the biggest question: How did the parachute open? Nobody really knows. There were a lot of theories, but they were just guesses. The fact is, the chute should not have opened. I just like to think that somebody up there really likes me.

21

SHOOTDOWN OF JIM POLLAK (PART II)

Kirk "KB" Clark, USAF, F-100D, January 4, 1968
{ Date of hire by Western Airlines: 10/28/1968 }

KB Clark, left, and Jim Pollak on the ramp at Tuy Hoa right after Jim's safe return. Jim Fogg had already departed to relieve Crown 3 over the Gulf of Tonkin.

I met KB Clark in the early 1980s during the dark days for Western Airlines. I had been flying as a second officer on the Boeing 727 at our San Francisco base, but the flying had been cut back quite a bit, and as the seniority system worked, I was bumped out of SFO by someone more senior and began to commute to the Salt Lake City base. Western had furloughed more than 200 pilots and the seniority list numbered just over 900 working pilots, down from nearly 1,200. I was happy to be among the working.

My commute lasted for nearly three years, and during that time I flew with a whole new group of pilots, many from our former Denver base who had been commuting for quite a bit longer. KB was a Denver commuter and was a very senior first officer on the 727. We flew together several times over that period, right up to 1986 when the Delta merger was announced and I was able to transfer back to SFO. KB was a pleasure to fly with and always had good stories to tell. As an Air Force Academy graduate, class of 1962, he was coincidentally a classmate of Dick Sell, whose story is also in this book. KB and Dick saw each other at the 50th *reunion of their graduating class in 2012.*

KB told me this incredible story when we were flying together, and years later I contacted him and asked if he would write it for this book. He graciously agreed, put me in touch with Jim Pollak, who related the involvement of Jim Fogg, and the rest is history. It reminds me of another Western pilot who had flown the F-100 in Vietnam and was shot down and rescued by an Army helicopter. Jerry Potter was in the reserves at Travis when I was first flying for Western, and he told a great story about being shot down in the Delta, south of Saigon, then landing in the middle of a wide river after he ejected. The most dangerous part of his ordeal was the rescue, as it seems the Army helicopter pilots were granted an additional one-week leave for every pilot they picked up. The helicopters were swarming like bees over him and he was in fear of a midair collision right over his head, but he figured the rotor wash that was forcing him underwater would probably drown him first. It was a great story, and I talked to Jerry a couple of times but lost track of him and never got his story in writing.

KB Clark is a wonderful guy, and I am happy to have had the opportunity to fly with him and hear this story, about three men I am proud to number among my friends. Now, here is KB Clark's story of January 4, 1968.

....

On January 4, 1968, I was an F-100 pilot assigned to the 308th TFS (Tactical Fighter Squadron) stationed at Tuy Hoa Air Base, RVN (Republic of Vietnam). Tuy Hoa was located on the coast of South Vietnam on the South China Sea, approximately equidistant from Saigon to the southwest and Da Nang to the north. On that day Captain Jim Pollak and I were assigned alert duty for the 308th TFS.

I had known Jim since August 1964 when we both reported to the 493rd TFS at RAF (Royal Air Force) Station Lakenheath, United Kingdom. We were both new lieutenants, having just completed F-100 combat crew training, and it was our first operational fighter assignment. I can't tell you how thrilled I was to get that assignment, as I had long dreamed of flying fighters in the same skies over Europe that had seen the great air battles of World War II.

A fighter squadron is a closely knit group. As a tour in Europe was an accompanied tour, which meant our families could be with us, we all got to know each other very well. By January 4, 1968, Jim and I had flown together a number of times in many different situations, both in Europe and in combat in Southeast Asia. I knew and respected Jim's abilities, and that is a good relationship to have with someone with whom you are flying combat. We were both married with young families: Jim and Bonnie had two daughters, while Cookie and I had two sons. During slack periods on alert or other times that we weren't flying, family was a frequent subject of conversation, so I usually knew the latest on Bonnie and the girls.

At Tuy Hoa, each squadron maintained two aircraft on alert. On January 4, 1968, Jim and I were on alert for the 308th, and when we pulled alert together, we alternated leading the flight. It was Jim's turn to lead so I would fly his wing; his call sign was Litter 03 and mine was Litter 04. Each alert aircraft was backed into a revetment that provided protection on three sides. Our aircraft were each loaded with four Mk-117 low-drag bombs (750 pound slick bombs), with no delay set in the fuses, and 800 rounds of 20mm high-explosive incendiary (HEI) shells. Each aircraft also carried two 335 gallon externally mounted fuel tanks called drop tanks. Hooked up to each was a start unit, a small jet engine that produces exhaust gas that is carried to the aircraft starter through a hose. This compressed air is used to turn the starter on the fighter's jet engine.

On that early afternoon, Jim and I were sitting in the alert shack in our flight suits and G-suits (our parachutes and helmets were in the aircraft) when the phone rang. A pilot from the 306th TFS picked up the receiver, answered, listened, then turned and looked at Jim and me and said, "Scramble 3 and 4." We jumped up and ran to our jets. My crew chief had the starter unit winding up as I hit the ladder to climb into the cockpit. As I settled into the ejection seat I hit the engine start button and signaled my crew chief for air from the start unit. He gave me air, the start-unit hose inflated, and my engine began to turn.

As my engine started, I put on my helmet. Our radios were preset to ground control frequency, so as soon as my engine had started and my radio warmed up, I radioed, "Litter 04 is on." Jim responded, "Roger. Tuy Hoa Ground, scramble two," and ground control cleared us to taxi to Runway 21. Jim taxied straight out of the revetment, then he turned about 15 degrees to the left and taxied across the ramp directly toward the arming area for Runway 21. I taxied behind Jim and to one side of his jet exhaust. We taxied at a good clip; time was critical as the alert birds were expected to be airborne ASAP (roughly 5 minutes) after being scrambled. As we taxied, I slipped into my parachute harness and snapped the leg and chest straps, then hooked up my shoulder straps and seat belt.

Jim pulled into the arming area and brought his plane to a stop. I taxied up next to him on his right side and stopped. We were parked next to the end of Runway 21, facing opposite the direction in which we would take off, with our guns pointed out over the beach and the South China Sea. A crew chief chocked my aircraft's main gear tires and I placed my hands in sight on top of the glare shield, so the armorers would be confident I wasn't touching any switches while they did their work. The armorers manually charged my guns and activated their electrical connections, pulled the pins from the bombs and pylons, and armed the pylons with explosive charges. There were two sets of explosive charges placed in each pylon. One set was to fire when I hit the bomb button to drop a bomb. This charge would thrust the bomb away from the aircraft by activating plungers in the pylon to ensure positive separation of the bomb from the aircraft. The other explosive charge was to blow the pylon off the wings if that became necessary during an emergency.

The crew chief made a last-chance walk-around inspection of my jet, pulled the gear pins and wheel chocks, and gave me a thumbs-up. I pulled the pins from my ejection seat, showed them to the crew chief, and returned his thumbs-up signal.

When all the ground personnel were clear of our aircraft, Jim instructed me to switch over to our command post frequency, where we would get our clearance. Once there, Jim radioed, "Surfside (call sign of the command post), Litter 03 ready to copy." Surfside responded, "Litter 03, your initial vector is 242 degrees for 64 nautical miles. You'll find your FAC (forward air controller), call sign Helix 41, on the 115 degree radial at 18 NM of channel 117." Then Surfside gave us a tactical frequency on which to contact Helix 41. We both copied this information on our mission data cards, and to confirm, Jim read this back to Surfside and we switched over to tower frequency.

The information we had gotten from Surfside told us a great deal. While it did not tell us what the target was, it told us just about everything else, certainly all we needed at that point. For example, it told us that after takeoff we should fly out the Tuy Hoa TACAN 242 degree radial to 64 NM on our distance measuring equipment. (TACAN, short for tactical air navigation equipment, is a navigation aid that we carried in the F-100. TACAN stations were strategically placed at secure ground locations throughout the war zone for our use as navigation aids.) The Tuy Hoa 242/64 position was approximately the 115 degree radial at 18 DME off channel 117, which was the Ban Me Thuot East TACAN. That put Helix 41, our forward air controller, about 23 NM east-southeast of Ban Me Thuot City. We could contact Helix 41 on the tactical frequency once we arrived in the rendezvous area. He would be flying a small, propeller-driven O-1 Cessna observation plane which carried white phosphorus (Willy Pete) marking rockets. He would direct the air strike. The 64 NM position from Tuy Hoa that Surfside had given us was valuable information, as Jim would use that distance, combined with the weather forecast for Tuy Hoa on our return, to determine a bingo fuel for the flight. Bingo fuel is the fuel state at which we would have to quit fighting and head for home.

On tower frequency Jim called for clearance to take off, and when we got clearance we lowered our canopies. As Jim pushed his power up and began to taxi, he transmitted, "Litter 03, canopy, pins, and lanyard." I responded, "Litter 04, canopy, pins, and lanyard." This provided verbal confirmation that we had our canopies down and locked, our ejection seat pins pulled (which armed the ejection seat), and the lanyard hooked to the parachute D-ring in the event a low-altitude ejection was necessary due to a major aircraft malfunction just after takeoff.

Coming out of the arming area, Jim turned left toward the runway and then, when on the runway, took another left to line up in the middle of the left side of Runway 21. I followed but stayed to the right of Jim, then passed behind him on the runway, turned left, and stopped in the middle of the right half of the runway with my aircraft slightly aft of his. By taxiing in this manner, at no time did either of us have armed guns pointed at the other. This precluded the possibility of stray voltage causing a 20mm round to fire accidentally and ruin the other guy's day!

As I braked to a halt next to Jim, he looked at me, raised his right hand with index finger extended, then whirled it around in a horizontal circle, his signal to run our engines up for takeoff. I stood on the brakes and eased the throttle forward to full military power. I looked the instruments and gauges over, and when I was satisfied I had a good airplane, I looked up again at Jim. He looked at me, I nodded "Yes" and he waved "Bye." As he released his brakes I punched the button on my clock and the second hand began to sweep. I watched the eyelids (the nozzle, the last couple of feet on the exhaust tail pipe on an afterburning jet engine) on Jim's engine snap to the full open position. Fire erupted from his tail pipe and almost instantly stabilized in that classic F-100 afterburner (AB) exhaust flame pattern. Jim had a good afterburner light and he accelerated down the runway. With a full combat load of fuel and ordnance, we did not make formation takeoffs for safety reasons, but made single-ship takeoffs with 30-second spacing, then joined up in formation on the way to the target. Single-ship takeoffs gave each pilot the whole runway to himself so he did not have to give up any power, as he normally would in a formation takeoff. So when my second hand hit 30 seconds I released my brakes, rolled a few feet, and then moved the throttle outboard to light the afterburner. The engine pressure ratio gauge needle dropped, indicating the nozzle had gone full open, and as the needle returned to the normal range, I felt the thrust of the afterburner as it lit. I had a good AB light and picked up speed as I raced down the runway.

After taking off and raising my landing gear and flaps, I kept the AB engaged until I had 400 knots indicated airspeed for the join-up. Jim held 300 knots so I would be able to overtake him. As I began to close on him I eased my throttle back to bleed off some airspeed while Jim made a gentle, 30 degree bank turn to the right to track out Tuy Hoa's 242 degree radial. I joined up on Jim in close formation to look him over and make sure all was well with his jet and ordnance. I looked over his right side, slid low and behind him, and then moved to his left side. His airplane and bombs all looked good so I gave him the "OK" sign, which he acknowledged with a nod. Jim then gave me a hand signal that he would look me over, so I rolled up in an 80 degree bank with my belly toward him. I held the aircraft there for a few seconds and then rolled back to wings level. Jim was satisfied with what he had seen so he gave me the "OK" sign, then signaled me out into route formation, two to four ship widths out, for the flight to the target.

Jim radioed to me, "Bingo fuel today will be 3,500 pounds." I acknowledged and thought it was a good figure, as it looked like the weather at Tuy Hoa might be somewhat marginal on our return.

As we proceeded toward the target, I began to think about some of the specifics of the airstrike. The clouds below were getting quite thick; it was turning into a pretty solid layer beneath us and becoming clear that the weather would be a factor on this mission. We had Mk-117 low-drag bombs with no delay set in the fuses, 750 pound slick bombs that would explode immediately upon ground impact. With low-drag bombs, we all preferred to drop from a 30 to 45 degree dive angle for several reasons. With a higher dive angle there is less exposure to anti-aircraft fire. In South Vietnam the Vietcong (VC) and North Vietnamese Army (NVA) had a significant number of automatic weapons that were very effective on aircraft below 6,000 to 8,000 feet. Thus a pilot in a steep dive would be exposed to effective anti-aircraft fire for a relatively short time. The lower the cloud level, the lower the dive angle we were able to use, and bombing under an overcast at about 1,500 feet above the ground required a level bomb attack, putting the aircraft in the high-threat envelope during the entire time of the airstrike.

The second reason to use a 30 to 45 degree dive has to do with the accuracy of the bombing, with a high dive angle being the most accurate and level bombing the least accurate, with much higher chance of the bomb falling short or long. Even a 5 to 15 degree dive angle was preferable to making a level bombing run, but as we approached the rendezvous with the FAC, we were looking at a solid layer of clouds below. From our position above the layer, my guess was that we would be lucky to get a 15 degree dive angle and might have to settle for 5 degrees or level bombing.

Jim signaled me to switch over to our tactical frequency, where we would work the air strike with our FAC. After we checked in on the tactical frequency, Jim contacted the FAC and the radio transmissions went as follows:

"Helix 41, Litter 03."

"Roger Litter 03, Helix 41 here, go ahead."

"Litter 03 is a flight of two F-100s. We have eight Mk-117 low-drag bombs and 1,600 rounds of 20mm."

As Jim looked for a hole in the clouds, Helix 41 gave us a target briefing. He said he had come under heavy automatic weapons fire in an area where there were no known enemy troops. This was not an unusual situation, as the enemy was quite good at secretly moving large numbers of troops from one point to another in South Vietnam, especially through the heavy jungle found in western South Vietnam in the vicinity of its borders with Laos and Cambodia. He went on to say that there were no friendly forces in the area. Helix said the target area was too hot for him to stay, so to mark the target he would fire one white phosphorus rocket and depart the area to the south. He would direct the attack from the south. He briefed us that the target was in a valley along the base of a range of large hills or small mountains. A stream flowed out of a pass in the mountains, and this would help us identify the target area. Because of the terrain and the weather, Helix 41 thought we might be restricted to a single run-in heading on our attacks—a long, straight-in final approach up the valley. Helix requested multiple bomb passes and asked that we drop one bomb per pass in order to do the most damage, because judging from the ground fire he had taken, he thought the enemy was well dispersed. He reported the ceiling was somewhat ragged, varying between 1,500 and 2,000 feet above the target elevation. He gave us a local altimeter setting and briefed us that a flight of five to seven Army Huey helicopters had just passed through the valley but was no longer in sight.

Although Helix had suggested the attack strategy, the final decision on the tactics we would use was Jim's (lead always made the tactical decisions), and he would make that call after we got below the clouds and took a look at the target, terrain, and weather.

During the target briefing by Helix there was one thing that struck a note of concern with me. It was uncommon for the VC or NVA to pick a fight with a FAC unless they felt confident they could knock him down quickly. They knew a FAC could get fighters on the scene in very short order so usually, when the VC or NVA knew they had been sighted, they would try to disappear into the jungle before the fighters arrived. This group seemed to be spoiling for a fight, and it could have been that they felt they had something they needed to defend. The VC and NVA had been very successful in conducting a secret and a very large buildup of their forces in South Vietnam, and it was just a few weeks after this mission that the Communists launched the Tet Offensive. In hindsight, it would seem that this force may have been part of that buildup.

Jim sighted a hole in the clouds and took us down through it. Once below the clouds, Jim signaled me to move into a more maneuverable and fluid position about 500 feet behind him and 30 to 45 degrees to one side. This allowed me to look around more, but most important, it allowed Jim to maneuver his aircraft more rapidly and aggressively if necessary. We were still some distance away from the FAC rendezvous point, so we worked our way around hills and weather towards the 115 degree radial at 18 DME (distance measurement equipment) point on the Ban Me Thuot TACAN. This put us in the valley where our target was located, and we headed east through it.

This valley was a couple of miles wide with mountains on the right (south) whose peaks were obscured by clouds. The ceiling looked like it might get a little lower the farther to the right you went in the valley, but it was difficult to say. Helix had called the ceiling correctly—it was ragged, and it varied from 1,200 to 2,000 feet. The left (north) side of the valley was defined by high terrain rising 1,000 to 2,000 feet. (In Eau Claire, Wisconsin, my hometown, we would call this sort of terrain mountainous, so for the purposes of this story, these were mountains.) Some of these mountaintops were in the clouds and some weren't. Just to the left of the target area was the pass through the mountains where the stream seemed to originate. This pass was V-shaped and the cloud base was nearly down on the mountains forming the pass. This pass would provide us a wee window through which to fly by breaking hard to the left after bomb release. The weather beyond the target was lousy, so we needed to stay out of that area.

As we flew low up the valley, Jim spotted Helix 41 and called out his position. I picked him up visually, and he saw us. We approached the target area and turned hard left, flying through the wee window and out over a wider valley that was perhaps three to four miles in width. The valley floor seemed to be a green, grassy meadow. Jim kept turning until he had turned 180 degrees and was set up on a downwind, flying west. Jim called me: "Litter 04, take spacing in the turn and set 'em up hot." After I had turned 90 degrees to the left and flown through the wee window, I rolled out and flew straight ahead toward the far side of the grassy meadow until I had about two miles of spacing on Jim. Then I turned left onto a downwind behind him.

Jim had briefed the tactics we would use. Because of the weather and terrain, we would fly a rectangular pattern with left-hand turns. The mountain range would be on our left throughout the bomb run. We would be restricted to one run-in heading with a long, low, straight run up the valley to the target, and then after bomb release, we would make a hard turn to the left and through the wee window. It would have been nice if there had been some alternatives to this plan, but there were none.

I thought it might be a good idea if I tried to mix things up a little bit, so I decided that coming up the valley I would fly toward a point as far to the right of the target as the weather would allow. Then I would turn left and start a 5 degree dive to deliver my bomb.

Additionally, I would fly at 450 knots while Jim would be carrying 500 knots during his delivery. The big question for me was whether the weather would cooperate. I remembered that on our first pass the ceiling was ragged and a bit lower to the right, just where I needed to fly for this plan to work. But I thought it would be worth a try.

As I proceeded on downwind, I set my armament switches and bombsight for 5 degree dive angle bombing. I noticed the meadow gave way to shrubs and a few trees, then increasingly heavy vegetation, and finally there was thick jungle below.

Suddenly, up ahead, I saw several vertical exhaust or condensation trails extending from the ground up into the clouds. I immediately thought that unguided rockets had been fired at Jim from the ground. I looked but couldn't see anyone. I called Jim and told him what I had seen and to keep his eyes peeled on downwind. Jim acknowledged my call and then radioed, "Litter 03 in hot. Request a mark ASAP." He was rolling into that long, low, straight run up the valley, accelerating to 500 knots.

Helix responded, "Litter 03, you're cleared in hot. There's my mark—hit the smoke. They're shooting and it's too hot for me. I've got to get out of here." Helix turned hard to the south.

As I turned base and then turned up the valley, I pushed up my throttle to accelerate to 450 knots and radioed, "Litter 04 in hot. I've got the target." Helix cleared me in hot. I hugged the mountains on my left as I raced up the valley. I saw Jim's bomb hit right on target as he radioed, "03 off left, with one away." Halfway up the valley I turned to the right to fly toward a point to the right of the target. As I crossed the valley at an angle, the clouds began to force me lower and the visibility became increasingly bad. I continued and then rolled left, moving my nose with the rudder about 5 degrees below the horizon. I rolled out of the turn and as the pipper on my bombsight came across the target, I realized I was too low to drop a bomb. I pulled up, broke hard left, and shot through the wee window without dropping a bomb. I radioed, "04 off dry."

I did not want to go through without dropping a bomb, as this was a freebie for their gunners. Because I hadn't done anything to cause them to keep their heads down, they were going to get another shot at me that I hadn't planned on. It now became obvious that I wasn't going to be able to get a 5 degree dive angle, so I would have to bomb straight and level for the rest of the mission. I adjusted the depression of the pipper on my bombsight for level bombing.

On downwind I saw more of those vertical exhaust trails from the ground up into the clouds, and Jim saw them too. He called turning base and then in on final, hot. Helix cleared him. As I called turning base and began my turn to final I heard Jim transmit, "03 is off with one away." I saw Jim's bomb explode and Helix 41 called, "Beautiful."

Then I heard a very faint, nearly inaudible, slightly broken transmission: "Fire—ejecting." I know Jim Pollak's voice, and I knew that if it was not my imagination, it was Jim transmitting. But it was so faint that I thought it must be my imagination. At least I hoped it was.

As I streaked toward the target I radioed, "Litter 03, this is Litter 04. Do you read?" There was no answer. Then I tried, "Jim, this is KB. Do you read?" Again there was silence. I knew that the transmission had not been my imagination and that Jim was probably down, but I had no idea where he might be. I also knew I might need all my ordnance, so I had to go through dry on this pass too—another freebie for the gunners, so I could keep all my ordnance for a possible RES CAP (Rescue, Combat Air Patrol) for Jim.

I asked Helix if he had heard Litter 03 radio that he was ejecting. He replied, "Negative." Just before the target I called, "Litter 04 is through dry," and broke left for the wee window. As I popped through the window, I saw Jim hanging in his parachute about a mile ahead of me. Then, just to the right of Jim and about three miles farther out, there was a huge explosion as Jim's aircraft impacted on a ridgeline. At that moment my mission changed from an airstrike to a rescue. We would employ every asset in the area to make a successful pickup.

Much of what happened next was compressed into a very short time frame and some things occurred simultaneously. I'm not able to tell the story in an instantaneous manner, so bear with me.

I kept my turn going to the left so Jim was about 1,000 feet to my right as I passed him. He was about 800 to 1,000 feet above the ground and seemed to be looking down at the valley where he was going to land. I moved the throttle outboard to light the afterburner and got a good light. I did this twice, hoping the noise of the after-burner lighting would signal Jim that I saw him and knew of his predicament. I was also rocking my wings as I passed him, but Jim didn't respond at all to the noise. I learned later that Jim had been knocked unconscious during the ejection sequence and I suppose he was unconscious when I tried to signal him.

I radioed, "Helix 41, Litter 03 is down. He has ejected and has a good chute. I'm going to guard." (Guard frequency is 243.0 MHz on the UHF radio and is reserved for emergency communications. Everybody monitors guard while working on other frequencies.) By saying I was going to guard, I meant I would transmit on guard frequency and everybody within radio reception range would hear me.

On guard I radioed, "Mayday, mayday, mayday. This is Litter 04 on guard. Litter 03 has been shot down and has ejected. He has a good parachute. I need a helicopter in here ASAP to pick him up. My position is on the 110 degree radial at 17 DME of Channel 117, Ban Me Thuot East." Almost immediately someone radioed back that they were a flight of Huey helicopters in the area and that they were on the way.

Then guard frequency exploded with radio transmissions. It seemed that everyone in Vietnam had something to say on guard and needed to say it right then and there! It just about rendered the frequency useless for the time being, and I couldn't get people to clear it. But the word about Jim was out and help was on the way. What amazing good fortune we had just experienced—helicopters had responded even before Jim hit the ground.

I needed to stay on guard frequency because Jim had an emergency radio with him that operated only on guard, so if I was to have any chance of communicating with him it would have to be there. I felt confident that, in spite of all the chatter on the emergency frequency, I would recognize Jim's voice through the din if he transmitted. I had to.

The helicopters were probably operating on their tactical frequency and monitoring guard. If they needed to talk to me or if I needed to talk to them, we could make contact on guard and then go to a discrete frequency to talk. I was sorely tempted to toss a couple of 750 pounders into the mountain pass that formed the V of the wee window, as I was sure there were guns there and possibly all over that mountain range. I resisted the temptation because I knew I might need those bombs if a big gun were to open up when the helicopters arrived.

Jim had landed almost in the middle of the meadow, which was fortunate for all of us. I was orbiting at the base of the clouds, and from my vantage point Jim stood out like a sore thumb. I thought that from the ground, depending on the height of the grass, he might be difficult to see. If the grass was high it would complicate the situation for any enemy troops sent out to capture him. I set my gun sight and armament switches for strafing and was prepared to roll in if I saw any movement toward him in that grassy meadow. Had the enemy been moving through the grass toward Jim, I think I would have seen them as the grass did not afford any cover or camouflage from eyes above.

Ejecting from an aircraft at low altitude and high speed, as Jim had just done, is extremely dangerous and can cause very serious and even fatal injuries, even if everything goes as advertised. I hadn't heard from Jim yet so I thought I'd better go down and take a look at him to see how he was doing. I chose to make one very low pass so I could get a good look, then pull up to the perch again and continue to watch for any threats to him in the grassy meadow. I decided on just one pass because I was sure the enemy would be shooting at me from the mountain range, and the last thing we needed was for a round fired at me to hit Jim hiding there in the grass.

I let down to about 20 feet above the grassy meadow and flew at 500 knots, planning to pass just a couple of feet to the left of Jim so I could see him really well. As it turned out I approached him from his back and he didn't see or hear me coming. He was sitting, looking at something in his hands which I believe was his emergency radio. I think he was trying to get it to work. The noise of an F-100 at full military power passing a few feet over a person's head at 500 knots is enough to knock that person over, so I knew that if Jim hadn't known I was in the area before, he surely knew now. As I pulled back up just below the clouds to resume my orbit, I transmitted on guard, "Litter 03, this is Litter 04. Do you read?" There was still no answer, but I felt better. I was confident Jim was in reasonably good shape, and if the helicopters arrived soon, we could get him picked up and safely out of there.

A moment later, in spite of all the radio chatter on guard, I recognized Jim's voice: "This is Litter 03 on guard. Does anyone read me?" I replied, "Roger Litter 03, this is Litter 04. I've got you in sight and helicopters are coming and should be here soon. If you need 20mm, let me know." I had no idea if he could hear me over all the other talk on guard.

It wasn't too long before I saw a flight of Huey helicopters approaching, really hugging the ground. I hoped they were gunships because that would provide more firepower in addition to mine if it were needed during the pickup or exit from the area.

With the arrival of the helicopters, I turned my attention to the mountain range. If the enemy had some 23mm automatic weapons on this side of the range, this would be the time they would bring them to bear on the helicopters. But I didn't see any big guns open up, and the helicopters didn't report any incoming fire. I watched them hover near Jim and it seemed that in no time one of the helicopters had him on board. The flight then moved up the valley in the same direction our downwind had taken us, heading for a point just south of Ban Me Thuot City. I didn't know where they were going to take Jim, but I knew he was in good hands.

As the helicopters disappeared into the haze, I transmitted on guard, "Helix 41, this is Litter 04. Let's go back to tactical frequency." I switched my radio and called, "Helix 41, Litter 04. Let's go back to work." He replied "Roger Litter 04, Helix 41. When you get set up, you'll be cleared in hot. Do you need a mark?" I replied, "Negative," and I think he was happy to stay away from the target.

I pushed my throttle up and turned to enter a downwind. I reset my sight depression and armament switches for level bombing and called turning base and turning final, hot. Helix 41 offered, "Litter, you might think about dropping all your bombs on this one pass. These guys are pretty good shots." For some reason, the idea of dropping all my bombs on one pass hadn't entered my mind; my thought process had been locked into dropping them singly on separate passes. But Helix's suggestion was clearly a good one. I could still get reasonably good target coverage by dropping my bombs in rapid succession on one pass.

As my bombsight passed about 100 meters short of the target, I pressed the bomb button three times. First the two outboard bombs blew off, then the left inboard, followed by the right inboard bomb. I broke hard left and shot through the wee window, out over the grassy meadow and onto a downwind, where I set my sight and armament switches for strafing. I came around base and onto final for that long run up the valley. I pushed the speed up to 500 knots and located my target just on the other side of the stream where a small road crossed, then put a good burst of 20mm into it. I made a 7-G left turn to pull out from the pass and again slipped through the wee window. I came around for a second strafe pass and this time I hit a position to the left of the first but still on the stream. I ran out of ammo, my guns went silent, and I made a 7½-G recovery straight ahead. I pulled up hard into the clouds, and as I climbed, I turned slightly left to set course for Tuy Hoa. I checked my fuel and saw that I had plenty to get home—I was still over bingo fuel. I turned off my sight and armament switches and at about 8,000 feet I popped out of the clouds into blue skies. Sunshine flooded my cockpit.

I called Helix for a bomb damage assessment report. I copied his report and then said, "*Adios*" as I leveled off at 19,500 feet for the trip home. At that point a tremendous sense of relief came over me that started at the top of my head and slowly flowed down my entire body. We had really dodged a bullet that day (although obviously not all of them). Jim could have been killed or captured, but instead he was safe and apparently in reasonably good shape, considering what he had been through. I wasn't going to have to write a letter to Bonnie telling her how we had lost Jim. Instead, he could write his own letter to his wife detailing the day's events.

This day gave all of us much for which to be thankful.

22

RESCUE OF JIM POLLAK

Jim Fogg, USAF, C-130P, January 4, 1968
{ Date of hire by Western Airlines: 5/26/1969 }

Jim Fogg at an awards ceremony, 1967.

I found the story of Jim Pollak's shootdown and rescue fascinating for several reasons. The coincidence that all three of the pilots involved ended up going to work for Western Airlines is the main reason, but more than that, my curiosity was piqued by the incident because I had flown throughout the Ban Me Thuot area in the C-7. When I was flying in Vietnam, late in 1968 and into 1969, we would spend days shuttling from Ban Me Thuot to the Special Forces camps in that part of South Vietnam. I am positive that I would have either flown into or known of the camp where the pickup was made. So I started a search. My research on the possibilities is included at the end.

Now here is Jim Fogg's story of the part he played in the rescue of Jim Pollak.

....

This particular story tells of my involvement in the rescue of Jim Pollak on January 4, 1968.

My Southeast Asia tour had started on March 14, 1967, as my buddy Captain Bill Delony and I flew a brand-new C-130P from the Lockheed factory in Marietta, Georgia, to Udorn Air Base, Thailand. During that one-year tour of duty, we would be stationed for three months at Udorn Air Base and for nine months at Tuy Hoa Air Base, Vietnam. My sole purpose in Southeast Asia was to save lives. I never hurt a soul during my tour, unless a night illumination flare accidentally fell on someone's head. On each and every mission I prayed that no American pilot would be shot down. However, if fate turned against us, my crew, as well as all rescue forces, was pre- pared to rescue and recover the downed airman as expeditiously as possible. Hopefully this could be done without further loss of air- craft or crew.

I have given more background on my mission and written about some of the interesting events that occurred during my tour in another story. This story is about the events of January 4, 1968, and it proves that this is a small world after all.

By January 4, 1968, several changes had been made in my life. First was my PCS (permanent change of station) move from Udorn Air Base, Thailand, to Tuy Hoa Air Base, Vietnam, a few months ear- lier. My crew was one of the first two crews sent from Udorn to Tuy Hoa to begin the transfer of the full squadron. Our C-130Ps were attached to the 39th ARRS (Air Rescue and Recovery Squadron) and joined the three F-100 squadrons at Tuy Hoa. Second, by January 1968 I had become a more seasoned veteran, with most of my 38 suc- cessful recoveries behind me. I could see light at the end of the tun- nel and was starting to think I would make it home after all, and there would be life after Vietnam. Only 10 more weeks and I would be heading back to the good old U.S.A. and a reunion with my wife, who had been teaching school in Maryland for the past year. I was getting short! But there was no time to celebrate yet, as anything could happen in 10 weeks. The enemy seemed more brazen than ever as the 1968 Tet (Lunar New Year) approached. Those Asians sure knew how to throw a holiday, as the next six weeks would prove. All Hades broke out as the war became more intense than ever during the infamous Tet Offensive of 1968.

My mission on January 4, 1968, was the afternoon watch over the Gulf of Tonkin. My call sign was Crown 4 and my duty was to relieve Crown 3, who had been on station over the gulf since before light that morning. Just as Crown kept its rescue forces over Laos for the overland missions (exclusively Air Force), each day a SAR (search and rescue) team was maintained over water for the Navy missions off the aircraft carriers in the gulf and for the Air Force missions that crossed into North Vietnam from over water. We were not prejudiced! We were just as happy to rescue a Navy or Air Force pilot, as they all displayed the same stars and stripes.

I was progressing up the coast of Vietnam, climbing through about 17,000 feet a few miles north of the city of Qui Nhon, when suddenly the silence was shattered by that all too familiar "Mayday, mayday, mayday." Reacting by instinct, I switched my radio over to guard frequency and copied down all the necessary particulars. An F-100 had been shot down to the west of my position.

Crown 3 could forget about being relieved now and would have to settle in for a longer day of duty, as I had a more pressing problem. Upon receiving the coordinates of the downed plane, I asked my navigator to plot its position and wheeled my aircraft in that direction. His response was that this crash site was just inside Cambodia. That surprised me because until then, I was unaware of any missions inside Cambodia. Maybe he was right, or he could have said it to dissuade me from taking off on another of my tangents. He was convinced I had a secret, strong yearning to get his tail blown off in combat, something he had expressed to me on several occasions. I wished him no harm, though, as I valued my tail also—even more than his! However, no matter where the downed pilot was, we were going to retrieve him if we could.

The call sign of the downed plane was Litter 03, and his wingman, Litter 04, was continuously flying over the area. It was he who had sent the initial distress call and relayed all the pertinent information. We were also told that the pilot was now located at a very small airfield whose runway appeared very inadequate in length and width for my plane. I was amazed that he had the good fortune to be shot down where I could personally recover him, if indeed I could land there. Years later, I learned that Litter 03 had actually crashed nearby and an Army helicopter had delivered him to this pea patch.

Upon approaching this field from the north, I spotted the pilot standing to the left of the runway at the far south end. Immediately I notified Blue Chip, our controller in Saigon. I told him that I had the "target" (a rescue term for a survivor) in sight and requested permission for a pickup. Obviously Blue Chip knew the area better than I did because the reply came back, "You may go in only at pilot's discretion," whatever that meant. To me it meant I was going in so I landed to the south. There was not an inch of room for error during this entire maneuver as I touched down on the first piece of runway and applied all available brakes and maximum reverse thrust to stop at the far end. My wings hung way over both sides of the runway, which was bad enough, but after landing I noticed a big hole, which looked like a bomb crater, on the left edge of the runway, made by goodness knows what. Naturally, I steered to the right edge to avoid the crater. This was not hospitable country, and not a place I wanted to spend any more time in than necessary, so I certainly didn't want to disable my aircraft.

Just as soon as I stopped at the extreme south end of the runway, my loadmaster quickly opened the ramp door and the pilot of Litter 03 ran aboard. Now only two major problems confronted me: how to get this big aircraft turned in the opposite direction, as there were no taxiways, and whether the runway would be long enough to allow my wings to generate enough lift to make a successful takeoff. Two things were certain. I didn't plan to ponder it all day, nor would I call the tower to get the current winds to determine if I would have adequate takeoff performance. (There was no tower to call!) Instead, I began a series of back-and-forth maneuvers, roaring my engines into reverse and then back to forward thrust as I rapidly executed a twisting reversal of direction, making sure not to proceed too far and slide off either side of the runway into the mud. Upon runway lineup, I held my brakes while applying every inch of power my four giant engines could muster and turned her loose. On nearing the far north end of the runway, it was apparent we didn't have desired speed but there was no time to turn back. I sucked the yoke back into my lap and prayed for the best. God is good! We may have given a tree or two a haircut on takeoff, but I delivered the pilot of Litter 03 to his home base of Tuy Hoa, which ironically was the same as mine. We chatted in the cockpit quite a bit during this return trip. There was a large welcoming committee awaiting this fallen comrade and hero when we returned to the Tuy Hoa ramp, including his wingman and good friend, Litter 04.

There was no time for my crew to join the gala event, however, as Crown 3 was still awaiting our arrival over the Gulf of Tonkin. We quickly took off and completed a long mission into the dark of night. Upon mission completion, my copilot and I dashed to the club to join the party. No one ever accused my crazy Indian sidekick or me of missing a party! The funny part was, there was no sign of Litter 03 or Litter 04. The Officers' Club was dull and orderly. Either the hour was now too late for sane aviators, or some people are just more subdued than others.

On March 14, 1968, I shipped back to the States after exactly one year in the war zone without ever laying eyes on that Litter 03 pilot again. Maybe he completed his tour and was reassigned stateside just after his rescue. Then there was another possibility. He, being a real pilot, a fighter pilot, did not want to be seen fraternizing with the likes of a multiengine driver. Shoot, someone might see us together and tell his wife or best friend! You know how pilots are. Heavens, I wouldn't have wanted to ruin the man's reputation. Put yourself in his place. If you went to the dance astride a thoroughbred and had to be brought home on a mule after your trusty steed was crippled, would you want to hang out with the muleskinner? No, you'd search out the company of other prestigious jocks—the Willie Shoemakers of the business!

Now the small world part: After I left the active Air Force in March of 1969, I became a pilot for Western Airlines. Unfortunately for me, Western decided to give 204 pilots an extended unpaid vacation in July 1969. Furlough! For two years and five months my

Western pilot's uniform hung on the rack collecting dust but no wear. Happily, I returned from furlough to resume my airline career in December 1971.

One day in early spring of 1972 I was awaiting the arrival of our airline crew bus to take me from the parking lot to flight operations for my flight at the Los Angeles base. As I gazed about, I noticed another of our pilots in uniform who appeared to be slyly studying me. I stared at him for a moment, thought I had seen him before, and then self-consciously looked away. However, each time I tried to look at him I caught him looking at me.

Abruptly he said, "I'm sorry, but don't I know you from some-place?" and I responded, "You seem familiar also."

We began to compare biographies. "What was your college?" His was Penn State; mine was Virginia Tech. "That's not it."

"Were you in the service?" Both of us were Air Force; now we were getting somewhere. He was stationed at Lakenheath in England while I was at Rhein-Main in Germany. "No, that's not it."

I said, "Were you ever stationed in Vietnam?" His face changed expression to a possible sense of recognition and he asked me, "Were you that rescue pilot who came and picked me up when I was shot down in 1968?"

I surveyed his worn uniform and mentally compared it to mine, much newer in appearance from just hanging in the closet for two years and five months. I gave him a steady stare. You see, the uniform tells the tale as to who is senior to whom, and in the airline world seniority is everything. Some pilots would give their firstborn for 100 seniority numbers!

With an amused, mischievous smile spreading across my face, I replied, "You're darn right. That was me who came in and got you and took you back to Tuy Hoa. But if I had ever known that you would rush back here and grab a seniority number over me, I would have left your ass in the jungle!" We both laughed heartily.

I spent 29 years being junior to him in seniority at Western and then Delta Air Lines until I retired at age 60 in August 1998. I never regretted for a moment rescuing his hide. He is a great guy, and the final irony is that not only did Jim Pollak fly for Western Airlines, but so did his close friend KB Clark, who was his wingman, Litter

04, the day he was shot down. It was KB who called "Mayday" and gave me much of the information needed for Jim's recovery. All three of us were based at Tuy Hoa at the same time and then all three flew for Western and then Delta for all these many years. Jim and KB have always been numbered among friends that I care about.

Isn't it a small world?

....

As I mentioned, after reading these three stories I got out my map, ONC K-10, Edition 5, which covered the area of this incident, and found the valley where the airstrike, shootdown, and initial helicopter pickup took place. That was easy, as the spot where Jim and KB met Helix 41, on "the 115 degree radial at 18 miles from Channel 117" (Ban Me Thuot TACAN), was in their initial clearance when they left Tuy Hoa. Then I selected all the Special Forces camps within a 40-mile radius of the estimated shootdown point to try and figure where Jim Pollak had been dropped off and Jim Fogg had landed his C-130 to pick him up. The fact that Jim said he landed to the south narrowed it down quite a bit. I came up with seven possibilities, but only two had north/south runways. I will list them below.

1) Ban Don, 24 miles northwest of Ban Me Thuot. The runway was 3,700 feet long with a clay/laterite surface and east/west orientation. It was approved for the C-130. There was no mention of trees off the end of the runway. This one is unlikely, especially with the runway orientation.

2) Buon Tsuke, 24 miles southwest of Ban Me Thuot. This would have been closest to the helicopter pickup point, but as you read, there are a couple of problems. The runway was 2,400 feet long but the aerodrome remarks said, "Security questionable. ABANDONED. Hills and trees ½ mile prior to approach end of either runway 18 or runway 36." The runway direction fits, as Jim says he landed to the south. These aerodrome remarks were in the 1969 edition, and since this incident took place in January 1968, it is possible this camp was open at that time.

3) Duc Lap #2, 30 miles west of Ban Me Thuot. The runway was 3,000 feet long but security was listed as questionable with the warning to "contact 5th Special Forces at Plieku for further information." This is a possi-

bility as the remarks also mention, "Runway and overruns soft and slick when wet, mudholes along runway edges and trees on the approach to runway 26." However, the runway orientation was east/west.

4) Duc Lap #1, 32 miles southwest of Ban Me Thuot. The runway was 2,200 feet long, clay/laterite surface, east/west orientation, and remarks show it was ABANDONED.

5) Duc Xuyen, about 50 miles south of Ban Me Thuot, seemingly in the wrong area. The runway surface was PSP (pierced-steel planking) and listed as VERY slick when wet, with uncharted minefields all sides of the runway. The runway orientation was northeast/southwest so that could fit, but I think it is too far from the valley.

6) Lac Thien, 16 miles southeast of Ban Me Thuot. The runway was 1,200 feet long, 60 feet wide, and unsuitable for either C-123 or C-130 aircraft. This is another possibility as it lists mountains and trees prior to the approach end of runway 29, but to get that big airplane stopped, then turn around and take off on a postage stamp–size runway like that seems nearly an impossibility for a C-130 (but maybe not for Jim Fogg). The east/west orientation of the runway also makes it unlikely.

7) Bu Prang, 55 miles to the west/southwest of Ban Me Thuot. The runway was 1,800 feet long, 70 feet wide, and had a north/south orientation. The camp was right on the Cambodian border, which fits with the first report the navigator gave Jim Fogg, but it seems a little too far away based on the reported length of the chopper ride. Jim Pollak says his helicopter ride was 10 to 15 minutes from pickup to drop-off at the camp, but that could be off by a bit due to his having just survived a high-speed, low-altitude ejection and the stress involved.

Only two camps really fit with a north/south runway orientation. Buon Tsuke is one, but it had been abandoned by 1969 due to security concerns. If it was still open in January 1968 it is most likely the place, but whether or not it was open is impossible to determine. Bu Prang is the other possibility with its proximity to the Cambodian border, its north/south runway, and some trees off the end of the runway. We know the pickup occurred at an established SF camp that had a team medic and a bunker-type complex where Jim Pollak was treated for his injuries. Take your pick; it had to be one of these camps. The amazing thing is that none of the camps I found were listed as suitable for the C-130 except Ban Don, and it is unlikely to be the one due to relatively flat terrain with no obstacles listed for takeoff or landing and the east/west runway orientation. Of the other six, all would have been a challenge for a small twin-engine STOL (short field takeoff and landing) aircraft like the C-7, much less a large four-engine aircraft like the C-130. As Jim Fogg tells the story, his controller in Saigon, Blue Chip, told him he could go in for the pickup only at "pilot's discretion," putting everything on Jim if there was an incident on landing or on the subsequent takeoff. That was the way it was. The guys in the office in Saigon did their CYA (cover your ass) maneuver while the guys in the field made the tough decisions. As it turns out, it wasn't a tough decision for Jim Fogg, as he had been making decisions like that for months.

23

RAVEN: "HE NO SURRENDER"

Anonymous, USAF/CIA, May 1968

This story, written by a Western pilot who wished to remain anonymous, is fascinating. It was contributed willingly by a good friend who then decided he didn't want it in the book due to the high level of secrecy that he felt still applied to the program he was involved in, when he wrote this in 1998. However, once I got the story, about a little-known piece of the air war in Southeast Asia that is often overlooked, I didn't want to let it get away. I asked his permission to run it anonymously and he agreed, so that is the way it will appear.

This contributor was quite an accomplished Air Force pilot flying the O-1 as a FAC (forward air controller) in Vietnam. He was interviewed and recruited while flying in Vietnam for something called the Steve Canyon Program. He ended up in Laos through a very circuitous routing, flying in civilian clothes for a clandestine organization on a leave of absence from the Air Force. The secrecy of this program is still maintained by the Air Force. According to the book The Ravens, *written in 1995 by Christopher Robbins, the level of secrecy is unprecedented. "The secret is still guarded today," Robbins wrote. "An official history of the war in which the Ravens fought, prepared by Air Force historians with Top Secret security clearances, will not be released for publication within the lifetime of anyone reading this." On the dust jacket of the book is a quote from the writer Tom Clancy, who calls it "a book of outstanding integrity. Here are the heroes no-one ever told you about." The book is an excellent reference for those who want to learn more about the Ravens, the Hmong, and the U.S. involvement in Laos.*

First, a little background on our involvement in Laos: The Hmong (Meo) tribesmen of Laos were our allies in a clandestine war with the Viet Minh (North Vietnamese Communists), who were moving men, equip-

ment, and supplies illegally through "neutral" Laos to South Vietnam along the Ho Chi Minh Trail. They were also using Laos as a giant supply dump that they thought would be untouched by the Americans due to the neutral status that was guaranteed by the Geneva Accords, signed by Khrushchev and President Kennedy in 1962. The North Vietnamese, of course, ignored the accords and mounted what was essentially an invasion of Laos. General Vang Pao, the leader of the Hmong, fought until the very end, when he saw his beloved people exiled from their ancestral mountain farms and villages by the Viet Minh. He immigrated to the United States with a large number of Hmong in 1975 at the end of the war.

The following story takes place in 1968.

. . . .

By the middle of May 1968 I had flown over 100 hours of combat that month in single-engine, light aircraft (O-1, U-17, U-10, AU-410, and the odd T-28D sortie), and I was beginning to get tired. We were wrapping up a campaign well north of the Plaine des Jarres (Plain of Jars) in the Muong Xon area of Laos. On the 12th or 13th of May I was on the ground directing air strikes as a forward air controller with a flight of two A-1s attacking enemy troops who were in contact with Meo guerrillas about a kilometer east of my ground location. I was on a ridge overlooking a broad valley with karsts, hills, and mountains all around. There was a little cone-shaped hill about 500 feet above the elevation of the valley floor, and a bunker had been dug into the top from which the enemy could adjust mortars and artillery on us.

The A-1s did their usual trick of dropping everything but the kitchen sink and then began strafing. On about the fourth strafing pass, the lead A-1 rolled in and about halfway through the pass took some hits. The aircraft started rolling uncontrollably and after one roll, when the aircraft came upright, the pilot bailed out. The airplane crashed at my 12 o'clock position, and the pilot came floating down very close to the target of his strafing, landing in a tree. Fortunately, some of the Meo guerrillas were near the tree and went over to try to help him. Unfortunately, he couldn't tell the difference between Meo and Viet Minh and began to blaze away at them with his trusty .38 revolver. The Meo called me on the radio and asked if I would come down to help them pluck him out of the tree, so we sent a Bell 203 Huey helicopter to go down and pick him up. The Huey couldn't manage the pickup due to the high elevation at that location (6,000 feet), so we called in another Air America helicopter, an H-34. (Air America was a CIA-funded organization.) He duly plucked said airman out of the tree and lifted him to my location, which had a STOL (short field takeoff and landing) strip next to it. Al Adolph, a Continental Air Services pilot (Continental Air Services was also CIA-funded, and a backup to Air America), landed his Pilatus Porter on the strip and we transferred the pilot from the helicopter to the Porter. He was banged up with a dislocated shoulder as well as bruises and contusions about the head, shoulders, and body, so Dave Kinney, the weatherman who was with me, and I jumped into the Porter and began to administer a little first aid.

Just a few days earlier I had been savoring a beer in the Sandy lounge (A-1 pilots used the call sign Sandy) at Udorn RTAB (Royal Thai Air Base). When I went to Udorn, in northern Thailand just a few miles across the border from Vientiane, Laos, I normally bunked with the 602nd Air Commando Squadron pilots, so there I was in the Sandy lounge. I was sitting with a 43-year-old Air Force lieutenant colonel who was reflecting on the fact that he had a kid in college, and if he wanted to see grandchildren he had better stop smoking. He told me he had actually quit that day. Well, the A-1 pilot we were patching up in the Porter turned out to be the same lieutenant colonel, who now reflected that "it's probably not going to be cigarettes that kill me. Does anybody have a smoke?" Dave did, and he lit up. We flew him down to Lima Site (landing site) 36, Na Khang, where a Super Jolly Green (long-range HH-53 rescue helicopter) landed and picked him up for rapid delivery to the hospital at Udorn. Last I heard, he had been flown back to the States on a medevac flight out of Udorn, and it probably was going to be cigarettes that killed him after all!

Just a couple of days later, I was flying an O-1, working targets (spotting and marking targets for air strikes) just south of Muong Xon with a backseater who was the Meo commander at Lima Site 36. His name was Major Uva Li. Unusual for a Meo, he had a rather large and prominent nose and very much resembled a Native American, so we called him the Indian. The Indian and I directed several air strikes that afternoon, and because we were just a few minutes south of the area where the A-1 had been shot down, I decided to go up and see what was going on in that area. As we approached, I could see the little cone-shaped hill with the bunker on top. Looking from a distance I could see puffs of dust kicking up around the very top, looking very much like the impacts of the little 60mm knee mortars the Meo used in the field. I said, "Wow, that's good shooting." As we got closer yet, I could tell that there were about two squads of Meo guerrillas ringing the hill about two-thirds of the way up, barely 50 feet from the bunker. The puffs of dust weren't mortar rounds exploding; they turned out to be hand grenades going off.

As we circled overhead, I saw a soldier pop up out of the little bunker on the top and spray the Meo with an AK-47. When he popped up the Meo would all hit the ground, and when he dropped back into the hole they would rise up again and start chucking grenades. He'd pop up again, they'd fall down, he'd spray them, and the cycle would repeat itself. It looked to me like he was in a world of hurt and would probably just as soon call this whole madness off before he got himself killed.

After two or three of these cycles, I sad to Uva Li, "He'd probably like to quit if he thought he could survive surrendering."

Uva said, "He no surrender."

I asked, "How do you know?"

He replied, "He Viet Minh, he no surrender."

I thought, "That's silly. He obviously would rather not get killed if he can help it."

I decided to call the strip where I had been the day the A-1 was shot down, and as luck would have it, General Vang Pao was there, personally running the show. I reiterated my statement that I thought the Vietnamese would like to surrender if he thought he would survive the attempt. Vang Pao said exactly the same thing the Indian had said: "He no surrender."

Well, having watched another cycle of hand grenades and AK-47 spray, I decided to take the situation into my well-meaning

American hands and personally urge the Viet Minh to surrender. I determined to do this by making a pass close by the bunker with my hands in the air just as he popped up to spray the grenadiers. I communicated my plan to the Indian, and he just said, "He no surrender." He probably was thinking, "This stupid American is going to get us both killed." In any case, we had all the windows open in the O-1, which was our normal configuration. There were a couple of reasons for this—first, it was hot, and second, you could hear the ground fire a lot easier. I made a diving turn toward the bunker, and as the Vietnamese popped up to spray, I was going by just behind him about 50 feet away, flying with my knees. I turned to face him with my arms and hands raised in the universal gesture of surrender. He, of course, had no way of knowing the altruistic purpose of my maneuver. As he popped up he probably got a glimpse of movement out of the corner of his eye. He probably couldn't hear my airplane, having been temporarily deafened by the grenades, but he spun around and sprayed a burst of automatic fire right in my face. Fortunately, he didn't do a good job of it and missed us all together. Unfortunately, he scared the bejesus out of me!

Now, I might be difficult to train but not impossible. My heart immediately went to high revs when he shot at us, and about two seconds later I went from scared to really mad. Instead of trying to save his life, now I was going to kill his ass. I shoved the throttle to the firewall and went chandelling up to roll in while arming the one smoke rocket I had left. He had obviously seen this maneuver before, because he ducked back into the hole. The entrance to the bunker was a hole about two feet wide by four feet high, and I was going to put that Willy Pete (white phosphorus) rocket right in the hole and fry him. Well, I was good but not quite that good. I missed the hole about one foot to the right, but I was so low when I launched the rocket that it didn't have time to arm and it just kicked a bunch of dirt into the hole. I pulled off and circled the hill, gnashing my teeth and loudly speculating upon his parentage and sexual orientation while the Indian quietly chuckled in the backseat.

After a couple of minutes he popped up out of the hole again, spraying the Meo. They put their faces in the dirt, but this time he didn't drop back into the hole but started climbing out. I guess he decided that now that air power was part of the equation, he had better *di-di* (Vietnamese for "go fast") and get out of there. But wait! He was pulling another soldier out of the hole with him while sending short bursts from the AK at the Meo, who were happy to stay flat. The other soldier was having a hard time moving, and the first guy was dragging him up and out of the hole, then down the hill. Now, the singular valor being demonstrated went right over my head at the time. I was still really angry at that guy for blazing away at me when I had been trying to save his life, so obviously I was still going to try to kill him. I was out of rockets, but I carried a 12-gauge Savage pump shotgun in the airplane with me, so I again dove down while I unlimbered the shotgun and the Indian got his M-16 hanging out the window. Flying with my knees again, I went swooping around the hill about 75 feet from the two stumbling Vietnamese and started blazing away with my scatter gun. Uva Li opened up with the M-16, putting a full 20-round magazine through it. The fleeing soldier sprayed his AK-47 at us, and nobody hit anybody. I was still mad, so I continued flying with my knees around the hill, shoving more shells into the shotgun. Uva Li slapped another magazine into the M-16 and around we came. Once again, I put all seven rounds of double-aught buck through the shotgun. Uva used up another magazine, the Vietnamese sprayed at us, and once again, nobody hit anybody. Yet again we reloaded and tried a third time to get that guy, he tried to get us, and nobody got anybody. By the time we got around a fourth time, the two Vietnamese had reached the tall grass and were gone.

As I cooled down, I began to reflect upon what I had just seen. It was really the most valiant act I had witnessed on either side in Vietnam or Laos. As my fright subsided, and with it my anger, I was really glad I hadn't gotten that Viet Minh soldier and his buddy. In fact, I really had to chuckle. Uva Li and Vang Pao were right. "He no surrender."

....

As a final note, Mr. Anonymous told me a story about one of the Hmong spotters who flew with him while he was working as a FAC. The spotters were there to talk to their troops on the ground and get information for the FAC to use while calling in air strikes. One day they came under heavy small arms fire and the spotter, sitting behind him, was badly wounded. After flying to the nearest Lima site where he could get medical attention, the pilot helped the spotter out of the airplane, thinking he could quite possibly have received fatal wounds. Mr. Anonymous soon returned home and separated from the service, never hearing the fate of his spotter. After the war General Vang Pao and a large number of Hmong immigrated to the United States, and one group settled in the Fresno, California area, establishing one of the largest Hmong communities in the country. At a reunion years after the war, Mr. Anonymous walked right into his spotter, now the proud owner of a landscaping company in Fresno.

24

ARC LIGHT

Ferd Fletcher, USAF, B-52D, 1968
{ Date of hire by Western Airlines: 10/7/1968 }

B-52 crew #E-92. Ferd Fletcher is at the far right in the back row.

In late 1998 I flew with Ferd Fletcher for the first time. The week before, I had driven to an air show at Gillespie Field in El Cajon, California, about 10 miles east of San Diego. That show was like being live at the History Channel. There were several groups sitting at tables, selling books and signing autographs. There was a long table with more than 10 World War II Flying Tigers, including Tex Hill, Chuck Older, Dick Rossi, and Eric Shilling; a group of Navajo code talkers, also selling and signing their books; and a big group of World War II Fighter Aces. Sitting at one table were Jim Swett, Jeff DeBlanc, and Robert Galer, all Medal of Honor recipients, with Fritz Payne and Bruce Porter, all five of them Marine aces from the early days at Guadalcanal. I had never seen one Medal of Honor, much less three, and here were a trio of the most humble, unassuming men, sitting side by side, wearing their medals and signing autographs. The five of them were telling stories about Joe Foss and Pappy Boyington and having a great laugh. Always a World War II history buff, it was a moment in time for me that I will never forget.

On the drive from San Diego to El Cajon we passed an exit for Fletcher Parkway. I filed that away, as I would be flying with Ferd Fletcher on my next trip and knew he was from the San Diego area. I reminded myself to ask him if there was any family connection. When I met Ferd I asked and he said, "Yes, that was named after my grandfather." Ferd is from one of the pioneering families of San Diego. His grandfather arrived there in 1888 and was involved in developing many of the roads and the water system for San Diego. Now I was flying with Ferd, a Vietnam veteran, Western pilot, and a nice guy to boot. He went to the University of Oregon, and my one vivid memory of our first day of flying was passing over Eugene on the way to Seattle and Ferd pointing out the campus and the football stadium where Oregon had just beaten Cal!

Ferd was another SAC (Strategic Air Command) pilot who was flying B-52 bombers and sitting on nuclear alert during those intense years of the Cold War. When the decision was made to use some of the B-52s for a conventional bombing mission in Southeast Asia starting in 1965 (the B-52D models were converted for this purpose), the crews were sent from various SAC bases in the States on TDY (temporary duty) to Anderson AFB, Guam, and later to Utapao Royal Thai Air Base in Thailand. Ferd's story begins in 1967 when he was based at March AFB in Riverside, California, and is preceded by a bit of biographical information.

....

I graduated from the University of Oregon in 1962 with a B.A. in history, and shortly thereafter I entered Air Force UPT (Undergraduate Pilot Training) at Laredo AFB, Texas, in class 63F. After pilot training I went to B-52 school at Castle AFB in Merced, California, and ended up being based at March AFB in Riverside. The story of the bomb run related here is lacking some of the detail I would like to have, as my memory of the incident is pretty hazy.

In 1967 I was based at March AFB as a B-52 crew member. Our primary mission was nuclear alert and our aircraft carried two Mark 53 nuclear weapons, each yielding 9.3 megatons. We also had the capability to carry nuclear armed missiles under each wing. On occasion we would fly airborne nuclear alert sorties called Chrome Dome, and these missions lasted approximately 24 hours, with two refuelings. The route of flight took us up over the northeastern U.S. and across the northern reaches of Canada near the BMEWS line (Ballistic Missile Early Warning System, which would alert us to a missile launch from the Soviet Union). After our second refueling, over Alaska, we would return south to our bases.

In the spring of 1967 our bomb squadron at March, along with others, was ordered TDY to Anderson AFB, Guam, where we would conduct operations, code-named Arc Light, in support of ground troops in Vietnam. Upon arrival we found Guam to be mostly a pleasant experience, with good facilities and Hawaiian-type weather. The BOQs (Batchelor Officer's Quarters) were more than adequate, and there was an abundance of sports facilities available. Then the missions started.

From Anderson, the flying time to our targets and back averaged 12 hours. Several hours after takeoff we would routinely refuel with KC-135 tankers from Kadena AFB, Okinawa, on refueling tracks north of the Philippines. From there several more hours would put us in our target areas, which were anywhere between the rice paddies along South Vietnam's border with Cambodia, south of Saigon, to the Mu Gia Pass in the southern part of North Vietnam. Our mission was to interdict supplies and NVA (North Vietnamese Army) troops moving south to join the war.

Our missions would start with comprehensive mission planning and target study. Most missions included from as few as nine B-52s to as many as 36. The weapons configuration varied, but most often we carried 105 500 pound bombs per airplane, both internally in the bomb bay and externally on wing-mounted pylons. Other weapons included 750 pound bombs and CBUs, which are clusters of anti-personnel bomblets that deployed above the ground and filled the area with grenade-like shrapnel designed to kill ground troops.

The takeoff gross weight for the B-52D on these missions was often near the maximum of 456,000 pounds, and we relied on all eight water-augmented engines for takeoff. The later models of the B-52 had more powerful fan jet engines. One day we lost water augmentation on our #7 engine during takeoff and had to abort, almost going off the end of the runway. On another occasion one of the B-52s on a maximum gross weight takeoff lost an engine shortly after decision speed (the maximum speed at which the pilot could abort the takeoff and stop on the remaining runway) and almost crashed into the Pacific Ocean off the end of the runway.

The bomb runs from the IP (initial point) inbound usually consisted of a three-aircraft cell operating at high altitude, between 28,000 and 33,000 feet. They approached the target in trail (in a line) with 500 feet vertical separation. When the bombing was directed from the ground, the targets were usually marked by a FAC (forward air controller) in a light observation aircraft (O-1 or O-2) or by a ground observer. The directions were relayed to a ground radar site that then guided us to the target by means of a transponder in the lead aircraft in the cell. Sometimes our targets were planned in our pre-mission briefing and were marked and plotted by our onboard radar navigator.

The aircraft would very noticeably pitch up after bomb release, when 52,000 pounds of bombs were dropped in what seemed like seconds. Then we would reverse course and climb to 41,000 to 43,000 feet for the return flight to Anderson. After landing, debriefings were always conducted, then food was regularly provided and beer was available regardless of the time of day.

On several occasions during our six-month TDY we flew over to Thailand and conducted missions from a small base south of Bangkok called Utapao RTAB (Royal Thai Air Base). From there the missions were considerably shorter (three to four hours), which gave us more time to spend at the local beach resort, Pattaya Beach. We also were able to get up to Bangkok several times on our days off. On one trip I got malaria, but that is another story!

There is a mission I remember vividly, but unfortunately I do not have my logbook so I don't know the exact date. It was in early 1968 and we were conducting a routine mission over the Mu Gia Pass in southern North Vietnam. Our call sign was Flame 19 and we were leading a cell with Flame 12 and Flame 24 in trail. Our target consisted of supplies and troops moving south on the Ho Chi Minh Trail that had been spotted by a fast FAC (a jet fighter as opposed to a small Cessna aircraft) earlier in the day. We had been informed in the pre-mission briefing that SAM (surface-to-air missile) sites had been installed in the area, but our concern was minimized because of the F-105 Wild Weasel missions that had been flown throughout the target area on an ongoing basis. The Wild Weasel aircraft carried Shrike missiles designed to destroy the SAM sites. If the SAM site turned on its radar to lock on to an aircraft before launching a missile, the Shrike would fly back down the radar beam and destroy the site. The North Vietnamese radar operators would turn on their radar only long enough to get a relative bearing and direction of flight, then turn them off to avoid allowing the Shrike missile to lock on to their radar signal.

On this day we had hit the IP and started our bomb run, but just as we released our bombs we heard a scream coming over the emergency radio frequency (243.0 MHz on the UHF radio, the guard frequency that we always monitored). "Missile launch, missile launch!" Our EWO (electronic warfare officer) immediately ejected chaff (small strips of metal) in hopes of decoying the missile. Shortly thereafter, a long plume of smoke appeared within a half-mile of our formation. It continued well above us before harmlessly exploding. This is exactly what happened when the SAM radar was turned off after launch and the missile was unable to lock onto its target. We all breathed a sigh of relief, sent a silent thank-you to the Wild Weasels, and turned to the east for our six-hour flight back to Guam.

I returned to March AFB after this TDY, separated from the Air Force later in 1968, and was hired by Western Airlines in October 1968. I was fortunate to miss the furlough in 1969 and worked straight through until my retirement as a Delta 767 captain in January 2001.

....

Since Ferd's story is about the B-52, I will add a postscript about how the B-52 was used to bring about a "peace treaty" and the signing of the Paris Peace Accords, "ending" the U.S. involvement in the war and bringing about the return of the prisoners of war.

In late 1972, after the North Vietnamese had walked out of the Paris Peace Talks, President Nixon ordered a massive bombing of North Vietnam called Operation Linebacker II. On the first day, December 18, 1972, 129 B-52s took off from Anderson AFB and Utapao RTAB, heading for Hanoi, a target previously off-limits to the B-52s. It was a massive effort that included most of the Air Force tactical aircraft in Thailand and South Vietnam, Marine and Navy carrier-based aircraft from ships in the Gulf of Tonkin, and Marine land-based aircraft from South Vietnam and a secret base in Thailand, Nam Phong. F-4s flew MIG CAP (combat air patrol), while Air Force F-105 Wild Weasels, F-111s, and Navy Iron Hand aircraft flew SAM and AAA (anti-aircraft artillery) suppression missions. To say it was massive is truly an understatement, as it dwarfed the initial bombing in Operation Rolling Thunder more than seven years earlier.

In anticipation of this bombing the Air Force had moved more than 200 B-52s to Anderson and Utapao, jamming the ramps and parking areas, and it reportedly took more than two hours for aircraft to take off and head southwest from Guam. Linebacker II lasted from December 18 to December 29, 1972, and in 11 days of bombing (called the 11-day war by some), the B-52s flew 729 sorties and dropped 15,000 tons of bombs, the North Vietnamese fired 1,240 SAMs, and 16 B-52s were shot down. There is no record of the amount of beer consumed during the debriefings, but it is estimated to have been considerable! It is reported that the B-52 crew members nearly revolted over the requirement to fly their bomb runs at the same altitude and over the same routes day after day.

A 36-hour Christmas stand-down allowed the North Vietnamese to restock their supply of SAMs and attempt to repair their shattered air defenses, but it also allowed Air Force planners to change their tactics. The bombing then continued for four more days, with one of the largest raids taking place on December 26 and involving 120 B-52s. The North Vietnamese, shocked by the ferocity of the attacks and defenseless when they ran out of SAMs, returned to the peace talks, and the Paris Peace Accords were signed on January 27, 1973. The accords brought about the end of the

U.S. air war over North Vietnam (but not over Laos and Cambodia), and in 60 days 591 POWs were returned in Operation Homecoming. Less than two years later, with Nixon gone after Watergate and Congress having cut off most of the aid to South Vietnam, the North Vietnamese violated the Paris Peace Accords and invaded the South. Saigon fell on April 30, 1975.

25

POISONOUS SEA SNAKES

Peter D. Nichols, USN, A-4F, 1967 – 1968
{ Date of hire by Western Airlines: 4/9/1973 }

Pete Nichols, photographed with an A-7.

This story is one of the most entertaining tales about what must have been an absolutely terrifying experience. It is so full of Navy Vietnam carrier and aviation jargon that I will try to translate for the uninitiated with my humble Air Force background. I think the easiest way to do that is to mark certain phrases with an asterisk and explain them at the end. I will do that the best I can without interfering with the story.

Pete Nichols was part of my peer group (more than 90 percent of whom were Vietnam veterans) hired by Western Airlines in the hiring cycle of late 1971 through mid-1973, when war in the Middle East and rising jet fuel prices put an end to airline pilot hiring for nearly three years. Because of the closeness in seniority, pilots in that group very seldom flew with each other unless it was a very senior first officer flying with a very junior captain. I did have the opportunity to fly with Pete on a couple of occasions when he was a brand-new and very junior captain and I was a senior copilot. We had a wonderful time, sharing stories and comparing backgrounds, and he gave me a lot of encouragement for this project.

I don't think I can use enough superlatives to describe the flying skill on display in this story. The closest thing I can compare it to is a night engine fire with hydraulic and electrical failures in the Delta flight simulator. That was part of our annual training, the dreaded compound-emergency scenario that took place in a multiengine aircraft with two pilots working together, sharing the flying, and using all forms of CRM (cockpit resource management) to complete the emergency checklists and get the aircraft safely on the ground. If you screwed up, you could take a break, climb out, and discuss what you could have done differently with the instructor over a cup of coffee. If it was really bad you could say you were sick and go back to the hotel. In Pete's story there was no opportunity for a do-over. I can't imagine a more difficult compound emergency to deal with at night in a heavy, single-engine aircraft than the one he encountered. When you see the photos of his fire damaged A-4, you will understand.

Here is Pete Nichols's story.

....

I was born May 28, 1943, and grew up in Ridgewood, New Jersey. I graduated from Penn State University in September 1965 and began flight training at Pensacola, Florida, the same month. I received my Navy wings in April 1967 at Beeville, Texas, and reported to NAS Lemoore, California, for A-4 training. I completed two western Pacific tours with VA-93 in the time frame 1967–1970, first in A-4Fs on the USS *Bonhomme Richard* and then in A-7Bs on the USS *Ranger*. After my second cruise I was assigned as an instructor in A-7Es with VA-122 from 1970 to 1972. When I left active duty I was hired by Western Airlines on April 9, 1973, as a GIB (guy in back), sitting on the ironing board (fold-down jump seat) on the Boeing 737—and glad to be there! I retired from Delta as a Boeing 757/767 captain in 2003. This adventure took place during my first cruise, on May 23, 1968.

Sometimes you don't even have to go across the beach* to have an interesting time. One particular night stands out for me. I was a lieutenant, junior grade, assigned to Attack Squadron 93 flying A-4Fs off the USS *Bonhomme Richard* (CVA-31). We were maintaining our normal position on Yankee Station in the Gulf of Tonkin, about 60 to 70 miles east of Vinh, North Vietnam. Most of our work was conducted in Route Packages III and IV,* with some hard targets, a lot of road reconnaissance* or targets of opportunity, and occasional Alpha Strikes or major air wing gaggles.

On May 23, 1968, I was scheduled for a night road recce* flight as wingman for Lieutenant Commander Art (Big Mother) Keen. We were flying the Polish cycle (midnight to noon) and I had a 2 a.m. briefing followed by a 3:30 launch. Briefing and man-up* were both normal. It was a black-ass night of course, hazy with no real horizon, but clear overhead. My call sign was Raven 310 and I was in A-4F Buno (tail number) 154989. The catshot* was its usual violent trip into an inkwell. We were both loaded out with a single centerline drop tank (fuel tank), three Mk-82 500 pound bombs on each wing, and flarepods* on the outboard stations. This was a lusty load for the little Scooter (nickname for the A-4). Eyeballs recaged, I began accelerating out to the prescribed distance ahead of the ship where I would then climb up to the overhead rendezvous circle. About 350 knots now, looking good; I started the pitch up to find Big Mother. Passing through about 7,000 feet, my oxygen supply suddenly turned rotten and then stopped. As I unhooked one side of my oxygen mask, the fire warning light came on bright—what other kind is there? Now the rest of the indications followed: Hydraulics* went away; fortunately the Scooter had manual reversion. Then the generator quit*; I threw out (deployed) the RAT* so I still had a radio. But the most ominous and hard to ignore clue was the orange glow from the aft end of the plane that grew brighter and was beginning to reflect off the bomb casings and flarepods. No doubt about it, lieutenant, you have a no-shit fire roaring in the back of this thing.

By now I had leveled off at about 10,000 feet. I made my "Mayday" call and cut the throttle to idle, which was the first half of the in-flight engine fire emergency procedure. The mayday call brought a flurry of advice from other aircraft still on the frequency. One of the second-tour pilots, whom I respected and whose voice I recognized, said, "Don't stay with that thing too long." I began to tighten up my straps and get rid of the kneeboard and flashlight, then to mentally gear up for the second half of the in-flight fire emergency procedure: ejection. The thought definitely shot through my mind about the sea snake stories the old guys would tell us new guys just to watch our expressions, the acres of ocean covered with mating poisonous sea snakes. No matter—time to go.

As I push myself back in the seat for a good firing position for the ejection seat, the nicest thing happens. The fire light blinks out and then comes back on, and then blinks several more times. Hold everything! I look outside; the glow is definitely fading. Maybe I don't have to run across the backs of all those snakes! Now the fire light goes out. This is good. Next I have to work on another problem. I'm losing altitude because of the idle throttle and I'm still carrying a full load of bombs. I call the *Bonhomme* to tell them that I am still here and that I need to jettison this ordnance. I have no navigation capability on the RAT and ask the ship if they have my position. I want to clean this stuff off now without dropping the bombs on the boat, where they might hit my stereo or someone else's. Naturally, the ship replies, "Negative—stand by." This is not good; I am coming down like a toolbox.* Finally, I get cleared to drop and quickly comply. I congratulate myself for coolly dropping the bombs, safely unarmed. I discovered later that I had cleaned the entire wing off: racks, drop tank, and all. No matter; now I'm flying again. I start to creep the throttle forward. If that fire light comes back on, I am out of options—but it doesn't.

Big Mother Keen has now joined up on me. He states that the fire appears out with just some occasional sparks coming out of the speed brake area. The bad news is that the tailhook, while still attached, has lost all hydraulic pressure and is just dangling in the slipstream. The ship is notified of this and starts an emergency pull forward of aircraft on the flight deck in order to rig the barricade to catch me. So I review. Let's see...manual reversion, no gauges,* it's still black-ass out here, and they want to put me into that net. My other option is to fly Art's wing about 200 miles down to Chu Lai AB (Air Base), South Vietnam, and land on a 10,000 foot concrete runway. Art and I head out for Chu Lai shortly thereafter.

The trip down the coast is uneventful, but the night has one more surprise for me. As Art and I arrive overhead Chu Lai Air Base, I can only vaguely make out the runway. There are no lights on. Questioned about this, the tower replies, "Negative lights—we are under rocket attack. Field is closed." Now I'm getting tired of all this. I tell them I'm making a high precautionary approach (because I'm still not sure what may happen if I jerk that throttle around, and I do respect rockets). I fly my precautionary approach and everything seems to be working so I come around for landing. I say that I'd appreciate a few seconds of runway lights as I roll out on short final, and bless 'em, they comply. Sure enough, as I roll out, I see several buildings burning off to one side. (It turned out a 122mm rocket went right through the front door of the base exchange* which was brand-new and set to be opened the next week.) I follow a director into a revetment and thankfully shut the plane down. I crawl out and walk around the aircraft; indeed it is a mess. A Marine warrant officer who was supervising the tie-down crew says, "Haw! Bet you wouldn't have stayed with that f***** if you'd knowed how bad it was!" I dunno—guess he never heard those sea snake stories.

NOTES

across the beach: Across the coastline into North Vietnam.

route package III and IV: The target areas in North Vietnam were listed as route packages with route package I being farthest south, butting up to the border between North and South Vietnam, and V and VI farthest north, extending to the border with China. Route package VI was divided into VI-A and VI-B.

road reconnaissance/road recce: Flying along roads looking for targets of opportunity like trucks and other military equipment.

man-up: Get suited up for a mission (with flight suit, G-suit, survival equipment) and strapped into the airplane.

catshot: A carrier takeoff, launched by a catapult.

flarepods: External pods to carry flares, which were used during night operations to illuminate ground targets.

hydraulics: The hydraulic system operated the flight controls, tailhook, and landing gear. In the event of loss of the hydraulic system, manual reversion switched operation of the flight controls to a system of cables to manually operate the ailerons, elevator, and rudder. The landing gear most likely was extended by free falling, with no system to raise it.

generator quit/RAT: The generator powered everything that required electricity, from flight instruments and radios to radar and lights. The RAT was a ram air turbine that was extended in an electrical failure and spun up by air flow across it in flight. It became a small generator to provide limited electrical power to essential items such as radios and basic flight instruments. Operation with the RAT was truly an emergency situation, especially at night.

coming down like a toolbox: This a great expression about losing power in a heavy airplane with limited glide ratio. The A-4 was a single-engine airplane with short, stubby wings, so there was not a great glide ratio when the throttle was at idle and the aircraft was heavy. We used the expression, "Coming down like a manhole cover," to describe descending in the Boeing 727 when one needed to get down to a lower altitude quickly. Coming down like a toolbox perfectly describes the situation.

no gauges: No flight instruments. In this situation the RAT would probably provide power for just a few essential instruments. This is a true emergency, especially at night. Being able to "fly Art's wing for 200 miles" meant Pete was able to fly formation on Art and basically use Art's instruments. He doesn't mention it, but he probably flew formation on Art through a good part of the landing approach at Chu Lai.

base exchange: The famous BX. Every large base had a base exchange where you could buy everything from toiletries to the latest cameras and stereo equipment to booze and cigarettes. There was an incredible barter system out in the boonies where the troops didn't have access to a BX. A carton of cigarettes or a bottle of Crown Royal Canadian whiskey were great for trading when flying into remote Army Special Forces camps. The SF guys had everything from Montagnard crossbows and bracelets to captured North Vietnamese and Vietcong flags and uniform items. A bottle of booze went a long way in a trade!

....

Pete Nichols had a second cruise around 1970 when he flew the A-7. I asked him if he could write a second story from that cruise, but he said he couldn't come up with anything worthy of print. Just to relay what he told me, that cruise involved mostly night bombing missions over the Ho Chi Minh Trail in Laos. In flying those missions he witnessed the most horrific waste of men and equipment imaginable, while attacking mostly meaningless targets. The difference between the two tours, 1967–1968 and 1970, was startling, both in the improvement in the enemy air defenses and in the targeting.

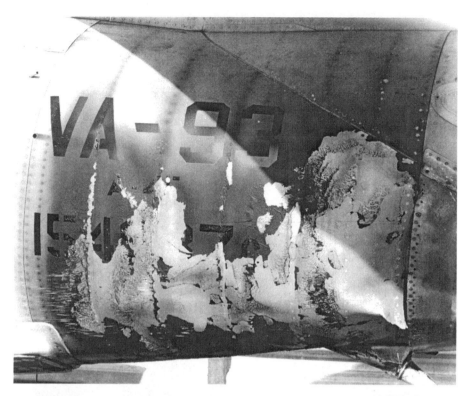

*4 Photos of Pete Nichol's fire damaged A-4F on the ground at Chu Lai AB,
Republic of Vietnam, after his emergency landing on May 23, 1968.*

26

MY MOST MEMORABLE MISSION

Don Chapman, USN, F-4B, 1967 – 1968
{ Date of hire by Western Airlines: 4/21/1969 }

Don Chapman, his VF-143 patch visible on his flight jacket, on the USS Constellation, 1968.

Although Don Chapman and I never had the opportunity to fly together, his name was on the list given to me by Gary Gottschalk when I first got started with this project. When I contacted Don back in 1997 he said he would be happy to write a story and was very enthusiastic about the whole idea of the book. In aviation terminology, my project stalled out for nearly eight years after I retired in 2004 and came back to life due to an e-mail I received from Don in early 2012. His good friend Jim Lee, who is featured in this story, had passed away, and Don wondered if I still had his story, as he wanted to forward a copy to Jim's family. Most of the stories had been sitting in a box in my garage for all those years. I found Don's, sent him a copy, and also sent a copy to Jim's son. Jim had made the Navy his career, retiring as a commander. Fortunately the story arrived in time for the family to see it and for his son to read it at Jim's memorial service. That experience gave new life to the project, and I have been working diligently on it ever since.

Today these stories seem far more special and meaningful than when I was collecting them some 15 years ago. I was entrusted with very personal and private things; some of the stories were thought through and put in writing for the first time for this book. Don's contact rekindled the sense of responsibility I have always felt to the men who trusted me to get this book finished, and I can't thank him enough.

Now here is Don Chapman's story about his good friend Jim Lee.

. . . .

I grew up in White County, Illinois, and graduated from Enfield High School in 1959. I attended the University of Illinois and joined the U.S. Navy in May 1963. I found out that you could enter Navy flight training with two years of college and I was paying my own way through school, so I signed up rather than spend two more years living in an unfinished attic! I entered flight training on May 11, 1963, at Pensacola, Florida, and finished on November 4, 1964, at Beeville, Texas. I flew 199 combat missions over North Vietnam in 1967 and 1968 in the F-4B Phantom off the aircraft carrier USS *Constellation*.

The following incident took place on August 25, 1968, in the Gulf of Tonkin off the coast of North Vietnam near the city of Vinh. This mission began like all other missions, with a catapult shot off the bow of the USS *Constellation*, but this one was into a totally black night so my eyes were glued to the flight instruments and nothing else. It was almost like a computer game, except the price for a mistake was instant death.

I, along with my radar intercept officer (RIO), Lieutenant Jack Hawver, was the wingman of a two-plane BAR CAP (Barrier Combat

Air Patrol) mission. Our mission was to fly between the coast of North Vietnam and all the Navy ships in the Gulf of Tonkin to protect the ships from an attack by North Vietnamese ships or aircraft. Commander Dave Grosshuesch, commanding officer of Fighter Squadron 143, based in San Diego, was my leader, and his RIO was Lieutenant Commander Jim Capps. It was a routine mission with occasional warnings about North Vietnamese radar sites on our APR-25 (an electronic countermeasure device) until we spotted a flash of light and then a trail of smoke in the limited predawn light.

I was flying to the seaward side of Commander Grosshuesch, looking beyond his aircraft into the North Vietnamese countryside just south of the city of Vinh. Instinctively, upon seeing the flash of light and trail of smoke, the commander and I dropped our noses and started to accelerate in order to evade the SAM (surface-to-air missile) that we thought was headed our way. However, it was soon evident that it was not a missile as its speed was much slower than a SAM. At about the same time, we heard, "Mayday, mayday, mayday, *I have been hit!*" over the radio. Commander Grosshuesch immediately turned our flight toward the stricken aircraft, and we crossed our fingers in hopes that the pilot would make it out over the water before he had to eject. (Very few crew members were recovered from overland ejections near heavily defended areas of North Vietnam.) As we watched the burning aircraft turn toward the Gulf of Tonkin just south of Vinh, we heard another transmission from the pilot, "I'm trying to make it to the water." The aircraft appeared to be flying quite normally at this time, even though it was on fire and leaving a long and dense trail of smoke.

Then our hearts sank and we watched helplessly as the aircraft abruptly pitched full nose down and proceeded to crash right on the beach at the very edge of the water. Then: a miracle! We saw a parachute drifting very slowly out to sea in the off-shore morning breeze. By this time we were flying directly overhead at about 5,000 feet.

Lieutenant Jim Lee of Attack Squadron 27 (VA-27) based at LeMoore, California, had been the leader of a three-plane mission of A-7 Corsair II aircraft targeted against a bridge near Vinh. As he was in his dive to deliver a Walleye missile against the bridge, he felt a thump in his aircraft and shortly thereafter saw fire coming out of his plane in his rearview mirrors. He immediately turned toward a large hill just south of Vinh, and when he realized he could make that point he proceeded toward the coast in order to be over the water when he ejected. Unfortunately, the control cables burned through prior to the coastline and his aircraft became uncontrollable. It crashed on the beach, but fortunately, after his ejection the pilot was caught in an offshore breeze and slowly drifted out to sea, landing about 100 yards from the beach.

The inhabitants of a nearby village began shooting at Lieutenant Lee as we flew overhead. We were only armed with air-to-air missiles for the BAR CAP mission and had no air-to-ground ordnance such as rockets, bombs, or bullets. However, we thought we could scare the villagers, so we made several high-speed, low-level passes, trying to convince them to leave the downed pilot alone until we could get a rescue helicopter into the area to pick him up. After a while, the villagers realized we did not have any weapons so they launched a small boat some 500 yards north of Lieutenant Lee. (North Vietnamese citizens were given rewards for capturing downed aviators.) Commander Grosshuesch, as the senior aviator present, was the on-scene commander for the rescue attempt, and he called on the radio for a helicopter and any other aircraft in the area that might have air-to-ground ordnance in an effort to help rescue Lieutenant Lee.

His chances for being rescued jumped dramatically when two A-7 Corsairs checked in and reported to Commander Grosshuesch that they both had a RES CAP (Rescue Combat Air Patrol) load of ordnance (bullets and rockets) and would be on the scene in approximately 10 minutes. The A-7s had been looking for an Air Force pilot who had been shot down the day before in the southern panhandle of North Vietnam. Fortunately for Lieutenant Lee, they had not found the Air Force pilot and had a full load of ordnance onboard.

Meanwhile, Lieutenant Lee had gotten rid of his parachute and was swimming out to sea at a rate that would make Mark Spitz seem like he was crawling! Each time we flew overhead there was more distance between the pilot and his parachute!! It was obvious to us even though we were flying overhead at 450 to 500 knots.

Then the unfolding drama took a turn for the worse when Commander Grosshuesch was informed that the rescue helicopter would take at least 30 minutes to arrive. The rescue chopper was based on a Navy destroyer and the ship had room for only one helicopter at a time in its landing area. Since they were expecting the mail chopper to arrive, they had folded the blades on the rescue helicopter and put it in the very small hangar onboard the ship. Now they had to pull the rescue chopper out of the hangar and unfold the blades before they could launch it for the rescue attempt.

Meanwhile, the situation off the beach improved when the two A-7s arrived on the scene. The villagers' boat was about halfway to Lieutenant Lee but was not proceeding very quickly, due to the rough seas, when the first A-7 rolled in on a strafing run. That Corsair missed the North Vietnamese boat on its first pass, but his wingman, flying westbound directly toward the north-south coastline, started firing his guns while still quite far from his target. His first bullets hit beyond the boat, but instead of the bullets continuing to hit farther and farther past the boat, as they would in a normal strafing run, we were extremely amazed to see the bullets start backing up! It was easy to see from our vantage point as the bullets were hitting the water. Each succeeding bullet was getting closer to the boat instead of farther away, which meant the pilot was continuously increasing the steepness of his dive instead of maintaining a constant dive angle as we had been taught. This very daring and unusual feat of airmanship succeeded in blowing the boat out of the water, causing it to sink. All of the occupants who had not been hit dived into the water and started swimming for shore while the small boat sank. At this point the villagers decided not to put any more boats in the water. Now the rescue effort had bought some time as we waited for the rescue helicopter to arrive and attempt a pickup.

The villagers did not give up, however, as they continued to shoot at Lieutenant Lee and waited for the helicopter they knew was coming. Lieutenant Lee called on his survival radio and asked for the A-7s to lay down some ordnance on the village because the villagers were firing at him, so Commander Grosshuesch directed the A-7s to strafe the village. That quieted them for a little while, but when the helicopter finally arrived, piloted by Lieutenant (junior grade) Tim Malokiski, the villagers really opened up with all their firepower as it was a much more visible target than Lieutenant Lee in the water, bouncing up and down with each wave.

Lieutenant Malokiski swooped in low at high speed (for a chopper) and reported that he was taking heavy fire, but would try to effect a rescue. Meanwhile, Commander Grosshuesch and I were still circling overhead at 5,000 feet, with Grosshuesch directing operations. The A-7s were also circling overhead in case they were needed again, as were several other aircraft that had arrived on the scene. Now the final stage of the rescue began as Lieutenant Malokiski reported he was going to pick up Lieutenant Lee.

Commander Grosshuesch directed several of the overhead aircraft to make high-speed, low-level runs over the village to try and divert the inhabitants' attention away from the helicopter while it made its approach to Lieutenant Lee. The helicopter was pitched forward as it made its approach at a high rate of speed, then abruptly pulled up to a very nose-high attitude as it slowed to a hover for a brief moment right over Lieutenant Lee and dropped its horse-collar rescue sling. This is the time when the chopper was most vulnerable, practically a sitting duck. Lieutenant Lee's first effort to get in the sling ended up with him in the harness backwards, but this was no time to quibble over such details. As soon as the air crewman on the chopper saw that he was in the harness, he signaled Lieutenant Malokiski to get the hell out of there as the villagers were still shooting. In fact, several bullets did hit the helicopter, but none in a critical area so the rescue was a success.

The chopper dropped the downed pilot at the North Star SAR (search and rescue) ship, the USS *Sterrett*, and after a brief physical he was returned to the USS *Constellation* that afternoon. In an ironic twist of fate, August 25 was the last day of combat operations for the *Constellation* crew before proceeding to Hong Kong for some well-deserved R&R. Hong Kong was a time of intense reflection for Lieutenant Lee and all the rest of us involved in his rescue. We were all risking our lives daily in a dangerous and violent war that was being run by politicians in Washington instead of warriors in the field.

As a postscript, Jack Hawver and I always carried a Super 8mm movie camera with us on every mission we flew in the daytime, but since this one had launched at night we didn't have my camera with us, thus missing the opportunity of filming this dramatic rescue.

EPILOGUE:

Lieutenant Jim Lee remained in the Navy and retired in 1985 as a commander. He served one tour as a commanding officer. He then became the site manager for Raytheon at Naval Air Station Lemoore in California. He passed away in early 2012.

Commander Dave Grosshuesch remained in the Navy and retired as a captain. He now lives in La Mesa, California.

The author left the Navy in 1969 and went to work for Western Airlines, which merged with Delta Air Lines in 1987. He retired from the Navy Reserve as a Navy captain in 1994 and from Delta as a Boeing 767 captain in 2001. He now lives in Newnan, Georgia.

Lieutenant Jack Hawver, a Naval Academy graduate, remained in the Navy and was selected for captain prior to retiring. He is now in business in the Washington, D.C. area.

The whereabouts of Lieutenant Commander Jim Capps and Lieutenant Tim Malokiski are unknown to the author.

27

PLAINE DES JARRES

David Schwartz, USAF, F-4D, 1968
{ Date of hire by Western Airlines: 5/9/1972 }

*David Schwartz beside his F-4D in a revetment
at Udorn RTAB in 1968.*

*As with several of the Western pilots who have written stories for this book,
I met David Schwartz when I arrived at the San Francisco pilot base in
early 1974. He was hired a few months before I was, and we were close
enough in seniority that we didn't fly together until many years later, after
the Delta merger. We got to know each other when we were both elected rep-*

resentatives and doing work with the Air Line Pilots Association (ALPA). We had a good group and got a lot accomplished as we worked our way through the difficult issues faced by the airline industry in general, and Western in particular, in the early to mid-1980s. The merger with Delta was announced in September 1986 and presented us with a new set of issues, as pay, pension, and seniority were addressed. The closure of the San Francisco pilot base by Delta ended our ALPA work in October 1989, and we both went on to commute from San Francisco until we retired. David is a good guy and one of many who told me they didn't do anything special in Vietnam but then came up with a great story.

It always fascinated me that my peer group at Western included so many Vietnam veterans who didn't know each other when they were in the service. They were in Vietnam, on a carrier in the Gulf of Tonkin, or at a base in Thailand during roughly the same time frame, but they wouldn't meet until later at Western Airlines. That became the common denominator for the authors of all these stories.

David's story begins with his biographical information.

....

My road to Southeast Asia started at the University of Connecticut, where I received a B.S. from the School of Business Administration in June 1966. Losing my student draft deferment upon graduation, my draft status changed to 1A and I immediately applied to USAF OTS (Officer Training School) and was accepted as a candidate. After my commissioning as a second lieutenant, I attended UPT (Undergraduate Pilot Training) Class 68C at Moody AFB, Valdosta, Georgia, and upon receiving my wings I was assigned to the F-4 Phantom and attended F-4 training at George AFB, California.

By the middle of 1969 the USAF began training navigators for the backseat of the F-4, but at this time, in 1968, they were using pilots as backseaters, and I was trained at George AFB in the use of radar, inertial navigation, and the many functions of the electronic equipment we carried, which was used for homing and jamming. The backseater had many nicknames and was affectionately called everything from the GIB (guy in back) to the PESO (pilot systems operator). The term

GIB seemed to stick, and I find it ironic that after being hired as a pilot by Western Airlines in May 1972, I found myself in training as a Boeing 737 second officer, also known as the GIB!

I attended World Wide Survival School at Fairchild AFB, Washington, Water Survival School at Homestead AFB, Florida, and Jungle Survival School in the Philippines. After all my combat and survival training was complete, I was assigned to the 555th TFS (Tactical Fighter Squadron), the famous "Triple Nickel" squadron, at Udorn Royal Thai Air Base (RTAB) in northern Thailand, and began to fly combat missions. As all combat orientation flights were actual combat missions, the in-theater training was fast, furious, and the real thing.

On November 8, 1968, I was a part of Ringo flight, a flight of four F-4Ds launched from Udorn to a target area on the Plaine des Jarres (Plain of Jars, or PDJ) in central Laos. Our takeoff time was 0730 and the eight crew members for Ringo flight met at the Wing Command Post for briefing just before 0600. I was the GIB on Ringo 3, flying with Lieutenant Colonel Ken Gutenkunst, while Ringo 4 was flown by Captain Joe Weinrich with First Lieutenant Jamie Gough as his GIB. The briefing began with intelligence, which included the location of friendlies on the ground, known hostile activity, and best egress routes from the target area. The crew members were then briefed by the lead pilot, Ringo 1, as to the targets; type of ordnance and how we should deliver it, such as in single or multiple passes; call signs of the refueling tankers; and times, altitudes, and location of the refueling track. Then the briefing covered the type of formation to be flown into and out of hostile territory, and escort procedures in the event one of our four aircraft had to return to Udorn with a problem.

After the briefing we proceeded to the PE (personal equipment) area in the 555th Squadron building and got our helmets, G-suits, survival vests, and radios, our handguns and parachute harnesses (the F-4 had the parachute built into the Martin-Baker ejection seat). The more sobering experience of removing all personal items and leaving them in the secure PE shop was next. This was in the event we were shot down and captured, so that personal information could not be used against us in captivity. Personal items such as wedding rings, school rings, personal photos, and letters were left behind before we were driven out to the aircraft.

Arriving on the flight line, we proceeded to do a preflight inspection of the aircraft and ordnance load. That day's ordnance was a mix of iron bombs and CBUs (cluster bomb units), totaling twelve, 500 pound bombs. Each aircraft also carried four air-to-air missiles, a mix of heat-seeking Sidewinders and radar-guided Sparrows. With the help of the crew chief we strapped in, completed our cockpit preflight, and checked in on the radio, "Ringo flight check in: Ringo 1, 2, 3, 4."

Just before 0730 we started engines and taxied to the arming area near the end of the runway. There, the EOD (explosives ordnance detail) did a final check on the ordnance load, removing safety pins and covers before takeoff. Throughout this arming procedure the pilots' hands were always visible to the EOD crew chief as his crew worked under the aircraft, to ensure nothing was inadvertently activated by the pilots during this critical procedure. After being armed and waved off by the EOD crew chief, we did a final flight control check and taxied onto the runway for takeoff. The takeoffs were at 30-second intervals; as Ringo 3, we were 1 minute behind Ringo 1, with Ringo 4 half a minute behind us. Departing to the southeast on Runway 12, we joined in formation as we made a left turn out of the traffic pattern and climbed toward Laos and our prestrike refueling, which was scheduled for 18,000 to 22,000 feet over southern Laos. The KC-135 tankers that refueled us were based at Utapao RTAB south of Bangkok, and they met us on the prebriefed refueling track at the briefed time. At such heavy weights, the refueling required varying power settings from minimum afterburner on one engine to adding or reducing power on the other engine to maintain position on the refueling boom.

Departing the tanker, we contacted Alleycat, the Airborne Command and Control Center (ABCCC), which was a C-130 flying as a command post that coordinated and controlled all aircraft to and from various target areas. The ABCCC controlled FACs (forward air controllers), fighters, and SAR (search and rescue) planes and helicopters that were standing on alert. Our target area was along Road Runner Lake, so called for its shape, on the PDJ in central Laos. Just south of the lake was a Chinese cultural center, off-limits to attack due to its diplomatic status. The Chinese cultural center was in fact a rest area and transshipment point for trucks coming down a road from China through Laos and then south to support the NVA (North Vietnamese Army) and VC (Vietcong) in South Vietnam. Our mission was to attack the trucks when they were not in the restricted diplomatic area.

Alleycat turned Ringo flight over to a FAC, call sign Firefly, who was an A-1 from NKP (Nakhon Phanom RTAB) in Thailand. In the event a crewman went down, Firefly's call sign changed to Sandy and he became the on-scene SAR commander. Firefly was currently working a flight of four F-105s against the target and directed Ringo flight to hold high and to the south. When the F-105s had expended their ordnance, they proceeded out of the area and Firefly cleared Ringo flight into the target. Ringo 1 and 2, as lead element, rolled in and began their attack while Ringo 3 and 4 remained on high perch to provide MIG CAP coverage (against enemy fighters or MiGs). The F-105s had received some ground fire but nothing too heavy, so the plan remained as briefed for the multiple passes on the target area.

On the first pass Ringo 1 and 2 picked up small arms ground fire and some AAA (anti-aircraft artillery). The intensity of the fire increased on their second pass and was heavier on their third and final pass. At this time, Ringo 1 and 2 left the target area and traded places with Ringo 3 and 4 on high perch as Firefly cleared us into the target. As Ringo 3 and 4 made our first pass, we received significantly more ground fire and noted there were three separate AAA batteries firing at us. We were now in a flak trap and the gunners knew our flight paths. The sky was filled with 37mm AAA and it looked like someone was blowing smoke rings all around us. We decided to expend the rest of our ordnance on the second pass, but as we pulled off the target, Ringo 4 was hit by the AAA. The canopies immediately came off and the backseater, Jamie Gough, ejected. Joe Weinrich in the front seat did not eject because, as we learned later, his ejection seat malfunctioned due to battle damage. He managed to pull Ringo 4 up to 2,000 to 3,000 feet AGL (above ground level) and we joined up on him to inspect the damage. With no other choice, Ringo 4 flew back to Udorn with no canopies, no backseater, and heavy battle damage from the AAA. Since we were undamaged, we landed first and Ringo 4 landed right behind us. As Udorn has only one runway and we were low on fuel, we would have faced fuel starvation and ejection if Ringo 4 had problems landing and closed the runway. As it was, both aircraft had uneventful landings.

Back on the PDJ, Firefly, now Sandy, coordinated coverage and the rescue attempt for Jamie Gough. Another flight of fighters covered him until an HH-53 Jolly Green Giant rescue helicopter could pick him up. The Jolly returned him to the Udorn base hospital and he was soon air evacuated to the United States due to his injuries from the high-speed, low-altitude ejection. Captain Joe Weinrich was required to fill out several forms to account for the missing canopies and rear ejection seat when he arrived at the 555th Squadron building after the debriefing for the flight.

As a postscript, I met Jamie Gough in September 1999 at a 555th TFS reunion at McDill AFB, Florida. He had recovered from his injuries, was able to regain his flight status, and had retired from the Air Force as a colonel. At the time of the reunion his son was an Air Force captain flying the F-16 in the 555th TFS!

David Schwartz, on the right, before flight, in the revetment at Udorn, 1968. Note fuse extenders (daisy cutters) on the bombs at right of photo. The fuse extenders cause the bombs to explode on contact to cause maximum damage above ground.

The bar at the Udorn Officers' Club (L), and the same Officers' Club bar (R) at 0130, New Year's Day, 1/1/69. Apparently, fun was had by all!

28

Bu Prang

Bruce Cowee, USAF, C-7A, 1968 – 1969
{ Date of hire by Western Airlines: 12/12/1972 }

Bruce Cowee in C-7A cockpit on the ramp at Cam Ranh Bay AB,
Republic of Vietnam, December 1968. The overhead throttles seemed
strange at first but soon became second nature.

I was born in 1945, and as I grew up, most of my boyhood friends had fathers who had served in World War II. My mom had a photo of her favorite cousin, Caleb Kendall, a Navy F4U Corsair pilot, who was killed by the kamikaze attack on the USS *Bunker Hill* off Okinawa on May 11, 1945, just six weeks after I was born. His son, my cousin Tim, was born just days after his father was killed, and when I was with him I would stare at his father's charred flight logbook with its three red "meatballs" marking the missions on which he'd had aerial victories. I thought I could still smell smoke on the pages from the fire that killed most of the VF-84 pilots, who were in the ready room after returning from a mission. My dad talked about watching the USS *Hornet* leave Alameda NAS (Naval Air Station) on April 2, 1942, with 16 B-25s for the Doolittle Raid strapped to the deck, as she passed under the Golden Gate Bridge. I grew up in the San Francisco Bay Area with MacArthur Boulevard, Army Street, and the Nimitz Freeway, Treasure Island and the Presidio, and a family friend, a Pearl Harbor survivor, who invited me to several of his group's monthly luncheons at Spenger's Restaurant in Berkeley. It was an area filled with patriotism and military history and surrounded by military facilities, including Oak Knoll Navy Hospital in Oakland, the Oakland Army Terminal, Mare Island Navy Shipyard, Moffitt Field, Alameda Naval Air Station, and Hamilton Air Force Base.

Watching *Victory at Sea* was a regular event on Sunday evenings for me. Thankfully, I grew up before *Mash* and the cultural change that came with it, because making fun of the military was never a part of my formative years. It seems I always wore a uniform, from Cub Scouts to Boy Scouts and on to ROTC, then the Air Force and the airlines, both Western and Delta; there were lots of uniforms in my life!

When I entered the University of California at Berkeley in September 1962, I joined the Air Force ROTC program without really having a plan to be a pilot but just knowing I wanted to serve. Since the ROTC programs were voluntary, they were small, and it was a good way to get my degree and my commission at the same time. Until about 1965, deferments from the draft were available to single male college students, and I can't remember any draft cards being burned when student deferments were available. When some deferments were taken away for single males in 1965 and 1966, two things happened: The anti-war movement (which I always thought was more anti-draft than anti-war, and motivated mostly by self-interest) really blossomed on the Berkeley campus, and the ROTC programs expanded somewhat. There were lines around the block to join and get an ROTC deferment, which guaranteed that you would be able to finish school and get a degree. As one of the early (pre-1965) participants in the program, I was encouraged to take the flight physical to see if I qualified for pilot training, so after a ride in a blue Air Force bus over to Hamilton AFB in Marin County, I took and passed the physical and moved onto the track for pilot training after getting my degree and my commission. Only a few eggs and tomatoes were thrown at the bus as we left the back entrance to the ROTC detachment, and it was one of my first experiences with what was to come. How the Bay Area had changed. And to think, I wasn't even getting combat pay yet!

(When UC Berkeley's Naval ROTC detachment was established in 1926, Commander Chester Nimitz became its first professor of Naval Science. Upon his death in 1966, five-star Fleet Admiral Nimitz left some of his memoirs and papers to be displayed there. The building was bombed and burned down by anti-war protesters in September 1968, and those memoirs were lost.)

I graduated from Berkeley and was commissioned a second lieutenant in the Air Force in December 1966. From there I went to UPT (Undergraduate Pilot Training), Class 68E at Williams AFB, Arizona, then to Air Force Survival School at Fairchild AFB, Washington, and to C-7 training at Sewart AFB, Tennessee. Within days of my arrival at Sewart, Martin Luther King was assassinated in Memphis and the Tennessee National Guard was patrolling the streets of the nearby cities of Smyrna and Nashville. Everyone was restricted to the base; we were unable to go into town for quite a while due to the unrest and the fear that racial strife would spread to the base, so my road to Vietnam, which began with a truly bizarre experience as an ROTC cadet at Berkeley, continued along an uncharted path. One of the lasting memories from my time at Sewart is the long lines of young men, restricted to the base, standing and waiting for hours at the handful of pay phones—something that is hard to believe in today's world of cell phones, laptops, and e-mail.

After C-7 training I went home for a short leave and then reported to Travis AFB, California, for my MAC (Military Airlift Command) charter flight to Southeast Asia. I think Travis was one of the busiest airports in the world in May 1968. There was a big sign over the entrance to the passenger terminal, "Travis AFB, Gateway to the Pacific." What an understatement! It seemed that everyone going to Vietnam or coming home went through Travis eventually, unless they were lucky enough to be a Marine and get to travel by ship!

Less than 24 hours after leaving Travis, I was at Clark AFB, Philippines, to attend Jungle Survival School, and from there my Vietnam experience began.

The MAC charter plane that took me from Clark AFB to Tan Son Nhut Air Base in Saigon on June 1, 1968, was a Continental Airlines Boeing 707—just another piece of the surreal experience that was the Vietnam War for hundreds of thousands of American boys. What country sends its young men off to war on a commercial airliner, with their last view of home a stewardess as they marched down the airstair into the war zone? It was a Continental Airlines airplane with real stewardesses, but all resemblance to a commercial airline flight ended there. As we began our descent into Saigon the captain came on the PA system to announce that we were going to enter a holding pattern for a period of time at 10,000 feet to accomplish a couple of things. It seemed there was a battle going on just off the north end of the runway at Tan Son Nhut, and we would have to wait for clearance to land until the air strikes were over. Now, we had read in the *Stars and Stripes* newspaper while at Clark that the Tet Offensive was officially over, but today's operation turned out to be, in typical military understatement, a mopping-up operation of some diehard VC (Vietcong) elements around Saigon. The captain told us that while we were in the holding pattern he would depressurize the airplane to make for quicker deplaning and that he would be leaving two engines running once on the ground to make for a faster departure (for him, of course) after we were deposited on the ramp. There were more than 200 of us, mostly Air Force and Army, jammed on an airplane that was configured in high-density, all-coach seating. All of our luggage, mostly military-issue B-4 and duffel bags for the Army guys, with a few suitcases thrown in for good measure (for guys like me), would be unloaded by the ground crew and thrown in a pile for us to sort through after the airplane was long gone. He thanked us in advance for our cooperation.

Now, unlike a lot of the other passengers on this flight, I knew exactly where that Continental 707 was headed after dropping off its passengers. The pilots were going back to Clark and the Officers' Club with the stewardesses, soon to be out at the pool. That made a lot more sense than sorting through a pile of bags on the Tan Son Nhut ramp. I knew this because I'd had to spend 10 days at Clark waiting for my survival school class to start. It seemed fighter pilots had priority for the classes, so as I waited, with my lower priority, I spent time at the club and studied the whole operation. If Travis was "Gateway to the Pacific," Clark was the Air Force "Hub of the Pacific," and in those days at Clark I ran into several of my pilot training classmates, going to their various assignments in-country after attending Jungle Survival School. I also spent some quality time watching the MAC charter stewardesses out at the pool in their bikinis, making the whole experience an unforgettable one. But, as I would soon learn, my Vietnam experience was about to get much better, with some unbelievable stories to file away.

As I stepped off that Continental 707, I was hit with what I can only describe as total sensory overload. Sound, sight, and smell were overwhelming. The noise was deafening from the two engines running on the 707 and the constant flight operations being conducted, with takeoffs, landings, and still a bomb or two being dropped just outside the airport boundaries. The heat and humidity hit me as if I had walked into a sauna, and the sights were almost too much to take in all at once. Barely 100 yards away, a line of aircraft waited for takeoff, including fighters with full bomb loads, F-5s and A-1s (both USAF and Vietnamese Air Force based at nearby Bien Hoa), C-130s, C-123s, C-47s, C-7s, and, in the middle, a Pan Am 707. The smell was something I can only describe as a bunch of stuff mixed together that shouldn't be mixed together: sweat, fear, smoke, gunpowder from the bombing, raw garbage, raw sewage, general rot—as a Supreme Court justice once said about pornography, "Maybe I can't describe it, but I know it when I see it." I have never smelled it before or since, but I'd sure know it if I smelled it again. It was really a smell puzzle, something that was going to be a part of my experience throughout the next 12 months.

Since it was a bit too much to process, I focused on finding my bag. After I was reunited with it, my next adventure was to find my way to Cam Ranh Bay. My orders told me where and when to report once I reached Cam Ranh but left the final leg of my journey a bit vague, as in, "You're on your own, lieutenant." I didn't want to end up like the young Marine lieutenant who, after flying in from Da Nang and wandering around Tan Son Nhut, asked someone how to get to Can Tho, south of Saigon in the Delta. It was suggested (with laughter behind his back) that he go out the main gate of the base and take a civilian bus. He did, lugging his M-16 rifle, his seabag, and all his gear. It turns out this was the most stupid, dangerous thing he could have done. That was Marine Lieutenant Zinni, later four-star General Zinni, and he tells that story often when he gives motivational speeches.

There's probably not a more pathetic sight than a brown-bar lieutenant (second lieutenant rank is a gold bar) wandering around the Tan Son Nhut ramp with a brand-new Samsonite suitcase, so I tried to look like I knew what I was doing—kind of hard with that new suitcase (a gift from my mom, of course). If there had been a bus to Cam Ranh Bay, I probably would have been directed to it by some seasoned veteran. Fortunately, after asking a few guys who looked like they had been around a while, I was directed to the in-country passenger terminal and was told that in a couple of hours I would be able to hitch a ride on a C-7 to Cam Ranh Bay. I made it to the in-country terminal, found a corner, and sat down.

While I waited, I made the mistake of using the men's room outside the so-called terminal. It was totally plastered with graffiti in several unknown languages, with the English messages consistent in their profane comments about Johnson and McNamara, saying in so many words that "Vietnam sucks," while the rest, in Vietnamese and every kind of script from Chinese to Korean to Thai, remains a mystery to this day. At 105 degrees and close to 100 percent humidity, the men's room uploaded the final piece of the smell puzzle to my afternoon's sensory experience. And to think, that Continental crew was already lounging at the Officers' Club pool at Clark! What I'd have given for a cold San Miguel and my corner table at the window overlooking the pool in the air-conditioned Officers' Club.

Arriving at Cam Ranh Bay Air Base late that afternoon, I reported in to the duty officer for the 458th TAS (Tactical Airlift Squadron), was assigned a room in the officers' quarters, and was told to report to the squadron building in the morning for in-processing. The quarters were called hooches, and they were set up as two small bedrooms with a connecting living room or common area between them. Each bedroom accommodated four pilots in two bunk beds, and we each got a metal locker. There was just enough room to go in, change clothes, and either go back out or go to bed. As a new guy, I was assigned an upper bunk. Outside the hooches, sandbags were piled four to five feet high against the walls to protect us from a rocket or mortar attack, and I did notice that the upper bunk was above the top row of sandbags, but fortunately a serious attack never came in the next 12 months. The bedrooms were air-conditioned, which was a real blessing, but we ended up spending most of our free time in the common living room or outside in the squadron area, which had picnic tables, a common bathroom and shower, and some exercise equipment. (It always intrigued me that after the Americans left Vietnam, Cam Ranh Bay AB was used by the Russians, before the Vietnamese got tired of them and began to ease them out. I'm sure they stayed in our hooches, but it was good to know that the local Vietnamese completely stripped the base after we left, including the air conditioners, toilet and shower fixtures, electrical wiring, and maybe even the sandbags. I'm sure the Russians had a primitive go of it, as I don't think the commissars cared much about the comfort or morale of the troops.)

The next morning I began my in-processing, which started with an in-country intelligence briefing. There were several new crew members, and we were told that South Vietnam was still recovering from the Tet Offensive, which had begun on January 30, 1968, and ended, for the most part, in February (except for the mopping-up operations around Tan Son Nhut the previous day). We were also told about the mission of the C-7 Caribou. We would be involved in tactical airlift and resupply of the Army Special Forces camps that were located mostly in the border areas between South Vietnam and Laos, and South Vietnam and Cambodia. The camps were near the border to monitor traffic on the Ho Chi Minh Trail, which ran from North Vietnam to the south through "neutral" Laos and Cambodia, and it was emphasized that under no circumstances would we cross the military operational boundary along the border and fly over Laos or Cambodia.

Designed for short field takeoff and landing, the C-7 was perfect for the job, as most camps had unimproved landing strips, some as short as 1,000 feet. Several of the camps had been under siege during the Tet Offensive, so a massive resupply and rebuilding effort was in its early stages. There would be no training flights; all in-country orientation and training would be conducted on regularly scheduled missions. The training would come fast and furious as we learned every way the Caribou could deliver cargo. We would learn about parachute air drops from 1,000 to 1,500 feet, and we would learn about LAPES (low-altitude parachute extraction system), in which cargo pallets were dropped from 200 feet right on top of a camp, sent out the rear of the aircraft via a cargo chute. There was another system in which we would land, make a 180-degree turn at the far end of the runway, and take off again. As we were rolling out from the landing, our flight mechanic would release the tie-downs and open the cargo door, and the pallets would slide out the back as we accelerated for takeoff. This could be done with minimum time on the ground, often little more than a minute. Then sometimes we would land, shut down the engines, and eat lunch with the Green Berets in the camp as their Montagnard soldiers off-loaded and guarded the airplane. (The Montagnards were mountain tribesmen who hated the Vietnamese in general, the North Vietnamese in particular, and were hired as mercenaries to fight with the Special Forces troops.)

We would carry everything from general cargo and mail, to food, ammunition, and troops. We also carried live animals to the camps for the Montagnards, including, on several occasions, cows. USAID (U.S. Agency for International Development) was trying to teach the Montagnards how to raise and breed the cattle, but that didn't work out well—they just killed and ate them, usually in some ritualistic sacrifice that I was spared from witnessing. (I think USAID had visions of Texas-style cattle ranches in the Montagnard villages. As you read in Jim Gibbs's story, this cattle airlift had been going on for four years by the time I arrived, without much success.) We even air-dropped live cows and pigs a couple of times; it was quite an experience.

Most interestingly, the Montagnard women and their young children would fly back to Ban Me Thuot with us after we dropped off our loads, to do their shopping and then fly back to the camp—part of the arrangement with the Montagnard troops, who were hired and supplied by the Special Forces. They didn't speak English and we didn't speak their language, but they knew the drill, and everything worked fine as they marched on the airplane, fastened their seat belts, and went to Ban Me Thuot with their woven shopping bags. The women carried a pungent liquid in small bottles that they used like perfume to keep from getting airsick, adding another smell to the others previously mentioned. When we flew through Ban Me Thuot, there would be groups of Montagnard women and children waiting patiently for a flight back to camp. Most of them had never ridden in a car but had more frequent-flyer miles than you could count! And they usually didn't get airsick, but their potion could make *us* sick on a hot, bumpy flight. This explains why we often flew with the cockpit side windows open. But I digress...

With all this information we began to fly and learned the ropes quickly. Our flying was mostly in daylight under visual flight rules; we never filed an instrument flight plan but instead kept in touch with our controller in Saigon, call sign Hilda (affectionately known as Mother), reporting our takeoff and landing times at each stop so they knew where we were. In the era before computers kept track of everything, the airplanes and crews were monitored and followed on a peg board and a handwritten log, believe it or not, as each daily mission had a call sign that could be tracked easily. The ACs (aircraft commanders) I flew with were a mix of more senior majors and lieutenant colonels and some young lieutenants and captains who had been in-country for six to eight months and had upgraded to AC. It was a great group, and I learned a lot.

The first time I saw Camp Bu Prang was July 6, 1968, and to this day, it is the most fascinating place I have ever been. Located on a hill near the Cambodian border, the camp looked like a cross between something out of a John Wayne western and a *National Geographic* article on the mountain tribes of Southeast Asia. The camp was built like a fort with huge sandbagged bunkers 10 to 15 feet high sitting on each side of the main gate. Machine gun barrels poked out of gun ports at the top of each bunker, with clear fields of fire across the runway and the approach to the camp from the east. The camp was surrounded by high barbed-wire fences and had a network of slit trenches several feet deep that ran around the camp so it could be reinforced at any point in the event of attack. The runway was outside the camp perimeter and sloped up, down, and sideways, ending at the north end near the camp gate, where there was a small unloading area. At night, rolls of barbed wire were pulled across the runway to form a portion of the camp's defensive perimeter. The Montagnard weapons ranged from crossbows to M60 machine guns (although the crossbows were mostly sold or traded as souvenirs, often carried by the Montagnard women to Ban Me Thuot for that purpose), and their dress from loincloths to Army jungle camouflage fatigues. The Green Berets were always in freshly starched uniforms with their ever-present berets, and since they didn't send their laundry out, I assumed they had a deal with the Montagnard women to take care of their fatigues.

Because the camp was so close to the border and the Ho Chi Minh Trail, it was a thorn in the side of the VC and the NVA (North Vietnamese Army) and was under constant harassment and attack. It became so dangerous and hard to defend that it was abandoned in late 1969 and moved seven miles east, away from the border, and renamed Bu Prang New.

On July 6, 1968, I had been flying in-country a little over a month, had close to 100 hours of combat flying time, and was flying copilot for Major Hunter Hackney, who was typical of my first aircraft commanders. I was learning everything about navigation in the war zone, where reaching our destination with whatever cargo we were carrying was critical to the troops on the ground. We used everything that was available to us, starting with the notoriously unreliable TACAN (tactical air navigation) stations, which would send a signal giving the pilot continuous information as to his range and bearing from the station. Each TACAN had a channel number that was dialed in on a receiver in the cockpit. But mostly we utilized basic pilotage to find the camps, with map reading and ground reference points, dead reckoning, flying headings, and timing. In the early morning, we often flew over a solid layer of clouds and had to look for holes to dive through to get beneath the layer when in the vicinity of our destination. I also learned the safest way to approach our destination and avoid areas that were guaranteed to draw ground fire. When near a camp it was easy to determine the direction in which to land: There were fires everywhere, and you just watched the way the smoke was blowing to decide on the landing direction. We always tried to land toward the unloading area so we could roll out, turn around, unload, and then take off in the opposite direction. It worked well.

As the designated navigator, the copilot carried the Tactical Aerodrome Directory for South Vietnam as well as a topographical air map, legend ONC K-10, that displayed all the aerodromes and Special Forces camps where we operated. There was no system of airways on the topographical map, and as mentioned, the TACAN stations were unreliable. It was always exciting, and although it was also challenging at first, we flew so much that it quickly became routine. Operating so close to the border kept us alert, and we rapidly learned the landmarks of the border areas.

The Tactical Aerodrome Directory, South Vietnam, dated 15 April 1969 (I failed to save an earlier edition), contains the following information on Bu Prang, on page 198:

> *Bu Krak* (the camp was also known as Bu Prang)
> *Runway 01-19* (It was basically a north–south runway, parallel to the border.)
> *1800' long, 70' wide* (the runway dimensions)
> *Clay/laterite surface* (Laterite, a striking reddish brown soil, is formed in tropical regions by the decomposition of underlying rocks containing iron, giving it the color of rust.)

After describing the runway, the next section, titled "Aerodrome Remarks," always got my attention:

> *Secure, SF* (Special Forces). *Do not land when runway is wet.* (I soon learned that all SF camps were listed as secure unless

they had been overrun or abandoned. However, the term *secure*, another good military term like *mopping up*, was a relative concept. And since it rained often, the runway was wet most of the time.)

Approach to RW 19 is over a canyon 100' from threshold. Unloading area is 90' x 325' W (west) side.

N (north) end is in poor condition and has numerous buildings and obstructions along its edge.

Hazards—minefields! and 6' concertina fence adjacent to both runway edges. There are bunkers and tents 10'–15' high as close as 25' from both edges of the runway. (This kind of note explains why I never had a problem landing in the center of the runway for the rest of my flying career!)

The chart for Bu Prang on page 198 also has an aerial photo of the camp and runway, showing that it is located 55 miles on a course of 242 degrees from the Ban Me Thuot TACAN, Channel 117.

Now, with enough information to give an FAA inspector a heart attack, Major Hackney was circling, waiting for heavy rain showers to pass, while I talked to the camp on our FM radio. When I dutifully pointed out to Major Hackney the note about landing when the runway was wet, he smiled and said, "The runway is wet most of the time. Those guys in the camp need the stuff we're carrying, so we'll just consider that note advisory in nature." Then he gave me some advice that served me well through the rest of my year in Vietnam and beyond. "It's a safe assumption that the runway surface will be wet because of the morning and evening ground fog or the constant rain showers. When the book lists the runway surface as clay/laterite like Bu Prang and so many of the SF camps, it will be slicker than greased owl snot." Now, "greased owl snot" was the perfect description of the wet runway surface. "Stay off the brakes and stop the airplane with reverse thrust; if she starts to skid, use differential reverse to keep her going in a straight line—and please stay out of the minefield!" Then he looked over at me and said, "You've got it." It was my first landing at Bu Prang and what a thrill it was. There was no FAA, no crusade against land mines (where was Princess

Diana when we needed her?), just our guys on the ground who depended on us to get in with their stuff. We landed. (Years later, while taxiing a Delta 757 to the gate in Fairbanks, Alaska, in mid-January, 30 degrees below zero and the ramp a sheet of frozen snow and ice, I could hear Hunter Hackney talking to me: "Stay off the brakes and stop her with reverse thrust.")

Some six weeks later, Major Hackney was awarded the Air Force Cross (the second-highest military decoration that can be given to a member of the U.S. Air Force) for a night airdrop that helped break the siege at Camp Duc Lap on August 25, 1968. The camp had been under attack for several days; "Snoopy" AC-47 gunships had been hosing down the area with their Gatling mini-guns to no avail. Hackney had to drop a load of ammunition, artillery shells, and water from 200 feet to the beleaguered Green Berets and their Montagnard troops. It was pitch dark and they were flying with no lights, and the ground fire was so intense that Hackney later described it as sounding like a flying through a hailstorm. When he landed at Ban Me Thuot, leaking fuel and hydraulic fluid from an airplane that had more holes in it than a sieve, it was miraculous that not one crew member had been scratched. The siege was broken the next day by a B-52 strike that all but vaporized the attackers and left the camp in the center of rows of bomb craters that crisscrossed the camp boundary. I never saw anything like that again during the rest of my tour. After the siege, Duc Lap was abandoned and moved several miles to a more defensible area, renamed Duc Lap #2.

Fast-forward six months, and I am now one of the "old heads." I had almost 600 hours of flying time in-country, and had completed the aircraft commander upgrade program, just awaiting my final check ride. On the evening of January 14, 1969, I learned that I was to be a late addition to the next morning's schedule and that I would be flying copilot for the wing commander, Colonel Keith L. Christensen. As commander of the 483rd TAW (Tactical Airlift Wing), he was in overall command of the six C-7 squadrons in-country, two at Cam Ranh Bay, two at Phu Cat, and two at Vung Tau. I was a likely candidate for this mission because the senior officers did not fly very often and were always paired with high-time copilots. The destination was—surprise!—Bu Prang. I was told only that we were to take a maintenance team to make a temporary repair on a Caribou that had landed at Bu Prang late in the afternoon of the 14th and had suffered some wing tip damage. "So get some sleep," I was told. "The briefing is at 0330."

The crew met for a pre-mission briefing on January 15 at the Wing Operations building near the flight line. In addition to the C-7 crew of three (two pilots and a loadmaster/flight mechanic), there were five C-7 maintenance men going with us to Bu Prang. The briefing was vague about what had happened to the damaged C-7, but the plan was to arrive at Bu Prang at sunrise, inspect the damage to the airplane on the ground, drop off the maintenance crew, then return to Ban Me Thuot to continue the daily scheduled 466 mission. All I knew was that the airplane at Bu Prang was damaged and unflyable, had spent the night on the dirt unloading area outside the security of the camp, and needed a temporary fix so it could be flown back to Cam Ranh Bay ASAP. You'll remember that Bu Prang sat right on the Cambodian border, so close to the Ho Chi Minh Trail that the Green Berets in the camp told me they could hear the vehicle traffic on the trail at night. "Sounded like commute hour on the Sepulveda Freeway," said one Special Forces trooper from Southern California.

It seemed like a simple enough plan. We got in the crew bus, swung by the armory where we picked up our .38 revolvers and M-16 rifles for our flight mechanic and the maintenance crew, then continued out to the flight line. It was pitch dark, and this was exciting enough because we seldom, if ever, flew at night. We didn't have a map with a low-altitude airway system for South Vietnam, and all our flying was under visual flight rules. The Air Force had even waived our annual instrument check ride that year since we seldom flew under IFR (Instrument Flight Rules), and for our daily missions we never filed an IFR flight plan. The majority of the camps we flew into were designated for daytime operation only because they were unlighted, with runways outside the perimeter and security of the camp. The only exception would be a severe tactical emergency when all the rules were waived, such as the siege of Duc Lap.

As the designated navigator for this mission, I reflected on the plan, knowing that finding Bu Prang in the dark or early sunrise was going to be a challenge. After six months of flying nearly 100 hours per month, I found daytime navigation pretty simple; ground references and landmarks were by then very familiar to me. This mission was going to require a mix of TACAN navigation and dead reckoning. We would fly outbound from CRB (Cam Ranh Bay) until we intercepted a course inbound to BMT (Ban Me Thuot). Then came the tricky part: flying a course outbound from BMT until we reached Bu Prang, which was located 55 nautical miles out the BMT 242 degree radial. It sounds straightforward enough but the BMT TACAN, Channel 117, had a nasty habit of losing its signal about 25 to 30 miles short of the Cambodian border, leaving ground references essential to finding the camp. The other nagging concern I had was the timing of our takeoff from CRB. I thought our scheduled takeoff time was too early and that it would still be dark when we reached Bu Prang; the geniuses in the "head shed" did not consult me on this detail, and flying with the wing commander, I was the "brief-ee," not the "brief-or." So off we went.

With the call sign Law 466 and flying aircraft tail number 171, we took off on runway 02R at Cam Ranh Bay at exactly 0430 and climbed out under a clear sky with little or no moonlight. A left turn over Nha Trang turned us westbound and took us over the coastal range, which rose sharply to 2,000 to 4,000 feet just west of Cam Ranh Bay. Once over the coastal peaks, we turned toward the west and leveled off at 4,500 feet MSL (mean sea level), which put us 2,500 to 3,000 feet above the flat plain of the Central Highlands. Colonel Christensen was flying and I was navigating. As we turned toward the BMT TACAN it gave us a good signal and a course lock-on, so we headed directly toward the station. It was still nearly pitch dark; the only lights below were from an occasional fire on the ground and some random tracer fire that was probably from a ground engagement and not directed at us. We finally saw the lights of Ban Me Thuot City and crossed overhead BMT (channel 117)—so far, so good. As mentioned earlier, according to the Tactical Aerodrome Directory Bu Prang was located 55 nautical miles away on a course of 242 degrees outbound from BMT, so we intercepted the 242 degree radial outbound, figured a heading to hold the course (with a minor wind correction) and started a time hack as a backup. It was still very dark outside as we headed toward Bu Prang, the Cambodian border, and all the hash marks and the "Military Operational Boundary" warning on the map. I had calculated a rough ground speed, heading, and time to fly those 55 nautical miles, but we certainly weren't going to find or land at Bu Prang in the dark, so we went on westbound, waiting for the sun to rise. As anticipated, the BMT TACAN lost its signal about 30 miles short of Bu Prang so we continued to fly the pre-calculated heading.

As we flew along in the dark, my only real concerns were the Cambodian border, which was less than a mile west of Bu Prang, and the target we presented to anyone who cared to shoot at us with a heavy weapon. At 4,500 feet we were out of range of most small-arms fire; we had our lights out and were in a moonless sky. But there was always the added prospect of friendly artillery or a B-52 strike. A B-52 strike was always preceded by a short announcement on guard frequency (243.0 MHz UHF) that said, "Heavy artillery at coordinates ____." This call always brought about a frantic check on the map to be sure we were clear of those coordinates and an evasive maneuver if we were too close. Watching a B-52 strike from even a couple of miles away was truly an awesome sight. More than a hundred 500 pound bombs per airplane, dropped from 35,000 feet by a flight of three B-52s and exploding in a line over a mile long, creates a scene that really gets your attention! And it gave emphasis to the first rule we learned about radio procedures: *always* monitor guard!

On we flew, following the predetermined heading and watching the time tick along. The sun started to come up behind us, but all we could see was a sea of low ground fog with the beautiful green trees and the jungle canopy sticking up through the fog. As I looked out, I took a few seconds to marvel at the beauty below and remember the dangers it held, also remembering that there was an old French airstrip just inside Cambodia, Camp le Rolland, which could be mistaken for Bu Prang if one was unfamiliar with the area. It was marked on the map "Abandoned, Probably Mined," which of course made it unsuitable as an alternate landing field! I knew Bu Prang was on a little hill that I could recognize on sight, but it was nowhere in front of us. I had been calling the camp on its FM radio frequency since about the 20 minute mark on the time hack, but I never got an answer as we continued traveling straight ahead to the west.

There was no question that we had flown too far to the west and were over Cambodia, but it took a while to convince Colonel Christensen to turn around and head back east. He was a man of few words; our longest personal conversation had taken place more than two hours earlier and consisted of, "Good morning, colonel." "Good morning, lieutenant." Then of course we had run the check-lists, but I don't really count that as conversation. As I became more and more insistent, Colonel Christensen finally made the long-awaited 180 degree turn and we headed back to the east. We flew for a good 15 minutes, calling Bu Prang on the radio and looking for the hill that should have been sticking up through the fog. Then, just ahead, was Camp le Rolland — and beyond, with a fog bank from the west reaching up nearly to the runway edge, Bu Prang.

We flew an abbreviated left hand traffic pattern, made a left base to final, landed to the north on runway 01, and taxied up to the unloading area at the north end of the runway next to the main gate of the camp. Now, of course, the radio decided to work, and the camp radioman told us that they had heard us fly overhead in the dark more than 30 minutes earlier; so much for my "old head" status and my navigation. The heading and timing worked out pretty well, but we had departed Cam Ranh Bay about 30 minutes too early. I can also claim about 30 minutes of flying time over Cambodia at a time when I thought it could have been a serious offense. Little did I know!

The most interesting part of the story was what we found on the ground at Bu Prang, and fortunately I had my camera to record everything. The damaged C-7 was missing 2 to 3 feet of the left wing tip, and a good part of that wing tip was imbedded in the rotor blades of a UH-1 helicopter parked nearby. Both aircraft were guarded by several heavily armed Montagnards. No crossbows for these guys; they were serious. The various stories I heard ranged from a mid-air collision on landing to a taxi accident, but the bottom line was a Caribou that was unflyable.

The UH-1 had an Air Force camouflage paint job, which I had never seen, and was totally unmarked. It was quite unusual, as we seldom saw an Air Force Huey and never at an Army SF camp. As I learned years after Vietnam, when much of the Special Operations activities had been declassified and written about, this Huey was most likely an Air Force Special Operations aircraft flown by the 20th SOS (Special Operations Squadron) called the Green Hornets. Outfitted with a rotating-barrel Gatling gun on each side for the door gunners, it put out a tremendous amount of firepower and was used on cross-border missions (remember the Military Operational Boundary along the border? Oh, well…). These same Gatling guns were used on the much larger HH-3 and HH-53 Jolly Green Giant rescue helicopters, but I had never seen them on a Huey. Interestingly, both Gatling guns had been removed and were most likely in the camp, so all we saw was an unarmed, unmarked Huey with an Air Force camouflage paint job and a big chunk of Caribou wingtip proudly mounted in the rotor blades.

If an incident like this had to happen, it was much better than sliding into the minefield! As for our foray over Cambodia, we were fortunate that the fog bank to the west had obscured the trail and probably saved us from being seen from the ground. Even if we had been seen, the NVA was extremely well disciplined and might have refrained from taking a shot at us because they didn't want to give away their positions by day. The fog kept us from ever knowing the answer to that question.

As a postscript, a few years ago I submitted this story to the Air Force Caribou Association for inclusion in its quarterly newsletter. I also sent several photos I had taken at Bu Prang that morning and ended up experiencing an incredible coincidence. I received a call from Pat Hanavan, vice president of the association. Unbeknownst to me, he had been the maintenance officer with the repair crew on the flight that morning, and he told me the rest of the story: The damaged wing on the C-7 was repaired with a temporary fix and it was flown back to Cam Ranh Bay late that afternoon by a crew brought in on another Caribou. At Cam Ranh it was permanently repaired. The only equipment the maintenance crew had at Bu Prang was a small camp generator for electricity and the tools they had brought with them. As for the 20th SOS Huey, it departed later in the morning with the Gatling guns reinstalled and the Caribou wing-tip removed from the rotor blades, heading off to the east. I never saw another Huey like it in my remaining months in Vietnam.

....

The military was famous for its acronyms, everything from AWOL to DNIF to DOS to SEA (absent without leave, duty not including flying, date of separation, Southeast Asia), but there are two that I want to mention at the end of my story because they were quite colorful and were a piece of every Vietnam veteran's experience. When we arrived in-country for our one-year tours of duty, each of us was given a DEROS (date eligible for return from overseas). Like a good acronym, DEROS became a word in and of itself. Just like an airline pilot who lives and breathes his seniority number, in Vietnam we all knew our DEROS, and as has been mentioned in several stories, the term *being short* or *short-timer* referred to how close you were to your DEROS. In our squadron and many of the others around the country, you were "short" when you were within 30 days of your DEROS, and many of us wore a short-timer's ribbon on the zipper of the small pocket on the left sleeve of our flight suit. Now, only the military can come up with names for uniform items such as a flight suit, but the one I wore (and still have) has the following designation on the label: COVERALLS, FLYING, MEN'S, W/R POPLIN, OG 10.COVINGTON INDUSTRIES, INC. 100% COTTON. DSA-100-67-C-344. 6 FEBRUARY 1967. The short-timer's ribbon that we wore was the gold cord from the purple bag that held a bottle of Crown Royal Canadian Whiskey. For whatever reason, the BX (base exchange) at Cam Ranh Bay would often run out of items like cameras and stereo equipment, but it never seemed to run out of booze or cigarettes! This was for troop morale, I suppose, and even though we had to use a ration card to buy them, there were always enough non-drinkers and non-smokers that there was plenty to go around—and the booze was very cheap. A bottle of Crown Royal or a carton of Marlboros went a long way in a trade at an SF camp on the Cambodian border. Every time I see a purple Crown Royal bag it takes me back in time. Some things change, but the Crown Royal bag and cord have remained the same to this day.

The second acronym was MPC (Military Payment Certificate). This was the only form of money that we were allowed to have in Vietnam, paper money in denominations from 5 cents to 20 dollars. Upon arrival in-country everyone was required to turn in their "green" dollars and coins, exchanging them for MPC. There was a thriving black market off base, with the demand for green dollars so great that the local Vietnamese money changers would buy them with MPC for several times their face value. Of course they ran a big risk in holding MPC, because periodically the powers that be would have an unannounced exchange, bringing out a new issue of MPC that made the old series worthless. In my year there were two MPC exchanges, and only the most nimble Vietnamese money changers survived.

I never kept a diary, but I did keep a very accurate logbook of my flights, took several hundred photos, and wrote at least once a week to my folks. A few years after I returned from Vietnam, separated from active duty, and was working for Western Airlines, my dad gave me a wicker basket that had all my letters in it, along with a wall-size map of South Vietnam showing all the Special Forces camps where we had operated. It was one of the first things I had sent home after arriving in-country and he had hung it on the wall and circled each camp as I wrote and told of my daily itinerary and where I had landed around the country. That basket of letters was as close to a diary as I could imagine. However, most of my letters sounded like a travel log, sanitized of most mentions of the war and written as if I were on a great *National Geographic* tour of Vietnam, visiting the most fascinating faraway places and getting some good flying lessons to boot. Reading between the lines today, I can see how concerned I was not to cause my parents any undue worry. I think I was more concerned about what was going on in Berkeley, but nothing could have prepared me for what I found when I got home. The funny thing was that I had gotten a lot of good-natured ribbing for being from Berkeley, Berzerkley as it was called, even earning the nickname "Berkeley Bruce" from some of my squadron mates. I had spent a great deal of time defending the city where I had grown up, delivered the *Berkeley Daily Gazette* on a three-speed Schwinn bike, became an Eagle Scout in Troop 41, and got an outstanding education in the public schools. To say that I didn't recognize Berkeley in May of 1969 and felt totally alienated from it, would be an understatement.

In closing, I would like to pay my respects and dedicate my story to the 38 Air Force Caribou crewmembers killed during the Vietnam War. The worst time for the Caribou came just under a year after I returned to the States, when three C-7s were shot down in a four-day period with the loss of all nine crewmembers. They were making airdrops at Special Forces Camp Dak Seang in early April 1970 while the camp was under siege. Dak Seang was just eight miles from the Laotian border, 50 miles northwest of Plieku. With the runway located outside the camp and under the control of North Vietnamese and Vietcong soldiers, airdrops were the only way to resupply the beleaguered American and South Vietnamese troops. There are several memorials around the country to those 38 Caribou crewmembers lost in the Vietnam War. I think the most beautiful is a bench just outside the entrance to the National Museum of the United States Air Force at Wright Patterson AFB in Dayton, Ohio.

．．．．．．．

It seemed over the years of airline flying that there were always questions from passengers about which airports were the most challenging for approach and landing. I knew they expected to hear LaGuardia or San Diego, even Butte, Montana, in a snowstorm, but I was tempted to say Bu Prang. You know that runway is slicker than greased owl snot when it's wet, and there are those minefields off the edge of the runway...

L) *Cows being offloaded at Camp Duc Lap from a C-7, 1968.* *R)* *Over my right shoulder is a Green Beret lieutenant supervising the Montagnard crew offloading the aircraft (and soon to eat the cows).*

L) *Camp Bu Prang from the air, Cambodian border at left less than one mile from the camp, late 1968.* *R)* *Setting up for a landing to the south at Bu Prang, Cambodia to the right, runway to the left of the camp, late 1968.*

Tactical Aerodrome
Directory South
Vietnam, 15 April 1969.

Top) Camp Bu Prang, January 15, 1969. There was always a mix of troops at the camps.
The man in the center with the blue scarf wears a yellow ARVN (Army of the Republic
of Vietnam) Ranger patch in a pocket hanger, and to his left the man wears LLDB
(Vietnamese Special Forces) jump wings. The others appear to be Montagnards. Really,
who gets to go to places like this? **Bottom)** Main gate at Camp Bu Prang, January 15,
1969. Note: freshly laundered, pressed and creased fatigues on the Green Berets—an
ongoing mystery. Here you see the Green Berets (usually 12 in an A Team at a camp),
2 ARVN LLDB troops, and to the left a mystery man in a non-US uniform, who has
been variously identified as a French Army "observer" of North African lineage.

L) *Damaged C-7 wingtip, Air Force Huey in the distance behind Montagnard troops, our C-7 is off to the right. All photos taken on January 15, 1969.* **R)** *C-7 wingtip in the Huey rotor blades. Dogs were always around the Special Forces camps.*

Maintenance crew examines damage to the C-7 wingtip. Colonel Keith Christensen is standing at the far left in the photo, talking to the Bu Prang camp commander, a Green Beret captain.

Another view of the unmarked Air Force Huey (and the dog).

29

PATRIOT'S DAY

Eric Jensen, USN, A-7A, 1969
{ Date of hire by Western Airlines: 6/6/1977 }

Eric Jensen, Western Airlines Logbook, 1986.

The contribution by Eric Jensen is a bit different from most of the others. I was given his name by Gary Gottshalk as one I should contact for a story, and after exchanging notes in our pilot mailboxes at the Los Angeles base, I received the following in the mail. There was no cover letter or other information, but it is an interesting and moving exchange between Eric and the City of Laguna Beach, California. Eric had been named Honored Patriot of the Year. The letters are undated, so I will assume it was for a year in the late 1990s. Both letters are presented as I received them and pay tribute to another Western pilot who distinguished himself in Vietnam.

HONORED PATRIOT OF THE YEAR:
CAPTAIN ERIC JENSEN

The Patriot of the Year award is given to a person who has served the nation gallantly or meritoriously in time of war or national emergency. This year's honored patriot is retired Navy Captain Eric Axel Jensen. Born in Los Angeles in 1942, Eric's ties to Laguna began as a baby during visits to his grandparents. As a teenager he worked at the Festival of Arts and later served as a Laguna Beach lifeguard for six years while attending Cal State Northridge.

After serving as an Aviation Machinist's Mate in the Navy Reserve, Eric was commissioned and designated a naval aviator in 1968. After qualifying in the A-7A Corsair II fighter attack aircraft, he joined the Marauders, of Attack Squadron 82, and then embarked on the aircraft carrier USS *Coral Sea*, for combat duties on Yankee Station in the South China Sea off the coast of Vietnam. In 1969, during the intense latter stages of the Vietnam War, Eric and his squadron were engaged in extremely hazardous night attack combat operations, and he flew a total of 113 combat missions over Vietnam. For his gallantry and meritorious service, he was awarded 11 Air Medals, 3 Navy Commendation Medals, the Navy Achievement Medal as well as two awards of the Meritorious Unit Citation.

Eric Jensen's Naval career spanned 26 years of active and reserve service and included tours in the Mediterranean Sea as an attack pilot instructor, and several staff tours at Point Mugu, North Island, and in Hawaii. For many years he has also been active at the Anaheim Veterans Center and elsewhere, assisting less fortunate fellow veterans. In civilian life, Eric joined Western Airlines in 1977, which later merged with Delta Air Lines where he now flies Boeing 767s. He is also president of his own company, Proud Traditions. Eric and his wife, Alice, have lived in Laguna for 27 years. The couple has two children, Dana, who is currently serving in the Marines, and Christian, a senior at Pepperdine University.

Now follows Eric Jensen's response to the city of Laguna Beach.

....

To my neighbors and fellow citizens of Laguna Beach,

March 6 is the Patriot's Day Parade, and it is a great honor for me to be chosen Patriot of the Year. (Patriot's Day is the anniversary of the Battle of Lexington in 1775.) I am writing this open letter to you so you will have a better idea of who I am and to share some thoughts with you.

When I was a junior in high school my family moved from Los Angeles to North Hollywood. As a new kid in the area I was lonely and unsettled. I met a person who became my friend while attending Walter Reed Junior High School. His name was Robin Andrew Pearce and he lived just half a block away from me. We quickly became best friends. In fact, my first date was with his sister Helen. We attended the same high school and university together and we shared a lot of life together. Robin was a year older than me, and when he received a draft notice he came to me to consider alternatives. We decided to visit the various service recruiters and choose our destiny. We joined the United States Navy Reserves so we could finish college uninterrupted. We put on our uniforms every Wednesday night to attend training meetings. We even tried to outdo each other in our appearance. We were sharp! In our "bell bottom trousers and coats of navy blue!"

By chance, on the way to class I met a Navy pilot recruiter who offered us a plane ride. Robin and I went to Los Alamitos Naval Air Station that following weekend but only one ride was available so we flipped a coin and I won. We were off on a new adventure. Robin scored off-scale high on his qualification tests. I was average. We went to pilot training and Robin got married. Being married, he chose the safe ride and became qualified in fairly safe multiengine land airplanes. I wanted to carry the challenge as far as I could and so I chose carrier-based single-seat jets. We focused all of our efforts on training, and after two years of pilot training we received our Navy wings of gold. And we became aware of Vietnam.

"I pledge allegiance to the flag of the United States of America, and to the Republic for which it stands, one nation, under God, with liberty and justice for all."

We had said those words in school for years. Now, simply because of our age, our country called. It was our turn to go, to become a part of our nation and history. Ladies and gentlemen, when our country calls, it is serious business because there are no points for second place!

Robin and I were the product of American society, and our role was now of greatest importance. Our job was to do our duty to the utmost of our ability. No man can do more, and no one calling himself a man could do less. I believe that those who are called upon to serve must expect nothing from our country, America. We in fact debase ourselves if we regard our country as merely a place in which to eat and to sleep. Our history resounds with the illustrious names of those who have given their all, and their accumulated sacrifice has resulted in an America where there is a measure of peace, justice, and freedom for all. A higher standard of civilization has evolved in our country and is still evolving more than anywhere else. As a result of personal sacrifices we have a history, and that history cries out to us: "For men and women of integrity, a moral obligation is a binding commitment fulfilled, even at the expense of personal sacrifice."

Today I count myself lucky and honored to have been at the right age and fully trained as a Navy pilot in 1969, to throw my full weight into the scale. My fellow veterans of my age group who had a chance to give and serve dared all for the principles of our history, like those who went before. God sends each one of us in this world to acquire a personality and a character that can never be taken from us. I firmly and absolutely believe that evil things in this world try us. They happen and we are put to the test and it is good for us. The Bible and our nation's history are full of cases where the easy way out has been discarded for the high ground of moral principles. You see, freedom must be nurtured by every succeeding generation. Failure to meet this obligation will lead to the erosion of liberty from the hearts of free people everywhere. With the final test of personally carrying America's banner to war, I considered my character fully developed.

This was my calling, and to have shunned this simple responsibility would mean my very life would have been in vain.

Robin and I carried our personal strengths and weaknesses to war in Vietnam. We were scared and frightened. With everything on the line, and in the face of combat, we learned to seek our reward with the inner satisfaction that comes from the knowledge that the task undertaken was performed well and to the best of our ability. We were predisposed to pray, too, and we learned to ask for strength and courage to overcome the vicissitudes of combat and not just deliverance from them. In short, we matured very rapidly.

For he today that sheds his blood with me shall be my brother.
—From William Shakespeare's Henry V, in the Crispin's Day speech before the battle of Agincourt in 1415. It expresses the essence of what it was to be a man in the Middle Ages.

I have 58,000 brothers whose names are etched in black granite in Washington, D.C. Those men of our nation's history who went before, and now these 58,000 new names, were the best our country had to offer. It is because of them that we bear the responsibility of our age and the making of our history today. Today I live by a credo linked to my brothers, and I charge you to consider it. "Behave honorably. You will be held personally accountable if you behave improperly, and undeservedly, your colleagues and organizations will also carry the burden of your shame." I say to you, "steadfastly seek moral excellence, a standard achieved when integrity, fidelity, honesty and the like, become a natural part of your inner person." If we heed these words, then I believe we are ALL patriots in the truest sense of the word.

I believe Lieutenant Robin Andrew Pearce purchased this opportunity for all of us. His name is etched permanently on panel 12W, line 8, on the Vietnam Memorial in Washington, D.C., as a monument to the price he paid for our opportunity to live in community as Americans.

I believe in you and I believe in us. God bless America.

See you at the parade March 6th.

—Eric Axel Jensen

30

Chinook Winds Of Bao Loc

Howard C. "Butch" Heinz, USAF, O-2A, July 1970
{ Date of hire by Western Airlines: 12/1/1976 }

Butch Heinz with his O-2A at Phan Rang AB, 1970. He is wearing his camouflage fatigues, posing with his CAR-15. Note: His flight helmet is hanging from a 2.75 inch rocket in the pod on the right wing.

Butch Heinz is another Western pilot who was among those in the big group of Vietnam veterans who poured out of the service and into the airlines in the early to mid-1970s. As with several others featured in this book, Butch and I were close enough in seniority that we never flew together, but when I found out that he had been a FAC (forward air controller) and had flown the O-2 with the 21st TASS (Tactical Air Support Squadron), I knew his story would be a great addition to this book.

There is an interesting history behind the O-2 and its introduction as a FAC aircraft by the Air Force in 1967. The civilian version of the O-2 was the Cessna 337 Skymaster. In 1966 the Air Force commissioned Cessna to produce a military variant of the two-engine, push-pull Skymaster (one engine was on the nose and a second engine was in the rear of the fuselage, providing two engines with centerline thrust).The O-2 was to replace the single-engine O-1 Bird Dog, and the first aircraft were delivered in 1967. The following statistic is staggering: Of the 532 O-2s delivered to the Air Force, 178 were lost in Vietnam to all causes, from combat to accidents. That works out to fully one-third of the O-2s. When you read about the types of missions they flew (casually mentioned by Butch), it is easy to understand.

The O-2s were produced at the Cessna factory in Wichita, Kansas, and one might wonder how the Air Force got them to Vietnam. That is a story in itself and worthy of mention here as a lead-in to Butch's story. The Air Force contracted with a company that hired some pretty dodgy civilian pilots and paid them $800 per trip to ferry the O-2s from Wichita to Saigon. This saved the Air Force money and also spared the Air Force pilots who were needed elsewhere. The civilian pilots flew the O-2s in groups of four, with the flight leader receiving $1,000 for the trip. The route was from Wichita to Hamilton AFB in California, then Hickam AFB in Hawaii, Midway, Wake Island, Guam, Clark AFB in the Philippines, and Tan Son Nhut AB, Saigon. Each pilot carried an airline ticket from Saigon back to Wichita for the next trip. The aircraft were fitted with extra fuel tanks and were so far over their maximum gross weight for takeoff that they had no single-engine flying capability for about the first five hours of flight. With no long-range navigation equipment, their pilots flew dead reckoning with a heading calculated for known winds and hoped for the best. The roughly 13-hour flight from Hamilton to Hawaii resulted in many "mayday" calls, with Coast Guard planes finding the distressed O-2s and leading them in to Hickam. Eventually the Air Force had to pair the O-2s with either C-7 or C-47 aircraft that had navigation capability and flew at about the same speed. Amazingly, only two O-2s were lost in the entire program, but it got off to a pretty shaky start.

When reading Butch's story I am taken back to a quote from the Preface. "It was a bunch of guys in their 20s who were thrust into situations of incredible excitement and danger, were given incredible responsibility, and responded with amazing, heroic performances."

....

REPUBLIC OF VIETNAM—II CORPS—1970

Phan Rang Air Base, located 25 miles south of Cam Ranh Bay and five miles inland from the South China Sea, was home to our small detachment of the 21st Tactical Air Support Squadron (TASS) and could get as hot as a firecracker on the 4th of July. In fact it was July, but near the end of the month. I had just put on a clean set of jungle camouflage fatigues (all the better to escape and evade in the event you were shot down), and they were already pitted out. This was our normal flying attire, though a few guys opted for the cotton gray/green K2-B flight suit.

Standing outside my hooch, I watched the cumulonimbus clouds that would build to over 60,000 feet again today while I reflected on the rocket attack that had hit the Officers' Club the previous night. Fortunately no one had been seriously injured, but curiously, the VC (Vietcong) always seemed to know when the O Club was having a function. As it later turned out, the most attractive cocktail waitress in the club was found to be the sister of a VC major. Regardless, it was going to be another scorcher today, and my assignment to fly into the cooler Central Highlands near the Cambodian border to participate in a search-and-rescue mission could not have been more welcome. Major Kerry Kicklighter, our air liaison officer (ALO) and commanding officer (CO), and Lieutenant Dave Wolfe had just flown a mission the previous night, coordinating with an AC-47 Spooky gunship near a village being attacked in the Central Highlands, so the fat-cat search-and-rescue mission fell to Lieutenant Ted Hallenbeck and me.

Our small detachment of the 21st TASS consisted of two O-2A aircraft, two Jeeps, three first lieutenant forward air controllers (FACs), two staff sergeant mechanics, and Major Kicklighter, the ALO/CO. Each FAC was assigned a tactical call sign when he arrived at his base, and this was his airborne name for his entire one-year tour. Mine was Walt 42. Ted and I had both arrived in-country six months earlier and had come to appreciate the marginal flight characteristics of our "beloved" Oscar Deuces (O-2s) and the tremendous challenges and variety of missions presented by our job as forward air controllers. Our missions included observation and visual reconnaissance, directing tactical air strikes, and working with troops in contact with the enemy. We coordinated artillery fire, flew search and rescue (SAR), and coordinated with AC-47 and AC-119 gunships. We flew air cover for convoys, coastal and river patrols, crop denial missions, and insertion/extraction of long-range reconnaissance and sniper patrols. Throw in an occasional maintenance run to 21st TASS Headquarters at Cam Ranh Bay, a typhoon evacuation to Pleiku in the Central Highlands, and a weekly produce run to the open market in the mountain resort of Dalat, and you have a pretty good idea of how we spent our year in Southeast Asia.

Although the O-2 had four hard points, two under each wing for attaching ordnance, weight and aircraft performance constraints limited us to one LAV-59/A rocket launcher per wing. Each rocket launcher held seven 2.75-inch MK4/40 rockets that could be launched individually or as a salvo via a cockpit toggle selector switch, and were fired with a "pickle" switch on the yoke. There was a variety of warheads that could be fitted to these rockets. We carried the white phosphorus smoke warhead, Willy Pete, to mark targets. When the mission dictated, we occasionally carried an entire launcher loaded with high-explosive warheads or the antipersonnel flechette warhead (this was loaded with small, pointed, steel projectiles that had a vaned tail for stable flight. The French word *flechette* means "little arrow" or "little dart"). However, since the large majority of our missions were routine day VFR (visual flight rules) observation and reconnaissance, the white phosphorus warhead was generally the order of the day. Essentially you had to be able to see the bad guys to do the job! Once they were identified we would call on our VHF radio to obtain the appropriate clearance from our Tactical Air Control Party (TACP) and Military Assistance Command Vietnam (MACV) before we could mark their position with Willy Pete smoke rockets and coordinate a fighter strike on their position over our UHF radio. There were more than a few occasions when the target disappeared before the lengthy clearance process could be completed.

The VC owned the night, and occasional night missions were a necessary part of the job. During these high-stress night missions we flew as a two-pilot operation since our primary means of navigation was pilotage with a case of 1:24,000 topographical maps of the area of operation. Besides all those pesky rules of engagement, forward air controllers had two principles to live by that were made exceedingly more difficult at night.

1. Don't fly into the side of a mountain! (This sounds easy enough, but at low altitude with no moonlight, no lights, few roads, negligible navigation aids, and plenty of triple canopy jungle, it wasn't.)

2. Avoid inflicting short rounds (friendly fire) at all costs without violating rule #1. Positive target identification was essential at all times, but with some nighttime operations it was all but impossible, especially if there was any weather in the area. Those missions were scrubbed (canceled).

Since we were based near the coast we didn't fly many night missions over the trail along the Cambodian border; most of our night missions were in the area of Phan Rang and west to the mountains. On those night missions I do remember plenty of tension, confusion, poor visibility from white phosphorus flares swinging from parachutes, being dangerously close to the terrain, and the occasional secondary explosion. Bomb damage assessment (BDA) was a real challenge at night, and usually everything was gone by morning except burned-out vehicles. The VC guerrillas were amazingly efficient at removing any evidence of their losses and melting back into the local population.

My recollection of the AC-47 Spooky and the AC-119 Shadow gunships was that they were very autonomous and very lethal. Their operations center did their targeting, and they carried a navigator to identify their target area. Our job was to coordinate with them and assist them in any way we could, including BDA. These gunships carried multiple mini-guns, six-barreled 7.62mm machine guns, each capable of putting out up to 6,000 rounds per minute, with every fifth round a red tracer. The AC-47 had three of these mini-guns, and when they fired it looked like a fire hose spraying a solid red stream of lead onto the ground and the enemy. Very impressive, to say the least! Most of their missions were night fire suppression for local villages under attack, while the AC-130 Spectres flew the majority of the night missions along the trail in Laos.

Shortly after our arrival at Bien Hoa AB, we attended in-country forward air controller orientation, informally known as "FAC U." (This clever acronym was also used for initial forward air control school at Hurlburt Field, Florida.) There we were instructed never to fly below 1,500 feet AGL (above ground level), which was effectively out of small arms range, but the reality was that you had to fly lower, typically 500 to 1,000 feet AGL to really find the VC. Generally speaking, in 1970 Charlie (the generic term for the enemy) was wary of the FACs and shot at us only after we had passed over-head, making his position more difficult to ascertain. They knew that if we could accurately determine their position, we would bring in heavy ordnance on top of them. That all changed in early 1972, when the Soviets started supplying the NVA (North Vietnamese Army) and later the VC with the SA-7 Strella shoulder-fired infrared ground-to-air missile. Then the minimum safe altitude for visual reconnaissance went to 6,500 feet AGL, where you couldn't see much without binoculars.

At this juncture let me back up and say that a month earlier, for most of the month of June 1970, our detachment had operated from Pleiku Air Base in the Central Highlands in support of the "incur-sion" into eastern Cambodia. The concept of this operation was to go into Cambodia, find and destroy 40,000 PAVN (Peoples' Army of Vietnam, or NVA) and NLF (Vietcong) troops, along with their weapons and supply caches, and to be out by the end of June, as President Richard Nixon had promised the international communi-ty. One very large problem that developed was that the caches were so plentiful and so deeply imbedded into Cambodia that we couldn't come close to getting them all, and more importantly, the U.S. armed forces could not be out of Cambodia with all of its equipment by the end of the month. So for the last two days of June 1970 my fellow FACs and I flew two four-and-a-half-hour missions per day directing U.S. fighter/bombers in dropping U.S. bombs on row after row of U.S. equipment: trucks, tanks, jeeps, armored personnel carriers, road graders, caterpillars, and all sorts of logistical supplies. Needless to say, I was staggered by the waste and the politics that had led to it. On the positive side, it was the best BDA (bomb damage assessment) I gave during the whole year!

While I was temporarily based at Pleiku AB in the Central Highlands, I got to know First Lieutenant John Ryder, who was a good friend and fellow Air Force Academy classmate of my roommate Ted Hallenbeck. John was a "Mike" (call sign) FAC, based at Pleiku, a good guy and a proficient pilot who took off one morning in his O-2 to do some visual reconnaissance, looking for a "suspected" 23mm anti-aircraft artillery (AAA) site northwest of Pleiku, near the Cambodian border. He never came back. A week of search-and-rescue missions yielded no clues. There had been no emergency distress "mayday" radio call. There had been no emergency locator transmitter (ELT) beeper heard. We had no success in attempting to raise him on his survival radio. No crash site was ever found, and his body was never recovered. John had simply been swallowed by the mountainous jungle of Vietnam.

As fate would have it, a month later a rated (pilot) U.S. Army brigadier general was sent up from Saigon to survey the devastation of our Cambodia incursion and flew his UH-1 Huey slick helicopter into the side of a mountain near the Cambodian border, killing all aboard. (Hueys were designated as either slicks or guns—the slicks were troop carriers and guns were gunships.) The search-and-rescue was being conducted from a tiny Army outpost called Bao Loc.

Bao Loc was situated on a small hill that was part of a larger mountain. A small river ran west to east just south of the hill, and on the east side of the hill a tributary joined the river from the north. These geographic features allowed us to find and land at Bao Loc under a very low overcast. Creating the outpost had been a marvel of modern, high-tech engineering: A 10,000 pound bomb with a 36-inch fuse extender was rolled out the back of a C-130 and impacted directly on the top of the hill, flattening everything in sight. A few thousand sand bags, some barbed wire, and 3,600 feet of pierced steel planking (PSP) and you had an outpost complete with an airstrip. I should mention that there was a pronounced hump in the middle of the runway so you couldn't see one end of the airstrip from the other.

On that day in July, Ted and I landed our O-2s to the west on Runway 27 at Bao Loc, and taxied to the auxiliary parking area very close to the runway. We set our parking brakes, chocked our nose wheels, and proceeded to the compound headquarters bunker for the search-and-rescue briefing being conducted by a non-rated Army major general. During the course of the briefing, the general stated that he wanted "those little Air Force planes to go up and check the weather for my choppers," which would also participate in the SAR mission. We young lieutenants were in the process of explaining to the non-rated general that it was neither reasonable nor safe for fixed wing aircraft to check weather for rotor aircraft in low overcast in mountainous terrain, when our appeal to the general was interrupted by the very distinctive sound of twin rotors of a heavy CH-47 Chinook approaching. Shortly after that, a private burst into the briefing with some very disturbing news. He said, "One of those Air Force planes has crashed into the river." Ted and I gave each other a horrified look, knowing that one of our Air Force careers had probably come to a premature end. Ted was an Air Force Academy graduate whose father was an Air Force brigadier general. My odds weren't looking so good. We excused ourselves from the briefing and sprinted to the crest of the runway to get a look at the parking area. On the runway sat the heavy Chinook helicopter. One O-2 remained just off the parking pad and the other had vanished. My brakes had held and Ted's had not. The rotor wash from the Chinook had blown both the O-2s over their wheel chocks, and his aircraft had rolled down the hill, torn through the perimeter barbed wire, and plunged into the ravine of the river.

The low overcast did not let up for two days, allowing us time to descend the ravine and scavenge radios, IFF (identification, friend or foe) transponder, voice encryption, and code books. The rest of Ted's airplane was a tangled, totaled mess and deemed unsalvageable, so our Army friends at Bao Loc filled his airplane with generic .30 caliber carbine rounds and it was written off as a combat loss. Ted came out of the deal smelling like a rose, and I believe may have been cited for meritorious action! Such are the fortunes of war.

As a tragic end to my story, Ted returned to Southeast Asia for a second tour and was killed at the age of 26 flying a T-28 in northern Thailand near the Laotian border in February of 1973.

This story is dedicated to Captain Ted B. Hallenbeck, Air Force Academy Class of 1968, panel 01W, line 115—my friend, roommate, and comrade-in-arms.

—*Howard C. "Butch" Heinz (USAF Captain Retired)*

．．．．．．．

When you read the basic mission of a FAC aircraft, be it a Cessna O-1, O-2, an OV-10,* or a jet fighter operating as a fast FAC, it seems pretty straightforward. Observing and then marking targets for air strikes with a white phosphorus rocket sounds simple enough, but finding the target in the first place was the bigger part of the story. As you read in the Jim Pollock story, the FAC involved in marking the target had drawn fire from the ground, called it in to his controlling agency, and requested fighters to bomb the target area. The fighters, in that case two F-100s sitting on alert at Tuy Hoa, were scrambled and flew to rendezvous with the FAC to be directed to the location of the target. The FAC in the Jim Pollock story flew his mission in South Vietnam in the daylight. Taking off at night in an O-2 and flying into Cambodia to rendezvous with a gunship or flying on a pitch-dark night in mountainous terrain west of Phan Rang is an entirely different story.

Now I would like to add a note about Bao Loc. Butch's description of the place brought back memories of flying down through a hole in the overcast and navigating along the river at treetop level to find the runway. I can't do Bao Loc justice without quoting from the Tactical Aerodrome Directory, South Vietnam, *dated 15 April 1969:*

BAO LOC
2750 ft. elevation
3500 ft. runway length, runway 09-27 (east-west orientation)

AERODROME REMARKS: Secure (as expected—they were always secure until they weren't, and you could be the last to find out). Approach to runway 09 over 200 ft. ravine (this ravine is where Ted's O-2 ended up after being blown over its wheel chocks), abrupt upslope, 4 ft. fence 153 ft. from threshold, 6 in. beveled lip between overrun and runway, first 600 ft. runway 09 closed, approach to runway 27 over downslope, 4 ft. fence 300 ft. from threshold. Runway in good condition, some deterioration in middle 2/3 of runway.

HAZARDS: Full runway cannot be seen from touchdown point. 2 ft. deep ditch 25 ft. from runway edge both sides. 4 ft. fence approximately 100 ft. north of runway. Runway depression at west entry to parking area. Mudhole south edge of runway between taxiways (mudholes and bomb craters were common obstacles when operating on unimproved runways).

[For navigation, Bao Loc was listed as being located 80 nautical miles on the 056 degree radial from Channel 102 (Tan Son Nhut–Saigon), so it was roughly 80 miles north east of Saigon.]

*The OV-10 Bronco was a twin turboprop aircraft produced by North American Aviation and introduced in Vietnam in 1969. It was flown by the Marines, the Navy, and the Air Force, and in addition to its mission as a FAC aircraft, it was able to carry close to 3,000 pounds of external munitions and operate in the role of armed reconnaissance. My classmate at Western Airlines, Mike Monagan, flew the OV-10 in the Navy in a very select unit known as the Black Ponies.

Two of Butch Heinz' squadron mates. Capt. Terry is being hosed down after his last flight in country, 1970.

31

THE BLACK PONIES

Mike Monagan, USN, OV-10A, 1970 – 1971
{ Date of hire by Western Airlines: 12/12/1972 }

Mike Monagan with his OV-10 "Black Pony" at Vung Tau, 1970.

When I walked into my new-hire training class at Western Airlines on December 12, 1972, I walked right into Mike Monagan. We all knew that the average class size for Western was 15 pilots, but this class was doubled to 30 because of an ongoing contract dispute between the company and the pilots' union that involved seniority issues and bidding rights. This pushed 15 of us into December from a January class and made a huge difference in seniority throughout our careers.

Seniority within a class was determined by date of birth, with the oldest being the most senior, so as we entered the classroom we were handed a class seniority list along with a pile of documents relating to company orientation, pay, benefits, insurance, etc. As it turned out, the seniority list

was the most important piece of paper to come out of that class. Pay, bene-
fits, and insurance were always subject to change, but your seniority num-
ber relative to your new-hire class was locked in concrete!

Mike was 26 and I was 27, with our birthdays just a few months apart,
so it ended up that I was a couple of numbers senior to him in the younger
half of the class. Western split the class, training the senior 15 as second
officers on the Boeing 737 and the 15 junior as second officers on the Boeing
707/720B. My recollection is that Mike and I sat together during the class-
room portion of the training and went through a standard set of questions
as we got acquainted:

"Where did you go to school?" Cal Santa Barbara, Cal Berkeley.

"What service were you in?" Navy, Air Force.

"What did you fly in Vietnam, and where were you based?"OV-10s,
Binh Thuy. Caribous, Cam Ranh Bay.

"OV-10s? I didn't know the Navy had OV-10s." It was a small unit
based in the Delta.

"When were you there?" 1970-71, 1968-69.

Then it was on to learning how to be flight engineers on the Boeing 707.
I was still in the Air Force Reserve at Travis AFB, flying on my days off
from Western and commuting back and forth to training in Los Angeles.
The training lasted nearly two months, so I rented what the commuters
called a "crash pad" apartment at the Skyways Motor Lodge just off
Century Boulevard in Inglewood. My main memory of the Skyways (which
has since been razed) was the thick plexiglass window the night clerk sat
behind and the stories of late-night robberies and occasional gunfire in the
lobby. Those were the days. It may have been a notch or two more danger-
ous than Vietnam, but then I had my seniority number and after all,
Vietnam had provided all the evidence I needed that I was bulletproof!
(Twenty years later, during the Rodney King riots in 1992, I would again
be flying in an environment where ground fire became an issue. Because of
gunfire from Watts and Compton, all aircraft inbound to LAX from the
east were required to cross the coastline at 10,000 feet and descend over the
water to land on runway 06 or 07, back to the east, while all departures
were to the west, over the water. Few people, other that the flight crews
involved, knew anything about that procedure.)

Mike and I went our separate ways after training, with me moving up
to the San Francisco base in early 1974 and Mike staying in Los Angeles.

Our paths would cross occasionally, but we didn't really get together again until becoming elected representatives of the Air Line Pilots Association in the early 1980s. We worked together through the dark days of ongoing financial crisis at Western in those years, watching Braniff cease operations and the Continental pilots go out on strike in 1983. It was a few years before the merger with Delta, and with the continuous labor strife and strikes at other airlines, things looked bleak for quite a while.

Mike decided to resign from Western in 1985 to take a job in Sacramento working in the Dukmejian administration on the Cal OSHA Appeals Board. Mike's father, Robert Monagan, had been a California State assemblyman for 12 years and was speaker of the assembly in 1969-1970, when Ronald Reagan was governor. Mike was a born politician, and it really showed while we were negotiating our way through various crises in the early 1980s.

It was many years after our first meeting in 1972 that Mike and I ever talked about Vietnam again, after he had left Western and was living in Sacramento. He called me one day in November 1988 and asked me to come to Sacramento for the dedication of the California Vietnam Veterans Memorial on December 10, 1988. We had a wonderful day together, listening to speeches and to the reading of the 5,000-plus names of the Californians who gave their lives in Vietnam. Then we had dinner and talked at some length about Vietnam, with Mike giving me some detail about his flying in the Navy and telling me how much he enjoyed flying the OV-10. I had not yet embarked upon my Vietnam book project but I knew it was a time to listen. Mike is a very private man, and it was a treat to spend the evening with him. It reminded me of one of my favorite airline expressions, which came from a captain describing a first officer nicknamed Gabby who was driving him crazy: "He is always transmitting when he should be receiving." I always knew when it was time to listen, and it served me well a few years later as I began putting the stories together for this book.

Mike and I get together for lunch or dinner once or twice a year. We always contact each other on Veterans Day and speak on the phone on December 12, the anniversary of our Western class date. Toward the end of 1999, Mike called me and told me to be on the lookout for the book Flying Black Ponies *by Kit Lavell, which was to be published in early 2000. It was this book that really told me what Mike did in Vietnam. He is mentioned, and his photo appears several times.*

We have just passed the 40th anniversary of our class date with Western Airlines. Mike Monagan is someone I will always remember fondly from that group of Vietnam veterans who were back from the war and thought they had hit the jackpot on December 12, 1972, with their new job as pilots for Western.

Here is Mike Monagan's story.

....

I didn't spend time as a kid at the local Tracy, California, airport watching small planes take off and land. Tracy, located in the Central Valley of California, is in the great agricultural basin of the nation, 60 miles east of San Francisco. As I was growing up, Tracy was small, with fewer than 10,000 people, and typical of many small towns in the valley. We were insulated from many big-city problems, but also isolated from educational and cultural outlets. My first airplane ride was as a passenger on a transcontinental flight from San Francisco to Washington, D.C. I was invited to look in the cockpit and it must have left some impression. I do remember gluing a few model airplanes together, like most small boys of the generation, but my first hands-on experience was still years away. It is a long journey from the San Joaquin Delta area of California to the Mekong.

After graduating from Tracy High School in 1963, with Vietnam just beginning to find its way into the daily lexicon of the TV news programs, I enrolled at the University of California, Santa Barbara. The Selective Service was going strong, but as a single male, if you were a full-time student, you could retain your student deferment. Within a couple of years that would change. The student deferment would be given only if you were making satisfactory progress toward a degree, defined as finishing college in four years. For many young, single, male college students, the 4½- to 5-year college plan was under siege. My roommate, Gary Miller (from San Mateo, California), and I were clearly in the gunsights of the local draft board.

Gary and I were strolling through campus one Friday morning, likely looking forward to the first of many Coors beers we would consume that weekend, when we came upon and spoke with a uniformed Naval officer with a fresh pair of Navy wings. We learned he was a lieutenant, junior grade, had just received his wings, and was looking for potential Naval Aviators. We both passed a few basic tests, and then he played his trump card: If we went to Los Alamitos Naval Air Station near Long Beach, California, passed a more comprehensive battery of tests, and agreed to enter the flight program, we would then be granted a student deferment in order to finish college. That sounded ideal to us, and we both raised our right hand that very day. Gary's eyesight was such that he could not be a pilot but could be a Naval Flight Officer (NFO). Safe to say, we were elated not to be at the mercy of the whims of the Selective Service.

A year later, April 1968, I made my way to Naval Air Station (NAS) Pensacola to begin Aviation Officer Candidate School (AOCS). AOCS was the Navy's way of converting scruffy college boys into officers and gentlemen in 67 days. Sure enough, they did it—with the able assistance of officers and drill instructors from the USMC. Gary was on a slightly different track. He arrived in Pensacola just after I received my commission, entered AOCS, and began the NFO course. Gary went on to become a Radar Intercept Officer (RIO) in F-4s, had two tours off Yankee Station in the Gulf of Tonkin, flew 175 missions, and went on to serve 26 honorable years in the Navy, retiring as a commander.

The Navy flight program began for all U.S. Navy, Coast Guard, and Marine officers with preflight ground school in Pensacola. From the Navy side it also brought together new ensigns from the various commissioning sources—AOCS, NROTC (Naval Reserve Officer Training Corps), OCS (Officer Candidate School), and the Naval Academy. Needless to say, within that group there was a vast difference in education, training, and of course, future opportunities. Training began with ground school at NAS Pensacola, then off to NAS Saufley for T-34 training, NAS Whiting Field for T-28 and carrier training, then on to NAS Corpus Christi for advanced multiengine training in the S-2, and upon successful completion, Wings of Gold.

Having been born and raised in California, spending time in Pensacola, Florida, and Corpus Christi, Texas, in 1968–1969 was a real culture shock. Do I need to mention the strange liquor laws? Nearing completion of the flight program, I placed VAL-4 (Light

Attack Squadron 4) and the OV-10A Bronco at the top of my wish list. Other opportunities were not very enticing: The P-3 mission seemed boring, and S-2 squadrons lived on aircraft carriers. Olde Navy wisdom (attributed to Samuel Johnson, circa 1750): "Living on a ship is like being in jail with a chance of drowning!" There was another reason to avoid carriers. While attached to VT-5 in training, I made four successful solo arrested landings in the T-28. During my fifth attempt the tailhook separated from the aircraft. Heeding the cries of *"Bolter! Bolter!"* from the Air Boss, I added full power and hoped there was enough air speed and altitude to stay out of the Gulf of Mexico. I returned to NAS Whiting none the worse for wear, but convinced that this was not what I wanted to do full time.

I received my wings in August 1969 with orders to VAL-4. I then returned to California, but before heading to Vietnam I went to NAS North Island with an intermediate stop at Marine Corps Air Station (MCAS) Camp Pendleton. Another session with the Marines, since the Navy had "borrowed" the OV-10s from the USMC and Camp Pendleton had the only OV-10 ground school.

VS-41 at North Island was the west coast Replacement Air Group training squadron for the S-2s, but it had taken on the responsibility for training new OV-10 pilots. Ground school, training flights, "rockets and bombs" at MCAS Yuma, and survival school did little to prepare one for combat. Our group of replacement pilots finished training in mid-December and took time off over the holidays, with most departing for Vietnam in early January 1970. The Navy, in its infinite wisdom, decided to send me and one other OV-10 pilot to admin/personnel school, conveniently located at the Naval Station in San Diego. Upon completion of the school, the two of us caught a MAC (Military Airlift Command) charter flight, arriving in-country around January 20. I still recall landing at Tan Son Nhut Air Base in Saigon and boarding a bus to the Navy in-country indoctrination facility. Riding a bus with wire mesh over the windows (to block grenades and firebombs thrown from motor scooters in heavy Saigon traffic) was a rude introduction to my new world. By the way, I never, ever served as an admin/personnel officer in the Navy!

Light Attack Squadron 4, call sign Black Ponies, was established to provide fixed wing, close air support for all the Navy assets in the

Mekong Delta. Those assets included all the river boats, swift boats, and of course the SEALs. VAL-4 was commissioned in late 1968 and went in-country in the spring of 1969. Ultimately, the squadron supported all U.S. assets in southern III Corps and all of IV Corps. (South Vietnam was divided into four Corps, with III Corps including Saigon and a bit north and IV Corps including all of the Mekong Delta south of Saigon.) I would recommend reading *Flying Black Ponies* by Kit Lavell, a former Black Pony pilot, published by the Naval Institute Press, as it tells the whole story of our mission in Vietnam.

The OV-10 was the result of the Defense Department's need for a fixed-wing, counterinsurgency, multipurpose aircraft. Operational in 1968, the planes were delivered to the Air Force and Marine Corps to be used as FACs (forward air controllers) and for observation and artillery spotting. The Bronco was a very spirited aircraft: a basic 10,000 pound plane with two pilots and a full load of fuel, perfect as a FAC and spotter. We would then add 3,000 pounds of ordnance (and the associated drag) to create an under-powered, heavily armed, light-attack platform that lacked air conditioning! The Bronco had five attachment points for ordnance below the fuselage, four internal 7.62mm guns, and two Zuni rockets on each wing. The under-fuselage attachments would carry pods for different combinations of ordnance: four Zunis or 19-shot pods of 2.75 rockets, mini-guns, a 20mm gun pod, or flares for night operations.

By the time I left Vietnam in January 1971 I had accumulated nearly 700 hours of combat flying time, half of that at night, and 342 combat missions. That was likely a pretty average tour for a junior pilot; during VAL-4s tenure in Vietnam, the pilots often flew more missions and more hours than any other fixed wing Navy squadron. But unless you were in the Mekong Delta area between April 1969 and April 1972, when the squadron was decommissioned, you probably never saw a Navy OV-10 in-country.

The squadron headquarters was located at the Naval facility in Binh Thuy and flew out of Vietnamese Air Force Base (VNAF) Binh Thuy.* I was assigned to Detachment Bravo, and we flew out of VNAF Vung Tau. At Detachment Bravo, away from the squadron command at Binh Thuy, we had more flying opportunities as well as many card games—Acey-Deucey—and maybe a beer or two after most missions.

Our missions started out as routine, two-hour patrols on a predetermined route. There were two aircraft, two pilots in each plane, talking to Navy, Army, or SEALs on the ground, searching for targets. Interspersed with the routine missions, every four or five nights we would be part of a scramble (alert) crew. This began when you returned from the 10 p.m. patrol and then slept in the bunker at the airfield. More often than not, your sleep would be interrupted and you would man the aircraft and head for a fight.

Normally there wasn't any problem finding boats or troops in contact with the enemy. We would identify the location of the friendlies and the bad guys, then decide on roll in/roll out headings to deliver our ordnance. The vast majority of the time we worked directly with the troops on the ground and only rarely did we work with a FAC, either Army or Air Force. The OV-10 was a very stable firing platform, making it ideal for working in very close proximity to friendly troops. There were times when we were asked to deliver five-inch Zuni rockets within 10 meters of friendly positions.

In *Flying Black Ponies*, Kit Lavell describes how we helped extract a SEAL team from Dung Island, at the mouth of the Bassac River. This was a daytime scramble from Vung Tau, and I was in the backseat of the lead aircraft. The SEALs had been inserted the night before, but when morning broke they were badly outnumbered, low on ammo, and unable to get helicopters in to extract the team because of the VC (Vietcong) automatic weapons fire. The Black Ponies had to intersperse dummy runs (strafing runs when we did not fire) in an effort to keep the VC at bay and conserve our own ammunition. We were able to stabilize the situation until another pair of Black Ponies arrived from Binh Thuy to continue the attack and enable the SEALs to be picked up by an LSSC (Light SEAL Support Craft). Both sets of Black Ponies made numerous dummy runs, making all this up as we went along, in order to ensure that the SEALs and their Vietnamese counterparts were extracted safely. None of the aircraft had much fuel remaining upon landing at Binh Thuy.

Kit also included an incident that describes me being slightly insubordinate to a senior officer. Allegedly, while being chewed out by a lieutenant commander for something I probably did but thought I had covered my tracks, when I said, "Excuse me a second, Mr. Becker. Hold that thought while I go out in the hall and see if I can find someone who gives a shit." All junior officers in our squadron were slightly irreverent. I believe it must have come from the job we were doing, in a country that was slightly inhospitable, with weather ill-suited to most of us. I had no idea what to expect when I arrived in-country and was not disappointed.

The flight back to Travis AFB in early January 1971 was uneventful, especially if you accepted the offer of sleeping pills from the squadron flight surgeon. Then it was off to VT-31, NAS Corpus Christie, for 22 months. During the first day with my new squadron, a commander came up and asked if I was assigned to VT-31. I replied in the affirmative, whereupon he ordered me to get a haircut. It turned out he was the executive officer of the squadron. Welcome back to the world! The Navy's *Approach* magazine, February 1970, had an article titled, "The Care and Feeding of the Vietnam Vet." According to the article, "The returning vet should be warned that 'mild' social drinking overseas might be considered by some uninitiated stateside folks as acute alcoholism." The transition from the war to stateside Navy duty was startling. Incidentally, in spite of having no fleet carrier experience, I was selected to be a carrier instructor, and I accumulated 50 traps (tailhook arrested landings). I even spent one night aboard the USS *Lexington* (CV-16), obviously not on purpose! After four years, six months, and five days (but who's counting?) I became a civilian.

On December 12, 1972, I wandered into the Tishman Building on Century Boulevard in Los Angeles to begin training at Western Airlines. It was there I met Bruce Cowee. We trained together, worked on Air Line Pilots Association issues together, and have remained dear friends to this day.

In 1988, Bruce and I walked together in the parade celebrating the dedication of the California Vietnam Veterans Memorial. More than 58,000 men and women lost their lives in Vietnam. Those who served will never forget them. Remember, "All gave some, some gave all."

Here is what the "Tactical Aerodrome Directory, South Vietnam" has to say about Binh Thuy, which was a VNAF base:

Non-U.S. controllers available 24 hours daily. U.S. controllers are available in the event instructions are not understood 24 hours daily.... Aircraft subject to hostile ground fire all quadrants... extensive unscheduled and uncontrolled helicopter traffic flying from taxiways. Soft terrain and shallow ditches each side of runway. Lips on both overruns, do not land short. Unlighted revetments south side of parallel taxiway.

In other words, normal operations like takeoff and landing were full of potential hazards, and this was nothing out of the ordinary for most of the airfields where we operated in South Vietnam. It was the perfect flying environment for a bunch of 20-year-olds who thought they were bulletproof and were up for an adventure and a challenge. And, to top it off, returning to Binh Thuy with battle damage, in a low-fuel state, or racing a heavy rainstorm down final approach, was not the time to have to request a U.S. controller and be told to "stand by" while awaiting landing clearance.

OV-10A "Black Pony" at Detachment Bravo, Vung Tau, showing the variety of armament it could carry, late 1970.

"Black Pony" firing a Zuni rocket near Binh Tuy, late 1970.

OV-10A "Black Pony," armed to the teeth, at Binh Tuy in late 1970.

$$32$$

ONE CHALLENGING MISSION

Dennis J. Dolan, USMC, F-4J, September 11, 1972
{ Date of hire by Western Airlines: 9/7/1976 }

Dennis Dolan with his F-4J configured for an attack mission, loaded with Mark 82, 500 pound bombs, on the flight deck of the USS America, 1972.

Dennis Dolan flew 333 combat missions in two tours of duty in Vietnam as a Marine fighter/attack pilot. His first tour was in 1969-1970 when he was based in-country at Chu Lai Air Base, flying the F-4B model. Chu Lai is on the South China Sea about 50 miles south of Da Nang, and this first tour consisted mostly of close air support and direct air support missions in South Vietnam and Laos.

This story took place during Dennis's second tour, when he was based aboard the aircraft carrier USS America and flying the F-4J. The second tour focused primarily on missions in North Vietnam. These missions were more challenging, mainly because the air defenses over North Vietnam were considerably more plentiful and more sophisticated than those in South Vietnam or Laos. I feel humbled and honored that someone as private as Dennis agreed to write about his experience for this book.

I knew Dennis mostly from work we did together at our union, ALPA (Air Line Pilots Association). He started work for Western Airlines in September 1976. In 1982 while he was flying for Western, he started law school, eventually graduating from St. Louis University School of Law, cum laude, in 1985. He first became involved with ALPA during the Western–Delta merger in 1986-1987 and continued to do work with ALPA throughout the remainder of his airline career. He was elected first vice president of ALPA for two four-year terms from 1999–2002 and 2003–2006 and worked at ALPA headquarters in Washington, D.C., until he retired in 2006. He also served as President of the International Federation of Air Line Pilots' Associations, which was headquartered in Chertsey, England, during the period 2003–2007.

When I met Dennis I never knew of this story, and he never talked about it. I knew he was a Marine but not much else. I was very surprised years later when I was asking various pilots I had flown with if they would write a story for this book. Someone advised me, "You've got to talk to Dolan. He got hit by a SAM over Hanoi and made it back to the ship with no instruments except his angle-of-attack indicator." I contacted him right away and he agreed to put the story in writing for the first time in his life. As you reach the end, you will see what a huge impact this experience had on him and how it changed his life.

Here is the story, from one of the most focused and driven men I have ever known, someone I am honored to call a friend.

. . . .

This event took place on September 11, 1972, in the Gulf of Tonkin while I was serving aboard the aircraft carrier USS *America*.

It was 1345 on a typical late-summer day on Yankee Station. It was hot, humid, and hazy, and the carrier task force was about 200 miles east of North Vietnam. My airplane was spotted aft on the port side of the ship, and I sat strapped in the jet within the hot confines of the cockpit as I waited for flight operations to commence. I watched as the signal flags were run up the halyard indicating that the carrier was turning into the wind for the launch. As the wind over the deck picked up, I waited for the American flag to go taut in the breeze, a ritual I tried to follow each time I was about to launch on a mission.

This day the embarked air wing, Air Wing Eight, was scheduled for an Alpha Strike with a 1400 launch time. A Navy Alpha Strike consists of a large number of tactical aircraft working closely in concert with each other to put a heavy concentration of ordnance on a particular site or point target, such as a power plant, munitions factory, or railroad yard. The tactical makeup of an Alpha Strike aboard the *America* was usually eight A-7 Corsair and four A-6 Intruder attack aircraft (these were primary bombers), two KA-6 Intruder tankers, one SH-3 Sea King rescue helicopter, one E-2B Hawkeye for radar surveillance, and eight F-4 Phantom fighters, for a total of 24 aircraft involved in the strike.

During an Alpha Strike the fighters aboard the *America* were used in two distinct roles. Four of the F-4s were designated to lead the strike force into the target area and drop munitions designed to suppress anti-aircraft fire. Once their ordnance was delivered, these fighters would loiter above the target area to protect the strike force from enemy aircraft attack, and continue to cover them until egress from hostile territory was completed. These fighters were designated as target combat air patrol (TAR CAP) aircraft. The other four fighters were assigned patrol stations geographically located between the route the strike force would take to and from the target and the nearest estimated enemy aircraft threat. The primary role of these fighters was to intercept and destroy enemy aircraft that posed a threat to the strike force. They were designated as MIG combat air patrol (MIG CAP) aircraft.

In the normal course of operations on the *America*, the two fighter squadrons alternated roles between TAR CAP and MIG CAP for each Alpha Strike. Our squadron, Marine Fighter/Attack Squadron 333 (VMFA-333)—Shamrocks, or "Trip Trey," as we were known colloquially—was assigned the MIG CAP fighter role on this particular Alpha Strike. In this role, our standard tactical doctrine was to fly our four F-4s in separate two-aircraft sections, with each section patrolling over a specific geographical area or station. Our sister F-4 squadron, VF-74 (the Be-Devilers), was assigned the TAR CAP fighter role on this mission.

Each Alpha Strike was preceded by an extensive strike briefing. This briefing was conducted by the strike leader and included aircrew from all of the participating squadrons. The briefing included, along with the particulars of each aircraft's targets, the location of each MIG CAP section's assigned patrolling station. Any known enemy aircraft threat in the target area of the strike force was also highlighted, and the responsibility for fighter cover in these areas belonged to the TAR CAP aircraft. This particular strike was directed toward a power plant just northeast of the port city of Haiphong. The nearest enemy aircraft threat that could be expected was from nearby Kep Airfield. In addition to the particulars covered in the general strike briefing, each section of MIG CAP fighters conducted a detailed briefing among themselves regarding engagement tactics, patrolling speeds, radio discipline, etc.

As was the case with a normal Alpha Strike, the fighters (MIG CAP and TAR CAP) were among the first aircraft airborne and were launched just after the tankers. Immediately after launch the fighters proceeded directly to the tankers, which were orbiting at 6,000 feet over the ship. Standard operating procedure on every fighter mission called for the fighters to be topped off with fuel prior to proceeding to their assigned targets or stations.

On this mission, our section was the second set of fighters launched from the carrier. When we arrived at the tanker the other section of fighters, our Trip Trey squadron mates, had just finished refueling and were headed toward their assigned station. Just as we were finishing our refueling and began departing the tanker, we were told by Red Crown, the ground control intercept (GCI) station located aboard a U.S. Navy cruiser in the Gulf of Tonkin which provided radar vectoring to U.S. air traffic, that there were MiGs airborne over enemy territory. Red Crown stated that our squadron mates in the other MIG CAP section that had just refueled ahead of us were being vectored toward these enemy fighters, and very shortly thereafter we were as well.

The vector we were given was toward Hanoi, which was in a different direction and quite a bit farther away from our originally assigned MIG CAP station. Hanoi is about 40 miles up the Red River Valley from the Gulf of Tonkin and about 75 miles west of Haiphong.

As we proceeded on our assigned vector, the controller informed us that there were six bogies (MiGs) airborne and that our playmates (the other section of fighters) were being vectored toward them. Shortly thereafter we were given an updated vector toward the bogies on a heading of approximately 330 degrees, which took us directly up the Red River Valley. At this time we took up our combat spread formation and began looking for the bogies, both visually and on radar.

About two minutes after we started our trek up the Red River Valley the controller told us that our playmates were engaged with the MiGs and that we needed to proceed toward the fight at the greatest possible speed so that we might be in a position to assist them. Based on this directive we accelerated our aircraft to 600 knots (approximately 690 mph) indicated air speed, which was a good engagement speed in the event we encountered the enemy fighters. I was on the right hand side of the formation, flying as the designated wingman on this particular mission. As we neared the location of the fight, my radar intercept officer (RIO), who was positioned in the backseat, was the first to spot our squadron mates, who were indeed engaged with enemy aircraft. He saw several missile contrails at our 1 o'clock position and directed me to turn hard right until we had the contrails on our nose and I had spotted them. (It should be noted that during this mission one of our squadron mates in the other section shot down one MiG-21 and had a probable kill on another. This activity had generated the missile contrails that my RIO spotted as we entered the fight.)

As previously briefed in our prelaunch, section-specific briefing, if our section was vectored toward an engagement the pilot who saw the enemy first would assume the lead of the formation, which I did at that time. I called for full afterburners, and as we rolled out of our turn, I called for the jettisoning of our empty centerline fuel tanks (this decreased the drag on the aircraft and made it more maneuverable) and pointed the nose of the aircraft directly toward the fight.

At this point I rechecked to make sure that our eight missiles—four radar-guided Sparrows and four heat-seeking Sidewinders—were armed and indicating ready for launch and that the master arm switch was in the on position, which would allow the missiles to be launched when I pulled the trigger. I also reconfirmed that my wingman's switches were set for action.

As we were proceeding toward the fight I took another glance at the missile contrails to see if I could detect any airplanes, but I couldn't pick up any quite yet. At this point I remember looking down toward the ground to orient myself—we were just about directly over the city proper of Hanoi—and what I saw was totally startling and at the same time breathtaking. There below me, and all around me, was the most intense display of anti-aircraft fire I had ever seen. It was an incredible amount of flak, with black, orange, and white puffs of smoke everywhere, and a constant stream of tracers streaking in the general direction of our aircraft. I remember thinking it was like being inside a popcorn popper, watching the kernels of corn explode. There were airbursts going off all around the aircraft. It was just an incredible display and I was mesmerized by it. In addition to the heavy flak, we were also receiving almost constant surface-to air missile (SAM) warnings, both on the electronic countermeasures (ECM) receivers located in the aircraft and verbally from Red Crown, who broadcast these warnings over the constantly monitored military emergency radio frequency of 243.0 MHz.

I then took my eyes off the enemy fire and looked back in the direction of the fight, where I saw one of our squadron airplanes in a steep climb. I called his position out to my wingman and informed him that we were joining the fight. I rolled in behind this aircraft and began looking for MiGs. Almost immediately I saw one in a steep descent at my 9 o'clock that appeared to be headed down and out of the fight. This type of exit maneuver was a standard tactic of the North Vietnamese air force when one of their pilots sensed that reinforcements were about to enter a dogfight. Their basic philosophy was to engage in a dogfight only if they could gain an immediate advantage that might lead to a kill. If this advantage did not materialize in a relatively short time, or if other U.S. fighters began to approach the area of the engagement, the North Vietnamese pilot was trained to exit the fight and head back to his base. Part of the strategy in this scenario was to ensure that the engagement took place in close proximity to a North Vietnamese airfield, to facilitate this ability to disengage. In this instance, Phuc Yen airfield was right below our position, and the MiG I spotted was most probably headed there.

I elected not to break from the formation at this time to chase the MiG because I wanted to provide mutual support for the aircraft I was now positioned on, and because the MiG I spotted was heading in a direction almost opposite the fight. As we proceeded further I was able to visually identify the other two aircraft from our squadron and felt that we were well positioned to provide them mutual support in the ongoing fight.

As I established my position on the aircraft in front of me a very strange feeling came over me—a feeling I had never experienced before. While I began the mental process of assessing the geometry of the fight, my sense of reality seemed to shift into slow motion. What this effectively did was allow me to evaluate the situation in many different contexts in a very short period of time. Even though we were traveling at great speed (almost supersonic at this point), I seemed to have all sorts of extra time to assess the overall situation, mull various tactical options over, and mentally debate with myself what my next maneuver should be to best position myself to continue providing mutual support for the aircraft in front of me. To give you a flavor for how rapidly my mind was able to work, I thought about the following things: the angle and position I currently had on the aircraft in front of me; what maneuver I would need to perform next to maintain the best mutual support position on the aircraft in front of me if he altered his flight path (this involved several different possibilities); the current fuel state of my aircraft, which I decided would allow me about five more minutes over the target area before reaching bingo fuel (minimum fuel required to return to the ship); the positions of the other three friendly aircraft from my squadron relative to my own; a scan around the periphery of the fight for enemy aircraft; an assessment of the volume and accuracy of the enemy fire currently being directed at me; an awareness that if I saw what I considered to be an enemy aircraft I must positively identify it before launching a missile because of the close proximity of friendly aircraft; and finally, that this was the real thing and I might get a missile shot at an enemy aircraft.

I estimate that all of this information was thought about, evaluated, and processed in about two or three seconds. Even today when I recount these moments I can't believe how my mind was working during this period of extreme tension and stress. Although I never again experienced anything like this particular mission, this experience taught me the true power and capacity of the human brain.

Very shortly after my section entered the fight, the Trip Trey airplanes found themselves in a tail chase with each other. We were flying in a vertical, egg-shaped pattern with all four F-4s continuing to go around and around, one behind the other in tight, 4-G (four times the force of gravity) turns. It didn't take me long to realize that all the MiGs had disengaged from the fight and exited the area, and our four F-4s were the only aircraft that remained in the immediate vicinity. It also became evident that a tremendous amount of anti-aircraft fire was now being directed toward the four of us, and we were getting a steady series of SAM warnings. It became clear to all of us that it was time to exit the area and head back toward feet wet (over water) and the ship.

One of the lessons we learned from this particular engagement concerned radio discipline. Prior to this mission it was our squadron policy that during an engagement with enemy aircraft, each section would remain on its own discrete radio frequency. This policy was intended to minimize the radio chatter, thus keeping as clear a frequency as possible so that the individual aircraft in a section could coordinate their maneuvers. After this particular mission we felt that philosophy was a mistake in a case where all four fighters were part of the same engagement, and that one section should have been pre-briefed to switch over to the other's frequency so that we could have communicated our plans. Such a procedure would have clearly enhanced our ability to mutually support each other in this particular situation.

As it turned out, the other section headed out of the area to the northeast while we elected to egress to the southeast. Shortly after our section began exiting the area of the engagement my aircraft received an active ECM warning that a SAM missile had been launched and was possibly guiding on my aircraft. During this latter phase of the war, the North Vietnamese had developed a tactic that triggered a very late warning for a SAM launch. It worked this way: The SAM missile launch commander would visually track an aircraft using a TV camera equipped with a powerful telescopic lens. The elevation and azimuth of the camera were aligned with the missile launch platform to ensure that the missile was effectively aimed by the camera. Once the parameters for a valid tracking solution were met, the missile operator would wait until he had a rear quarter view of the aircraft and then launch the missile. At this juncture in the launch sequence, because no radar guidance was being provided, the missile was basically just a dumb—or ballistic—missile. But because there was no electronic guidance, there was also no electronic warning displayed inside the targeted aircraft.

The most common surface-to-air missile used by the North Vietnamese was the Russian-made SA-2. The SA-2 was an extremely high-speed missile and covered a lot of distance very quickly. In the visual launch scenario described above, several seconds after the initial trajectory of the missile was established, the missile operator would be required to turn the radar on for about four or five seconds to establish electronic tracking and guidance, which would allow the missile to make a course correction toward the rear quadrant of the targeted aircraft. If this maneuver was successful, it placed the missile in a position that made evasion by the targeted aircraft very difficult. However, when the tracking radar was turned on to enable this course correction, it also gave a distinct electronic warning on the targeted aircraft's ECM receiver.

Once the missile was within 60 degrees of the rear quadrant of the aircraft, the missile operator would switch the radar off again and allow the missile to home in on the aircraft mechanically. These missiles were equipped with either acoustical or infrared homing devices and were designed to explode when they came in close proximity to the aircraft.

Our intelligence briefings had made us aware that this SAM launch tactic was being employed by the North Vietnamese. Consequently, as soon as we received the missile tracking warning with no other warnings preceding it, our countermeasure was to roll the aircraft upside down and look directly to our rear quadrant, or 6 o'clock, in an attempt to visually acquire a missile if one was tracking the aircraft. The SA-2 was a relatively easy missile to spot since it had a prominent streak of exhaust flame and left a huge white smoke trail in its wake.

Therefore, following the recommendation given to us by the intelligence community, I rolled the aircraft upside down for a better look toward the rear of the aircraft. My RIO had the best view of this area and looked at our deep 6 o'clock. He reported that he didn't see any missiles. Since I didn't see anything either, I rolled the aircraft back upright.

Almost immediately after rolling the aircraft upright we felt a heavy thump below and to the rear of the aircraft. The nose of the aircraft then pitched down violently, followed by a slight yaw (sideways movement), and then by an immediate full hard-over rudder to the left (the rudder went full deflection to the left and remained in that position). As a result of the hard-over rudder input, the aircraft yawed so violently that it bounced my head off the canopy, momentarily stunning me. After regaining my senses I gathered my thoughts and looked down at my hand on the control stick. I consciously told myself to reach down slightly below the pistol grip of the stick and grab what was called the paddle switch. The paddle switch was an emergency disconnect for all electrically generated stability augmentation commands to pitch, roll and yaw dampers, devices attached to the control surface actuators that were designed to enhance the stability of the aircraft. About the time I began to accomplish this task, I became aware that the aircraft was rudder-rolling hard to the left and was now upside down. It became very apparent to me I was now wrestling with a high-speed, severely wounded, uncontrolled beast.

When I depressed the paddle switch the stability augmentation systems disengaged, and after a few moments the airplane began to fishtail and wallow around in an ungainly fashion. At the high rate of speed the aircraft was still traveling (approximately 600 knots indicated airspeed), the lack of stability augmentation caused the airplane to enter some very unusual gyrations. After a few moments I felt like I was beginning to regain control of the aircraft, although it still reacted very sloppily whenever a control input was made. I knew it would take some time for the oscillations in pitch, roll, and yaw to dampen out aerodynamically at this high rate of speed, and that the best course of action under the present circumstances was to let the inherent stability of the aircraft assist me in completing the recovery to a sustained controlled flight condition.

Once a stable flight regime was regained, I slowly rolled the wings back upright and tried to collect my thoughts about the situation. I checked the engine instruments and they were all normal, as was the hydraulic system pressure. However, we had lost our air-speed and altitude indications, and all other controls related to the pitot/static instruments (airspeed, altimeter and vertical speed indicators), appeared to be inoperative. Additionally, the control stick felt very heavy, as though it had a large amount of nose-down pressure, making control of the aircraft to sustain level flight a very laborious task.

It was at this time that I began to consider the possibility that the airplane could become uncontrollable, forcing us to eject. The fact that we were right above the city of Hanoi gave me a chilling feeling; I knew an ejection in this geographical area would mean certain incarceration as a prisoner of war. This realization immediately triggered thoughts about what effect such an event would have on my family, particularly my mom and dad. I know they suffered a great deal of emotional distress during my combat tours, and I was very concerned how they might react to my not coming home for a while, or ever.

I began praying that I would have the strength to overcome the adversity that I now faced and to return safely to the ship. I prayed a lot during this particular tour, regularly reciting a prayer my mom had given me before I left on this cruise. It is a prayer to my patron saint, St. Joseph. Legend has it that this prayer had been given to kings and emperors to recite before they went into battle so that their safety would be assured. I carried this prayer with me on every mission I flew, and I still carry it with me in my wallet today.

Once these thoughts had registered with me, I returned to the task at hand and sized up the situation. I decided our best bet would be to make an expeditious run back to feet wet. With this plan in mind, I physically disengaged the roll and yaw augmentation systems by turning their respective control switches off. I decided to leave the pitch augmentation system on, hoping it would function properly when I released the emergency paddle switch. Since our plan was to egress at a high rate of speed, this system would be necessary to enhance aircraft controllability, which I considered to be marginal at this time.

Next, I held my breath and released the paddle switch. As the switch disengaged, I carefully monitored the aircraft's flying characteristics. After a short period I determined that the aircraft was flying in a relatively stable state. I again checked the engine instruments and everything there was still normal. I was, of course, communicating with my RIO during all of these maneuvers, keeping him advised about what was going on and what we were going to do. I also told my wingman that we had been hit and were going to make a high-speed exit from the target area. We then asked Red Crown for a vector toward feet wet. He gave us a heading of 120 degrees and informed us that feet wet was 40 miles away.

After a quick discussion with my RIO, we elected to make the run to feet wet as quickly as we could. His assessment was that we had no ECM gear, and he informed me that there were no airspeed or altitude indications on his instruments in the backseat. We estimated we were at 16,000 feet and our speed was approximately 600 knots, so I elected to engage both afterburners and make a straight and level run for the beach. We both realized that a high-speed egress entailed a lot of risk because of the uncertainty of the structural integrity of the aircraft. But because of the dire nature of our circumstances, we agreed that this would be the best course of action. As an aside, we later listened to an audiotape that my RIO had made of this whole incident and calculated that we covered the 40 miles to feet wet in just over two minutes. We were moving at a rate of about 20 miles per minute, or almost 1,200 mph, and an ejection from the aircraft at this speed would probably not have been survivable.

During the flight back toward the water we were getting constant calls from Red Crown about SAMs in the area. This was of great concern to us since we no longer had any operable ECM equipment and would have to rely on our ability to visually sight a missile in order to have a chance to evade it. In addition, as we left the target area it became apparent to me that the aircraft had a serious pitch control problem. This problem manifested itself by a lack of control response when I pulled or pushed on the stick. During such inputs the stabilator (horizontal tail-control surface on the F-4) was not properly responding in that there was a lag in control response for about a second or so after the stick was moved forward or aft. This type of pitch malfunction would probably have ruled out the ability to outmaneuver a SAM fired at our aircraft even if we had been fortunate enough to see it in time.

After we reached feet wet, Red Crown informed us that our squadron mates in the other section of F-4s were under attack by MiGs and by SAMs as they made their way out of the target area. As previously stated, they had exited the area of the engagement on a heading that took them farther to the north of the route we had elected to take. Red Crown further stated that both refueling tankers designated for emergency use in situations like ours had been vectored toward the other section since one of those aircraft had been hit by enemy fire and was headed out over the water. We told Red Crown we had also been hit and would need a tanker as soon as possible. The Red Crown controller responded by stating that he would vector one of the tankers south toward us.

As it turned out, because both tankers had been vectored toward the other two fighters, when we finally arrived feet wet they were 25 to 30 miles north of our position and in the area where the other two F-4s had exited North Vietnam. About this time the aircraft in the other section that had been hit by a SAM went out of control and the crew ejected over the water. The second aircraft in that section was critically low on fuel, and one of the tankers was desperately trying to reach it before its fuel was exhausted and the crew had to eject.

Meanwhile, the other tanker turned south toward us. We were over the water now and our situation had stabilized. I checked our fuel state and the gauge showed we had about 2,000 pounds of fuel remaining. In the F-4 this is a very low fuel state; in fact, the low-fuel warning light was already illuminated on the instrument panel. I estimated we had less than 20 minutes of fuel remaining. We were still about 150 miles from the carrier and there was no way we could make it back to the ship with that amount of fuel. Our alternatives were now very limited. We would have to either obtain additional fuel from the tanker headed in our direction, or eject from the airplane.

Another mechanical problem manifested itself when I slowed the aircraft just after reaching feet wet. It became even more apparent to me that there were severe control difficulties with the stabilator, and the aircraft was responding even more sluggishly at the slower speed we were maintaining as we searched for the tanker. The hesitation in movement of the stabilator was now accompanied by a jerky motion when the control surface actually moved, making pitch control very rough. Additionally, it was even more difficult to maintain level flight now because the nose-down pressure from the control stick had grown heavier still. I felt like I was holding a 10-pound weight in my hand.

Our next priority was to rendezvous with the tanker so we could avert a flameout and certain ejection from the aircraft. The tanker that had been vectored toward us was still quite some distance away and we did not have visual contact with it yet. Although we still had radar and were desperately searching for the tanker, we had no speed or altitude indications with which to determine our vertical orientation or closure rate in the event we were able to gain a visual sighting of the tanker. Red Crown had us in radar contact and was vectoring both the tanker and our aircraft in directions that would bring about a rendezvous of the two aircraft, but his ability to assist us in estimating the altitude of our aircraft was very limited.

During this whole sequence of events, my wingman, who had been separated from the formation and lost sight of us just prior to our aircraft being hit, had still not reestablished formation integrity by locating and joining up with our aircraft. Hence he was unable to give us any assistance in rendezvousing with the tanker.

As the tanker was being vectored toward us I again checked the fuel gauge, and it now read below 1,000 pounds, giving us less than 10 minutes of flying time. Considering the current control problems with my aircraft, the prospect of completing a rendezvous with the tanker and accomplishing in-flight refueling prior to flaming out did not look promising. I informed my RIO of this critical fuel situation and told him that while I would do my best to get to the tanker and get plugged in, we would probably not make it and that we would have to eject from the aircraft. Accordingly, I reminded him that our procedures for a controlled ejection called for us to stow our loose equipment, tighten up our harness straps, review the proper seat position for ejection and prepare to eject from the aircraft if we flamed out.

About this time we established radio contact with the tanker and shortly thereafter we spotted him on radar. Soon after that we sighted him visually about two miles away. I told him to go into a hard left turn so I could attempt to rendezvous with him, and I also requested that he deploy his refueling drogue (which looks like a large basket) and have it ready to dispense fuel. I told him we were so low on fuel that I would be lucky to get one attempt to engage the drogue, and if I flamed out just prior to engagement I wanted him to start a slow descent and toboggan his aircraft downhill so I could attempt to plug in as I coasted my aircraft downhill behind him. I figured that if we wound up in this situation and I subsequently was able to engage the drogue as we descended, I might possibly be able to restart the engines as we continued our descent while taking on fuel. I also deployed my emergency generator (the RAT, a ram air turbine that was propelled by the slipstream) so I could be assured of maintaining radio contact and have electrical power for engine start if that became necessary.

He said he understood those instructions and entered a 30 degree bank turn. I then rolled into a tight turn to establish a rendezvous with him and was able to complete the join-up fairly expeditiously in spite of the sluggishness of the controls. I rolled in behind him and reached down to put the refueling probe switch to the extend position. The refueling probe switch on the F-4 had both an extend and a refuel position, and the advantage of using the extend position in a situation like the one we were in was that the fuel received from the tanker would go right into the number-one fuel cell and immediately into the engines to keep them running. The refuel position would not have provided such immediate access to the fuel and the aircraft might have flamed out even though fuel was being transferred from the tanker.

I completed the rendezvous and flew directly up under the tanker to make my pass at the refueling drogue. Since we had in-flight refueled so many times while operating from the ship, this procedure had become a straightforward task for me. The sight picture for engaging the refueling probe in the refueling drogue was the same every time. In this particular situation, however, I was very conscious of the extreme nose-down pressure on the stick. I knew I had to concentrate fully and put the probe into the drogue on the first try, which I managed to do. As I engaged the drogue, the light indicating that fuel was being transferred came on and we began taking on fuel. At that moment I looked down at the fuel gauge and it indicated 200 pounds.

If you look in the F-4 operating manual, 200 pounds is the tolerance of the fuel gauge, so essentially the gauge was indicating that we had virtually no fuel left when we began taking fuel from the tanker. The fact of the timing of all this maneuvering and the ultimate, critical moment when my airplane began receiving fuel to keep the engines running was nothing short of a miracle, in my estimation.

After we engaged the drogue, the tanker pilot gave us 1,500 pounds of fuel, which he stated was all that he was allowed to dispense. I said that wasn't enough and that I needed at least another 2,000 pounds to return to the ship and have a reasonable chance of getting the aircraft back aboard. He said he couldn't give us another 2,000 pounds without permission from the commander of Task Force 77. I said, "Well, get the permission, because I'm not unplugging the aircraft until I get the 2,000 pounds of fuel." So he got the permission, we got the additional fuel, and then we headed back toward the *America*.

Just after we reached the tanker our wingman finally caught up with us. When we had finished refueling I asked him to take a look at our aircraft. He pulled up close and took a look from the side but stated that he couldn't see anything amiss. He then flew up underneath the aircraft and initially stated he couldn't see anything there either but then said, "Let me take another look." He flew closer under the aircraft on his second look and stated the whole bottom of the airplane was full of holes. That didn't surprise me. I told him we were without airspeed and altitude indications and were experiencing pitch control problems. He said he would lead us back to the ship and get us lined up for our approach to the carrier. Since there was no divert field within reasonable range, going back to the ship was really our only option at this point.

As we headed back to the ship I thought to myself about all that had happened to us up to that point and how fortunate we had been to get the aircraft safely out over the water and to the tanker. Suddenly, however, it dawned on me that the toughest challenge was still ahead. I realized that getting this badly damaged aircraft back aboard the carrier would take every ounce of flying skill that I possessed, but after coming this far, I was not about to give up.

As we neared the ship I told my wingman I was concerned about the controllability of the airplane because of the pitch control problems I was experiencing. I also thought other aircraft systems might be affected when I attempted to configure the airplane for landing. That being the case, my desire was to "dirty up" (lower the landing gear, flaps, and tail hook) about five miles behind the ship at about 3,000 feet altitude. I wanted at least this much altitude and distance from the ship to establish my landing configuration. This would assure that in the event the aircraft became uncontrollable, we'd have enough altitude to eject far enough away from the ship so that an abandoned airplane wouldn't pose a hazard. I also knew that dirtying up at this point would mean that we would have enough fuel for only two passes at the deck, and there was no hope of getting back to a tanker if we didn't get aboard on one of these two attempts.

We coordinated this strategy with the Combat Information Center (CIC) on the *America* and they cleared us to the designated spot aft of the ship to configure the airplane for landing. By this time we had declared an emergency and the ship's Air Boss (commander in charge of the ship's control tower) had told us we were number one in the traffic pattern and the deck was ready.

The weather was still hot, humid, and hazy as we lined up behind the ship and lowered the landing gear, the flaps, and the tail hook. At this point, with the exception of the pitch problem, everything seemed normal from a controllability standpoint. The wingman checked us and said everything looked good to him. His visual check confirmed the indications we had in the cockpit that the landing gear and flaps were down. He then took the lead, and as I flew his wing we checked our angle of attack indication against his airspeed (the angle of attack gauge is used in carrier operations to determine the optimum approach attitude and speed for landing; fortunately it was still operating normally), and he confirmed that it looked good for the approach. He "kissed us off" (broke out of formation) and we were cleared for a straight-in landing.

While flying the final approach to the carrier I continued to struggle with the pitch control. At this lower landing speed it was intermittently unresponsive to my control inputs, making it very difficult to safely maneuver the aircraft into a position for landing. I was doing my best to be as smooth as I could, since I had no trim and the stick was still very heavy with a full nose-down feel. And after flying for so long, fighting with this heavy nose-down input (it had been about 40 minutes since the SAM had hit us), my arm felt extremely tired and cramped. At this point I was struggling just to hold onto the stick, and I realized that my chances of getting this heavily damaged aircraft back aboard the carrier in one piece were iffy at best. Nevertheless, the adrenaline surge from setting up for a carrier landing under these conditions was more than enough to overcome these feelings of discomfort. We proceeded toward the ship.

Remember, I was flying this approach without an airspeed indicator or an altimeter and was relying completely on my angle of attack indicator and outside visual cues. It was a tough task for me to make the small control corrections required to maneuver the airplane into the proper attitude and to line up for the arrested landing. It resulted in my being a little high at the ramp (aft end of the ship) during the last, most critical phase of the landing. However, I managed to get the airplane down in the landing zone and hooked the number four arresting wire on the first pass (there are four arresting wires, and number four is the last). The sudden and violent jerk of the arrested landing brought one of the most welcome feelings of relief I have ever experienced. As we taxied clear of the landing area and parked the airplane, our squadron maintenance chief came toward us. He went under the aircraft to take a look, and after he viewed the damage he came out and stared up at me. I'll never forget the look on his face. He just shook his head and seemed to say, "How did you ever get this airplane back here?"

After I parked the aircraft and descended from the cockpit I realized how physically exhausted I was. My arm was extremely tender and sore, and I was very thirsty. I remember walking around and looking at the aircraft. There were numerous small fragmentation holes from the mid-wing area all the way aft to just above the tail hook. I also saw several large holes four to six inches across, as well as chunks of metal missing from around the empennage and stabilator area. There were several other large holes in the aircraft as well as numerous chip marks on the tail hook. Fortunately, the area that was subjected to the most damage, right underneath and right above the tail hook, is probably one of the strongest areas on the airplane. In the tail hook area, where most of the heavy damage occurred, it appeared that a large piece of metal had gone through the tail from bottom to top. This particular hit was most probably what damaged the control system, the pitot/static instruments, and the ECM gear. Maintenance personnel discovered that the pitch control malfunction was caused by the hydraulically powered stabilator actuator arm having been bent by a piece of shrapnel from the SAM that struck our aircraft. They also discovered that when we took the SAM hit the bellows system, which is an artificial pitch feel control system (which gives positive and negative pressure on the control stick to give a realistic feel of the flight characteristics of the airplane) had been wiped out by shrapnel. This resulted in a loss of the artificial pitch feel, which normally produced a very light feel on the stick. With the loss of the bellows system, the stick felt like it had full nose-down pressure, and that is why it seemed so heavy.

The official report of this incident indicated that there were more than 90 holes in the airplane. One area that had a large number of fragmentation holes was the underside of the left wing around the rear wing spar. A close inspection of this area revealed that the wing spar had been cracked as a result of the shrapnel damage. As a result of this report, the aircraft was deemed unflyable without extensive repairs. During the USS *America*'s next port call in the Philippines, the damaged aircraft was removed from the ship by a cargo crane and put on a barge to be taken to a rework facility in Japan for repairs. More than 2,000 man-hours were necessary to return the aircraft to a flyable condition.

As an aside, when I came back to Trip Trey approximately three years later, this same aircraft was back in service with the squadron. In fact, when I rejoined the squadron it was deployed aboard the USS *Nimitz* for that ship's shakedown cruise. While on this cruise the airplane was involved in a midair collision and crashed into the sea. Regrettably, it now lies at the bottom of the North Atlantic Ocean. I always felt that it was a sad ending for a great airplane, an airplane that, despite sustaining an enormous amount of physical and structural damage, had managed to get me safely back to the *America*. I have nothing but high praise for the durability and survivability of the F-4 Phantom in combat, and particularly for this airplane.

After I made my post flight inspection of the aircraft, the captain of the *America* summoned my RIO and me to the bridge. He wanted a full report about our mission as well as all of the details we could give him about the MiG engagement. He informed us about our squadron mates, telling us that one had been shot down by a SAM and the other had run out of fuel and the crew had ejected into the South China Sea. We had lost those two airplanes but all four crewmen had been safely recovered. I told him that our squadron mates had gotten at least one MiG kill and one probable kill. Maybe the score was even.

After we left the bridge I went to the ready room to debrief our squadron commanding officer. After I finished debriefing "the skipper," I realized how much my arm was bothering me. I rolled up the right sleeve of my flight suit and noted that a number of blood vessels in my right arm had popped, leaving my forearm black and blue. This injury was caused by having to constantly pull against the extreme nose-down pressure on the stick. The flight surgeon also met us in the ready room and briefly checked both of us over. He gave each of us a bottle of "medicinal brandy" to help us relax from the tension of the mission. He said the popped blood vessels in my right forearm were nothing to worry about and that there would be soreness for a few days, not unlike the tenderness experienced from a bad bruise.

After an extensive debrief with the Combat Intelligence Center about all aspects of the flight, I ate dinner and returned to my stateroom to think about the events of the day. I must have recounted those events 100 times in my mind that night, in an attempt to let the full impact sink in. The fact that I had come so close to losing the airplane, not once but twice that day, really had an impact on me. I also remember thinking to myself, in a philosophical moment, that the North Vietnamese had been given a golden opportunity to get me, and they had missed. The realization that I had managed to escape the best they had to throw at me gave me a measure of both comfort and confidence that is hard to describe. In essence, it was a cathartic moment. I remember a strange feeling of peace coming over me, stemming from the sense that if I were ever tested like this again, I could expect to make it back, as long as I was fully prepared to fly and fight.

At this point I would like to pay tribute to my RIO on this mission, Captain George Harper. He was a consummate professional and displayed an enormous amount of cool-headedness during this whole incident. I am convinced that without his capable assistance I would not have been able to return this aircraft safely to the ship. He provided a huge amount of support for my efforts while constantly supplying a stream of critical and useful information that enabled me to concentrate on keeping the aircraft flying. Because of these efforts he will always have my deepest respect, admiration, and friendship. I don't think I'll ever find the words to adequately thank him for his contributions that day.

Eventually, when the emotion of the day finally began to wear off and my adrenaline level returned to normal, I went to bed and slept for about 12 hours. The next day we briefed for and flew another Alpha Strike on a target just west of Haiphong. Although this one went according to plan, it was difficult flying with my sore arm. I wrapped it in an Ace bandage, which gave me some relief.

I flew a total of 333 combat missions during two combat tours of duty in Vietnam. This mission certainly ranks as the most challenging of all of them, and it completely changed my outlook on life. As the days passed into weeks and the weeks into months, I realized just how close I had come to dying on that September afternoon in 1972. With that realization as a backdrop, I made several promises to myself.

First, I would strive to use the talent and ability I had been given to the utmost of my capability. No more settling for just getting by; if there was a job to be done, it would be done with all of my energy and to the best of my ability, each time, every time. It occurred to me that God had spared me for a reason—a reason that was unclear to me at the time, but nevertheless a reason for me to fulfill some special role in my life. I concluded that to accomplish whatever this role might be I would be required, just as I had been on September 11, 1972, to use all of my talent and skill to accomplish this task as well. I became a driven person. I wanted to learn everything, see everything, and do everything I could for the rest of my life. No challenge would be too tough and no task too difficult.

Second, I realized how very much my family meant to me, and from that day forward they would always come first in my life.

Third, I would keep promises that I made and not make promises that I couldn't keep.

Finally, I would always be honest with myself and operate within the limits of my capabilities.

I also realized what an important and stabilizing role my religion had played in giving me a sense of balance and steadiness when everything around me seemed to be in chaos or in danger of collapsing. There have been many times when I have had to draw upon this strength to keep myself focused on what I needed to do to get through a difficult period in my life. These feelings have stayed with me and have given me a deeper appreciation for life and for all that I have been able to accomplish since that fateful day.

I will close by saying that because I am a very private person it has been difficult for me to share these feelings in a public forum. I hope my story has been insightful and entertaining to those with whom I am now sharing it, after keeping it to myself for more than 40 years.

This story is dedicated to all those warriors who were unable to return home to tell their stories.

UNITED STATES SEVENTH FLEET

The President of the United States takes pleasure in presenting

Gold Star in lieu of the Second Navy Commendation Medal to

Captain Dennis J. DOLAN
United States Marine Corps

for service as set forth in the following:

CITATION

"For heroic achievement as a pilot of jet aircraft while attached to Marine Fighter Attack Squadron THREE HUNDRED THIRTY THREE embarked in USS AMERICA (CVA-66). On 11 September 1972, Captain DOLAN was the wingman in an element of MIG Combat Air Patrol in support of a coordinated air wing strike in North Vietnam. On egressing from the area his aircraft received severe structural damage from antiaircraft fire. In spite of serious control limitations, Captain DOLAN skillfully effected rendezvous with a tanker aircraft and engaged in inflight refueling. With very little response from his controls, Captain DOLAN then expertly maneuvered his crippled aircraft to an arrested landing aboard the carrier on his first attempt. As a result of his ability and calmness, a severely damaged, highly valued aircraft was saved. Captain DOLAN's superb airmanship, courage, and devotion to duty reflected great credit upon himself and were in keeping with the highest traditions of the Marine Corps and the United States Naval Service."

For the President

J. L. HOLLOWAY III
Vice Admiral
United States Navy

Dennis Dolan received the Navy Commendation Medal for his performance on 11 September 1972 (Citation above).

Photos taken after landing on the USS America, September 11, 1972, showing SAM damage to Dennis Dolan's aircraft. Damage shown here is around and above the tail hook, where much of the significant damage occurred during this flight.

Dennis Dolan in the cockpit of his F-4J.

VMFA-333 F-4 alongside Navy VF-74 F-4 preparing for launch on the deck of the USS America, 1972.

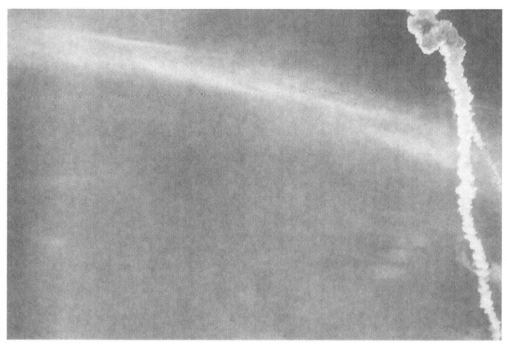

A SAM missile explodes harmlessly after being successfully evaded.

VMFA-333 F-4 on final approach for landing on the USS America, 1972.

33

TWILIGHT OVER THE TRAIL

Sam Reiter, USAF, F-4E, Early 1973
{ Date of hire with Western Airlines: 12/1/1976 }

Sam Reiter at Ubon RTAB, F-4E in the background, 1973.

My friendship with Sam Reiter goes back to his early days as a new-hire pilot with Western Airlines in 1976. The connection we had was Dave Beach, a classmate of mine at Western in December 1972 and a former squadron mate of Sam's from the 523rd TFS (Tactical Fighter Squadron) at Clark AB in the Philippines. Sam and I never flew together at Western, but our paths crossed many times over the years as we both commuted from San Francisco after the base closure in 1989. We are close in age, and with the FAA-mandated age 60 retirement, we were both coming up on retirement in 2004 and talked often to compare notes on our best course of action.

Delta Air Lines was talking bankruptcy; we wanted to retire before that happened and try to preserve as much of our pension as we could.

Over the years I talked to Sam about writing a story for this book, but he always told me he couldn't think of anything really worth writing about. As you read his story you will see how wrong he was and know how good I feel about bugging him over the years! The photos he provided are priceless. Sam's story came to me in a very interesting way. On October 5, 2012, the annual Navy Fleet Week celebration was beginning in San Francisco and the Blue Angels, the U.S. Navy's precision flying team, were having a practice performance over San Francisco and the Bay that afternoon. I met Sam and we took a long hike, ending up on the Marin County end of the Golden Gate Bridge. About halfway across the bridge we watched the Blue Angels do their practice performance, with most of their maneuvers ending in a low pass over the bridge, heading west, away from the city. It was an awesome experience and gave me one final opportunity to talk to Sam about writing a story. He agreed to give it some thought, and less than two weeks later this story arrived. Written over 40 years after the fact, it is a wonderful account that covers every area from how he ended up in the Air Force, his pipeline to the war, his experiences and his observations about them, and his hiring by Western Airlines. I asked Sam how he was able to come up with this in such a short time and he told me he had been "inspired." The story ends with a very touching experience that makes me realize again how fortunate I have been to have known, become friends with, and worked in the company of such men.

Now, here is Sam Reiter's story.

....

My personal odyssey into aviation started in my last quarter at Penn State in 1966. The Vietnam War was raging and the draft was still in effect, except for people who were moving on to graduate school, getting married, or moving to Canada. My GPA ruled out the first option, I couldn't find anyone to marry me, and it was too cold in Canada. Since my brother-in-law was an officer in the United States Air Force and spoke so highly of it, I decided to join. My recruiter asked me if I wanted to try for pilot training and I said, "Why not?" To my surprise, after testing they accepted me for OTS

(Officer Training School) and UPT (Undergraduate Pilot Training).

I had a few months between graduation and OTS so I took a job in New York City as a marketing analyst for Freeport Sulfur Company and commuted daily from our family home in New Jersey. I liked the job, except when we all went to lunch the topic of conversation was always sulfur; no sports, no politics, just sulfur. It was not exactly a topic that keeps you on the edge of your seat. Shortly before I left for Air Force OTS my boss called me into his office and told me that they would guarantee me a job when I returned. Of course, he was required to say that, so I thanked him, said a silent *"Adios,"* and never looked back; at 21, office work did not appeal to me.

OTS at Lackland Air Force Base in San Antonio was a mind-altering experience from the get-go. I remember being awakened at 0400 hours (4 a.m.) the first day and immediately deciding to hunt down my Air Force recruiter. Of course, it got better with time, and in between classes, marching drills, and physical training, I made many wonderful friends that have lasted to this day. After each course there were stacks of paperwork to be read: documents, rules and regulations, and all the "fine print." We were required to sign a statement that we had read (we hadn't) those mountains of paper. They had to be kidding, but everyone else was signing, so of course I did too.

Most of us graduated from OTS and were commissioned second lieutenants in the USAF. Leaving San Antonio, I had my first Air Force PCS (permanent change of station) move which took me exactly 145 miles west of Lackland AFB to Laughlin AFB in Del Rio, Texas, for my year of undergraduate pilot training. Laughlin AFB was not what I had seen in the movies, but it was my home for a year in class 68G. Frankly, I didn't care that the place was terrible because I was learning all sorts of wonderful stuff.

As our class was nearing completion I found out that the academic portion of training counted more toward class rank than my flying scores. Although at the time I couldn't understand why, I soon learned that good class rank was important because it assured a better flying assignment. Thank God I was first in my class in flying. That landed me a backseat F-4 assignment and not a B-52 (affectionately known as the BUF, or "big, ugly f...er"), as I had acquired a love for fast, maneuverable aircraft.

Pilot classes were graduating every month and to celebrate one class' graduation, the Air Force precision flying team, the Thunderbirds, performed. One of the highlights of their demonstration was the "bomb burst," which consisted of four F-100s in fingertip formation pulling up in front of center field, flying vertically, and then pulling 90 degrees away from each other as in a bomb burst. A fifth F-100, flying low at 500 knots, followed up through their vertical smoke doing victory (aileron) rolls. At least that was the plan. Actually the 5th aircraft pulled up in front of the crowd and both wings came off in a massive structural failure attributed to a broken wing spar. There was a huge fireball, and as the fuselage exited the fireball, still climbing and safe from the fire, the pilot ejected. Amazingly, he survived while the F-100 crashed near the Base golf course and scared the hell out of a bunch of jackrabbits. Shortly thereafter, we all received our assignments, graduated from UPT in May 1968, and took leave to go home.

All of us F-4 backseaters were put in the pipeline to combat, and for an F-4 backseater at that time it was about six weeks at Davis Monthan AFB in Tucson, Arizona, to learn the backseat systems, radar, etc. Then I moved on to nine months at George AFB, in Victorville, California. This was a wonderful time and the flying was great, even if you were in the backseat. There were gunnery range rides, intercept missions, air combat, low-level navigation and practice bombing missions. Upon completion of that training, about eight of us were assigned to Ubon RTAB (Royal Thai Air Base) in Thailand.

We were all thinking about the war, which was still roaring. There were group photos of previous classes hanging in the halls outside our classrooms at George, with sobering notations if an individual had been KIA (killed in action) or was MIA (missing in action), and it was impossible not to feel the war getting closer — closer, but not quite here yet.

Before we could leave for Thailand we needed to complete basic Survival School at Fairchild AFB in Spokane, Washington, and Sea Survival School at Homestead AFB, Florida. On my first day at Homestead, the group that was going to Thailand learned that our assignments had been changed, sending us to the 523rd TFS (Tactical Fighter Squadron) at Clark Air Base in the Philippines for a PCS tour of duty lasting a year and a half. I immediately got out a map to see where the hell the Philippines was.

Looking back, I can say that this was an incredible experience, with some of the best flying with some of the best people of my Air Force career. The 523rd TFS had a wonderful and charismatic leader by the name of Charlie Goodwin, and our main mission was to have four aircraft on continuous 24-hour nuclear alert at a Nationalist Chinese AFB at Tainan, Taiwan. This commitment required each of us to go TDY (temporary duty) to Taiwan and sit on five-minute nuclear alert (we had to be airborne within five minutes of being alerted) for one week each month. It was all business while we were there, but somehow we all became fond of playing poker during our 24/7 duty at the "alert pad."

For the remainder of the time back at Clark, we flew and socialized. We would meet at the squadron in the morning and plan a low-level mission to our gunnery range north of Clark called Crow Valley. We were free to fly in the "Clark/Cubi Control Area" from 0 to 50,000 feet. We flew low-level wherever we wanted, as high or as low as we wished, and this accounted for some wild undocumented stories.

All the backseaters, affectionately called GIBs (guys in back), became range officers. We were provided helicopter transportation to the range, but we all had trail bikes by this time and that was the way we traveled when it was our turn to be the range officer. It was a long ride to the range through a number of Filipino villages, and all the small children would line the streets and yell, "Hi Joe" to us. I missed the briefing and still have no idea why they did this. At the range we were range safety officers. We would score the practice bomb drops, score the holes in the strafe panels for hits, and control the flights so the F-4s wouldn't run into each other or hurt anyone on the ground. As the day progressed, Filipinos would come out of the villages and form a long line at the range border. When the last flight departed and the range was safe, we would step out of the range tower onto the surrounding deck and signal to them that it was safe to go ahead. A hundred or so would charge onto the range and pick up the brass 20mm shell casings that had been ejected overboard from the range flights for the day. They would then sell the brass.

I flew frequently with "Clip" Clippinger, the 523rd Weapons Officer, a truly intelligent man and a gifted pilot. Whenever we flew, I knew something different was about to happen. Sometimes after a mission when we had some fuel left, he would contact the long-range radar station on a mountaintop near Leyte Gulf. He would challenge them to find us on their radar while we tried to sneak up on them. Clip would mask us by using mountain ranges and flying at really low level until they spotted us. Then the game was over. He would also test bomb delivery methods we didn't normally use. There is a delivery method for a nuclear bomb called a loft, and we practiced it using an inert practice bomb. You essentially perform a maneuver called an Immelmann (basically a half-loop pull-up where the aircraft ends up heading in the opposite direction from the run-in) from a low altitude traveling at 500 knots. When your aircraft is at 45 degrees in the pull up, the bomb is released a mile or so from the target, and it continues to arc downrange. Normally at the end of this maneuver your aircraft is moving away from the target so you can survive the nuclear blast. That's not how Clip did it. Right after bomb release he would roll inverted and fly formation, canopy to bomb, as it looped toward Crow Valley. On another mission we were doing a Mach 2 (twice the speed of sound) run to test a new engine that had been installed. Clip had the airplane climbing through 60,000 feet and passing through Mach 2.3 with no indication that it had reached peak speed or altitude. As the Phantom exceeded its design limits, he finally gave the plane an A-OK for operations and ended the high-speed test run. Never again in my life have I flown that high or that fast.

The 523rd TFS was hands-down the most professional and the best-run of any squadron I flew with in the Air Force. The survivors have a reunion every five years to celebrate our time together and relate all the stories we couldn't tell from more than 40 years ago.

When my tour at Clark was over, I was assigned to the 309th TFS in the 31st TFW (Tactical Fighter Wing) at Homestead AFB in Homestead, Florida, and became combat-ready (meaning that I was eligible to be sent TDY to Thailand) on January 21, 1971. After my departure from Clark, the 523rd was sent TDY to Ubon RTAB, Thailand, and over the next year 25 percent of the squadron was reported KIA or MIA, including the front-seater I flew with most of my time at Clark, Steve Cuthbert. He was a truly fine and professional individual and a San Francisco Bay Area native. He was lost and declared KIA on a mission over Laos in 1970 (more on him later). When a pilot was shot down and there was an observable parachute, he was listed as MIA unless rescued. If no parachute was observed by his wingmen or other aircraft in the area, he was usually listed as KIA unless there were special circumstances. If the pilot was considered to be alive and MIA, his family continued to receive his pay, but if he was listed as KIA they received his service life insurance ($10,000).

My first assignment at Homestead was to be sent TDY to MacDill AFB near Tampa, Florida, where I was upgraded to the F-4 front seat. Of course, I felt this was long overdue and it was something I really wanted to do! At this time I also went to other schools such as FAC (forward air controller) training. Forward air controllers were pilots who traveled with the ground troops or flew as airborne FACs, spotting targets and calling in air strikes if needed, and directing the strikes when fighters arrived. I never worked as a FAC, but the knowledge I received was helpful when I was flying combat missions over the Ho Chi Minh Trail in Laos. And Laos was beginning to appear on my radar!

After upgrading to the front seat I returned to Homestead and found it was a bit of a drag after Clark. We were permitted to fly only one "canned" (always the same profile) low-level route, which we had memorized after the first mission. The rest of our flying was also very standardized and uncreative. Flying time was also restricted as we were flying only 15 hours a month. Later, I was sent to the Command Post for extra duty and received flying hours only on sporadic cross-country missions. All of this was about to change dramatically, though, as Homestead was increasingly being called upon to send TDY crews and aircraft to Thailand to replace returning crews and "attrition" losses. Sometimes a pilot would receive orders and be mobilized almost overnight. A squadron mate, John Cerak, was mobilized one day, was on a C-141 transport the next day, and was shot down and captured on his first mission, four days after he was mobilized. John was released with the POWs in Operation Homecoming in 1973. Some 591 American POWs were released between February 12 and April 4, 1973, after the Paris Peace Accords were signed on January 27, 1973. John was hired by Delta Air Lines in July 1973, and we met again after the Western/Delta merger in 1986.

On December 11, 1972, I finally signed out of Homestead AFB along with my best bud, "Long John" Dietrich, and several others. Some of us boarded a C-141 transport aircraft for a long flight to Thailand to replace returning personnel. After fuel stops at Elmendorf AFB in Anchorage, Alaska, and Yokota AB, Japan, we arrived at Ubon RTAB and checked in with the 308th TFS, after in-processing and being assigned quarters on the base. Obviously we were more than curious as to what our missions would be, but to our surprise we didn't fly until the following month. Our arrival closely coincided with Operation Linebacker II, which commenced on December 18, 1972, and ended December 29. Peace talks involving the North Vietnamese, South Vietnamese, and the U.S, represented by Henry Kissinger, had been on and off for some time and had reached an impasse on December 13, with no further meetings scheduled. President Nixon wanted to pressure the north into resuming the peace talks, so Linebacker II was planned to make them "see the light" and return to the negotiating table. Linebacker II was an all-out, 100 percent bombing mission, but since the new air crews had not had their local orientation ride by the time of commencement on the 18th, we could not participate.

Linebacker II utilized every available aircraft at Ubon, in addition to those at all the other bases in Thailand and South Vietnam, plus all available carrier-based aircraft from the carriers in the Gulf of Tonkin. It was a massive effort, with the fighters being launched during the daytime for raids on North Vietnam and the B-52s from Anderson AFB, Guam, and Utapao RTAB in southern Thailand used mostly for nighttime raids. For days we would sit on the roofs of our hooches (living quarters) and watch the base aircraft take off. Ubon had only one runway and there was little or no wind, so as a flight of four F-4s was taking off, another flight of four was on the other end running up. This unconventional crisscross takeoff procedure continued until every available combat aircraft had left the base, and the base cleared out quickly. Our ringside seats gave us an eerie perspective of events. There was a bulldozer at center field that would push a disabled aircraft off the runway if needed; nothing was going to slow down or stop this operation. After the takeoffs all would be quiet until the fighters began to return a few hours later. They would straggle back individually or in flights of two or four and land. To my recollection, not one Ubon aircraft was lost in all of Linebacker II. President Nixon announced a 36-hour pause over Christmas to encourage the North Vietnamese to return to the peace talks, but unfortunately it only allowed them to resupply their dwindling stock of SAMs (surface-to air-missiles) and rebuild their shattered air defenses.

On January 2, 1973, I had my orientation ride, and on January 3 we "new guys" were sent to Clark AB for Jungle Survival School. It was great to see the old squadron and the familiar sights around Clark. We learned how to survive in the jungle if we were unfortunate enough to be shot down: where to find water, what was safe to eat, etc. We also learned how to E and E (escape and evade) the enemy, who would undoubtedly be hunting us down to catch us and give us a paid vacation, assuming we survived, at the Hanoi Hilton. Maybe we would even be lucky enough to meet Jane Fonda.

The highlight of that training was the day we went off to hide in the jungle and hope we weren't found by the Negritos, a diminutive tribal people who were sent out to find us. The Negritos lived in the Negrito Village adjacent to Clark Air Base, and they had been fierce allies of ours in the later stages of World War II. We were each given a chit that we had to surrender to them when they found us so they could trade it in for a ration of rice. It was great fun for them but not for us city dwellers, as this was their back yard and they knew it well. We all were found, the Negritos got their rice, and we completed jungle survival school.

We returned to Thailand on January 10 and flew real combat missions until the Paris Peace Accords were signed and took effect on January 28, 1973. Once again we were wondering what the future would hold—but not for long. Almost immediately we began missions into Cambodia supporting the Cambodian government's battle against the Khmer Rouge. The peace treaty was only with North Vietnam, but they continued to support insurgents in South Vietnam with supply lines moving through Laos and Cambodia on the Ho Chi Minh Trail. We continued with interdiction missions, night and day, trying to keep these supplies from reaching the forces killing our soldiers in South Vietnam.

On days that I wasn't scheduled to fly, I would try to go on an OV-10 or an AC-130 gunship mission and ride as a copilot or auxiliary pilot. The OV-10 was a twin-engine FAC aircraft, flying medium-altitude FAC missions in Cambodia, directing fighters to the targets. The OV-10 pilots were really good! We would take off from Ubon and fly a four-hour mission, land at Phnom Penh, Cambodia, and take a break for lunch. On the ground it was obvious that the capital of Cambodia was suffering badly from this war. After lunch we would take off and fly another four hours before landing back at Ubon.

The AC-130H Spectre gunship of the 16th SOS (Special Operations Squadron) was an intimidating machine, charged with countering the flow of weapons and personnel down the Ho Chi Minh Trail. The AC-130 was a large, four-engine aircraft, and for self-preservation it flew only at night with all its lights extinguished, and never flew when the moon was out. Its weapons were impressive, with the left side of the aircraft bristling with gun barrels and sensors. Moving aft from the flight deck, there were two M134 miniguns, each capable of firing 6,000 rounds of 7.62mm shells per minute. Next came two M61 Vulcan Gatling guns, which fired larger, 20mm shells at the same rate of fire. A later model of the gunship soon arrived, designated the AC-130U, nicknamed Spooky, and in addition to the above weapons it sported a 40mm Bofors or a105mm howitzer cannon mounted toward the rear of the aircraft. There was also a laser designator onboard so the crew could mark targets and guide "smart bombs" from fighters like the F-4 and F-105.

They flew with the aft cargo ramp down and a crew member located there, tethered to the plane. His only job was to look aft in the darkness for any sign of incoming missiles. The missiles were heat-seeking and would lock onto the heat signature of the engines, so if he spotted one, decoy flares would be released to draw the missile away from the aircraft. The cargo bay of the AC-130 contained large, condo-sized pallets that housed sensor operators, whose responsibility it was to find the targets. When a target was found by the sensor operator, he would lock onto it. This would then supply navigation information to the aircraft's electronic flight director, which would give flight instructions to the pilot, who would fly to and circle the target area. In conjunction with the sensors, the pilot would align two computer-generated, doughnut-shaped red circles projected on the left window. When the pilot superimposed the circles, the gunnery parameters were complete and the pilot would fire the selected weapon. In later versions of the AC-130, sighting and firing were incorporated into the autopilot system. Typically, when a Spectre or Spooky found a truck convoy, it would hit the lead and trailing vehicles and then destroy all in between. By this time the entire enemy supply force would be scattering because they knew what was coming.

I flew many night missions in support of the AC-130 gunships. My backseater, Bill Reiter (no relation), and I would report at dusk to the squadron. Usually at this time the gunships were taking off and circling the field, sighting in their weapons and doing final checks before flying off to Laos for the evening's activities. After our flight briefing, Bill and I would go to our aircraft, preflight, then start and taxi with our flight of two F-4s to the runway. We would usually carry 500 pound dumb bombs with daisy cutters (fuse extenders that detonated the bombs upon contact with the ground, so most of the blast would be above ground) and CBU (cluster bomb unit) canisters. Due to the weight of the ordnance, we needed to reduce our fuel load to stay under our maximum gross weight for takeoff. We were always at a very heavy weight for takeoff, so after rejoining with our flight we would go immediately to a pre-briefed refueling track and meet our KC-135 tanker, where we would hang out until Hillsborough (C-130 airborne command post) would assign us a mission. The "gathering of eagles" at the tanker was a sight to be seen. There would often be many aircraft of different vintages and from different bases waiting for their mission assignments.

Once assigned, our flight of two would top off our fuel tanks from the tanker and proceed to the rendezvous point, where we would establish contact with our gunship. The Spectre and Spooky C-130s had luminescent strips on the top of their wings so we could see and identify them from above, but they were not observable from the ground. Our job was to protect the gunship from ground fire and help in demolishing any targets found, and since we were much faster than the AC-130, we had to fly slowly and do S turns behind and high above them.

On the ground, Laos was always dark at night and the people living there knew that anything that gave off light would get bombed or shot at, so it was the definition of pitch dark! We always joked that on nights when Charlie (the VC or the NVA) was bored, he would send a new guy down into a valley to start a fire, then come back up the hill and be entertained by the firepower demonstration.

Charlie would try to shoot down these dreaded gunships, and at that time their only weapon was AAA (anti-aircraft artillery). We were told that they would dig a hole and lower the gun into it, then when they heard the engine noise of the AC-130, four guys would lift the gun up and another would shoot at the noise. They didn't fire for long because they had learned what to expect. When AAA is fired it is invisible until the rounds are 1,500 feet from the gun barrel. Then every fifth shell turns into a tracer, that familiar red/orange color as the rounds streak into the blackness. The tracer rounds eventually top out, curve back, and extinguish as they fall back toward earth. From our viewpoint above we could see the AAA being fired but could not see the exact location of the gun, so we had to extrapolate (big word for guess) to try to determine where the firing came from. We had the perfect weapon for attacking the gun and its crew, the CBU 24. A canister of these CBUs would open up when reaching a certain altitude above the ground and spread its bomblets over a wide area. The bomblets would not all go off at the same time but over a period of 20 minutes, keeping the enemy heads-down while the gunship performed its mission. Sometimes we would ripple off a few 500 pound bombs on the suspected position.

So, there we'd be, S-turning above and behind the gunship. When we saw some tracer rounds coming up, we would immediately roll in and dive toward the point we thought they came from and deliver a CBU canister or two. We didn't need to be too accurate, so we released from a safe altitude and didn't worry too much about the mountainous terrain.

The gunship would also use our 500 pound dumb bombs to good effect on the convoys they found winding down the trail. If they were working (firing on and destroying) a convoy and had it burning, they would have us use our ordnance for a bigger punch. There was a forward air controller onboard the AC-130, and when he found a target that needed some heavy ordnance and it was burning, giving us a visual reference, he would direct us in for a bomb run. We had to deliver these at a lower altitude for accuracy, so the FAC would give us a safe heading and altitude to fly on our bomb run and our pull out. We relied on him to be accurate about this; otherwise we could fly into a Laotian mountainside without ever seeing it. Night bombing was always challenging, but it was extremely so over Laos. Normally you have a visual horizon to guide you, but at night, in a steep dive angle in total darkness, with your own aircraft lights turned off and your instrument panel and instrument lights turned nearly off, you needed to cross-check your attitude indicator frequently. After delivering our ordnance we would typically pull out of our dive at an altitude lower than the surrounding mountains.

One dive bomb pass in particular will always stand out to me. The night was pitch dark, with no moon and only starlight illuminating our area of Laos. Bill and I were orbiting in our usual position above the gunship with our number two in extended wingtip formation, and we were on deck when the gunship found its next target. Suddenly we received the request. The gunship wanted us to lay down some 500 pound bombs on a target area burning visibly on the ground. The onboard FAC gave us a roll-in and pull-out heading and the target's elevation. Bill and I quickly maneuvered into a steep (45 to 60 degree) dive into the darkness. Coming down the chute (as we called it), Bill was reading off the altitudes to our bomb release altitude and I was maneuvering the aircraft so as to put the pipper, the aim point on my bombsight, onto the target at the pickle (bomb release) altitude. When Bill said, "Pickle," I mashed the pickle button, releasing our ordnance, and began to pull out of the dive. But the circling AC-130 was in front and above me, so I had to flatten my pull out. This is something you do not want to do because it is possible to blow yourself up with your own slick bombs if you press the target (delay bomb release) and don't pull up immediately. As our bombs, detonating below and behind us, lit up the Laotian darkness, for the first time I saw the nighttime ground of Laos. We were in a deep valley, and in our peripheral vision, Bill and I picked up the towering mountains on either side of our Phantom. The FAC, who had given us our roll-in heading and target elevation, had done his job well. The belly of the AC-130 was illuminated by the orange light of exploding bombs as we passed close but safely underneath. Then I lit the afterburners and soared safely to altitude. When our flight of two had expended our ordnance and another flight arrived to protect our Spectre, we rejoined and flew back to Ubon. After landing we were off to the O Club for a few too many Singha beers.

This was just a typical, routine night mission flown thousands of times over the course of the air war in Southeast Asia, and looking back while I'm writing this, I still can't believe I was even a small part of this incredible piece of history. Before long the Vietnam conflict will just be a footnote in a history book.

Later-model Spectres had a laser generator onboard, and we began using laser-guided smart bombs, or LGBs. This allowed us to deliver our ordnance from a much higher altitude with better accuracy, and we didn't need a ground reference point for our bomb runs. Spectre would fire some rounds called "mish" at the target, and these rounds would twinkle when they hit the ground, giving us a visual cue that would allow us to determine an aim point for our LGB pass. Once we released our weapon we would transmit, "Pickle, pickle, pickle," over our common radio frequency with Spectre, giving the laser operator on the gunship the signal to concentrate a laser beam onto the intended target. On the five to six second trip to earth, the LGB would pick up the laser signal and guide itself to the laser point, allowing us to pull out thousands of feet above the small arms danger altitude of 4,500 feet AGL (above ground level). This saved many airplanes and aircrews but removed a lot of the drama and cut back significantly on the flow of adrenaline!

We always dropped our ordnance whether we had a good target or not—hell, even if we didn't have a target. It was not recommended to return to base and land with any bombs or CBUs onboard, and if you had "hung" ordnance (pickled bombs that had failed to release), you had a serious problem.

Bill and I also flew plenty of daytime missions. In the beginning, I was always the wingman for someone who had more time and combat experience, and one in particular was Major Hank Canterbury. On the last pass over the target he would tell me to "go in first and then head back to the base." Bill and I would say to each other, "Not again." As we were heading back toward Ubon, the major would love to surprise us, sometimes flying freakingly fast right under us and pulling up sharply in front of our plane. This would cause us to fly through his jet wash and turbulence. He thought this was great fun, but he was also training us to expect the unexpected. He had been a Thunderbird, and one time he joined up on us upside down. I can't even imagine where to put the stick to do that!

My tour of duty and commitment to the Air Force was to end officially on May 24, 1973. The USAF needed to send me back to Homestead AFB to process out and separate from the service, so my last combat mission was April 12, 1973, in an F-4E Phantom, tail number 345. Today this beautiful aircraft is either corroding away in the boneyard at Davis Monthan AFB in Arizona or sitting on a pedestal in front of a library or in a museum. Or maybe it's been cut up for scrap.

Long John and I left Ubon on April 28, 1973, on a C-141. After a stop at Utapao RTAB, we flew to Clark AB and remained overnight. We left the next day with a hangover, flew to Yokota AB in Japan and then on to Travis AFB, California, where my mother, sister, brother-in-law, and their children were waiting. Soon I left for Homestead and my separation from the Air Force. Whatever one thinks of war, there is an excitement, good or bad, that you never forget. A big part of me said that I didn't want to leave and was sorry that I had missed so much of the adventure. But when your turn is over, you move on to the rest of your life.

The rest of my life at the time wound up with me and Rick Beach (Dave Beach's brother) at the Nevada County Fair in Grass Valley, California, charging kids $5 each to fly around the Grass Valley Airport traffic pattern for 10 minutes. Nearly 2½ years earlier I had been flying the fastest fighter in the free world and sitting on top of that world. My God, what happened?

Long John Dietrich and I had started OTS together back in 1967 and now we were both separating on the same date in May 1973. We were looking forward to a long and profitable airline career. However, 1973 was a bad economic time, and no airline had plans to hire pilots for quite a while. We decided to prepare ourselves to look better on our resumes when things turned around. With GI Bill benefits in hand, we got some extra flight ratings and, while living in Florida, enrolled at Burnside-Ott Aviation Training School in Opa-locka, Florida, where we earned our Airline Transport Pilot (ATP) rating and a Boeing 727 Flight Engineer (FE) rating. Later we both moved on to California, meeting up again and earning our Certified Flight Instructor (CFI) rating.

John and I had stayed in touch with a friend of ours from the 523rd at Clark AB by the name of Dave Beach. Dave was smart, personable, and always lucky. He had landed a job with Western Airlines in December 1972 (coincidentally a classmate of Bruce Cowee) before the industry turned south, and while being on a roll, purchased a restaurant in Sacramento. John and I went to work for Dave at the Great Northern Food and Beverage Company. Dave had also purchased a Cessna 210, a turbocharged, single-engine aircraft that could carry up to six passengers. Dave wanted me to start a Part 135 (aircraft for hire) company, and over the next few months I got the operating certificate and prepared myself for my new career. Great Northern Aviation was born!

Light-airplane flying was very enjoyable, with none of the regimentation of the Air Force. You were *free!* Free to choose your own route through mountainous terrain at night, free to go in weather conditions that were marginal; free to land at places you never would have, had you seen them beforehand; free to fly at altitudes that would normally require oxygen, even though you didn't have any; free to almost kill yourself a couple of times to try and please a customer. This was a different kind of excitement, with none of the glory.

All of us wanted airline careers, and Western Airlines was our best shot. I had, of course, applied to Western and all the others, sending in monthly updates of my flight time and changes in ratings. I had endorsements from several Western captains I had met through Dave at the restaurant, and finally, toward the end of 1976, I was called for an interview and a pre-hire physical. It was almost for naught. Western was using a company in Texas to call pilot candidates and make the job offer and tell them the date their class would begin. Day after day I was sitting on the edge of my seat in anticipation of moving on. But somehow my name had changed by the time Western had them call me. I was sitting in the office when the phone rang and Marylou, our secretary, answered. The conversation went on for a short while until she finally said, "No, there is no Ralph Ruchter here." I don't know why, but I yelled, "*Do not hang up!*" I picked up the phone, and it turned out to be my invitation for second officer training at Western Airlines. If I had not been there at that time, I don't know what would have happened.

I graduated in December of 1976 as a Boeing 737 second officer for Western Airlines and had my first line trip on December 28. I had a very good holiday season!

The choice to join the Air Force led me on a journey filled with events and people I will never forget, plus a lifelong career in flying. It included having the honor of flying troops to Kuwait as a Delta captain, flying Delta Boeing 767ERs chartered by the military during the buildup to the invasion of Iraq in 2003.

I would like to add one final note. In 1990, when I was living in Marin County, California, I received a phone call from a man named Bill Schmol, whom I had never met. He had met and married Janey Cuthbert, the widow of Steve Cuthbert, my front-seater from Clark AB in the 523rd TFS who was shot down and killed over Laos in 1970. A long time after Steve was confirmed as KIA, Janey and Bill had met and married. Janey was a wonderful woman whom everybody loved, and when her husband died she was left to raise two young children. In 1989 she received a phone call from the Air Force informing her that Steve's remains had been recovered in Laos and transported to Travis AFB in Fairfield, California. After processing, Steve was to be laid to rest at the Presidio in San Francisco.

John Dietrich, Rick Cunliffe, Rocco Aicale, and I had been in the 523rd and had known Steve well. We were invited to the funeral and traveled together to the ceremony. The Air Force conducted the whole ceremony wonderfully and respectfully. "Taps" is a beautiful and melancholy tune, whenever you hear it. As we drove up to the grave site we were struck with an image of Steve we hadn't seen for 20 years. It was his son. It was a vision none of us will ever forget. We had a somber and respectful reception afterwards. Most of us can't imagine what the families of those service members missing and killed in action must suffer. I hope they can find the peace their hearts are yearning for.

L) Control tower at the Clark gunnery range. R) Strafe panels at the Clark gunnery range.

L) Various types of ordnance being taken to revetments to load F-4s for missions, Ubon 1973. R) Bomb load for a typical night mission in support of the AC-130 gunships, includes CBUs and Mk 82 500 pound bombs with daisy cutters (fuse extenders).

L) 1000 pound LGBs (Laser Guided Bombs) on an F-4E at Ubon, 1973. R) F-4 with ordnance load of air to air missiles for a MIG CAP mission (guarding fighter/bombers from attack by MiGs), 1973.

L) *A gathering of Eagles at the tanker.* **R)** *The boom operator's view during the refueling of an F-4.*

Sam Reiter, standing, 3rd from left, with fellow pilots of the 308 TFS at Ubon RTAB, 1973.

34

EXCITEMENT OVER THE TONLE SAP

Jim Erdos, USAF, EC-121, June 16, 1973
{ Date of hire with Western Airlines: 8/4/1986 }

Jim Erdos, not knowing that he would eventually fly for five different airlines, leans against a museum piece, his EC-121D, on the ramp at Korat RTAB, 1973.

I met Jim Erdos in October 1983 on a picket line in front of the San Francisco International Airport. I had been an elected Air Line Pilots Association representative for our Western SFO pilot base for about a year, and we were taking turns dropping by the Continental pilots' picket line to lend our support. Jim was a Continental pilot and was one of the strike coordinators for San Francisco. We would see one another at the ALPA field office in Burlingame or on the picket line, and we hit it off right away. Jim had talked our SFO chief pilot, Marty Farber, into letting him store his picket signs in the Western pilot lounge in the terminal. As chief pilot, Marty was a direct representative of Western management and didn't think much of the militancy being expressed by the striking Continental pilots, but he liked Jim and let him bring the signs in at the end of the day. This lasted for a while, but the best part of the story is that Marty was instrumental in seeing that Jim was called for an interview by Western when the company started pilot hiring again in 1986. Jim was offered a job and has the distinction of being the only Continental striker hired by Western Airlines.

Our friendship has spanned close to 30 years. I always felt that I was akin to a voyeur as I watched the labor problems of the airline industry back in the 1980s through Jim's experience. As I have said before, the industry was a minefield, and the fortunes of an individual pilot were seldom in his own hands. I watched Braniff declare bankruptcy and cease operations in 1982, and then a series of terrible strikes rocked the industry. The pilot strikes at Continental in 1983 and United in 1985 caused rifts among the pilots and other employees that are still felt today. Western, on the other hand, made it through that period until September 1986, when Delta came along and bought the company, taking all the employees with the deal. Jim was hired in a class starting August 4, 1986, and it turned out to be the last pilot class hired by Western before the Delta merger was announced. He has five pilot uniforms hanging in his closet (Continental, People Express, Air Cal, Western, and Delta). From the time we met in 1983 until he was hired by Western in 1986, he worked for People Express on a contract basis, fit in a stint teaching flight engineer ratings for Sierra Academy of Aeronautics at Oakland International Airport, went to work for Air Cal, and then was called for his Western interview and offered a class date.

Chronologically, Jim's story is the last in the series of Western pilots who flew in the Vietnam War, as this period in 1973 came after the Christmas bombing in 1972 that brought about the Paris Peace Accords and the return of the POWs. In Vietnam the U.S. was in the midst of the "Vietnamization" of the war, with the Americans leaving and a lot of the aircraft and equipment being turned over to South Vietnamese units. In Thailand, busy, modern bases like Korat were beginning to wind down.

On a personal note, Jim went to Notre Dame, and one of my biggest college football thrills was to go with him to South Bend to the Boston College game in 2002. Notre Dame was 9-0 and scalpers were offering tickets for $400 to $500—unheard of in my neck of the woods! A football weekend in South Bend certainly puts West Coast football to shame. Getting to see everything from the pep rally Friday night to the acres of tailgating Saturday morning to the game itself was a high point for me! The weekend was an event to remember.

Here is Jim's story.

....

I had never heard of the Tonle Sap before 1973. I had barely heard of Cambodia, never mind the largest lake in that country. I *had* heard of Thailand, and it was from there that I flew the Lockheed EC-121 Warning Star. We were based at Korat Royal Thai Air Base on TDY for two months at a time, and our call sign was Disco. Many other types of aircraft called Korat home. There were F-4s, A-7s, C-130s, and also F-105s, both the one and two-seat versions. The EC-121 was a small piece of the big picture. We were part of what was known as the College Eye Task Force. Stateside, the College Eye Task Force was based at McClellan AFB in Sacramento, California. We were part of ADC, the Air Defense Command, where our mission was known as AEW&C, Airborne Early Warning and Control. It was a high-priority endeavor. There were three squadrons that made up the 552nd AEW&C Wing, and I was attached to the 963rd AEW&C Squadron. Our sister squadron was the 964th, while the 965th was responsible for training.

ADC was at its heyday from the mid-1950s to the late 1960s when EC-121 radar picket aircraft laid down a pattern of radar coverage on both coasts of the United States, 24/7. The search radar on each aircraft had a radius of approximately 250 miles, and the overlapping radar pattern ballet proceeded north on the hour and south on the half hour. The objective of the mission was to detect any hostile intruder into U.S. airspace, scramble interceptors such as the F-101, F-102, or F-106, and direct them toward the bogey until their radar could complete the intercept. If necessary, the hostile aircraft would be shot down. As the technology of land-based radar improved, the mission of the EC-121 became less and less important and, although verboten to say it, ADC was dying. However, there was this Southeast Asia conflict going on, and maybe some of those guys could use some airborne radar assistance....

How I went from flying the supersonic T-38 over West Texas to the aviation museum of the EC-121 is a story for another time. Nevertheless, some details might be helpful.

The EC-121 was an offshoot of the Lockheed Constellation L-1049 airliner. I flew mostly the EC-121D and the EC-121T models, with the suffix referring mostly to the radar and radio equipment that was carried, but each had four Wright R-3350-93A radial engines driving a Hamilton Standard prop. Each engine had 18 cylinders, two spark plugs per cylinder, and three PRTs, Power Recovery Turbines. These 144 spark plugs helped burn 115/145 fuel and produce a total of 14,000 horsepower. Each engine had a 42-gallon oil tank, and we had the capability of replenishing engine oil in flight from two (later one) 67-gallon auxiliary tanks. The fuel was loaded in nine or occasionally ten tanks, including two 600-gallon wingtip tanks. The aircraft electrical system had AC generators, DC generators, inverters, converters, batteries, and a transformer rectifier. There were primary, secondary, and emergency hydraulic systems, again with in-flight replenishing capability. The T models even had an auxiliary air-conditioning system whose compressor was driven by the secondary hydraulic system. I mention the foregoing to point out three things. There was an incredible number of moving parts, you soon learned that the flight engineers were your best friends, and Rube Goldberg was alive and well on the EC-121. I was involved in a total of 36 engine-out landings in the EC-121 in my four years of flying the airplane.

The distinctive triple tail design with the slender fuselage was modified (some would say desecrated) by the addition of two radomes (a search radar on the belly and a height-finder radar on top of the fuselage) and two wingtip fuel tanks. This made for a sort of airborne radar approach control with about a 250-mile radius of surveillance. This capability could help intercept hostile aircraft, provide tanker rendezvous assistance, assist in SAR coordination, or give directions to whoever needed them. In 1973 the air war in Vietnam was on-again, off-again, so our mission became radar surveillance of activity in Cambodia from an orbit over the Tonle Sap, the big lake.

Our unit was tasked with two missions per day in order to provide radar coverage during daylight hours. The early mission had a pickup time of about 0300 in order to launch before sunrise. The late mission would assume the duty around midday until sunset. The flying time from Korat to the orbit was about an hour, and the average length of each mission was around eight hours. Despite the ungodly wake-up, most crews preferred the early mission so if things went as planned, you could easily make it back to Korat for happy hour. It was important to keep such things in perspective.

On June 16, 1973, my crew was assigned the early mission with the call sign Disco 309. The extensive preflight routine started with the intel briefing: "Who are the good guys in Cambodia, and who are the bad guys? At least for today…" The intel briefing was held in a building known as Fort Apache, and it was here that I first encountered a Korat legend named Roscoe. Roscoe was a large, straw-colored shepherd-husky mix who had come to Korat from Japan in 1966. He was the pet of an F-105 pilot and soon became the mascot of the 388th TFW (Tactical Fighter Wing). Roscoe had the run of the base and was everybody's friend, especially if you gave him a tidbit from your plate while eating at the Officers' Club. The junior officer in the 388th assumed the additional duty of "Roscoe control officer," in charge of the pooch's well-being. In order to keep the canine population under control, the base commander allowed Roscoe to have one *teelock*, Thai for "girlfriend." A front-row seat in the auditorium at Fort Apache was reserved for Roscoe at intel briefings and his behavior was carefully observed by the pilots. Tradition had it that if he slept through the briefing it would be an easy mission, but if his ears pricked up or he was restless, it was going to be tough slugging.

The next stop was BEMO (base equipment) to pick up our chest-pack parachutes, survival vests, and a small wooden box containing .38 caliber pistols. After a swing by the flight kitchen for box lunches, we went on to the flight line to preflight the aircraft. By this time the crew bus began to resemble a scout troop going on a three-day outing. The crew composition was roughly as follows: one aircraft commander, one copilot, two flight engineers (usually very experienced senior NCOs), one navigator, one radio operator, two radar techs (airborne radar fixers), one weapons controller, and about seven radar operators. Sometimes an additional weapons controller (or two) would be added, and maybe even some security service people. To this day I'm not sure what they did as they sat behind a black curtain. They did not even wear name tags.

The lake was situated roughly on a northwest-to-southeast axis, and depending on the season, it was about 100 miles long and 10 to 20 miles wide. The city of Siem Reap was near the north shore, and it was important to avoid this area because of the proximity of Angkor Wat, the ancient temple complex. Not far from the south shore was the capital, Phnom Penh, with a big airport and lots going on. Once the aircraft arrived at the orbit and the radar was up and running, the two pilots took turns at the controls with shifts of about 90 minutes on and 90 minutes off. The on-duty pilot worked the autopilot and coordinated with the navigator to fly the desired heading. In addition to navigation, the navigator was responsible for the stabilization of the radar. This involved a sort of voodoo, inputting data to the radar system that allowed the scopes to present a stabilized display. If the radar picture was moving along with the aircraft and the targets on the radar were also in motion, chaos would result. In essence, the navigator tricked the radar into thinking it was stationary. Don't ask.

Boredom was cultivated. The flight engineers made sure the fuel was burned in the proper tank sequence and monitored each engine's health by means of a three-inch-diameter cathode ray tube gizmo imbedded in their panel. It was called an ignition analyzer, and the engineers were truly able to predict the future with it, as far as engine behavior went. The off-duty pilot snoozed (we had a few bunks), read, or ate his box lunch.

The radar part of the mission was conducted from the rear portion of the aircraft, where there were five radar operator stations.

Each operator sat behind a large scope and could access numerous radios. The radar compartment was supervised by an officer, usually a captain, known as the weapons controller, also called the CICO (combat information center officer). The rest of the radar crew was made up of enlisted men headed by a crew chief, an experienced NCO. From the standpoint of the aircraft commander, it was an unusual situation. As the AC he was responsible for the entire aircraft and crew, but the farther aft he walked, the less he understood what was going on.

It was my turn in the seat, and I had just taken a sip from a can of Coca Cola when the unmistakable, piercing "*whoop, whoop, whoop*" of an emergency locator beacon blared in my headset. The radio lit up.

"Beeper, beeper, come up voice!"

"This is Cricket on guard. All aircraft stand by!"

"I see a good chute!"

"Calling Red Crown, say call sign!"

We were approaching the northern end of the lake, and the navigator called for a left turn to the reciprocal heading. The chaos on the radio continued. I switched to interphone and tried to call the radar guys.

"CICO, pilot." Nothing. Again, "CICO, pilot."

After a few seconds the reply came back.

"Pilot, CICO. I'll get back to you—we're awfully busy back here."

Sergeant Krantz was seated at the flight engineer's panel, and Sergeant Danvers, the second flight engineer, was seated on the step that separated the cockpit from the next compartment. I asked Sergeant Danvers to ask the copilot, John Sims, to come up front. Lieutenant Sims was in the forward galley area reading a magazine. When he came to the cockpit, I transferred control of the aircraft to him and explained I was going to go to the radar compartment and see what was happening.

I got out of my seat and hurried past the navigator's station and the radio operator's desk. The farther I walked toward the radar compartment, the darker it got. The scope at each radar operator's station gave off a green glow, and I could hear the muffled chatter between crew members as I tried to stick my nose into their business. I got the attention of a young airman who was writing on a clipboard.

"Booglie. What's going on?" I asked. He smiled when I used the nickname given him by the radio operator a few weeks ago—something to do with swamp rats in Louisiana.

"I think two F-111s ran into each other over downtown Phnom Penh," he replied while continuing to write.

"Were they under our control?" I asked. He turned a page in the radar crew chief's log and said, "No sir. They checked in at 0417 Zulu and said they were going tactical."

In essence, going tactical meant that they would take care of themselves. The CYA had already begun! (For those who have not heard the expression, CYA means "Cover your ass.")

The F-111 was a pretty rare beast in Southeast Asia. I remember seeing some film back in Air Force ROTC in the mid-60s about how it was going to be all things to all people. It would be an interceptor, a bomber, a fighter, a fleet defender, and just about whatever else you wanted. I also remembered that the entire program was riddled with politics, problems, and finger-pointing.

The drama continued to unfold.

After a few minutes I got the attention of Rick Kirby, the weapons controller. He was busy shuffling papers, making radio calls, and pointing to his scope. He lifted his headset from his ears and said, "Two F-111s from Takhli, call signs Popper and Whaler, ran into each other. Popper's crew ejected, and it looks like they're OK. Whaler has part of his wing missing and is trying to fly back to Takhli. The rescue guys are on their way to Papa Papa (Phnom Penh). Everybody who should know what's going on has been notified. If you want to monitor the SAR, tune to UHF channel 4. I gotta go now!"

I could see that my presence was not helping things, so I walked back to the cockpit. I was glad to hear that the ejection from Popper had gone well. I remembered reading that the F-111 had a capsule ejection system. During the ejection sequence, the cockpit became a sort of cocoon after electrical, hydraulic and pneumatic connections were severed by a guillotine-type device. The parachute would then deploy and the two crew members would float to earth. I got back to the cockpit, told John and the two flight engineers what was going on, and asked John to continue to fly the aircraft while I listened to the rescue.

After about 30 minutes I could hear the radio calls between the rescue helicopter and one of the crew members on the ground. The guy on the ground told the chopper that he could hear him but couldn't see him. He said they were in a line of trees just south of a water tower. The rescue chopper said he couldn't descend any lower until he had a visual on both crew members. A discussion ensued about who was going to do what until the helicopter pilot said, "Look. I've got five minutes of fuel left before I have to RTB (return to base). If I don't pick you up, you're going to have to spend the night."

There was a slight pause, and Popper Alpha replied, "We'll be right out!" The two crewmen were picked up and the rescue was a success, or so we thought.

About 15 minutes later, Kirby, the weapons controller, called on the interphone. "Pilot, CICO."

"Go ahead," I replied.

"Our relief aircraft took off from Korat on schedule and should be taking over for us shortly. Also, you're gonna love this one, the head shed is wondering what's going to happen to the ejection capsule." I couldn't believe it. What were they afraid of? Did they think that the Khmer Rouge were going to build an F-111 around the ejection capsule and mount an offensive? I have no idea what happened to the capsule.

We flew back to Korat and turned in our survival gear, our parachutes, and our box of guns. We debriefed the maintenance troops. The crew bus stopped by our detachment headquarters, where we dropped off the classified documents, code books, etc. The detachment executive officer poked his head in the bus and pointed at me.

"Colonel Grimes wants to see you."

"He wants to see me? You're kidding."

"Nope. He's waiting in his office."

It was hot, I was tired, and my flight suit had sweat stains on it. Now I had to go see the detachment commander. I'll just say that he never won any Miss Congeniality awards from any of the aircrew.

I put on my hat, walked into his office, saluted smartly, and said, "Captain Erdos, reporting as ordered, sir."

He glared at me and barked, "What the hell happened out there?"

"Well sir, let me get Captain Kirby and have him tell you."

"Dammit! YOU are the aircraft commander, and YOU are responsible for that aircraft and crew!"

"Yes, sir, but I was in the cockpit looking out the window when all the excitement happened."

After he found out that the F-111s had not been under our control he calmed down a bit. The CYA exercise was to be continued the following day when he and Kirby had to go to 7th Air Force headquarters at NKP (Nakhon Phanom Royal Thai Air Base) and do a "rug dance" (explain your actions on the rug in front of the Commander's desk).

Finally he dismissed me and I went out to the waiting crew bus. It looked like we'd be in time for Happy Hour after all. Maybe I'd even get a chance to pet Roscoe.

As a final note, the second F-111, Whaler, made a successful landing at Takhli Royal Thai Air Base with four feet of one wing missing.

Jim, with another three-tailed, four-engine, "Eye in the Sky," 1973.

EC-121 cockpit—talk about a museum piece!

EC-121D at McClellan AFB, California, 1973.

35

PSY OPS GOON

Robert E. Moore, USAF, C-47D, 1969

The last stories in the book are written by my friends
Bob Moore and Peter Foor, with an addendum to Peter's
story by Nick Kosturos. Since they were not Western pilots,
their stories appear out of chronological order.

Bob Moore, standing, 2nd from the left, with his C-47D crew at Nha Trang, 1969.

*Bob Moore is the only pilot in the book who did not end up working for
Western Airlines. It was not for want of trying, as Bob is a native
Californian, born in San Francisco, who tried his best to get hired by
Western and stay on the West Coast. Bob graduated from Lincoln High
School in San Francisco in 1962, where he received a baseball scholarship
to attend the College of William and Mary in Virginia. Scouted by the
majors in his senior year in college, he was told, "You're an outstanding*

southpaw first baseman. We've been watching you all year, and it's too bad you can't hit the ball." With a career in the majors off the table, Bob graduated, signed up for Air Force OTS (Officer Training School), took the tests to qualify for UPT (Undergraduate Pilot Training), and soon found himself at Williams AFB, Arizona, in pilot training class 69-04. After getting his wings he went right to Vietnam, along with 75 percent of his class. The other 25 percent would go eventually because going to pilot training meant you were going to Vietnam, one way or another.

After separating from the Air Force, Bob missed the hiring cycle that had ended at Western but was offered a job by Eastern Airlines in 1973 and took it. Bob and I met in the Air Force Reserve after he had been furloughed by Eastern and had transferred from McGuire AFB, New Jersey, to Travis in the C-141 reserve. We became good friends, and when Western began to hire pilots again in 1976 he was called for an interview. The best we could figure was that the contact that opened the door for his interview also closed it for a job. Bob's mother was a secretary for the Teamsters Union in Los Angeles, and since the Western mechanics were represented by the Teamsters, Bob's mom made a call, her boss made a call, and Bob got an interview. Somewhere along the line the connection to the Teamsters must have done him in, as he was politely declined for a job and went back to Eastern when they recalled their furloughed pilots in 1978. Eastern's bankruptcy and liquidation in 1991 ended Bob's airline career but opened up a career at the FAA, where he worked in Atlanta with Delta, retiring in 2010.

Bob and I had several exploits together while flying in the Travis reserves. The most notable was our being selected to fly a C-141 in a high-speed, low-altitude fly-by at the Travis air show honoring the bicentennial in 1976. Now "high-speed, low-altitude" means different things in different airplanes. For those of us in MAC (Military Airlift Command), it was permission to fly 250 knots at 600 feet above the ground, down the runway, in front of a reviewing stand and a large crowd on the ramp. Bob and I discussed various options for the fly-by, and the one we decided on was 350 knots at 200 feet, 350 knots being the red-line on the airspeed indicator at that altitude. We did give some thought that it might end our reserve careers but not much more, and apparently it looked so good from the reviewing stand that we never heard a word about it. Interestingly, I was flying at Western that month with Barry Harmon from our San Francisco base; he was planning to come to the show and promised to take a couple of photos. Barry's most memorable remark was, "I have never seen anything that big, going so fast, so close to the ground." It may not have matched Bill Wilson's high-speed, low-altitude pass at Ubon, or the low pass over his house, but we have to seize our opportunities when they arise!

Bob's position with the FAA and his role with Delta Air Lines were instrumental in my being able to fly my retirement flight over Memorial Day weekend 2004. My wife, Angie, had passed away unexpectedly a week before that flight, and Delta Operations had called and suggested I stay home, saying that they would put me on bereavement leave and pay me for that last trip. I did not want to end my 37 years of flying sitting at home, but unknown to me, Bob had intervened on my behalf. He had talked to Delta's VP of operations and told him that if I said I could handle it, then I could handle it. He said he would fly at least one leg of that trip in the cockpit with me, more if they wanted. They paired me with a high-time Los Angeles–based first officer and sent me off for the trip of a lifetime. Bob flew with us from LaGuardia to Orlando on day three of that four-day trip and took a video that I treasure to this day. My brother Dave flew with us on the last leg from JFK to LAX, and my family was waiting at the gate in LAX when we arrived. Bob is on a list of dear friends, and that list is a constant reminder of my good fortune in life. The fact that almost every name on that list is a Vietnam veteran is not lost on me.

....

JUNGLE SURVIVAL SCHOOL: MARCH, APRIL 1969

My road to Vietnam actually began one Saturday afternoon in the Officers' Club at Williams AFB, Arizona, in the summer of 1968. I was having a beer with three pilot training classmates, and the topic of conversation turned to the classes graduating ahead of us. We had a list of assignments for a couple of classes that were six months ahead of us, and the reality of those assignments did not escape us. All indications were that we would receive flying assignments to Vietnam because 80 percent of the assignments for the classes ahead of us were for Vietnam or SEA (Southeast Asia). Sure enough, when our assignments came through in December, roughly 75 percent of our class was headed to Vietnam. I received a C-47 (civilian DC-3, affectionately known as the Gooney Bird) with an assignment to the 9th SOS (Special Operations Squadron) at Nha Trang AB, Vietnam. The 9th SOS was a psychological warfare squadron, made up of C-47Ds and O-2B aircraft; the O-2A was the forward air control version of the civilian Cessna 337 Skymaster, while the O-2B was set up for the psy-war mission. We would conduct leaflet drops, loudspeaker orbits, flare support at night, and other special operations. We were affectionately known as the Bullshit Bombers.

After graduating from pilot training in December 1968, considerable training was scheduled before I would ever set foot in Vietnam. Beginning in January 1969, I attended Basic Survival School at Fairchild AFB near Spokane, graduating on February 4. From Spokane I made a low pass through home (San Francisco) to see family and my girlfriend, then departed for Louisiana for C-47 and Special Operations Force Training at Alexandria AFB, graduating on March 18. As I recall, very few days remained before I was scheduled to depart Travis AFB for Clark AFB in the Philippines, so I drove home to San Francisco in two days with a quick overnight stop in Yuma, Arizona.

In what seemed like the blink of an eye, one evening I found myself walking out of the terminal onto the tarmac at Travis to get on an ugly green Braniff Airlines stretch DC-8 bound for Southeast Asia. I remember looking back at the terminal before entering the aircraft and I could see my mom, sister, and girlfriend standing there waving and probably wondering if they would ever see me again. Quite honestly, I don't remember having that sort of thought, as I believed very strongly that I would see them and my beautiful hometown of San Francisco again.

I arrived at Clark AFB on March 25, 1969, to begin PACAF (Pacific Air Force) Jungle Survival School. I grew up near the beach in San Francisco, and my childhood experience had revolved around the beaches of San Francisco and down the coast to the beautiful town of Santa Cruz, walking to Harding Park to play golf, or hitchhiking to the Olympic Club to pack two rounds of doubles as a caddie on Saturdays and Sundays—if I could sweet talk my way out of Sunday school.

Jungle Survival training—you've got to be kidding me! Much to my surprise, though, my experience at the school was exhilarating. By the time we graduated, on April 9, my whole attitude toward the Asian jungle had changed and I had gained the confidence and knowledge that I could survive in that environment if called upon to do so. My best experience was the E and E (escape and evasion) portion of training. We were paired up, dropped off in the jungle in the mountains outside Clark, and given coordinates for a clearing in the jungle where a Navy helicopter would pick us up the next morning. The Air Force hired local Negrito natives to try to find us during the day and night, while our job was to evade and find our way to the pickup point. We were given chits worth a certain amount of money, and if caught, we had to give the chits to the Negritos as a reward. My partner and I evaded successfully along the ridgelines during the daytime, but as night approached we struggled to come up with a place to hide. With less than an hour of daylight remaining, we stumbled across some cliffs where there were all sorts of strong vines hanging over the edge. We decided to wrap the vines around our waist and arms in a manner that would allow us to hang off the edge of the cliff and out of view of any Negritos who might be passing by. We found an area where we could rest our feet on a small ledge. So, there we were, hanging by vines all night looking at the lights of Clark AFB and Angeles City off in a distant valley. We were not discovered that night and managed to make it to the designated spot in time for the helicopter pickup. The next day was graduation day, April 9, 1969, and my next stop was Vietnam.

FROM CLARK TO NHA TRANG: ON OR ABOUT APRIL 14, 1969

Early in the day I made my way to the passenger terminal at Clark AFB to check in for my flight to Vietnam. I knew my ultimate destination was Nha Trang and that I was set up for an initial flight from Clark to Saigon's Tan Son Nhut Airport/Air Base. Lo and behold, about an hour before departure time the same ugly green Braniff DC-8 taxied up to the loading tarmac in front of the terminal. I learned many years later that this DC-8 was affectionately called "the pickle" by the troops. Roughly 165 of us boarded the pickle bound for Saigon, all of us unsure about what sort of future was waiting for us. Inbound to Tan Son Nhut, I remember the approach being quite steep and relatively close to the airport. Apparently, the military charter airlines trained their crews to conduct special approach and departure procedures in conjunction with the military, in order to limit exposure to ground fire. After landing, and much to my surprise, we were dropped off on the civilian side of the airport, in front of the international terminal. That was it—no connecting flight to Nha Trang and no information regarding how I might get there.

After getting my bearings and retrieving my baggage, my recollection is that I asked a ticket agent in the terminal for information and was told that my best bet would be to try to hitch a ride to Nha Trang over on the Air Force side of the base. It was located on the opposite side of the airport and a long distance away, but I spotted several U.S. military guys and asked them how I might get over to the other side without having to take a local taxi. One of them had just dropped off a group of short-timers about to go home and offered me a ride in his crew van to the Air Force side. I gladly accepted and about 45 minutes later was dropped off at base operations. When I went inside, the duty officer happened to be at the counter and I asked him if he knew of any flights that might be headed to Nha Trang. He said there was a C-130 flight crew in the flight planning room and I should ask the aircraft commander, a major, if he had space for me. I found the flight planning room, introduced myself to the major, and asked him if I might catch a ride to Nha Trang. He politely said hello, looked at his copilot and navigator, then sternly looked me in the eye and said I could ride in the back as long as I promised never to tell anyone what I observed back there. Of course I had no idea what that meant, but I promised him I would never tell anybody about the flight—just like a good second lieutenant should! He said they would take a few more minutes to flight-plan and would meet me in the snack bar. He told me to be sure to eat something as it could be a long night. After about 20 minutes the flight crew joined me in the snack bar. After eating, we hung around for a while due to a maintenance problem with the aircraft. It was about 6:30 p.m. when the crew called for a crew bus and we departed base operations for the aircraft. When we arrived at the C-130 the loadmaster introduced himself as he came off the airplane, told me to board the aircraft, turn right immediately, walk to the back and take a seat. He said he would take care of my baggage.

I climbed up the stairs of the C-130, turned right and began the strangest walk of my life. On both sides of the aircraft, seated on fold-down troop seats, were Asian men dressed in military uniforms, staring straight ahead and not speaking. In the middle of the aircraft, with troops on either side, silver coffins were stacked and strapped three high all along the length of the aircraft. The clamshell doors in the back were closed. I found my place at the end of the troop seats and realized it was the last seat available on the aircraft. When I sat down, I looked up and down the row of troops looking for any sign that they recognized my existence. No acknowledgment – just silence and staring straight ahead. So I basically joined them, staring straight ahead and wondering what the hell this was all about. After looking at their uniforms, my gut feeling was that they were Chinese uniforms, khaki with red epaulets on the collars and a red star in the middle of the caps.

Not long after I sat down, I could see the loadmaster closing the forward entry door. Then the engines started up, and soon we were taking off into the dusk for Nha Trang. I don't know how long the flight lasted but I do remember that it seemed to take forever. During the entire flight not one person in the back of the aircraft spoke. The loadmaster walked back to check on me once, looked over, gave me a thumbs up to make sure I was OK, and then went back to his station. I didn't see him again until we were parked on the ramp at Nha Trang. He walked back to my seat and said I should follow him to the front and off the aircraft. When I got off he told me to jump into the back of the follow-me truck that had led us to our parking spot and wait for my baggage. He indicated that the follow-me truck would take me to transient quarters, and in a minute or so he brought my bags to the truck, turned around, and went back to the aircraft without saying a word. The follow-me truck driver said hello and drove me to the transient quarters where I jumped off the truck and grabbed my bags. The driver said, "Welcome to Nha Trang and have a good night," and then sped off. Standing there alone, I remember it being very dark outside. I never saw the flight crew of that aircraft again.

I checked in at the office and went to the barracks building next door to find a place to sleep. As I walked up the steps I noticed little or no activity and the base was very quiet. I believe by then it must have been close to 10 p.m. I left my bags out of the way in the foyer of the barracks and quietly entered. The only light was the illumination of the street lights through the small windows located above the long row of bunk beds. Each bunk, including the top bunk, was draped with mosquito nets, and I tried to be as quiet as I could because everyone else was sound asleep. It was very hot and humid so I took off everything but my shorts and slowly crawled into a lower bunk—the upper bunk was also empty. I remember lying there on my back, in the dark, surrounded by mosquito netting and wondering what the future would bring. I'm sure I fell asleep instantly because the next thing I remember was being awakened from a deep sleep by an extremely loud explosion, which scared the hell out of me and literally sent me flying into the bottom of the mattress of the upper bunk. Then another explosion went off and I realized the Army was firing 105mm howitzers. They didn't tell us about that in survival school! It was 1:30 a.m., and I'd had my first introduction to, "Good Morning Vietnam."

Regarding the C-130 flight, I later discovered that this C-130 was one of the few MC-130E Combat Talon aircraft manufactured by Lockheed and it belonged to the 15th SOS based at Nha Trang. If you went into base operations and studied the base diagram on the wall, you would see all aircraft based at Nha Trang depicted on that diagram, with the exception of the MC-130s. They were physically there but you couldn't find them on any base map or diagram. Painted green and black with the scissor-like blades on the nose for the Fulton Recovery System, they were completely unmarked.

MAMA SAN

I couldn't write about my Vietnam experience without acknowledging my "mama san" at Nha Trang. The Air Force hired local women to work as housekeepers and do laundry for the officers living on the base, and they were all called "mama san." From day one, I knew my mama san and I would have a special relationship. She spoke absolutely no English but somehow we managed to communicate using just a few English and Vietnamese words. Looking back at this experience reminds me how lucky I was to be assigned to Nha Trang and to be a young Air Force pilot rather than a young Army or Marine officer commanding a platoon of teenagers somewhere out in the jungle of South Vietnam. Not much in the way of mama sans for those guys.

In any case, my mama san and I became good friends, and I have some cherished memories of her. She was married with two young children and her husband was serving in the ARVN (Army of the Republic of Vietnam), so she was raising her family alone. One afternoon the base came under rocket attack, and when that occurred, in order to protect ourselves we would pull the mattresses off the bunks, crawl under the lower bunk and pull the mattresses on top of ourselves. For about two hours one afternoon, mama san and I hid under that bunk, each of us praying in our own way and in our own language that a 122mm rocket would not come in on top of us. She was truly frightened, and all I could do was hold her hand, try to make her laugh and keep her talking, even though I couldn't understand 99 percent of what she was saying.

My mama san and her colleagues did a wonderful job for us, including doing our laundry by hand on the floor of our showers when we were out of the barracks for the day. Nearly 44 years later I still think of her and wonder how her life turned out once we cut and ran from Vietnam. I wonder whether her husband survived once the Communists came to power and what sort of life her children have experienced. She was 37 when I knew her and already beginning to look old. In my wildest dreams, I imagine mama san and her family were somehow able to leave Vietnam on a C-141 for a new life in the United States. If not, I pray that they survived the transition and have lived a reasonably good life in Vietnam.

FIRST MISSION AND SUBSEQUENT TRAINING:
APRIL 19-MAY 31, 1969

Unfortunately, I failed to keep a daily record of events during my stay in Vietnam. The only records I have in hand are my old Air Force Form 5 flight time records; my personal logbooks disappeared many years ago. I flew my first mission on April 19, 1969, with Captain Bill Sargent. During the next several weeks he would teach me everything I needed to know in order to survive in combat and to succeed as an aircraft commander. Bill's guidance and counsel provided a solid foundation for me when flying the C-47 and provided me with the knowledge required to work with a diverse group of crew members and support personnel during both good and difficult times.

When I arrived at Nha Trang, the squadron was very short on mission-qualified pilots, so the pressure was on for new pilots like me to become proficient as soon as possible. The qualified pilots, like Bill Sargent, were flying their tails off to the point of exhaustion. On May 31 I went out on a mission with Bill Jones, our squadron standardization pilot (the chief check pilot) to check out as aircraft commander. In order to fly as an aircraft commander, pilots were required to have 400 hours of total flight time. When we departed on the mission that day, my total time was about 396 hours, including pilot training time. Our mission lasted about 4.4 hours, so by the time we returned I had cracked the 400-hour barrier and was a new aircraft commander. During those six weeks leading up to my check ride, I learned to fly the C-47 in a hostile environment and gained confidence in making crosswind landings in very strong winds. (It seemed as if the runways in Vietnam were all oriented for maximum crosswinds!) I learned to fly diverse missions involving low-altitude speaker orbits and leaflet drops, flare support at night for fighter strikes, psychological support missions for the ROK (Republic of Korea) Marines, and other very unusual missions.

ENGINE FAILURE

I flew my first mission as an aircraft commander on June 2, 1969. The mission that day involved three stages. First, we were to drop off the 14th SOW (Special Operations Wing) commander in Saigon for a meeting, then from Saigon we were to fly to the Phan Thiet–Vung Tau area, east/southeast of Saigon, and drop leaflets over several targets. (Most leaflet drops involved the Chieu Hoi ("Open Arms") program, with the leaflet to be used as a "safe conduct pass" for defecting Vietcong insurgents.) After completing the leaflet portion of the mission we were to fly back to Saigon, pick up the commander, and fly back to Nha Trang. The weather was clear and very hot and humid, somewhere in the mid-90s. We had a full load of fuel and were loaded with 100 boxes of leaflets, putting us very close to maximum takeoff weight for the conditions.

Runway 12 was approximately 5,500 feet in length and required a special departure procedure after takeoff to avoid overflight of Hon Tre Island, located not far off the end of the runway. Hon Tre and two or three other, smaller islands were off to the southeast and in the gap we would normally fly through if headed to Cam Ranh Bay and other points south. Although Nha Trang was known as the Vietnamese Riviera and was an in-country R&R center for American and South Vietnamese troops, it was also used for R&R by the Vietcong. However, the VC would try to shoot an aircraft down if it overflew Hon Tre Island, so we always followed the special departure procedure.

The takeoff roll on Runway 12 was normal but quite long due to the temperature and our weight. When flying through about 200 feet on departure, the right engine experienced a massive failure, losing all its engine oil instantaneously. Before I could call, "Feather #2 engine," Bill Sargent was already doing so, demonstrating the value of having a highly experienced copilot flying with you on your first trip as an aircraft commander. He made my task of flying the aircraft much easier as I started a slow left turn over the water, trying to avoid flying over the island. For a moment, I wasn't sure that I could maintain altitude and picked out a ditching spot just off Nha Trang beach where I knew an American lifeguard station was located. I wasn't sure I'd be able to complete the nearly 110 degree turn in time to avoid the island, but fortunately I was able to stabilize the aircraft between 200 and 300 feet above the water and continued turning until I was essentially on a downwind leg. We completed our emergency procedures, declared an emergency with the tower, and requested clearance to make a visual approach and landing on Runway 12. While I continued on a downwind leg, I had our navigator call operations and ask them to prepare another C-47 and crew to take the wing commander to Saigon. The downwind, base, and final legs of the approach went quite well considering our low altitude, but the landing was another story. Being new to the aircraft, I was very tense and bounced the first touchdown quite hard. The aircraft bounced two more times before I could stabilize it, but the last half of the landing roll was uneventful. We stopped at the end of the runway and advised the tower we would need to be towed in to our parking spot. Bill Sargent had to pry my hands off the yoke!

The squadron jeep reached the end of the runway about the time we stopped, and after shutting down the left engine the loadmaster assisted the wing commander off the aircraft. The squadron had another aircraft and crew ready to take him to Saigon, and after we were towed off the runway, that aircraft took off with the wing commander aboard. Later that day we learned that the wing commander was very upset at the landing and directed our squadron commander to ground Bill and me until further notice, but after we briefed our squadron commander, Colonel Fred Kuhlengel, he managed to get us both back in the air within two or three days. I can't remember the name of the wing commander, but he never once thanked us for saving his butt that day despite the landing—he never knew how close we came to ditching in Nha Trang Bay. The following month, karma caught up with the wing commander when he was fired by 7th Air Force Headquarters in Saigon and sent home.

(A note regarding Hon Tre Island and Nha Trang: Today the island is a resort, hosting a five-star hotel called the Vinpearl, which features wonderful secluded bays, world-class pools, and a superb golf course. Nha Trang was always a very special place. From the air, the city looks very much like a European city along the Mediterranean. There were very few places in Vietnam where an American soldier could walk the streets with relative safety, and other than during the Tet Offensive in early 1968, Nha Trang was one.)

Few people understand that the U.S. military accomplished many missions that were not related to the war, and I'm not sure the story of those missions has been adequately told. A case in point was the dedication to and support of the Catholic orphanage in the heart of the city of Nha Trang by the 9th SOS. We would visit the orphanage once or twice a week, bringing clothes, food, and other items that the nuns needed for the children. The greatest part of the experience was the opportunity to spend quality time with those kids. They didn't ask for much, just a little love and companionship. I'll always cherish that experience, and I often wonder what happened to them and their loving teachers, the Vietnamese Catholic nuns.

PSY OPS

During the Tet Offensive in 1968, the Vietcong and North Vietnamese Army lost thousands of troops, with estimates of up to 240,000 killed by the end of 1968. Those losses had a huge psychological effect on the VC and NVA soldiers who survived. The U.S. Army controlled the psychological warfare efforts in Vietnam and provided targets and strategies for the Air Force. After Tet, the Army increased both ground and airborne psy ops missions in an attempt to get demoralized VC and NVA soldiers to come over to the South Vietnamese side. This effort went unnoticed by most people but was considered a huge success. Most of the missions we flew during my time in country were associated with the Chieu Hoi program. The 9th SOS had C-47D and O-2B aircraft flying speaker and leaflet missions night and day, primarily in the coastal and highland provinces of South Vietnam. We were affectionately known as the B.S. Bombers.

Although our government denied it, we were also flying missions at night in Laos and Cambodia. The sorties that I flew to Laos were all leaflet-drop missions. Due to the politics involved, we had grave concerns about our well-being should we be required to make an emergency landing anywhere in Laos. We knew there was a high probability that we would be treated as men without a country.

Other flights were psychological speaker missions in support of the ROK Marines, our South Korean allies who were involved in many active ground operations at night as part of their mission to protect the perimeters of our bases. Once over the target, usually in a dark, mountainous valley about 1,000 feet above the ground, a Korean specialist would speak to his comrades on the ground with tales of valor and bravery and play tapes of Korean military motivational music. We supported AC-119 Shadow and AC-47 Spooky gunship aircraft in their night missions, and the squadron rotated crews into Pleiku to fly flare support for nighttime fighter strikes in the highlands. These were usually 30-day TDY assignments. We also flew missions dropping newspapers into small villages and hamlets in order to provide information from the South Vietnamese government in Saigon.

In part due to the Paris Peace Talks that started in 1968, the U.S. presence at Nha Trang began to wind down in the summer of 1969, and the 9th SOS closed up shop entirely and moved up the coast to Tuy Hoa AB. The date was September 5, 1969, and I vividly remember flying in the formation of C-47D and O-2B aircraft, heading up the coast to our new home.

MAJOR GEORGE THOMPSON, NAVIGATOR EXTRAORDINAIRE

I owe my life and the lives of my crew members to Major George Thompson. Major Thompson was my navigator one dark and stormy night off the coast of South Vietnam, perhaps 10 miles south of Tuy Hoa. We were on the way back from a very long mission, dropping leaflets on several targets between Vung Tau and Phan Thiet, southeast of Saigon. The date was October 8, 1969, and as nightfall approached, thunderstorms were rapidly cropping up in all flying quadrants. We learned that a weather front would pass through the coastal area later in the evening.

As was often the case, we would fly feet wet off the coast on the way back to Nha Trang or Tuy Hoa. When we departed Phan Thiet the weather was good, but we could see the dark skies of the approaching front far off to the north. We started our cruise back at about 6,000 feet and in the clear, but as we progressed to the north the weather forced us to descend as the ceilings were getting lower. There was no air traffic control other than the tower control facilities at Phan Rang, Cam Ranh, and Nha Trang. When we reached 2,500 feet we became a bit concerned about the weather and considered diverting into Cam Ranh Bay. We made the decision to press on; however, by the time we passed Cam Ranh, the weather had forced us down to 1,500 feet in order to stay in the clear beneath the clouds. It was very dark and raining off the coast of Vietnam. We could make out the lights of Nha Trang to the northwest beyond Hon Tre Island, so I decided to stay to the east of the islands off Nha Trang and then pick up a heading to Hameau Mo hamlet, located just south of Tuy Hoa. My only concern was that the mountains just south of Tuy Hoa rose to 2,000 feet or more—I knew the area well, as my favorite beach in Vietnam was located near Hameau Mo.

We proceeded on a northerly heading and continued to be forced lower due to the deteriorating weather. At times, in order to maintain any sort of visual reference, we were forced down to 500 feet, but we were able to maintain 1,000 feet most of the time. The closer we got to the point just east of Hameau Mo, the more concerned I became that our track could be farther west than we wanted due to the frontal winds. Remember, this aircraft was built in 1944, and we were without GPS or FMS to assist in navigation. Under the clouds it was very dark, as there were no hamlets of any size in that vicinity and it was raining very hard. I also became very aware that the cockpit had become quiet. About the time I started thinking about making a safe turn to the east, Major Thompson called out in a very loud, stern voice, "Make an immediate right turn to 090 degrees." The voice was so unlike Major Thompson's normal manner of speaking that I'm sure I was halfway through the turn before he finished the command. I completed the turn to 090 (east) and remember observing the altimeter at 700 feet. Almost immediately after I completed the turn, the clouds started breaking up and, looking to the left, I began to see the dim lights of Tuy Hoa city way off to the north. Then, quite mysteriously, I distinctly remember seeing the silhouette of the mountain ridge sloping down to the South China Sea, and I

knew we had dodged the "big one" thanks to our navigator extraor-
dinaire, Major George Thompson. We proceeded to Tuy Hoa and
landed to the southwest on Runway 21L without incident, the whole
crew feeling very lucky after our near miss with the mountain. (I
recently duplicated this experience by flying Google Earth's flight
simulator to assist my recall of the flight. We certainly were very
lucky.)

QUICK CHANGE

Just a few weeks later I was sitting around in our operations
office at Tuy Hoa. It was November 5, 1969, and by then I was considered one of our more experienced aircraft commanders. My
squadron commander, Colonel Fred Kuhlengel, suddenly came out
of his office, looked at me, smiled, and said, "Lieutenant Moore,
how'd you like to go home?" I stared back at him and asked him to
please repeat what he had just said to me. You see, I had been in-
country less than seven months and did not expect to be going home
until April 1970. He repeated himself and said, "You don't have
much time if you want to make a flight out of Cam Ranh Bay at
1500." The time then was about noon, so that was just three hours. I
asked him how this could be happening and he indicated I should
thank Richard Nixon and the Paris Peace Talks. He said I needed to
get moving, now!

He said there would be an O-2B waiting to fly me to Cam Ranh
and I should be able to make the flight. So off I went in a state of
shock. I packed my stuff, including my dirty laundry, went back to
operations to out-process, went to the base personnel office to out-
process, and then found myself getting on one of our O-2B aircraft,
still wearing my flight suit, for the flight to Cam Ranh. The flight was
not long, about 45 minutes, and the guys dropped me off on the
ramp in front of—yes—that ugly green Braniff DC-8, which had suddenly become beautiful! I carried my bags into the terminal just in
time to check in, hit the bathroom to change out of my flight suit, and
get on the airplane. I sat down in my seat with my head spinning,
not believing that I could possibly be going home. I thought I was

dreaming until I heard the engines crank up on that DC-8. Within just a few minutes we were climbing out of Cam Ranh Bay and 165 lucky guys were yelling, cheering, and crying, all at the same time.

The irony of the story of my abrupt return home is that just two days earlier I had traveled to Cam Ranh with another pilot from the squadron to go on R&R to Australia for a week. The charter flight was overbooked; my partner managed to get the last seat and left me at Cam Ranh. What a surprise for him when he returned from R&R to find that I was already home in San Francisco!

I was happy to be going home, but I regret to this day that I didn't have time to say good-bye properly to the dedicated airmen I flew with during my time with the 9th SOS. Our maintenance, ground support, and flight crew personnel were the best, and I am honored to have served with them. I always thought I would see them again at a reunion one day, but that hasn't happened. I was never able to thank Major Thompson appropriately—we had a few beers at the club, but I don't think he really knows how much he meant to me and the rest of the crew members for saving our butts that dark, stormy night. This writing project has managed to get me off my rear-end, and has motivated me to start a search for some of these guys before I'm too late.

The Braniff flight stopped at Yokota AB in Japan to refuel. I didn't even know the final destination stateside until we left Yokota and I discovered we were headed for McCord AFB near Seattle. We arrived in Seattle around midday and I found a pay phone to call my mother at work to give her the news. I flew commercial to Sacramento and took a bus to San Francisco. I remember being on that bus on the east side of the bay when I got my first view of the city. What a wonderful view!

*L) Bob Moore at the helicopter pick-up point, after successful completion of the E & E portion of Jungle Survival School, April 8, 1969. **R)** Mama San at Nha Trang, 1969.*

A dazed but happy Bob Moore, in the backseat of the O-2, arrives at Cam Ranh Bay for his early departure from Vietnam, November 5, 1969.

Chieu Hoi leaflets dropped by the C-47Ds to encourage VC and NVA to come over to the South Vietnamese government side. Also used as a safe conduct pass.

The navigator who saved our lives, Major George Thompson.

36

ON THE GROUND

Peter Foor, First Lieutenant USMC, Kilo Company, 3rd Platoon, 3/26 Marines, 1968 – 1969

Lt. Peter Foor, USMC, leaving for Operation Meade River with Kilo Company, 3/26 Marines, November 1968.

In the spring of 1962 there were four friends who were seniors at Berkeley High School in Berkeley, California. They were coming up on their 18th birthdays and facing Selective Service registration for the draft. The war in Southeast Asia was on the back burner, not really registering much with them, and it certainly wasn't in the papers or on the nightly news. On the University of California's Charter Day, March 23, 1962, President Kennedy had spoken at Memorial Stadium on the UC Berkeley campus and talked about a New Frontier, not a war in Southeast Asia.

These four friends faced a more immediate problem, and that was who could get the family car on Friday night and who looked the oldest and could go into Bill's #2 Liquors at 54th and Grove in Oakland and buy a couple of six-packs of beer. On this particular Friday night Charlie had his mother's 1961 Ford Falcon. It was bright red and really stood out as we sat parked on 54th Street, waiting for him to buy the beer. He looked the oldest and had a good enough "fake" ID for Bill's #2 Liquors. Someone had the brilliant idea that smoking a rum-soaked Wolf Brothers Crook cigar would go well with the beer, so it was quite a Friday night, curing most of us of smoking and getting Charlie permanently banned from driving his mother's car.

Those four friends all ended up in the service. Charlie joined the Marine Corps a year or so after graduation from high school, following in his father's footsteps. His dad had survived Iwo Jima, so there was never much doubt as to where Charlie would end up. His dad was an intimidating presence for any 17-year-old, at about 6 feet 6 inches tall, and from all I've read about the Marines and the island battles in World War II, the tall guys didn't have much of a life expectancy in combat because they were the easiest targets. That alone was enough to scare us half to death, and I'm sure the smoke-soaked Falcon got Charlie an early initiation to boot camp. Peter, Craig, and I went off to college. Peter and I became officers after graduation, Peter through OCS (Officer Candidate School) and I through ROTC (Reserve Officer Training Corps). After graduation, Craig was drafted in 1967 and spent two years at Fort Rucker, Alabama, learning to be an air traffic controller. As a college graduate, he received an Army offer to attend OCS and become an officer, or to become a warrant officer and a UH-1 Huey pilot. Remembering the advice that he should not volunteer for anything, he spent his two years at Fort Rucker, got out of the Army, and went back to school.

Charlie was the first of us to go to Vietnam, landing at Da Nang with the III MAF (Marine Amphibious Force) in 1965, while Peter and I arrived in Vietnam in May and June 1968, spending a year when the number of Americans in Vietnam hit its peak and the yearly casualty total was the highest. All four of us survived and went on with our lives. In hindsight, sitting in that bright red Ford Falcon at 54th and Grove in Oakland may have been one of the more dangerous things we did. Certainly it would be today, when Bill's #2 Liquors is long gone and 54th and Grove, now 54th and Martin Luther King Boulevard, is close to ground zero in the war zone of one of the most dangerous cities in the country.

Of the four of us, three used GI Bill benefits to go to school, Peter and Craig to law school and Charlie to finish his undergraduate degree and then go to law school. I stayed in the Air Force Reserve and was hired by Western Airlines a few months after I left active duty, so all four of us went on to live very productive lives. That was the way for the vast majority of those who survived the service and Vietnam. As I had mentioned earlier, I lost track of Peter until I read in the news that he had been appointed a judge for the California Superior Court in Solano County by Governor Pete Wilson. The following is taken from an article about his appointment in the San Francisco Chronicle *on November 29, 1997:*

A year ago Peter Foor was a virtual unknown among a crowded field of prosecutors, private attorneys, and Municipal Court Judges jockeying for a bench spot created by the Legislature.... About the same time he decided to send his name up to Sacramento for consideration, Foor cut off the ponytail he sported for years in court.

Foor, 53, defies easy definition. He served as a Marine Lieutenant in Vietnam and was decorated in 1968 for leading his troops in a firefight with the North Vietnamese Army near Da Nang. He was a Deputy District Attorney in Tulare County from '73 to '75 then worked in private practice before becoming a public defender in 1984. He has handled what one attorney called the county's "most obnoxious cases."

Foor, who voted for Wilson, says he has a moderately conservative philosophy and called himself the "closet conservative" of the Public Defender's Office.

News of Foor's appointment roiled Solano County's close-knit legal community.

....

I called and spoke with Peter on the phone after reading about his appointment, but we didn't meet again until nearly 10 years later at our 45th Berkeley High School reunion in 2007. It was then that I learned more

about his service with the Marine Corps in Vietnam. The coincidence that
we had been there at exactly the same time was another bond, like the one
forged over those Wolf Brothers Crooks in the 1961 Ford Falcon.

Below is Peter's citation for the Navy Commendation Medal he received
for heroic achievement in combat.

....

The Secretary of the Navy takes pleasure in presenting the
Navy Commendation Medal to First Lieutenant Peter B. Foor,
United States Marine Corps Reserve, for service as set forth in
the following citation:

For heroic achievement while serving as Commanding Officer
of Company K, Third Battalion, Twenty-Sixth Marines, Ninth
Marine Amphibious Brigade in connection with combat operations against the enemy in the Republic of Vietnam. On 9
December 1968, during operation Meade River, Company K
was heavily engaged with a large North Vietnamese Army
force occupying a bunker complex. During the battle, First
Lieutenant Foor fearlessly maneuvered throughout the fire-
swept terrain shouting instructions and encouragement to his
men and ably directing their fire against the enemy. Skillfully
leading an assault on the hostile emplacements, he was instrumental in defeating the North Vietnamese Army force and
securing the designated objective. Shortly thereafter, he alertly
observed an enemy soldier in a tunnel and, boldly moving
toward the enemy, persuaded him to surrender. Subsequently
coming under fire from several hostile soldiers who were occupying the cave, First Lieutenant Foor rushed to the tunnel
entrance and throwing 3 hand grenades, silenced the North
Vietnamese fire. His heroic and timely actions inspired all who
observed him and contributed significantly to the accomplishment of his unit's mission. By his courage, aggressive leadership and steadfast devotion to duty in the face of great personal danger, First Lieutenant Foor upheld the finest traditions of
the Marine Corps and of the United States Naval Service.

The Combat Distinguishing Device is authorized.
For the Secretary of the Navy
H. W. Buse Jr.
Lieutenant General, U.S. Marine Corps
Commanding General, Fleet Marine Force, Pacific

....

Now, all I could think when I read this citation is what was I doing and where was I on December 9, 1968? A quick check of my logbook and I find that I was about 200 miles away from Peter, flying the 470 mission, call sign Law 470. We were shuttling back and forth from Ban Me Thuot to several Army Special Forces camps along the Cambodian border, Buon Blech, Tieu Atar, and the already famous Bu Prang. The most excitement for me that day was a UH-1 Huey gunship escort near the final approach at Tieu Atar due to sniper fire from a nearby treeline.

My vision of Peter had always been of a nine-year-old playing dodgeball at Hillside School or a 17-year-old smoking a Wolf Brothers Crook in the backseat of that 1961 Ford Falcon. It was certainly not a 24-year-old man, a Marine lieutenant, throwing grenades into a tunnel and leading a Company of 18 and 19-year-old Marines in combat. When I visited Peter recently I saw a Superior Court judge presiding over a murder trial involving the killing of a Vallejo police officer by a bank robber. The only feeling that comes to mind is one of gratitude for my incredible good fortune in knowing such a man and being his friend.

I know that Peter doesn't talk about Vietnam with many people, yet in his chambers at the courthouse he has a few things framed and hanging on the wall. The above citation is there, yet when I asked about it he told me it was nothing and he really didn't do that much. I can only refer back to a previous mention of awards and decorations and how each unit did things differently. Peter and I went to the Marines' Memorial Club in San Francisco in September 2011 to hear Karl Marlantes speak and sign his books about Vietnam, Matterhorn *and* What It Is Like to Go to War. *As a Marine lieutenant he was involved in a very similar action in Vietnam for which he was awarded the Navy Cross.*

Peter's citation has something very special with the notation, "The Combat Distinguishing Device is authorized." That means it was an award for valor and combat heroism, authorizing the wearing of the Combat V (for valor) on the ribbon. The Marine Corps expects such behavior in combat from its officers and would look on it as just doing your job. To be recognized for it is a big deal! His conduct was noted and appreciated by his young Marines, whose trust in him and his decisions had to be absolute, as their lives depended on it. My friend Peter—I just wish he hadn't talked me into smoking that Wolf Brothers Crook.

Peter Foor's story is unique for a couple of reasons. Other than at reunions over the past few years, he told me that he hardly talks about Vietnam at all, and in fact has spent more than 40 years trying to forget most of it. As the S.F. Chronicle *said, Peter "defies easy definition." I knew it would require the right moment to sit down and ask him a few questions, get him started talking, and see where it went. I had that opportunity on March 8, 2013, and ended up with more than eight pages of notes. Peter's memory of events is quite good. I can understand why he wanted to forget a lot of the things he saw, and why he asked me not to write many of the things he talked about.*

When we were 11 or 12 years old, Peter and I had adjoining paper routes, delivering the Berkeley Daily Gazette *after school. I'll never forget the rules: Porch the papers, deliver them by 6 p.m. at the latest, make sure they don't get wet in the rain, and collect and turn in the money to the* Gazette *office in downtown Berkeley every month. Our pay for the month was usually $10 to $15, in a good month $20. But the paper boy got stuck with the deadbeats! Going from there to Vietnam and back was an adventure we were both fortunate enough to survive, and it is an incredible honor to be entrusted with Peter's story. The fact that we both came back from Vietnam to a city that was so utterly changed from our childhood home that we felt alienated and divorced from it, is the ultimate statement on the times.*

I am proud to number Peter Foor among my friends.

....

I spent quite a bit of time in my senior year at Whittier College, and a few months after graduation, trying to get lined up to enter a military aviation program. I wanted to be a pilot and would soon be facing the draft, so there was a little pressure to get something set up. I took the aptitude and physical exams for both the Air Force and the Navy, but both had the same criteria for the eye exam and I failed both tests for depth perception. Meeting a Marine Corps recruiter after these setbacks changed my life. I took a similar exam for the Marines and was told I had passed, so I signed up for OCS (Officer Candidate School). OCS was at Quantico, Virginia, and I arrived in September 1967 for class. In early December 1967, with about two weeks left in the three-month course, I was told I needed to retake the eye exam, which I failed, and had my MOS (Military Occupational Specialty) assigned as infantry officer. I was commissioned as a second lieutenant in December 1967 and went to Basic School, which was the Marine Corps school to teach the fundamentals of being a Marine officer. They taught us everything from etiquette to basic infantry training, down to map reading and ground navigation, in an accelerated program necessitated by the losses the Marines were sustaining in Vietnam.

There was a huge emphasis on learning from the lessons of Vietnam, and most of the instructors were combat veterans. Our weapons training primarily involved the M-14 rifle, which fired the 7.62mm NATO or .308 caliber round. The M-16 fired a smaller 5.56mm NATO or .223 caliber round, but since the M-16 rifle was new, it was not widely available for training at that time. At the range we also fired the Model 1911 A-1 .45 caliber pistol. We ran practice patrols in as realistic conditions as they could create, right down to practice ambushes with "enemy" soldiers hiding in spider holes and setting booby traps along the trails. We learned the safest ways to walk along the trails and how to approach a jungle village — they even had constructed a realistic Vietnamese village, complete with thatched-roof hooches and "enemy" troops wearing black pajamas. To prepare us for casualties they had simulated ambush sites that we would come upon while on a patrol with simulated wounded and dead troops on the ground — right down to raw hamburger and ketchup to simulate serious wounds. It was realistic and got our attention. One bizarre thing was seeing snow on the ground at our Vietnamese "jungle" village in the Virginia winter. I graduated from Basic School in May 1968, went home for a 30-day leave, then I flew to San Diego for five days of additional training at Camp Pendleton.

The Camp Pendleton training was hurried and compressed. It was basically a continuation of training for patrols, ambushes, escape and evasion in the event we were captured, and ground navigation. We were subjected to simulated ambushes along the trails by "aggressors" who taught us how to identify and defend against potential ambush sites. We were given training on the new M-16 rifle at this point, but the early models were prone to jam, and as officers, we were able to draw other weapons once in-country. The five-day course was totally oriented to what we would be seeing in Vietnam.

After I finished training at Camp Pendleton, I was with a large group of Marines taken by bus to Norton AFB in San Bernardino. We flew on a MAC (Military Airlift Command) charter flight to Honolulu and then to Kadena Air Base and the adjacent Marine base on Okinawa. I arrived at Kadena with five other new second lieutenants, none of us having ever commanded anything. I was told to report to a barracks area where there was a large group of Marine enlisted men waiting to go home after their 13-month tours. They were veterans of some of the worst fighting, including the Tet Offensive of January and February 1968, the siege of Khe Sanh, and the battle to retake the city of Hue after Tet, which involved some of the worst street-to-street and house-to-house fighting imaginable. I was to be in charge of organizing them into groups for their flights home, but as most of the flights were overbooked it was a nightmare. Fortunately I was able to delegate almost everything to the NCOs (non-commissioned officers), who were more than able to handle it.

I was put in charge of a second group of Marines that was headed to Vietnam and, like me, had just arrived on Okinawa. The expression at Kadena for those who were headed to Vietnam was "going south." After three days I got on an Air Force C-141 with a big group and flew from Kadena to Da Nang AB, Vietnam. My main recollection of the flight into Da Nang was seeing the ground full of craters with grass growing in them as we crossed the coast and the area outside the airbase. I also have a vivid memory of the steep approach prior to landing. On the ground we walked to the Marine area, passing rolls of concertina razor wire and sandbagged machine gun emplacements, with the smell of the shitters (latrines) almost over-powering in that hot, humid air.

It was late June 1968 and I was on my own to get to Dong Ha, where I was issued my gear, including my weapons: .45 pistol and black leather shoulder holster, with a double magazine pouch taped to the holster with black electrical tape, a Ka-Bar knife, M-2 carbine with several 30-round magazines taped end to end for quick change in combat (all explained by the gunnery sergeant in the Dong Ha armory, even though we had been taught in training). I was then issued my 782 gear (named after Form 782, which every Marine for-mally signed as a receipt for the equipment), which included web gear, like ammo pouches, belts, canteens, etc.

I then went to Quang Tri, where I spent a couple of days before I caught up with my new unit, Kilo Company of the 3rd Battalion, 26th Marine Regiment (3/26, as they were called). I was assigned to be platoon leader of the 3rd platoon of Kilo Company. The platoon was made up of 30 to 35 young Marines, all veterans of Khe Sanh and most with six to eight months in-country. After the siege and battle for Khe Sanh, which had lasted nearly six months, the deci-sion had been made to abandon the base, and 3/26 was just return-ing to Dong Ha from Khe Sanh. An untested second lieutenant was-n't going to inspire much confidence in these battle-hardened guys, so the challenge was to earn their confidence and to stay alive in the process. The senior NCOs were the key to doing that, and any new lieutenant who didn't work with and learn from his NCOs was not destined to have a good experience.

When I joined Kilo Company we began running patrols, and I learned fast. We only wore flak jackets and helmets when our oper-ations were in flat areas like rice paddies. When in the field and in mountainous terrain we did not wear the heavy flak jackets and wore a soft cover field hat. For about four weeks we patrolled north of Dong Ha, along the DMZ. Later in July, the battalion moved south to Da Nang and Kilo Company took up positions along Highway 1 at the Hai Van Pass. The road had a series of switchbacks as the ele-vation rose from sea level to over 1,600 feet at the Hai Van Pass, and there were culverts along the switchbacks for rain runoff. The NVA and VC tried to blow up the culverts in an attempt to close the road and shut down traffic along that critical stretch, and we were constantly alert for ambushes along the road. During this time we were taken into the field mostly by truck but occasionally by helicopter. The trucks were known as "deuce and a half," 2½-ton cargo and troop-carrying trucks, and the convoys were reminiscent of movies I have seen about World War II. The little kids lined the sides of the road as we passed through villages while the Marines threw them candy bars and chewing gum.

Later in August we moved to Hill 55, southwest of Da Nang. As we looked to the west from the top of the hill, everything was called "Indian country," and was basically a free-fire zone where anything that moved was considered a legitimate target. The Marine Corps operated a sniper school on the hill, and Carlos Hathcock, the famous Marine Corps sniper, had been based there in 1967 and had many of his kills around Hill 55. In this time frame we ran patrols out of Hill 55 back and forth to the Rock Crusher (the quarry used by the Navy Seabees for their many construction projects).

By September, after about three months in-country, I had become more comfortable in my job and had begun to earn the confidence and trust of the young Marines in 3rd platoon. While still out in the field (or in "the bush," as it was also called), I received a radio message that I was to go to a pickup point and be flown out by helicopter, as 3rd Battalion Headquarters had a new assignment for me. I was to fly to Okinawa to attend a two to three-week school to learn to be the "embarkation officer" for 3/26. The battalion was going on "the float" in a couple of months. That meant that 3/26 and all the related armament and equipment was going to be boarded on ships that would cruise off the coast of South Vietnam, ready to land at any hot spot where it might be needed. The little flotilla would also include a hospital ship. I told them I really didn't want to leave my Marines but was ordered to the pickup point. Beginning with that helicopter ride, I embarked upon one of the most bizarre experiences of my 13 months in Vietnam.

The helicopter landed in a rough LZ (landing zone) and I was the only passenger to board. I had been out in the field for nearly two weeks without bathing, without much sleep, eating sporadically and only C-Rations, most of which were of World War II vintage. I always had a rule not to eat any C Rats that were older than me, but many were dated 1943 and early 1944 (I was born in September 1944), so I checked them carefully. I had the only piece of paper we were allowed to carry in the field, my Geneva Convention Card. I didn't have my military I.D. card, my pay card, my wallet, money, or any other personal items, as they were all left behind in the battalion rear when we went out on operations.

The helicopter was not the usual CH-46 that the Marines used to carry troops and supplies or medevac in the field, and to this day I am not sure what it was. The interior was narrow, and I was carrying all my gear: my pack, which was very heavy, my rifle, an M-2 carbine with seven or eight loaded 30-round magazines, my Ka-Bar knife, a bag attached to my web belt containing several hand grenades, and a quarter-pound block of C4 explosive. I was wearing a soft cover field hat and my jungle utilities, which were as foul as they can get after that long in the field. Shortly after takeoff the crew chief came over and said they were making an unscheduled stop to pick up a casualty, and then they would have to stop at the morgue before dropping me off at Da Nang for my flight to Okinawa.

The helicopter landed in a very desolate spot on an LZ that had been hastily cut out of the tall grass. Two young Marines ran over carrying the body of another Marine wrapped in his poncho, and they proceeded to push and pull him into the narrow cabin right in front of where I was sitting. They both were very upset and barely acknowledged me. I was carrying so much gear that it was a tight fit, with no room for my feet as the helicopter lifted off. I tried to keep from putting my feet on any part of the body.

The stop at the morgue was my one and only visit, and the sight and smell were quite simply staggering. We soon lifted off for my drop-off point, and when I arrived I was told to board a Marine C-130 that was just getting ready to taxi out for departure to Okinawa. I still had all my weapons and gear, no I.D. or other paperwork, no written orders authorizing my travel, and nobody said a word about it.

After the C-130 had been airborne for a couple of hours, with me sitting on a side-facing, fold-down seat, the loadmaster came over and told me that because of a typhoon over Okinawa, we were going to mainland Japan. Next thing I knew it was about 10 p.m. and we had landed at MCAS (Marine Corps Air Station) Iwakuni, Japan. With enough weapons to start a small war, I checked into the transient officer quarters, got cleaned up with a new set of utilities, left my grenades and other weapons in the closet, and went to the bar at the Officers' Club. When the Marines at the bar heard I had just come from "the bush," I couldn't buy a drink. One of them loaned me $40 for anything I might need and that's pretty much the way it stayed until the typhoon passed and I got on another C-130 and took off for Okinawa. Arriving at Kadena, weapons intact and accounted for, I attended embarkation school, and after about three weeks I flew back to Da Nang and rejoined Kilo Company.

In early October 1968 we were flown by helicopter into an area west of Happy Valley (an area west of Da Nang, and west of Happy Valley would be near the Laotian border), where we were dropped off for what was called a "search and destroy" mission. We were looking for enemy emplacements and supplies, and our plan was to engage the enemy and destroy his supply caches. We moved along a ridgeline in a state of high alert, looking for signs of enemy activity in the area, and then walked down the side of the mountain into a draw. There was a stream flowing in the direction in which we were moving, and as we got into the draw and deeper into the jungle we could see bamboo sections that had been cut, hollowed, and formed into a pipe to carry water from the stream to what turned out to be a large casualty center, set up almost like a hospital. Invisible from the air, there were hooches with beds, fresh bloody bandages on the ground, and bowls of still-warm rice. The NVA had just left, so we set up a guard and began a search of the area.

It was a large complex, and in one of the hooches we made a find that I will never forget. There were stacks of cardboard boxes full of medical supplies marked, "Cutter Laboratories, Berkeley, California," and boxes of sweatshirts from UC Berkeley featuring UC's mascot, Oski the Bear. I was struck with an immediate, overwhelming reaction of disbelief that these items had been sent from my hometown and were being used by the enemy that was trying to kill me and my fellow Marines. It was hard to believe that we found this stuff in the middle of the jungle near the Laotian border. It must have traveled from Berkeley and roundabout to a ship that took it to

Haiphong Harbor, then by truck down the Ho Chi Minh Trail to that casualty center west of Happy Valley. (As decreed by the target planners in the White House, Haiphong Harbor was one of the many targets in North Vietnam that were off-limits to U.S. bombing. It wasn't until Operation Linebacker II in 1972 that Haiphong Harbor was mined and targets around Hanoi were bombed.) I had my camera with me and took several photos, but unfortunately my camera was lost sometime in the next few months with the film still in it.

My mind flashed to a book I had read in a college course: *You Can't Go Home Again,* by Thomas Wolfe. I was struck that the place of my youth was gone, that it didn't exist anymore. Berkeley was no longer my home, and I never wanted to be associated with it again. The quote came to me: "You can't go back home to your childhood... back home to a young man's dreams of glory and fame."

We burned the complex to the ground.

Kilo Company continued on routine patrol activities until late November and into December, when 3/26 was involved in a large operation called Meade River. It was a mission to cordon off the area south and west of Da Nang and capture or kill VC or NVA troops while cutting off any avenue of escape. I was acting company commander for Kilo for most of this operation, and we left Hill 55 both on foot and in trucks while other blocking units were carried in by helicopter. The operation lasted until December 9 and was considered very successful.

By the end of December, 3/26 was preparing for "the float," and I was sent to Subic Bay Naval Base in the Philippines to perform my duties as embarkation officer. When I arrived, the loading of the ship, an LPH (landing platform, helicopter), was being supervised by two very senior, crusty Navy chief petty officers who suggested that I go to the bar and said they would call me if they needed me. So much for being embarkation officer! I spent New Year's Eve 1968 at Subic Bay, and the ship was loaded and ready to depart for Da Nang in early January. With the equipment and ammunition onboard, the ship set sail for Da Nang, and I flew back to join 3/26. At this point I was no longer attached to Kilo Company but was attached to 3rd Battalion while I served as embarkation officer.

When the LPH arrived off Da Nang, 3/26 was south of the city, along Red Beach. We went out in small boats and climbed up rope nets onto the ship, carrying all our gear. It was just like the World War II scenes I used to watch on *Victory at Sea*. During the period of "the float," Kilo Company engaged in two operations where troops and equipment were landed by boat and helicopter. These operations, Bold Mariner and Taylor Common, occurred in February and March, 1969, and Kilo Company suffered a significant number of casualties in a mine field, during this time. I was onboard the ship when this occurred, having been assigned duties as embarcation officer. As I watched the helicopters returning with the dead and wounded, it was one of the low points of my Vietnam experience.

On a lighter note, the first night onboard ship the Marine junior officers were invited to join their Navy counterparts for dinner in the junior officers' mess. It was a disaster and so shocked the executive officer (XO) of the ship that we were segregated from then on so we wouldn't teach our bad manners to the Navy. It started when the Filipino steward walked through the mess ringing a bell announcing that it was time to go to the table. There were large, round tables with seating for eight, with Navy officers mixing in with the Marines. The tables were piled high with bread and butter, fruit, meat, and vegetables, things we had not seen for months. As everyone was standing behind their chairs and not knowing the protocol, staring at the china, silverware, tablecloths, and cloth napkins, the Marines started to pick up the bread and fruit laid out on each table and soon everyone was standing up and eating with their hands. The Navy officers were horrified, and when the XO entered the room (which was the signal to sit down) we had finished eating and left the room. From then on, we ate alone. Our colonel was called in to the XO's office but backed us up, saying he didn't see any problem and that we were obviously hungry.

In late March I went on R&R, and when I returned in early April, I rejoined Kilo as the executive officer. The 3/26 was gearing up to go on Operation Oklahoma Hills, which took us by helicopter to a mountainous area west of Da Nang. Two distinct parts of this area were called Charlie Ridge and Happy Valley, and they contained supply and infiltration routes, base camps, and storage facilities that always posed a threat to Da Nang. I was out in the field for the duration of Oklahoma Hills, which ended on May 29, 1969. It was the last time I was a platoon commander, returning to Da Nang after the operation. For the next few weeks I went out on local patrols and then spent my last 30 days in-country as executive officer for Kilo Company, remaining in the Da Nang area and at 3/26 headquarters.

(The areas where we operated were all named, prior to my arrival, with some having names from the Old West and some from incidents that had occurred there. The names ranged from Dodge City, Happy Valley, and Charlie Ridge, to Arizona Territory and Elephant Valley, and most were south and west of Da Nang extending to the Laotian border.)

One final note has to do with weapons and how they were carried. We always had our weapons with us, and when we entered or departed a Marine facility there were signs reminding us to "lock and load" on the way out and "clear" our weapons on the way in. There was an upscale bar in Da Nang city that we frequented on the very few occasions we could (five or six times for me in 13 months). It was called the Stone Elephant and was air-conditioned, which for us was like heaven. There was a requirement to check our weapons at the entrance, and a small storage room just inside the front door looked like an armory. You could find any weapon imaginable in that room, as we were all armed to the teeth.

I would like to close by saying that I do not think anything I did or was involved in was unique or out of the ordinary. Those who should receive recognition are those who did not come home or who came home damaged either physically or mentally. I consider myself extremely fortunate.

L) Lt. Peter Foor, USMC, in front of his "5 star, luxury hooch" on Hill 55, southwest of Da Nang, 1969. R) Looking out over an M-60 Machine Gun from a Kilo Company position west of Da Nang, 1969.

L) Kilo Company Radio Operator carrying AN/PRC-25 radio with its very visible whip antenna. Several "deuce and a half" truck-loads of Kilo Company Marines going out on an operation, 1968.
R) Lt. Peter Foor on patrol, 1969.

Lt. Peter Foor, kneeling on the left, with Kilo Company Marines and a Russian flag captured on Operation Oklahoma Hills, April 1969. There is a story here, but, like "the bush," it will remain a mystery to those who weren't there.

37

ADDENDUM TO PETER FOOR

Nick Kosturos, Lance Corporal USMC,
Kilo Company, 1st Platoon, 3/26 Marines, 1968-1969

L/Cpl. Nick Kosturos, USMC, Kilo Company, 3/26 Marines, 1969.

The following is a brief addition to Peter Foor's story, confirming the presence of medical supplies in the hands of the NVA that were sent by "the people of Berkeley, California." It was provided by Nick Kosturos, a lance corporal who served with Peter in Kilo Company.

My name is Nick Kosturos, and I was a lance corporal with Kilo Company, 1st Platoon, 3/26 Marines. I was involved in Operation Meade River, which began on November 20, 1968, and ended December 9, 1968.

Operation Meade River took place in an area 10 miles south of Da Nang that was about five miles wide and three miles long, honeycombed with caves, tunnels, and man-made bunkers. The area was nicknamed Dodge City, and the ultimate goal was to trap the NVA and destroy their headquarters and supply caches.

On December 4, after two weeks of continuous day and night firefights, Kilo Company, 1st Platoon moved to reinforce a company that had suffered heavy casualties and was trapped in a trench between fortified bunkers and a river. A helicopter flew over in the early evening and broadcast a message to the NVA, telling them that they were surrounded and must surrender or die. One soldier gave up and about 30 minutes later an artillery barrage, both land-based and from Navy guns offshore, began to pound the area. It continued for most of the night along with an AC-47 gunship, nicknamed Puff the Magic Dragon, which fired into the complex for several hours.

At first light, Kilo 1st Platoon walked into the area and found many NVA bodies but no sign of life. There was a large bunker with an entrance that was partially covered, so another member of the platoon, Lance Corporal James "Tex" Evans, and I cleared the opening and entered in single file, due to the narrow size of the tunnel. I was armed with a .45 pistol and held a Zippo lighter. I crawled about ten feet into the tunnel where there was a sharp right turn. I extended the Zippo around the corner and heard voices very close by, so we backed up and I yelled for them to come out and give up.

The first of three NVA soldiers came out, wounded and bandaged. I had him on his knees with his hands up when he started to move his right hand toward his shirt. I stuck the .45 in his ear, pulled the hammer back, and he stopped moving his hand but pointed to his shirt pocket. (Unknown to me, a photo was taken at this point by a Vietnamese reporter for the *Stars and Stripes* newspaper who had flown into the area by helicopter. He had accompanied a colonel who had arrived with his staff to check on the progress of the operation. The photo first appeared in the *Stars and Stripes* with a feature article about Operation Meade River.) I reached into his pocket and pulled out a pill bottle with a label that read, "Penicillin, donated by the people of Berkeley, California." I handed it back and directed him to two Vietnamese-speaking interrogators waiting at the bottom of the slope.

We continued "search and destroy" and on December 9 Kilo Company walked out of Dodge City.

I was born and raised in San Francisco and worked at my father's grocery store in the Haight-Ashbury neighborhood when I was growing up. I wasn't surprised finding medicine from Berkeley in the hands of the enemy. The Marines who gave all allowed us to keep the traitors busy supplying the replacement NVA troops entering South Vietnam.

One of three NVA that did not get away. Semper Fi Kilo, 3/26.

The author, Bruce Cowee (C), with two Kilo Company, 3/26 Marines.
Nick Kosturos (L) and Peter Foor (R), July 2013.

EPILOGUE

It is fitting that when put in chronological order these stories begin and end at the same base, Korat RTAB (Royal Thai Air Base), Thailand. Jerry Stamps arrived at Korat in August 1964, TDY (temporary duty) from Yokota AB, Japan, with his F-105 squadron. This was the first major Air Force expansion into Thailand and was for all intents and purposes a secret deployment of 18 F-105s and 25 pilots. It was soon followed by a massive construction project that built the base into one of the largest in Southeast Asia. Jim Erdos arrived at Korat in June 1973, nine years later, and found a very modern base, starting to wind down from all those years of the air war. He was also TDY, with his EC-121 squadron from McClellan AFB, California. Fittingly, Jerry had one of the earliest hire dates with Western, February 26, 1968, while Jim was in one of the last classes hired by Western, August 4, 1986, just before the merger with Delta.

In the middle of that nine-year period, from 1964 to 1973, are stories that span the entire Vietnam War and give some very interesting perspectives of the air war. This group of more than 30 just scratches the surface of the hundreds of Vietnam veterans who were hired by Western Airlines and literally thousands that were hired in the airline industry. I think this book presents a good cross-section of military services, airplanes, and most important, the missions that were flown during the war.

With all the talk we hear today about hiring veterans, I don't think that the airline industry of the 1960s and 1970s was ever given the credit it deserved for all the Vietnam veterans that were hired. During that time frame, Western's management hired Vietnam veterans almost exclusively, and even though Western was a relatively small airline, it hired as many Vietnam veterans on a percentage basis as any of the other airlines—or more. It makes me proud to have been a part of that group. When Frank Borman was the CEO of Eastern Airlines, from 1975 to 1986, he made a standing offer to hire any of the POWs who had come home in 1973 and wanted an airline job. When Eastern resumed pilot hiring in 1978, the first few classes had most of the slots reserved for former POWs, and many were hired, sadly to lose their jobs when Eastern declared bankruptcy and ceased operations in 1991.

I would like to relate a wonderful experience I had back in October 2007 when I was invited to speak to a high school class about Vietnam. A friend in Napa, California, told me of her daughter's reading assignment in her English class that was a very anti-war, anti-military book about Vietnam. The author claimed to be a Vietnam veteran, but if you have read the book *Stolen Valor* by B. G. Burkett, you know it is easy to put yourself forward as a decorated Vietnam combat veteran and not have to back it up, especially if you are telling the audience what they expect to hear. This is especially true today when the Supreme Court has ruled that it is a First Amendment right of free speech and expression to wear or claim to hold any military decoration, up to and including the Medal of Honor.

The book assigned in that English class perpetuated every negative stereotype about Vietnam veterans in a fictional story, purported to represent the author's combat tour. It was generally a sick portrayal of rampant drug use, rape and pillage on a monumental scale, burning of villages, and indiscriminate killing of women, children, animals—you name it. I told my friend's daughter that I would be happy to talk to the class about my experience in Vietnam, and was surprised to receive an invitation from her teacher. I had never done anything like that before and only had a short time to prepare, but I gave it my best shot. I immediately contacted my Marine buddy, Peter Foor, and asked for his input as an infantry officer on the ground. Then I put together a few statistics and some photos from my tour and wrote a basic outline of what I wanted to say. My first surprise was that the teacher never made any effort to check my credentials to see if I was a Vietnam veteran. I introduced him to the Defense Department Form 214, which documents your military service. It shows quite clearly whether or not you had foreign or SEA (Southeast Asia) service, the military awards and decorations to verify that service, and the category of discharge, whether it was honorable or otherwise. I think that embarrassed him a bit as he said he had invited a Vietnam veteran to speak to a prior class and, after my presentation and the question-and-answer period, told me his attitude had been quite different from mine.

I gave a short presentation stressing that it was strictly my experience, but I had never seen the kinds of things written about in the book. I told them that my tour of duty had been very positive and that I had ended up working with some of the most competent professionals I have ever worked with in my life. I received incredible training, was given more responsibility than I have ever been given since, and most important, my military experience opened the door to a wonderful career as an airline pilot. I stressed that the Vietnam veterans I know all lead productive and successful lives and I really hate to see the negative stereotypes about them perpetuated and not answered.

I also quoted extensively from an article titled, "RVN Wannabes! Vietnam Facts vs. Fiction," by retired Army First Sergeant Nick Bacon. This was a young man who had forged his mother's signature when he was 17 to join the Army, and received the Medal of Honor for an action on August 28, 1968, during his second tour in Vietnam. Here are a few of the statistics from his extensive research and from VA (Veterans Administration) studies:

1. Vietnam veterans represented 9.7 percent of their generation.

2. 97 percent of Vietnam veterans were honorably discharged.

3. 91 percent of Vietnam veterans say they are glad they served.

4. 74 percent say they would serve again, even knowing the outcome.

5. There is no difference in drug usage between Vietnam veterans and non-Vietnam veterans of the same age group (according to the VA study).

6. Vietnam veterans are less likely to be in prison.

7. 85 percent of Vietnam veterans made successful transitions to civilian life.

8. A common belief is that most Vietnam veterans were drafted. In fact, two-thirds of the men who served in Vietnam were volunteers.

9. Another common belief is that a disproportionate number of African-Americans were killed in the Vietnam War. In fact, 86 percent of the men who died in Vietnam were Caucasians, 12.5 percent African-American, 1.5 percent other races. These figures are proportionate to the racial makeup of the country at the time.

10. It is commonly believed that the war was fought largely by the poor and uneducated. The fact is that servicemen who went to Vietnam from well-to-do backgrounds had a slightly elevated risk of dying because they were more likely to be pilots or infantry officers. Vietnam veterans were the best-educated forces our nation had ever sent into combat—79 percent had a high school education or better.

11. My favorite statistic: Vietnam wannabes. According to the August 2000 census count used by Nick Bacon for this article, there were just over 1,000,000 Vietnam veterans still living. In the same census, the number of Americans claiming to have served in-country was 13,800,000! More than 90 percent of those claiming to be Vietnam veterans are not! I find it most interesting that so many want to claim participation in a war we have been told was so unpopular. My recommendation is the same one I gave the English teacher at Napa High School. Ask to see a DD Form 214, and that should settle the issue.

Then I added some additional statistics that are of interest. As many as 125,000 young draft age men moved to Canada to evade the draft through those years, but were given an unconditional pardon by Jimmy Carter as the first act he took upon assuming the presidency on January 21, 1977. All officers were volunteers no matter what their commissioning source, OCS, OTS, ROTC, AOCS, or the Service Academies. All pilots who served in Vietnam, regardless of service, were either commissioned officers or warrant officers, and all were volunteers. 333 West Point graduates fell in Vietnam, with the classes of 1964 to 1969 being the hardest hit. And finally, a little known fact is that the Marine Corps suffered more casualties in Vietnam than in World War II, with 101,689 killed and wounded in Vietnam and 87,890 killed and wounded in World War II. Every bit as much heroism was on display in Vietnam as in World War II. There were 248 Medals of Honor received in the Vietnam War, 156 of them received posthumously.

I then took questions for about 45 minutes and was very impressed with the quality of the questions and the thoughtful things I was asked. Only one in the class of over 30 even knew someone who had served, and the students' feelings about Vietnam and the military in general were mostly shaped by books like the one they were reading and by the movies. After Saigon fell in 1975, Hollywood began to treat the American people to a series of movies about the Vietnam War, assaulting Vietnam veterans by portraying them as everything from rapists to murders, drug dealers and addicts, deserters to suicidal crazies, to just plain stupid. Starting with *The Deer Hunter* in 1978, *Apocalypse Now* in 1979, *Platoon*, *Full Metal Jacket*, and *Born on the Fourth of July* in the 1980s, and ending with *Forest Gump* in 1994, the stage was set for the negative stereotypes of Vietnam veterans that still exist today. At the same time, Hollywood and the press were getting ready to present a very different image of our fathers' generation, kicking it off in 1998 with Tom Brokaw's book, *The Greatest Generation*, followed by the movie *Saving Private Ryan*, then on to *Band of Brothers* in 2001 and *The Pacific* in 2010. The same studios, actors, and directors seemed adept at moving from one generation to another while creating a totally different "stereotype." What my generation did to deserve such treatment has never been adequately explained: we answered our country's call and served honorably in a war that was horribly mismanaged by the politicians in Washington. We came home and for the vast majority, got on with our lives and became productive, law abiding, tax paying citizens. If you are looking for reasons why a lot of Vietnam veterans have never talked about their war experience, you don't have to look far. I can only do my small part to try to change those stereotypes, but the experience at Napa High School was very gratifying.

About two weeks after my presentation I received an envelope with an individual thank-you note from each member of the class. To say I was floored is an understatement. I would like to include quotes from a few of those notes, starting with the young lady who invited me to speak to her class. These thoughts will always stay with me.

I know that you said you always wanted to do this, but I really appreciated you coming in to talk. We really never had the chance to sit down and talk about your war experience. It was very interesting to hear you speak, watching you stand up there sharing your feelings and stories....It was comforting to know that even though the war was horrible, men did come back and lead normal lives. I think your next job is to write your side in our history books. You were very organized and I thought you gave an excellent presentation. I am lucky to have you as a resource. —Stephanie T.

Thank you so much for taking the time to come to our classroom and discuss such an important time in your life. It is very uplifting to hear someone talk about the Vietnam War in a positive way so as not to get such a biased opinion on it. Thank you for being so open and allowing us to ask such open questions on such a personal topic. —Audrey P.

Thank you for coming in and presenting your experiences and thoughts on the Vietnam War. I found them very interesting and some of the things you said really surprised me. The war from your perspective sounds very different from a lot of those found in novels and movies and it was nice to hear a difference of opinion. It must have been hard to come home to such chaos in Berkeley but it sounds like you adapted well. —Peter S.

Thank you for taking the time to address our English class about the experiences you had in Vietnam, the friends you made, and the memories that will forever remain with you. You gave us an entirely different perspective on the war and your involvement in it through the Air Force. We are extremely fortunate to have another person's perspective and outlook on the war, especially one that was positive. —Ethan G.

I really appreciate you coming to our class and sharing your stories and experiences with all of us. It was really interesting to hear the perspective of a person who was actually involved in the war. It was also very interesting to hear what Berkeley was like in the 1960s. It makes me very sad to hear how the people treated the soldiers... You were very open about your experiences and it meant a lot to me. —Lucas N.

I will end with a final note that tells me I succeeded in some small way on that day in October 2007. Every note had the same theme as the quotes above and this one sums it up.

I really enjoyed our English class last Friday. You seem really different from the character in the book we are reading. It was nice to hear a different point of view and a different perspective on the war. Thank you for taking the time to come and talk to us. I am thankful that you were open with us and that you could share your opinions and experiences with us. —Nick P.

There was a note from the teacher along with the students' thank you notes. "Bruce, thank you so much for your incredible presentation. I thought you might want to see what the students had to say about it."

When I left the class, I extended an open offer to the teacher to come and speak again, at any time and to any class. I have yet to be invited back.... but then, it has only been five and a half years. Unfortunately, I doubt the class reading list has changed.

In closing I would like to leave the reader with two quotes. The first quote sums up my feelings about my generation. It is from Jim Webb, author of several books including a classic novel about the Vietnam War, *Fields of Fire*. He is an Annapolis graduate, decorated Marine veteran of Vietnam, former Secretary of the Navy and Senator from Virginia, and the quote is from an article titled, "Vietnam Generation." In that article Jim Webb wrote:

> *Those of us who grew up on the other side of the picket line from that era's counterculture can't help but feel a little leery of the sudden gush of appreciation for our elders from the leading lights of the old counterculture....In truth, the "Vietnam generation" is a misnomer. Those who came of age during that war are permanently divided by different reactions to a whole range of counterculture agendas, and nothing divides them more deeply than the personal ramifications of the war itself....The men and women who opted to serve in the military during the Vietnam War are quite different from their peers who for decades have claimed to speak for them. In fact, they are much like the World War II generation itself....The men who fought World War II were their heroes and role models. They honored their father's service by emulating it, and largely agreed with their father's wisdom in attempting to stop Communism's reach in Southeast Asia.*

Speaking of the young Marines he served with in Vietnam:

It would be redundant to say that I would trust my life to these men. Because I already have, in more ways than I can ever recount. I am alive today because of their quiet, unaffected heroism. Such valor epitomizes the conduct of Americans at war from the first days of our existence. That the boomer elites can canonize this sort of conduct in our fathers' generation while ignoring it in our own is more than simple oversight. It is a conscious, continuing travesty.

The second quote is from the well-known author of *Flight of the Intruder*, Vietnam veteran and former Navy pilot Stephen Coonts. He wrote the forward to the book, *Flying Black Ponies* by Kit Lavell, a book recommended to me by my good friend and Western classmate, Mike Monagan, who flew Black Ponies. It is always reassuring to me when I read things that confirm my thoughts about such weighty issues as war and the reasons men volunteer to do dangerous things. His quote could easily have been in the introduction to this book because it applies to all those who wrote their stories here. In the forward to *Flying Black Ponies*, Coonts wrote:

One of the essential points of American military history often missed by students is that the people in the critical skill positions in all our wars were volunteers....Since the invention of the airplane, cockpits have been exclusively reserved for those who wanted to be there, those willing to put forth the effort and pay the price to earn their seat. Even in that most unpopular war, Vietnam, it was so. The men you will meet in this book were not the sons of the privileged elite. Their fathers were not senators, officers of major corporations, or decorated with inherited fortunes....They usually hailed from small towns or farms...had fathers and uncles who served in World War II or Korea, and—universally—were patriots. Those who survived combat had their patriotism and faith in their fellow Americans tempered like fine steel. As you read this book I invite you to speculate on the motivations that took these men to Vietnam, that put them in the cockpit....

The men featured in this book probably cover the entire political spectrum. Politics was never discussed as these stories were put together, and was never a part of this book. It is all "living history" as these guys experienced it. This is a group of men who, when they were in their 20s, volunteered and served honorably when their country called. No matter what they might have thought of the war, of the politicians who managed every bit of it from Washington, or of the press that distorted it at every opportunity, universally, they were proud of their service.

ABOUT THE AUTHOR

 *Bruce Cowee* was born in Berkeley, California in 1945 and attended Berkeley public schools and the University of California. His road to Vietnam began as an Air Force ROTC cadet, and he still talks about filing a claim for combat pay for his last two years at Cal, 1964-1966! After a year in Vietnam and three years at Travis AFB, California, flying the C-141, he separated from active duty on July 1, 1972 and was hired as a pilot by Western Airlines on December 12, 1972. After Western's merger with Delta Air Lines on April 1, 1987, he flew for an additional 17 years and retired from Delta as a Boeing 757/767 Captain based in Los Angeles on June 1, 2004.

His flying career began with Vietnam and ended with 9/11. He left Boston on a Delta 767-300 at midnight on 9/10/2001, flying a "red-eye" to Las Vegas, departing Boston six hours before the hijackings. Flying New York layovers the whole month of October 2001, the crew could see the eerie dull glow of the fire that still burned at Ground Zero from nearly 100 miles away, as they flew at night from Atlanta to LaGuardia. Described by some as similar to a blast furnace at a steel mill, it was truly the devil's work. He will never forget.

Bruce currently resides in Northern California.

ABOOKS

ALIVE Book Publishing and ALIVE Publishing Group
are imprints of Advanced Publishing LLC,
3200 A Danville Blvd., Suite 204, Alamo, California 94507

Telephone: 925.837.7303 Fax: 925.837.6951
www.alivebookpublishing.com

CPSIA information can be obtained at www.ICGtesting.com
Printed in the USA
LVOW07*0020021113

359565LV00003B/8/P